Theodor Hertzka, Arthur Ransom

Freeland

A Social Anticipation

Theodor Hertzka, Arthur Ransom

Freeland
A Social Anticipation

ISBN/EAN: 9783743418066

Manufactured in Europe, USA, Canada, Australia, Japa

Cover: Foto ©Suzi / pixelio.de

Manufactured and distributed by brebook publishing software (www.brebook.com)

Theodor Hertzka, Arthur Ransom

Freeland

FREELAND

A Social Anticipation

BY

DR THEODOR HERTZKA

TRANSLATED BY

ARTHUR RANSOM

London
CHATTO & WINDUS, PICCADILLY
1891

TRANSLATOR'S NOTE

This book contains a translation of *Freiland: ein sociales Zukunfts-bild*, by Dr. Theodor Hertzka, a Viennese economist. The first German edition appeared early in 1890, and was rapidly followed by three editions in an abridged form. This translation is made from the unabridged edition, with a few emendations from the subsequent editions.

The author has long been known as an eminent representative of those Austrian Economists who belong to what is known on the Continent as the Manchester School as distinguished from the Historical School. In 1872 he became economic editor of the *Neue Freie Presse*; and in 1871 he with others founded the Society of Austrian National Economists. In 1880 he published *Die Gesetze der Handels- und Sozialpolitik ;* and in 1886 *Die Gesetze der Sozial-entwickelung.* At various times he has published works which have made him an authority upon currency questions. In 1889 he founded, and he still edits, the weekly *Zeitschrift für Staats- und Volkswirthschaft.*

How the author was led to modify some of his earlier views will be found detailed in the introduction of the present work.

The publication of *Freiland* immediately called forth in Austria and Germany a desire to put the author's views in practice. In many of the larger towns and cities a number of persons belonging to all classes of society organised local societies for this purpose, and these local societies have now been united into an International Freeland Society. At the first plenary meeting of the Vienna *Freilandverein* in March last, it was announced that a suitable tract of land in British East Africa, between Mount Kenia and the coast, had already been placed at the disposal of the Society ; and a hope was expressed that the actual formation of a Freeland Colony would not be long delayed. It is anticipated that the English edition of *Freiland* will bring a considerable number of English-speaking members into the Society ; and it is intended soon to make an application to the British authorities for a guarantee of non-interference by the Government with the development of Freeland institutions.

Any of the readers of this book who wish for further information concerning the Freeland movement, may apply either to Dr. HERTZKA in Vienna, or to the Translator.

A. R.

St. LOYES, BEDFORD : *June*, 1891.

AUTHOR'S PREFACE

THE economic and social order of the modern world exhibits a strange enigma, which only a prosperous thoughtlessness can regard with indifference or, indeed, without a shudder. We have made such splendid advances in art and science that the unlimited forces of nature have been brought into subjection, and only await our command to perform for us all our disagreeable and onerous tasks, and to wring from the soil and prepare for use whatever man, the master of the world, may need. As a consequence, a moderate amount of labour ought to produce inexhaustible abundance for everyone born of woman ; and yet all these glorious achievements have not—as Stuart Mill forcibly says—been able to mitigate one human woe. And, what is more, the ever-increasing facility of producing an abundance has proved a curse to multitudes who lack necessaries because there exists no demand for the many good and useful things which they are able to produce. The industrial activity of the present day is a ceaseless confused struggle with the various symptoms of the dreadful evil known as ' over-production.' Protective duties, cartels and trusts, guild agitations, strikes—all these are but the desperate resistance offered by the classes engaged in production to the inexorable consequences of the apparently so absurd, but none the less real, phenomenon that increasing facility in the production of wealth brings ruin and misery in its train.

That science stands helpless and perplexed before this enigma, that no beam of light has yet penetrated and dispelled the gloom of this—the social—problem, though that problem has exercised the minds of the noblest and best of to-day, is in part due to the fact that the solution has been sought in a wrong direction.

Let us see, for example, what Stuart Mill says upon this subject:
'I looked forward . . . to a future' . . . whose views (and institutions) . . . shall be 'so firmly grounded in reason and in the true
exigencies of life that they shall not, like all former and present
creeds, religious, ethical, and political, require to be periodically
thrown off and replaced by others.' [1]

Yet more plainly does Laveleye express himself in the same
sense at the close of his book 'De la Propriété': 'There is an order
of human affairs *which is the best . . . God knows it and wills it.
Man must discover and introduce it.*'

It is therefore an *absolutely best, eternal order* which both are
waiting for; although, when we look more closely, we find that
both ought to know they are striving after the impossible. For Mill,
a few lines before the above remarkable passage, points out that all
human things are in a state of constant flux; and upon this he
bases his conviction that existing institutions can be only transitory.
Therefore, upon calm reflection, he would be compelled to admit
that the same would hold in the future, and that consequently
unchangeable human institutions will never exist. And just so
must we suppose that Laveleye, with his '*God* knows it and wills
it,' would have to admit that it could *not* be man's task either to
discover or to introduce the absolutely best order known only to
God. He is quite correct in saying that if there be really an
absolutely best order, God alone knows it; but since it cannot be
the office of science to wait upon Divine revelation, and since such
an absolutely best order could be introduced by God alone and not
by men, and therefore the revelation of the Divine will would not
help us in the least, so it must logically follow, from the admission
that the knowing and the willing of the absolutely good appertain
to God, that man has not to strive after this absolutely good, but
after the *relatively best,* which alone is intelligible to and attainable
by him.

And thus it is in fact. The solution of the social problem is not
to be sought in the discovery of an *absolutely good* order of society,
but in that of the *relatively best*—that is, of such an order of human
institutions as best corresponds to the contemporary conditions of

Autobiography, p. 166.

human existence. The existing arrangements of society call for improvement, not because they are out of harmony with our longing for an absolutely good state of things, but because it can be shown to be possible to replace them by others more in accordance with the contemporary conditions of human existence. Darwin's law of evolution in nature teaches us that when the actual social arrangements have ceased to be the relatively best—that is, those which best correspond to the contemporary conditions of human existence —their abandonment is not only possible but simply inevitable. For in the struggle for existence that which is out of date not only *may* but *must* give place to that which is more in harmony with the actual conditions. And this law also teaches us that all the characters of any organic being whatever are the results of that being's struggle for existence in the conditions in which it finds itself. If, now, we bring together these various hints offered us by the doctrine of evolution, we see the following to be the only path along which the investigation of the social problem can be pursued so as to reach the goal :

First, we must inquire and establish under what particular conditions of existence the actual social arrangements were evolved.

Next we must find out whether these same conditions of exist- tence still subsist, or whether others have taken their place.

If others have taken their place, it must be clearly shown whether the new conditions of existence are compatible with the old arrangements; and, if not, what alterations of the latter are required.

The new arrangements thus discovered must and will contain that which we are justified in looking for as the ' solution of the social problem.'

When I applied this strictly scientific method of investigation to the social problem, I arrived four years ago at the following conclusions, to the exposition of which I devoted my book on ' The Laws of Social Evolution,' [1] published at that time :

The actual social arrangements are the necessary result of the human struggle for existence when the productiveness of labour was such that a single worker could produce, by the labour of his

---

[1] *Die Gesetze der Sozialentwickelung.* Leipzig, 1886.

own hands, more than was indispensable to the sustenance of his
animal nature, but not enough to enable him to satisfy his higher
needs. With only this moderate degree of productiveness of labour,
the exploitage of man by man was the only way by which it was
possible to ensure to *individuals* wealth and leisure, those fundamental essentials to higher culture. But as soon as the productiveness of labour reaches the point at which it is sufficient to satisfy
also the highest requirements of every worker, the exploitage of man
by man not only ceases to be a necessity of civilisation, but becomes
an obstacle to further progress by hindering men from making full
use of the industrial capacity to which they have attained.

For, as under the domination of exploitage the masses have no
right to more of what they produce than is necessary for their bare
subsistence, demand is cramped by limitations which are quite
independent of the possible amount of production. Things for
which there is no demand are valueless, and therefore will not be
produced ; consequently, under the exploiting system, society does
not produce that amount of wealth which the progress of science
and technical art has made possible, but only that infinitely smaller
amount which suffices for the bare subsistence of the masses and
the luxury of the few. Society wishes to employ the whole of the
surplus of the productive power in the creation of instruments of
labour—that is, it wishes to convert it into capital; but this is
impossible, since the quantity of utilisable capital is strictly dependent upon the quantity of commodities to be produced by the aid
of this capital. The utilisation of all the proceeds of such highly
productive labour is therefore dependent upon the creation of a new
social order which shall guarantee to every worker the enjoyment
of the full proceeds of his own work. And since impartial investigation further shows that this new order is not merely indispensable
to further progress in civilisation, but is also thoroughly in harmony
with the natural and acquired characteristics of human society, and
consequently is met by no inherent and permanent obstacle, it is
evident that in the natural process of human evolution this new
order must necessarily come into being.

When I placed this conclusion before the public four years ago,
I assumed, as something self-evident, that I was announcing a

doctrine which was not by any means an isolated novelty; and I distinctly said so in the preface to the 'Laws of Social Evolution.' I fully understood that there must be some connecting bridge between the so-called classical economics and the newly discovered truths; and I was convinced that in a not distant future either others or myself would discover this bridge. But in expounding the consequences springing from the above-mentioned general principles, I at first allowed an error to escape my notice. That ground-rent and undertaker's profit—that is, the payment which the landowner demands for the use of his land, and the claim of the so-called work-giver to the produce of the worker's labour—are incompatible with the claim of the worker to the produce of his own labour, and that consequently in the course of social evolution ground-rent and undertaker's profit must become obsolete and must be given up—this I perceived; but with respect to the interest of capital I adhered to the classical-orthodox view that this was a postulate of progress which would survive all the phases of evolution.

As palliation of my error I may mention that it was the opponents of capital themselves—and Marx in particular—who confirmed me in it, or, more correctly, who prevented me from distinctly perceiving the basis upon which interest essentially rests. To tear oneself away from long-cherished views is in itself extremely difficult; and when, moreover, the men who attack the old views base their attack point after point upon error, it becomes only too easy to mistake the weakness of the attack for impregnability in the thing attacked. Thus it happened with me. Because I saw that what had been hitherto advanced against capital and interest was altogether untenable, I felt myself absolved from the task of again and independently inquiring whether there were no better, no really valid, arguments against the absolute and permanent necessity of interest. Thus, though interest is, in reality, as little compatible with associated labour carried on upon the principle of perfect economic justice as are ground-rent and the undertaker's profit, I was prevented by this fundamental error from arriving at satisfactory views concerning the constitution and character of the future forms of organisation based upon the principle of free organisation. *That* and *wherefore*

economic freedom and justice must eventually be practically realised,
I had shown ; on the other hand, *how* this phase of evolution was to
be brought about I was not able to make fully clear. Yet I did not
ascribe this inability to any error of mine in thinking the subject
out, but believed it to reside in the nature of the subject itself. I
reasoned that institutions the practical shaping of which belongs to
the future could not be known in detail before they were evolved.
Just as those former generations, which knew nothing of the
modern joint-stock company, could not possibly form an exact and
perfect idea of the nature and working of this institution even if
they had conceived the principle upon which it is based, so I held
it to be impossible to-day to possess a clear and connected idea
of those future economic forms which cannot be evolved until the
principle of the free association of labour has found its practical
realisation.

I was slow in discovering the above-mentioned connection of my
doctrine of social evolution with the orthodox system of economy.
The most clear-sighted minds of three centuries have been at work
upon that system ; and if a new doctrine is to win acceptance, it is
absolutely necessary that its propounder should not merely refute
the old doctrine and expose its errors, but should trace back and
lay open to its remotest source the particular process of thought
which led these heroes of our science into their errors. It is not
enough to show *that* and *wherefore* their theses were false ; it must
also be made clear *how* and *wherefore* those thinkers arrived at
their false theses, what it was that forced them—despite all their
sagacity—to hold such theses as correct though they are simply
absurd when viewed in the light of truth. I pondered in vain over
this enigma, until suddenly, like a ray of sunlight, there shot into
the darkness of my doubt the discovery that in its essence my work
was nothing but the necessary outcome of what others had achieved
—that my theory was in no way out of harmony with the numerous
theories of my predecessors, but that rather, when thoroughly
understood, it was the very truth after which all the other economists had been searching, and upon the track of which—and this I
held to be decisive—I had been 'thrown, not by my own sagacity,
but solely by the mental labours of my great predecessors. In

other words, *the solution of the social problem offered by me is the very solution of the economic problem which the science of political economy has been incessantly seeking from its first rise down to the present day.*

But, I hear it asked, does political economy possess such a problem—one whose solution it has merely attempted but not arrived at? For it is remarkable that in our science the widest diversity of opinions co-exists with the most dogmatic orthodoxy. Very few draw from the existence of the numberless antagonistic opinions the self-evident conclusion that those opinions are erroneous, or at least unproved ; and none are willing to admit that—like their opponents—they are merely seeking the truth, and are not in possession of it. So prevalent is this tenacity of opinion which puts faith in the place of knowledge that the fact that every science owes its origin to a problem is altogether forgotten. This problem may afterwards find its solution, and therewith the science will have achieved its purpose ; but without a problem there is no investigation—consequently, though there may be knowledge, there will be no science. Clear and simple cognisances do not stimulate the human mind to that painstaking, comprehensive effort which is the necessary antecedent of science ; in brief, a science can arise only when things are under consideration which are not intelligible directly and without profound reflection—things, therefore, which contain a problem.

Thus, political economy must have had its problem, its enigma, out of the attempts to solve which it had its rise. This problem is nothing else but the question ' *Why do we not become richer in proportion to our increasing capacity of producing wealth ?* ' To this question a satisfactory answer can no more be given to-day than could be given three centuries ago—at the time, that is, when the problem first arose in view, not of a previously existing phenomenon to which the human mind had then had its attention drawn for the first time, but of a phenomenon which was then making its first appearance.

With unimportant and transient exceptions (which, it may be incidentally remarked, are easily explicable from what follows) antiquity and the Middle Ages had no political economy. This was not because the men of those times were not sharp-sighted enough to discover the sources of wealth, but because to them there was nothing enigmatical about those sources of wealth. The nations became richer the more progress they made in the art of producing; and this was so self-evident and clear that, very rightly, no one thought it necessary to waste words about it. It was not until the end of the sixteenth and the beginning of the seventeenth centuries of our era, therefore scarcely three hundred years ago, that political economy as a distinct science arose.

It is impossible for the unprejudiced eye to escape seeing what the first political economists sought for—what the problem was with which they busied themselves. They stood face to face with the enigmatical fact that increasing capacity of production is not necessarily accompanied or followed by an increase of wealth; and they sought to explain this fact. Why this remarkable fact then first made its appearance will be clearly seen from what follows; it is unquestionable *that* it then appeared, for the whole system of these first political economists, the so-called Mercantilists, had no other aim than to demonstrate that the increase of wealth depends not, as everybody had until then very naturally believed, upon increasing productiveness of labour, but upon something else, that something else being, in the opinion of the Mercantilists, money. Notwithstanding what may be called the tangible absurdity of this doctrine, it remained unquestioned for generations; nay, to be candid, most men still cling to it—a fact which would be inconceivable did not the doctrine offer a very simple and plausible explanation of the enigmatical phenomenon that increasing capacity of production does not necessarily bring with it a corresponding increase of wealth.

But it is equally impossible for the inquiring human mind to remain permanently blind to the fact that money and wealth are two very different things, and that therefore some other solution must be looked for of the problem, the existence of which is not to be denied. The Physiocrats found this second explanation in the assertion that the soil was the source and origin of all wealth, whilst human labour, however highly developed it might be, could add nothing to what was drawn from the soil, because labour itself consumed what it produced. This may look like the first application of the subsequently discovered natural law of the conservation of force ; and—notwithstanding its obvious absurdity—it was seriously believed in because it professed to explain what seemed otherwise inexplicable. Between the labourer's means of subsistence, the amount of labour employed, and the product, there is by no means that quantitative relation which is to be found in the conversion of one physical force into another. Human labour produces more or less in proportion as it is better or worse applied ; for production does not consist in converting labour into things that have a value, but in using labour to produce such things out of natural objects. A child can understand this, yet the acutest thinkers of the eighteenth century denied it with the approval of the best of their contemporaries and of not the worst of their epigones, because they could not otherwise explain the strange problem of human economics.

Then arose that giant of our science, one of the greatest minds of which humanity can boast—Adam Smith. He restored the ancient wisdom of our ancestors, and also clearly and irrefutably demonstrated what they had only instinctively recognised—namely, that the increase of wealth depends upon the productiveness of human labour. But while he threw round this truth the enduring ramparts of his logic and of his sound understanding, he altogether failed to see that the actual facts directly contradicted his doctrine. He saw that wealth did *not* increase step by step with the increased productiveness of labour ; but he believed he had discovered the cause of this in the mercantilistic and physiocratic sins of the past. In his day the historical sense was not sufficiently developed to save him from the error of confounding the—erroneous—explanations of an existing evil with its causes. Hence he believed that the course of economic events would necessarily correspond fully with the restored laws of a sound understanding—that is, that wealth would necessarily increase step by step with the capacity of producing it, if only production were freed from the legislative restraints and fiscal fetters which cramped it.

But even this delusion could not long prevail. Ricardo was

the first of the moderns who perceived that wealth did not increase
in proportion to industrial capacity, even when production and
trade were, as Smith demanded, freed from State interference and
injury. He hit upon the expedient of finding the cause of this
incongruity in the nature of labour itself. Since labour is the
only source of value, he said, it cannot increase value. A thing is
worth as much as the quantity of labour put into it; consequently,
when with increasing productiveness of labour the amount of
labour necessary to the production of a thing is diminished, then
the value of that thing diminishes also. Hence no increase in the
productiveness of labour can increase the total sum of values. This,
however, is a fundamental mistake, for what depends upon the
amount of labour is merely the *relative* value of things—the exchange relation in which they stand to other things. This is so
self-evident that Ricardo himself cannot avoid expressly stating
that he is speaking of merely the ' relative ' value of things; nevertheless, this relative value—which, strictly speaking, is nothing
but a value relation, the relation of values—is treated by him as if
it were absolute value.

And yet Ricardo's error is a not less important step in the
evolution of doctrine than those of his previously mentioned predecessors. It signifies the revival of the original problem of political
economy, which had been lost sight of since Adam Smith; and
Ricardo's follower, Marx, is in a certain sense right when, with
bitter scorn, he denounces as ' vulgar economists ' those who, persistently clinging to Smith's optimism, see in the *productiveness*
of labour the measure of the increase of *actual* wealth. For all
that was brought against Ricardo by his opponents was known by
him as well as or better than by them; only he knew what had
escaped their notice, or what they saw no obligation to take note
of in their theory—namely, that the actual facts directly contradicted the doctrine. It by no means escaped Ricardo that his
attempted reconciliation of the theory with the great problem of
economics was absurd; and Marx has most clearly shown the absurdity of it. The latter speaks of the alleged dependence of value,
not upon the productiveness of labour, but upon the effort put forth
by the labourer, as the ' fetishism ' of industry; this relation,

being unnatural, contrary to the nature of things, ought therefore —and this, again, is Marx's contribution to the progress of the science—to be referred back to an unnatural ultimate cause residing, not in the nature of things, but in human arrangements. And in looking for this ultimate cause, he, like his great predecessors, comes extremely near to the truth, but, after all, glides past without seeing it.

On this road, which leads to truth past so many errors, the last stage is the hypothesis set up by the so-called Historical School of political economy—the hypothesis, namely, that there exists in the nature of things a gulf between economic theory and practice, which makes it quite conceivable that the principles that are correct *in thesi* do not coincide with the real course of industrial life. The existence of the problem is thereby more fully established than ever, but its solution is placed outside of the domain of theoretical cognisance. For the Historical School is perfectly correct in maintaining that the abstractions of the current economic doctrine are practically useless, and that this is true not only of some of them, but of all. The real human economy does *not* obey those laws which the theorists have abstractedly deduced from economic phenomena. Hence it is only possible either that the human economy is by its very nature unfitted to become the object of scientific abstraction and cognisance, or that the abstractions hitherto made have been erroneous--erroneous, that is, not in the sense of being actually out of harmony with phenomena from which they are correctly and logically deduced, but in the sense of being theoretically erroneous, deduced according to wrong principles, and therefore useless both *in abstracto* and *in concreto*.

Of these alternatives only the second can, in reality, be correct. There is absolutely no reasonable ground for supposing that the laws which regulate the economic activity of men should be beyond human cognisance; and still less ground is there for assuming that such laws do not exist at all. We must therefore suppose that the science which seeks to discover these laws has hitherto failed to attain its object simply because it has been upon the wrong road—that is, that the principles of political economy are erroneous because, in deducing them from the economic phenomena, some fact has been overlooked, some mistake in reasoning has been committed. There *must* be a correct solution of the problem of political economy; and the solution of the social problem derived from the theory of social evolution offers at once the key to the other.

The correct answer to the question, ' Why are we not richer in proportion to the increase in our productive capacity ? ' is this : *Because wealth does not consist in what can be produced, but in what is actually produced ; the actual production, however, depends not merely upon the amount of productive power, but also upon the extent of what is required, not merely upon the possible supply, but also upon the possible demand : the current social arrangements, however, prevent the demand from increasing to the same extent as the productive capacity.* In other words : We do not produce that wealth which our present capacity makes it possible for us to produce, but only so much as we have use for ; and this use depends, not upon our capacity of producing, but upon our capacity of consuming.

It is now plain why the economic problem of the disparity between the possible and the actual increase of wealth is of so comparatively recent a date. Antiquity and the middle ages knew nothing of this problem, because human labour was not then productive enough to do more than provide and maintain the means of production after covering the consumption of the masses and the possessors of property. There was in those ages a demand for all the things which labour was then able to produce ; full employment could be made of any increase of capacity to create wealth ; no one could for a moment be in doubt as to the purpose which the increased power of producing had served ; there was no economic problem to call into existence a special science of political economy. Then came the Renaissance ; the human mind awoke out of its thousand years of hibernation ; the great inventions and discoveries rapidly followed one upon another ; division of labour and the mobilisation of capital gave a powerful impulse to production ; and now, for the first time, the productiveness of labour became so great, and the impossibility of using as much as labour could produce became so evident, that men were compelled to face the perplexing fact which finds expression in the economic problem.

That three centuries should have had to elapse before the solution could be found, is in perfect harmony with the other fact that it was reserved for these last generations to give us complete control over the forces of nature, and to render it possible for us to *make use* of the knowledge we have acquired. For so long as human production was in the main dependent upon the capacity and strength of human muscles, aided by the muscles of a few domestic animals, more might certainly be produced than would be consumed by the luxury of a few after the bare subsistence of the masses had been provided for; but to afford to *all* men an abundance without excessive labour needed the results of the substitution of the inexhaustible forces of nature for muscular energy. Until this substitution had become possible, it would have availed mankind little to have attained to a knowledge of the ultimate ground of the hindrance to the full utilisation of the then existing powers of production.

For in order that the exploitage of man by man might be put an end to, it was necessary that the amount of producible wealth should not merely exceed the consumption of the few wealthy persons, but should be sufficient to satisfy the higher human needs of all. Economic equity, if it is not to bring about a stagnation in civilisation, assumes that the man who has to depend upon the earnings of his own labour is in a position to enjoy a considerable amount of wealth at the cost of moderate effort. This has become possible only during the last few generations ; and herein is to be sought the reason why the great economists of the seventeenth and eighteenth centuries were not able to rise to an unprejudiced critical examination of the true nature and the necessary consequences of the exploiting system of industry. *They* were compelled to regard exploitage as a cruel but eternally unavoidable condition of the progress of civilisation; for when they lived it was and it always had been a necessity of civilisation, and they could not justly be expected to anticipate such a fundamental revolution in the conditions of human existence as must necessarily precede the passage from exploitage to economic equity.

So long as the exploitage of man by man was considered a

necessary and eternal institution, there existed no motive to prompt men to subject it to a closer critical investigation; and in the absence of such an investigation its influence upon the nature and extent of demand could not be discovered. The old economists were therefore *compelled* to believe it chimerical to think of demand as falling short of production; for they said, quite correctly, that man produces only to consume. Here, with them, the question of demand was done with, and every possibility of the discovery of the true connection cut off. Their successors, on the other hand, who have all been witnesses of the undreamt-of increase of the productiveness of labour, have hitherto been prevented, by their otherwise well-justified respect for the authority of the founders of our science, from adequately estimating the economic importance of this revolution in the conditions of labour. The classical system of economics is based upon a conception of the world which takes in all the affairs of life, is self-consistent, and is supported by all the past teachings of the great forms of civilisation; and if we would estimate the enormous force with which this doctrine holds us bound, we must remember that even those who were the first to recognise its incongruity with existing facts were unable to free themselves from its power. They persisted in believing in it, though they perceived its incompatibility with the facts, and knew therefore that it was false.

This glance at the historical evolution of economic doctrine opens the way to the rectification of all the errors of which the different schools of political economy have—even in their quest after truth—been guilty. It is seen that the great inquirers and thinkers of past centuries, in their vast work of investigation and analysis of economic facts, approached so very near to the full and complete cognisance of the true connection of all phenomena, that it needed but a little more labour in order to construct a thoroughly harmonious definitive economic theory based upon the solution, at last discovered, of the long vexed problem.

I zealously threw myself into this task, and had proceeded with it a considerable way—to the close of a thick first volume, containing a new treatment of the theory of value; but when at work on the classical theory of capital, I made a discovery which at once threw a ray of light into the obscurity that had until then made the practical realisation of the forms of social organisation impossible. *I perceived that capitalism stops the growth of wealth, not*—as Marx has it—*by stimulating 'production for the market,' but by preventing the consumption of the surplus produce; and that interest, though not unjust, will nevertheless in a condition of economic justice become superfluous and objectless.* These two fundamental truths will be found treated in detail in chapters xxiv. and xviii. ; but I cannot refrain here from doing justice to the manes of Marx, by acknowledging unreservedly his service in having been the first to proclaim—though he misunderstood it and argued illogically—the connection between the problem of value and modern capitalism.

I consider the theoretical and practical importance of these new truths to be incalculable. Not merely do they at once give to the theory of social evolution the unity and harmony of a definitive whole, but, what is more, they show the way to an immediate practical realisation of the principles formulated by this theory. If it is possible for the community to provide the capital for production without thereby doing injury to either the principle of perfect individual freedom or to that of justice, *if interest can be dispensed with without introducing communistic control in its stead, then there no longer stands any positive obstacle in the way of the establishment of the free social order.*

My intense delight at making this discovery robbed me of the calm necessary to the prosecution of the abstract investigations upon which I was engaged. Before my mind's eye arose scenes which the reader will find in the following pages—tangible, living pictures of a commonwealth based upon the most perfect freedom and equity, and which needs nothing to convert it into a reality but the will of a number of resolute men. It happened to me as it may have happened to Bacon of Verulam when his studies for the 'Novum Organon' were interrupted by the vision of his 'Nova Atlantis '—with this difference, however, that his prophetic glance saw the land of social freedom and justice when centuries of bondage still separated him from it, whilst I see it when mankind is already actually equipped ready to step over its threshold. Like him, I felt an irresistible impulse vividly to depict what agitated my mind. Thus, putting aside for awhile the abstract and systematic treatise which I had begun, I wrote this book, which can justly be called a ' political romance,' though it differs from all its predecessors of that category in introducing no unknown and mysterious human powers and characteristics, but throughout keeps to the firm ground of the soberest reality. The scene of the occurrences described by me is no imaginary fairy-land, but a part of our planet well-known to modern geography, which I describe exactly as its discoverers and explorers have done. The men who appear in my narrative are endowed with no supernatural properties and virtues, but are spirit of our spirit, flesh of our flesh ; and the motive prompting their economic activity is neither public spirit nor universal philanthropy, but an ordinary and commonplace self-interest. Everything in my ' Freeland ' is severely real, only one fiction underlies the whole narrative, namely, that a sufficient number of men possessing a modicum of capacity and strength have actually been found ready to take the step that shall deliver them from the bondage of the exploiting system of economics, and conduct them into the enjoyment of a system of social equity and freedom. Let this one assumption be but realised—and that it will be, sooner or later, I have no doubt, though perhaps not exactly as I have represented—then will ' Freeland ' have become a reality, and the deliverance of mankind will have been accomplished. For the age of bondage is past ; that control over the forces of nature which the founder of modern natural science, in his ' Nova Atlantis,' predicted as the end of human misery has now been actually acquired. We are prevented from enjoying the fruits of this acquisition, from making full use of the discoveries and inventions of the great intellects of our race, by nothing but the phlegmatic faculty of persistence in old habits which still keeps laws and institutions in force when the conditions that gave rise to them have long since disappeared.

As this book professes to offer, in narrative form, a picture of the actual social life of the future, it follows as a matter of course that it will be exposed, in all its essential features, to the severest professional criticism. To this criticism I submit it, with this observation, that, if my work is to be regarded as a failure, or as the offspring of frivolous fancy, it must be demonstrated that men gifted with a normal average understanding would in any material point arrive at results other than those described by me if they were organised according to the principles which I have expounded; or that those principles contain anything which a sound understanding would not accept as a self-evident postulate of justice as well as of an enlightened self-interest.

I do not imagine that the establishment of the future social order must necessarily be effected exactly in the way described in the following pages. But I certainly think that this would be the best and the simplest way, because it would most speedily and easily lead to the desired result. If economic freedom and justice are to obtain in human society, they must be seriously *determined upon*; and it seems easier to unite a few thousands in such a determination than numberless millions, most of whom are not accustomed to accept the new—let it be ever so clear and self-evident—until it has been embodied in fact.

Nor would I be understood to mean that, supposing there could be found a sufficient number of resolute men to carry out the work of social emancipation, Equatorial Africa must be chosen as the scene of the undertaking. I was led, by reasons stated in the book, to fix upon the remarkable hill country of Central Africa; but similar results could be achieved in many other parts of our planet. I must ask the reader to believe that, in making choice of the scene, I was not influenced by a desire to give the reins to my fancy; on the contrary, the descriptions of the little-known mountains and lakes of Central Africa adhere in all points to sober reality. Any one who doubts this may compare my narrative with the accounts given by Speke, Grant, Livingstone, Baker, Stanley, Emin Pacha, Thomson, Johnston, Fischer—in short, by all who have visited these paradisiacal regions.

Just a few words in conclusion, in justification of the romantic accessories introduced into the exposition of so serious a subject. I might appeal to the example of my illustrious predecessors, of whom I have already mentioned Bacon, the clearest, the acutest, the soberest thinker of all times. But I feel bound to confess that I had a double purpose. In the first place, I hoped by means of vivid and striking pictures to make the difficult questions which form the essential theme of the book acceptable to a wider circle of readers than I could have expected to reach by a dry systematic treatment. In the second place, I wished, by means of the concrete form thus given to a part of my abstractions, to refute by anticipation the criticism that those abstractions, though correct *in thesi*, were nevertheless inapplicable *in praxi*. Whether I have succeeded in these two objects remains to be proved.

THEODOR HERTZKA.

VIENNA: *October* 1889.

FREELAND

A SOCIAL ANTICIPATION

BOOK I

CHAPTER I

In July 18 . . . the following appeared in the leading journals of
Europe and America :

'INTERNATIONAL FREE SOCIETY.

'A number of men from all parts of the civilised world have
united for the purpose of making a practical attempt to solve the
social problem.

'They seek this solution in the establishment of a community
on the basis of perfect liberty and economic justice—that is, of a
community which, while it preserves the unqualified right of every
individual to control his own actions, secures to every worker the
full and uncurtailed enjoyment of the fruits of his labour.

'For the site of such a community a large tract of land shall be
procured in a territory at present unappropriated, but fertile and
well adapted for colonisation.

'The Free Society shall recognise no exclusive right of property
in the land occupied by them, either on the part of an individual or
of the collective community.

'For the cultivation of the land, as well as for productive
purposes generally, self-governing associations shall be formed, each
of which shall share its profits among its members in proportion to
their several contributions to the common labour of the association.

Anyone shall have the right to belong to any association and to leave it when he pleases.

' The capital for production shall be furnished to the producers without interest out of the revenue of the community, but it must be re-imbursed by the producers.

' All persons who are incapable of labour, and women, shall have a right to a competent allowance for maintenance out of the revenue of the community.

' The public revenue necessary for the above purposes, as well as for other public expenses, shall be provided by a tax levied upon the net income of the total production.

' The International Free Society already possesses a number of members and an amount of capital sufficient for the commencement of its work upon a moderate scale. As, however, it is thought, on the one hand, that the Society's success will necessarily be in proportion to the amount of means at its disposal, and, on the other hand, that opportunity should be given to others who may sympathise with the movement to join in the undertaking, the Society hereby announces that inquiries or communications of any kind may be addressed to the office of the Society at the Hague. The International Free Society will hold a public meeting at the Hague, on the 20th of October next, at which the definitive resolutions prior to the beginning of the work will be passed.

' For the Executive Committee of the
International Free Society,
' KARL STRAHL.

' THE HAGUE, *July* 18 . . .'

This announcement produced no little sensation throughout the world. Any suspicion of mystification or of fraud was averted by the name of the acting representative of the Executive Committee. Dr. Strahl was not merely a man of good social position, but was widely known as one of the first political economists of Germany. The strange project, therefore, could not but be seriously received, and the journals of the most diverse party tendencies at once gave it their fullest attention.

Long before the 20th of October there was not a journal on either side of the Atlantic which had not assumed a definite attitude towards the question whether the realisation of the plans of the Free Society belonged to the domain of the possible or to that of the Utopian. The Society itself, however, kept aloof from the battle of the journals. It was evidently not the intention of the Society to win over its opponents by theoretical evidence; it would attract to itself voluntary sympathisers and then proceed to action.

As the 20th of October drew near, it became evident that the largest public hall in the Hague would not accommodate the number of members, guests, and persons moved by curiosity who wished to attend. Hence it was found necessary to limit the number of at least the last category of the audience; and this was done by admitting gratis the guests who came from a distance, while those who belonged to the place were charged twenty Dutch guldens. (The proceeds of these tickets were given to the local hospital.) Nevertheless, on the morning of the 20th of October the place of assembly—capable of seating two thousand persons— was filled to the last corner.

Amid the breathless attention of the audience, the President— Dr. Strahl—rose to open the meeting. The unexpectedly large number of fresh members and the large amount of contributions which had been received showed that, even before facts had had time to speak, the importance of the projected undertaking of the International Free Society was fully recognised by thousands in all parts of the habitable globe without distinction of sex or of condition. 'The conviction that the community to the establishment of which we are about to proceed'—thus began the speaker—' is destined to attack poverty and misery at the root, and together with these to annihilate all that wretchedness and all those vices which are to be regarded as the evil results of misery—this conviction finds expression not simply in the words, but also in the actions, of the greater part of our members, in the lofty self-denying enthusiasm with which they—each one according to his power— have contributed towards the realisation of the common aim. When we sent out our appeal we numbered but eighty-four, the funds at our disposal amounted to only 11,400*l.*; to-day the Society consists of 5,650 members, and its funds amount to 205,620*l.*' (Here the speaker was interrupted by applause that lasted several minutes.) 'Of course, such a sum could not have been collected from only those most wretched of the wretched whom we are accustomed to think of as exclusively interested in the solution of the social problem. This will be still more evident when the list of our members is examined in detail. That list shows, with irresistible force, that disgust and horror at the social condition of the people have by degrees taken possession of even those who apparently derive benefit from the privations of their disinherited fellow-men. For—and I would lay special emphasis upon this—those well-to-do and rich persons, some of whose names appear as contributors of thousands of pounds to our funds, have with few exceptions joined us not merely as helpers, but also as seekers of help; they wish to found the new community not merely for their suffering brethren, but also for themselves. And from this, more than from anything else, do we derive our firm conviction of the success of our work.'

Long-continued and enthusiastic applause again interrupted the President. When quiet was once more restored, Dr. Strahl thus concluded his short address :

'In carrying out our programme, a hitherto unappropriated large tract of land will have to be acquired for the founding of an independent community. The question now is, what part of the earth shall we choose for such a purpose ? For obvious reasons we cannot look for territory to any part of Europe ; and everywhere in Asia, at least in those parts in which Caucasian races could flourish, we should be continually coming into collision with ancient forms of law and society. We might expect that the several governments in America and Australia would readily grant us land and freedom of action ; but even there our young community would scarcely be able to enjoy that undisturbed quiet and security against antagonistic interference which would be at first a necessary condition of rapid and uninterrupted success. Thus there remains only Africa, the oldest yet the last-explored part of the world. The equatorial portion of its interior is virtually unappropriated ; we find there not merely the practically unlimited extent and absence of disturbing influences necessary for our development, but— if the selection be wisely made—the most favourable conditions of climate and soil imaginable. Vast highlands, which unite in themselves the advantages of the tropics and of our Alpine regions, there await settlement. Communication with these hilly districts situated far in the interior of the Dark Continent is certainly difficult ; but that is a condition necessary to us at first. We therefore propose to you that we should fix our new home in the interior of Equatorial Africa. And we are thinking particularly of the mountain district of Kenia, the territory to the east of the Victoria Nyanza, between latitude 1° S. and 1° N., and longitude 34°–38° E. It is there that we expect to find the most suitable district for our purpose. Does the meeting approve of this choice ? '

Unanimous assent was expressed, and loud cries were enthusiastically uttered of ' Forwards ! To-day rather than to-morrow ! ' It was unmistakably evident that the majority wished to make a beginning at once. The President then resumed :

' Such haste is not practicable, my friends. The new home must first be found and acquired ; and that is a difficult and dangerous undertaking. The way leads through deserts and inhospitable forests ; conflicts with inimical wild races will probably be inevitable ; and all this demands strong men—not women, children, and old men. The provisioning and protection of an emigrant train of many thousand persons through such regions must be organised. In short, it is absolutely necessary that a number of selected pioneers should precede the general company. When the pioneers have accomplished their task, the rest can follow.

' To make all requisite provision with the greatest possible vigour, foresight, and speed, the directorate must be harmonious and fully informed as to our aims. Hitherto the business of the Society has been in the hands of a committee of ten ; but as the membership has so largely increased, and will increase still more largely, it might appear desirable to elect a fresh executive, or at least to add to the numbers of the present one from the new members. Yet we cannot recommend you to adopt such a course, for the reason that the new members do not know each other, and could not become sufficiently well acquainted with each other soon enough to prevent the election from being anything but a game of chance. We rather ask from you a confirmation of our authority, with the power of increasing our numbers by co-option from among you as our judgment may suggest. And we ask for this authorisation—which can be at any time withdrawn by your resolution in a full meeting—for the period of two years. At the expiration of this period we shall—we are fully convinced—not only have fixed upon a new home, but have lived in it long enough to have learnt a great deal about it.'

This proposition was unanimously adopted.

The President announced that all the communications of the executive committee to the members would be published both in the newspapers and by means of circulars. He then closed the meeting, which broke up in the highest spirits.

The first act of the executive committee was to appoint two persons with full powers to organise and take command of the pioneer expedition to Central Africa. These two leaders of the expedition were so to divide their duties that one of them was to organise and command the expedition until a suitable territory was selected and occupied, and the other was to take in hand the organisation of the colony. The one was to be, as it were, the conductor, and the other the statesman of the expeditionary corps. For the former duty the committee chose the well-known African traveller Thomas Johnston, who had repeatedly traversed the region between Kilimanjaro and Kenia, the so-called Masailand. Johnston was a junior member of the Society, and was co-opted upon the committee upon his nomination as leader of the pioneer expedition. To take charge of the expedition after its arrival at the locality chosen, the committee nominated a young engineer, Henry Ney, who, as the most intimate friend of the founder and intellectual leader of the Society—Dr. Strahl—was held to be the most fitting person to represent him during the first period of the founding of the community.

Dr. Strahl himself originally intended to accompany the pioneers and personally to direct the first work of organisation in the new home, but the other members of the committee urged strong objections. They could not permit the man upon whose further labours the prosperous development of the Society so largely depended to expose himself to dangers from which he was the more likely to suffer harm because his health was delicate. And, after mature reflection, he himself admitted that for the next few months his presence would be more needed in Europe than in Central Africa. In a word, Dr. Strahl consented to wait and to follow the pioneers with the main body of members; and Henry Ney went with the expedition as his substitute.

CHAPTER II

THE account—contained in this and the next five chapters—of the preparations for and the successful completion of the African expedition, as well as of the initial work of settling and cultivating the highlands of Kenia, is taken from the journal of Dr. Strahl's friend :

My appointment as provisional substitute for our revered leader at first filled me with alarm. The reflection that upon me depended in no small degree the successful commencement of a work which we all had come to regard as the most important and far-reaching in its consequences of any in the history of human development, produced in me a sensation of giddiness. But my despondency did not last long. I had no right to refuse a responsibility which my colleagues had declared me to be the most fitted to bear ; and when my fatherly friend Strahl asked me whether I thought failure possible on the supposition that those who were committed to my leadership were fired with the same zeal as myself, and whether I had any reason to question this supposition, then my courage revived, and in place of my previous timidity I felt an unshakable conviction of the success of the work, a conviction which I never lost for a moment.

The preparatory measures for the organisation of the pioneer expedition were discussed and decided upon by the whole committee of the International Free Society. The first thing to determine was the number of the expedition. The expedition must not be too small, since the race among whom we proposed to settle—the nomadic Masai, between the Kilima and the Kenia mountains—was the most warlike in Equatorial Africa, and could be kept in check only by presenting a strong and imposing appearance. On the other hand, if the expedition were too numerous it would be exposed to the risk of being hampered by the difficulty of obtaining supplies. It was unanimously agreed to fix the number of pioneers at two hundred of the sturdiest members of the Society, the best able to endure fatigue and privation and to face danger, and every one of whom gave evidence of possessing that degree of general intelligence which would qualify him to assume, in case of need, the whole responsibility of the mission.

In pursuance of this resolve, the committee applied to the branch associations—which had been formed wherever members of the Society lived—for lists of those persons willing to join the expedition, to whose health, vigorous constitution, and intelligence the respective branch associations could certify. At the same time a full statement was to be sent of the special knowledge, experience, and capabilities of the several candidates. In the course of a few weeks offers were received from 870 strongly recommended members. Of these a hundred, whose qualifications appeared to the committee to be in all points eminently satisfactory, were at once chosen. This select hundred included four naturalists (two of whom were geologists), three physicians, eight engineers, four representatives of other branches of technical knowledge, and six scientifically trained agriculturists and foresters; further, thirty artisans such as would make the expedition able to meet all emergencies; and, finally, forty-five men who were exceptionally good marksmen or remarkable for physical strength. The selection of the other hundred pioneers was entrusted to the branch associations, which were to choose one pioneer out of every seven or eight of those whose names they had sent. The chosen men were asked to meet as speedily as possible in Alexandria, which was fixed upon as the provisional rendezvous of the expedition; money for their travelling expenses was voted— which, it may be noted in passing, was declined with thanks by about half of the pioneers.

Thus passed the month of November. In the meantime the committee had not been idle. The equipment of the expedition was fully and exhaustively discussed, the details decided upon, and all requisites carefully provided. Each of the two hundred members was furnished with six complete sets of underclothing of light elastic woollen material—the so-called Jäger clothing; a lighter and a heavier woollen outer suit; two pair of waterproof and two pair of lighter boots; two cork helmets, and one waterproof overcoat. In weapons every member received a repeating-rifle of the best construction for twelve shots, a pocket revolver, and an American bowie-knife. In addition, there were provided a hundred sporting guns of different calibres, from the elephant-guns, which shot two-ounce explosive bullets, to the lightest fowling-pieces; and of course the necessary ammunition was not forgotten.

At this point the weightiest questions for discussion were

whether the expedition should be a mounted one, and whether the
baggage should be transported from the Zanzibar coast by porters,
called *pagazis*, or by beasts of burden. Johnston's first intention
was to purchase only eighty horses and asses for the conveyance of
the heavier baggage, and for the use of any who might be sick or
fatigued; and to hire 800 *pagazis* in Zanzibar and Mombasa as
porters of the remainder of the baggage, which he estimated at about
400 cwt. But he gave up this plan at once when he discovered
what my requirements were. He had made provision merely for
six months' maintenance of the expedition, and for articles of
barter with the natives. I required, above all, that the expedition should take with it implements, machinery (in parts), and such
other things as would place us in a position, when we had arrived
at our goal, as speedily as possible to begin a rational system of
agriculture and to engage in the production of what would be necessary for the use of the many thousand colonists who would follow
us. We needed a number of agricultural implements, or, at least,
of those parts of them which could not be manufactured without
complicated and tedious preparation; similar materials for a field-
forge and smithy, as well as for a flour-mill and a saw-mill; further,
seeds of all kinds and saplings in large quantities, as well as many
materials which we could not reckon upon being able to produce at
once in the interior of Africa. Finally, I pointed out that, in order
to make the way safe for the caravans that would follow us, it
would be advisable to form friendly alliances, particularly with the
warlike Masai, for which purpose larger and more valuable stores
of presents would be required than had been provided.

Johnston made no objection to all this. He estimated that the
necessary amount of baggage would thus be doubled, perhaps trebled,
and that the 1,600 or 2,400 *pagazis* that would be required would
make the expedition too cumbrous. Dr. Strahl proposed that transportation by *pagazis* should be relinquished altogether, and that
beasts of burden should be used exclusively. He knew well that in
the low lands of Equatorial Africa the tsetse-fly and the bad water
were particularly fatal to horses; but these difficulties were not to
be anticipated on our route, which would soon take us to the high
land where the animals would be safe. And the difficulty due to
the peculiar character of the roads in Central Africa could be easily
overcome. These roads possess—as he had learnt from Johnston's

descriptions, among others—where they pass through thickets or bush, a breadth of scarcely two feet, and are too narrow for pack-horses, which have often to be unloaded at such places, and the transportation of the luggage has to be effected by porters. This last expedient would either be impossible or would involve an incalcul-able loss of time in the case of a caravan possessing only beasts of burden with a proportionately small number of drivers and attendants. But he thought that the roads could everywhere be made passable for even beasts of burden by means of an adequate number of well-equipped *éclaireurs*, or advance-guard. Johnston was of the same opinion: if he were furnished with a hundred natives—whom he would get from the population on the coast—supplied with axes and fascine-knives, he would undertake to lead a caravan of beasts of burden to the Kenia without any delay worth mentioning.

When this question was settled, Dr. Strahl again brought forward the idea of mounting the 200 pioneers themselves. He had a double end in view. In the first place—and it was this in part that had led him to make the previous proposition—it would be necessary to provide for the introduction and acclimatisation of beasts of burden and draught in the future home, where there were already cattle, sheep, and goats, but neither horses, asses, nor camels ; and he held that it would be best for the expedition to take with them at once as large a number as possible of these useful animals. Moreover, he thought that we could travel much faster if we were mounted. In the next place, he attached great importance to the careful selection of animals—whether beasts of burden or for the saddle—suitable for breeding purposes, particularly in the case of the horses, since the character of the future stock would depend entirely upon that of those first introduced. This also was agreed to ; only Johnston feared that the expenses of the expedition would be too heavily increased. According to his original plan, the expenses would not exceed 12,000*l.* ; but the alterations would about quad-ruple the cost. This was not questioned ; and Johnston's estimate was subsequently found to be correct, for the expedition actually consumed 52,500*l.* But it was unanimously urged that the funds which had been placed so copiously at their disposal, and which were still rapidly pouring in, could not be more usefully applied than in expediting the journey as much as possible, and in establishing the new community upon as sound a foundation as the means allowed.

The detailed consideration of the requisite material was then proceeded with. When everything had been reckoned, and the total weight estimated, it was found that we should have to transport a total burden of about 1,200 cwt., as follows :

150 cwt. of various kinds of meat and drink ;
120 „ „ travelling materials (including fifty waterproof tents for four men each) ;
160 „ „ various kinds of seed and other agricultural materials ;
220 „ „ implements, machinery, and tools ;
400 „ „ articles of barter and presents ;
120 „ „ ammunition and explosives.

At Johnston's special request, in addition to the above, four light steel mortars for shell were ordered of Krupp, in Essen. His object was not to use these murderous weapons seriously against any foe ; but he reckoned that, should occasion occur, peace could be more easily preserved by means of the terror which they would excite. At the last moment there came to hand 300 Werndl rifles, together with the needful cartridges—very good breechloaders which we bought cheaply of the Austrian Government, to use partly as a reserve and partly to arm some of the negroes who were to be hired at Zanzibar.

The baggage was to be borne by 100 sumpter-horses, 200 asses and mules, and 80 camels. Since we also needed 200 saddle-horses, with a small reserve for accidents, it was resolved to buy in all 320 horses, 210 asses, and 85 camels, the horses to be bought, some in Egypt and some in Arabia, the camels in Egypt, and the asses in Zanzibar.

All the necessary purchases were at once made. Our authorised agents procured everything at the first source ; buyers were sent to Yemen in Arabia and to Zanzibar for horses and asses. When all this was done or arranged, Johnston and I—we had meantime contracted a close friendship—started for Alexandria.

But, before I describe our action there, I must mention an incident which occurred in the committee. A young American lady had determined to join the expedition. She was rich, beautiful, and eccentric, an enthusiastic admirer of our principles, and evidently not accustomed to consider it possible that her wishes should be seriously opposed. She had contributed very largely to the funds of the Society, and had made up her mind to be one of the first to set foot in the new African home. I must confess that I was sorry for the noble girl, who was devoured by an eager longing for adventure and painfully felt as a slight the anxious solicitude exhibited by the committee on account of her sex. But nothing could be done ; we had refused several women wishful to accompany their husbands who had been chosen as pioneers, and we could make no exceptions. When the young lady found that her appeals failed to move us men of the committee, she turned to our female relatives, whom she speedily discovered ; but she met with little success among them. She was cordially and affectionately received by the ladies, for she was very charming in her enthusiasm ; but that was only another reason, in the eyes of the women, for concluding that the men had been right in refusing to allow such a delicate creature to share in the dangers and privations of the journey of exploration. She was petted and treated like a spoilt child that longed for the impossible, until Miss Ellen Fox was fairly beside herself.

She suddenly calmed down ; and this occurred in a striking manner immediately after she became acquainted with another lady who also, though for other reasons, wished to join our expedition. This other lady was my sister Clara. While the former was prompted to go to Africa by her zeal for our principles, the latter was fired with the same desire by detestation and dread of those same principles. My sister (twelve years my senior, and still unmarried, because she had not been able to find a man who satisfied her ideal of personal distinction and lofty character) was one of the best—in her inmost heart one of the noblest—of women, but full of immovable prejudices with which I had been continually coming into contact for the twenty-six years of my life. She was not coldhearted—her hand was always open to those who needed help ; but she had an invincible contempt for everything that did not belong to the so-called higher, cultured classes. When for the first time the social question was explained to her by me, she was seized with horror at the idea that reasonable men should believe that she and her kitchenmaid were endowed with equal rights by nature. Find-

ing that all efforts to convert her were in vain, I long refrained
from telling her anything of my relations with Dr. Strahl, or of the
founding of the Free Society and the *rôle* which I played in it. I
wished to spare her as long as possible the sorrow of knowing of
my going astray; for I love this sister dearly, and am idolised by
her in return. For many long years the one passion of her life was
her anxious solicitude about me. We lived together, and she always
treated me as a small boy whose bringing up was her business.
That I could exist more than at most two or three days away from
her protection, without becoming the victim of my childish inexpe-
rience and of the wickedness of evil men, always seemed to her an
utter impossibility. Imagine, then, the unutterable terror of my protectress when I was eventually compelled to disclose to her not only
that I was a member of a socialistic society, had not only devoted
the whole of my modest fortune to the objects of that society, but
had actually been selected as leader of 200 Socialists into the interior
of Africa! It was some days before she could grasp and believe the
monstrous fact; then followed entreaties, tears, desperate reproaches,
and expostulations. I might let the fellows have my money—over
which, however, she felt that she should have kept better guard—
but, for heaven's sake, could I not stay like an honest man at
home? She consulted our family physician as to my responsibility
for my actions; but she came back worse than she went, for he was
one of our Society—indeed, a member of the expedition. At last,
when all else had failed, she announced that, if I persisted in rush-
ing to my ruin, she would accompany me. When I explained to
her that this could not be, as there were to be no women in the
expedition, she brought her heaviest artillery to bear upon me;
she reminded me of our deceased mother, who, on her deathbed,
had commissioned my sister never to leave me—a testamentary
injunction to which I ought religiously to submit. As I still
remained obdurate, daring for the first time in my life to remark
that our good mother had plainly committed me to my sister's care
only during the period of my childhood, she fell into hopeless
despondency, out of which nothing could rouse her. In vain did I
use endearing terms; in vain did I assure her that among our 200
pioneers there would certainly be some excellent fellows between
whom and myself there would exist kindly human relations; in vain
did I promise her that she should follow me in about six months'

time : it was all of no avail. She looked upon me as lost ; and as
the day of my departure drew near I became exceedingly anxious
to find some means of allaying my sister's touching but foolish
sorrow.

Just then Miss Ellen visited my sister. I was called away by
business, and had to leave them together alone ; when I returned I
found Clara wonderfully comforted. She no longer wailed and
moaned, and was even able to speak of the dreadful subject without
tears. It was plain that Miss Ellen's exaltation of feeling had
wrought soothingly upon her childish anguish ; and I inwardly
blessed the charming American for it, the more so that from that
moment the latter no longer troubled us with her importunities.
She had gone away suddenly, and I most heartily congratulated
myself on having thus got rid of a double difficulty.

On the 3rd of December Johnston and I reached Alexandria,
where we found most of our fellow-pioneers awaiting us. Twenty-
three were still missing, some of whom were coming from great distances, and others had been hindered by unforeseen contingencies.
Johnston set to work at once with the equipment, exercising,
and organisation of the troop. For these purposes we left the
city, and encamped about six miles off, on the shore of Lake
Mareotis. The provisioning was undertaken by a commissariat of six
members under my superintendence ; each man received full rations
and— unless it was expressly declined—2*l.* per month in cash. The
same amount was paid during the whole of the time occupied by the
expedition—of course not in the form of cash, which would have been
useless in Equatorial Africa, but in goods at cost price for use or
barter. After such articles as clothing and arms had been unpacked,
the exercises began. Eight hours a day were spent in manœuvring,
marching, swimming, riding, fencing, and target-practice. Later
on Johnston organised longer marches, extending over several days,
as far as Ghizeh and past the Pyramids to Cairo. In the meantime
we got to know each other. Johnston appointed his inferior officers,
to whom, as to him, military obedience was to be rendered -a necessity which was readily recognised by all without exception. This
may appear strange to some, in view of the fact that we were going
forth to found a community in which absolute social equality and
unlimited individual liberty were to prevail. But we all understood
that the ultimate object of our undertaking, and the expedition

which was to lead to that object, were two different things. During the whole journey there did not occur one case of insubordination ; while, on the other hand, on the side of the officers not one instance of unnecessary or rude assumption of authority was noticed.

When the time to go on to Zanzibar came, we were a completely trained picked body of men. In manœuvring we could compete with any corps of Guards—naturally only in those exercises which give dexterity and agility in face of a foe, and not in the parade march and the military salutes. In these last respects we were and re-mained as ignorant as Hottentots. But we could, without serious inconvenience, march or sit in the saddle, with only brief halts, for twenty-four hours at a stretch ; our quick firing yielded a very respectable number of hits at a distance of eleven hundred yards ; and our grenade firing was not to be despised. We were quite as skilful with a small battery of Congreve rockets which Johnston had had sent after us from Trieste, on the advice of an Egyptian officer who had served in the Soudan—a native of Austria, and a frequent witness of our practising at Alexandria. The language of command, as well as that of our general intercourse, was English. As many as 35 per cent. of us were English and American, whilst the next numerous nationality—the German—was represented by only about 23 per cent. Moreover, all but about forty-five of us understood and spoke English more or less perfectly, and these forty-five learnt to speak it tolerably well during our stay in Alexandria.

On the 30th of March we embarked on the ' Aurora,' a fine screw steamer of 3,000 tons, which the committee had chartered of the English P. and O. Company, and which, after it had, at Liverpool, Marseilles, and Genoa, taken on board the wares ordered for us, reached Alexandria on the 22nd of March. The embarkation and providing accommodation for 200 horses and 60 camels, which had been bought in Egypt, occupied several days ; but we were in no hurry, as, on account of the rainy season, the journey into the interior of Africa could not be begun before May. We reckoned that the passage from Alexandria to Zanzibar—the halt in Aden, for taking on board more horses and camels, included—would not ex-ceed twenty days. We had therefore fully two weeks left for Zan-zibar and for the passage across to Mombasa, whence we intended to take the road to the Kilimanjaro and the Kenia, and where, on account of the danger from the fever which was alleged to prevail on the coast, we did not purpose remaining a day longer than was necessary.

Our programme was successfully carried out. At Aden we met our agents with 120 superb Yemen horses, and 25 camels of equally excellent breed. Here also were embarked 115 asses, which—like the camels—had been procured in Arabia instead of Zanzibar or Egypt. On the 16th of April the 'Aurora' dropped anchor in the harbour of Zanzibar.

Half the population of the island came out to greet us. Our fame had gone before us, and, as it seemed, no ill fame; for the European colonists—who during the last few years had increased to nearly 200—and the Arabians, Hindoos, and negroes, vied with each other in friendliness and welcome. Naturally, the first person to receive us was our Zanzibar representative, who hastened to give us the agreeable assurance that he had exactly performed his commission, and that, in view of the prevailing public sentiment respecting us, there would be no difficulty whatever in engaging the number of natives we required. The English, French, German, Italian, and American consuls welcomed us most cordially; as did also the representatives of the great European and American houses of business, who were all most zealous in pressing their hospitality upon us. Finally appeared the prime minister of the Sultan, who claimed the whole 200 of us as his guests. In order to avoid giving offence in any quarter, we left ourselves at the disposal of the consuls, who distributed us among the friendly competitors in a way most agreeable to everyone. Johnston and sixteen officers—myself being one of the company—were allotted to the Sultan, who placed his whole palace, except that part devoted to his harem, at our disposal, and entertained us in a truly princely manner. Yet, ungrateful as it may seem, I must say that we seventeen elect had every reason to envy those of our colleagues who were entertained less splendidly, but very comfortably, in the bosom of European families. Our host did only too much for us: the ten days of our residence in Zanzibar were crowded with an endless series of banquets, serenades, Bayadère dances, and the like; and this was the less agreeable as we really found more to be done than we had expected. A great quantity of articles for barter had to be bought and packed; and we had to engage no fewer than 280 Swahili men—coast dwellers—as attendants, drivers, and other workmen, besides the requisite number of guides and interpreters. In all this both the consuls and the Sultan's officials rendered us excellent service ; and as the negroes had a very favourable opinion of our expedition, in which they anticipated neither excessive labour nor great danger, since we had a great number of beasts and were well armed, we had a choice of the best men that Zanzibar could afford for our purpose. But all this had to be attended to, and during the whole of the ten days Johnston was sorely puzzled how to execute his commission and yet do justice to the attentions of the Sultan.

At last, in spite of everything, the work was accomplished, and, as the issue showed, well accomplished—certainly not so much through any special care and skill on our part as through the good will shown to us on all sides. The merchants, European and Indian, supplied us with the best goods at the lowest prices, without giving us much trouble in selection; and the Swahili exercised among themselves a kind of ostracism by whipping out of the market any disreputable or useless colleagues. In this last respect, so fortunate were we in our selection that, during the whole course of the expedition, we were spared all those struggles with the laziness or obstinacy of the natives which are generally the lot of such caravans ; in fact we had not a single case of desertion—an unheard-of circumstance in the history of African expeditions.

On the 26th of April we left Zanzibar in the ' Aurora,' and reached Mombasa safely the next morning. We had sent on, in charge of ten of our men, the whole of our beasts and the greater part of our baggage in the ' Aurora ' a week before, together with a number of the attendants who had been engaged in Zanzibar. We found all these in good condition, and for the most part recovered from the ill-effects of the sea voyage. In order to muster the people we had engaged, and at the same time to allot to each his duty, we pitched a camp outside of Mombasa in a little palm-grove that commanded a beautiful view of the sea. To every two led horses or camels, and to every four asses, a driver and an attendant were allotted. This gave employment to 145 of the 280 Swahili; 35 more were selected to carry the lighter and more fragile articles, or such things as must be always readily accessible ; and the remaining 100—including, of course, the guides and two interpreters— served as *éclaireurs*. By the 2nd of May everything was ready,

c

the burdens distributed, and every man had his place assigned; the journey into the interior could be at once begun.

As, however, we could not start until we had received the European mails, due in Zanzibar on the 3rd or 4th, by which we were to receive the last news of our friends and any further instructions the committee wished to give us, we had several days of leisure, which we were able to employ in viewing the country around Mombasa.

The place itself is situated upon a small island at the mouth of a river, which here spreads out into a considerable bay, with several dense mangrove-swamps upon its banks. Hence residence on the coast and in Mombasa itself is not conducive to health, and by no means desirable for a length of time. But a few miles inland there are gently undulating hills, clothed with fine clumps of cocoa-palms growing on ground covered with an emerald-green sward. Among the trees are scattered the garden-encircled huts of the Wa-Nyika, who inhabit this coast. These hills afford a healthy residence during the rainy season; but it would be dangerous for a European to live here the year through, as the prevailing temperature in the hot months— from October to January—would in time be injurious to him. In May, however, when the heavy rains that fall from February to April have thoroughly cooled the soil and the air, the heat is by no means disagreeable.

The French packet-ship was a day behind, and did not arrive at Zanzibar until late in the night of the 4th; but, thanks to the courtesy of the captain, we received our letters a day earlier than we had expected them. The captain, learning at Aden that we were awaiting our letters at Mombasa, when off that place hailed an Arabian dhow and sent us by that our packages, which we consequently received on the same morning; we should otherwise have had to wait for them until the evening of the next day. Of the news thus brought us only two items need be mentioned: first, the intimation that the committee had instructed our agent in Zanzibar to keep up constant communication with Mombasa during the whole period of our journey, and for that purpose to have in readiness several despatch-boats and a swift-sailing cutter; and, secondly, the information that on the 18th of April, the day of despatching the mails, the membership of the Society had reached 8,460, with funds amounting to nearly 400,000*l*.

Together with our letters there came another little surprise for us from home. The dhow brought us a pack of not less than thirty-two dogs, in charge of two keepers, who were the bearers of greetings to us from their master, Lord Clinton. His lordship, a warm espouser of our principles and a great lover of dogs, had sent us this present from York, believing that it would be very useful to us both on our journey and after we had arrived at our destination. The dogs were splendid creatures—a dozen mastiffs and twenty sheep-dogs of that long-legged and long-haired breed which looks like a cross between the greyhound and the St. Bernard. The smallest of the mastiffs was above twenty-seven inches high at the loins; the sheep-dogs not much smaller; and they all proved themselves to be well-trained and well-mannered creatures. They met with a cordial welcome from us all. The two keepers told us that they were perfectly indifferent to our plans and principles, for they ' knew nothing at all about such matters '; but, if we would allow them, they would gladly accompany us along with their four-footed friends. As they looked like strong, healthy, and, in spite of their simplicity, very decent fellows, and as they professed to be tolerably expert in ·iding and shooting and experienced in the training and treatment of different kinds of animals, we were pleased to take them with us. A cordial letter of thanks was returned to Lord Clinton; and when our mails had been sent off to Zanzibar, and all arrangements for the morrow completed, we retired to rest for the last time previous to our departure for the dark interior of the African world.

CHAPTER III

On the 5th of May we were woke by the horns and drums of the Kirangozis (leaders of the caravan) at three o'clock, according to arrangement. The large camp-fires, which had been prepared overnight, were lighted, and breakfast—tea or coffee, with eggs and cold meat for us whites, a soup of meat and vegetables for the Swahili—was cooked; and by the light of the same fires preparations were made for starting. The advance-guard, consisting of the hundred *éclaireurs* and twenty lightly laden packhorses, accompanied by thirty mounted pioneers, started an hour after we awoke. The duty of the advance-guard was, with axe, billhook,

c 2

and pick, so to clear the way where it led through jungle and
thicket as to make it passable for our sumpter beasts with the
larger baggage; to bridge, as well as they were able, over watercourses; and to prepare the next camping-place for the main body.
In order to do this, the advance-guard had to precede us several
hours, or even several days, according to the character of the
country. We learnt from our guides that no great difficulties were
to be anticipated at the outset, so at first our advance-guard had no
need to be more than a few hours ahead.

It was eight o'clock when the main body was in order. In the
front were 150 of us whites, headed by Johnston and myself; then
followed in a long line first the led horses, then the asses, and
finally the camels; twenty whites brought up the rear. Thus, at
last, we left our camp with the sun already shining hotly upon us;
and, throwing back a last glance at Mombasa lying picturesquely
behind us, we bade farewell to the sea foaming below, whose dull
roar could be distinctly heard despite a distance of four or five miles.
To the sound of horns and drums we scaled the steep though not
very high hills that separated us from the so-called desert which
lay between us and the interior. The region, which we soon
reached, evidently deserves the name of desert only in the hot
season; now, when the three months' rainy season was scarcely
over, we found the landscape park-like. Rich, though not very
high, grass alternated with groves of mimosa and dwarf palm and
with clumps of acacia. When, after a march of two hours, we had
left the last of the coast hills behind us, the grass became more
luxuriant and the trees more numerous, and taller; antelopes
showed themselves in the distance, but they were very shy and
were soon scared away by the dogs, which were not yet broken of
the habit of useless hunting. About eleven o'clock we halted for
rest and refreshment in the shade of a palm-grove which a dense
mass of climbing plants had converted into a stately giant canopy.
All — men and beasts — were exhausted, though we had been scarcely
three hours on the march; the previous running and racing about
in camp for four hours had been the reverse of refreshing to us, and
after ten o'clock the heat had become most oppressive. Johnston
comforted us by saying that it would be better in future. In the
first place, we should henceforth be less time in getting ready to
march, and should therefore start earlier—if it depended upon him,

soon after four—doing the greatest part of the way in the cool of
the morning, and halting at nine, or at the latest at ten. Moreover, the district we were now going through was the hottest, if
not the most difficult, we should have to travel over; when we had
once got into the higher regions we should be troubled by excessive
heat only exceptionally.

Reinvigorated by this encouragement, and more still by a
generous meal—the bulk of which consisted of two fat oxen bought
on the way—and by the rest in the shade of the dense liana-canopy,
we started again at four o'clock, and, after a trying march of nearly
five hours, reached the camping-place prepared by our advance-
guard in the neighbourhood of a Wa-Kamba village between Mkwalé
and Mkinga. We did not come up with the advance-guard at all;
they had rested here about noon, but had gone on several hours
before we arrived, in order to keep ahead of us. However, they had
left our supper in charge of one of their number—eleven antelopes
of different kinds, which their huntsmen had shot by the way. The
Swahili who had been left with this welcome gift, and who mounted
his Arab horse to overtake his companions as soon as he had
delivered his message, told us that they had unexpectedly come
upon a large herd of these charming beasts, among which the white
huntsmen had committed great havoc. Five antelopes had furnished
his company with their midday meal, as many had been taken away
for their evening meal, and the rest—among which, as he remarked,
not without a little envy, were the fattest animals—had been left
for us. This attention on the part of our companions who were
ahead of us was received by us all the more gratefully as, in the
Wa-Kamba villages which we had passed through since our midday
halt, we had found no beasts for sale, except a few lean goats, which
we had refused in hopes of getting something better; and we had
been less fortunate in the chase than our advance-guard. Nothing
but a few insignificant birds had come within reach of our sportsmen, and so we had already given up any hope of having fresh meat
when the unexpected present furnished us with a dainty meal, the
value of which only those can rightly estimate who have left an
exhausting march behind them, and have the prospect of nothing
but vegetables and preserved meats before them.

On the morning of the next day, mindful of the inconvenience
experienced by us the day before, we began our march as early as

half-past four. At first the country was quite open; but in a couple
of hours we reached the Duruma country, where our advance-guard
had had hot work. For more than half a mile the path lay through
thorny bush of the most horrible kind, which would have been absolutely impassable by our sumpter beasts but for the hatchets and
billhooks of our brave *éclaireurs*. Thanks, however, to the ample
clearance they had made, we were quickly through. Towards eight
o'clock the way got better again; and this alternation was repeated
until, on the evening of the third day, we left Durumaland behind
us and entered upon the great desert that stretches thence almost
without a break as far as Teita. We once got very near to our
advance-guard; I gave my steed the spur, in order to see the men
at their work, but they made it their ambition to prevent us from
getting quite close to them. With eager haste they plied knife and
hatchet in the thick thorny bush, until a passage was made for us;
and they then at once hurried forward without waiting for the main
column, the head of which was within a mile and a quarter of them.

Nothing noteworthy occurred during these days. We left our
camp about half-past four each morning, made our first halt about
nine, resumed our march again before five in the afternoon, and
camped between eight and nine in the evening. The provisioning
in Durumaland was difficult; but we succeeded in procuring from
the pastoral and agricultural inhabitants sufficient vegetables and
flesh food, and of the latter a supply large enough to last us until
we had passed through the Duruma desert. The soil seems to possess
a great natural fertility, but its best portions are uncultivated and
neglected, since the inhabitants seldom venture out of their jungle-
thickets on account of the incessant inroads of the Masai. We heard
everywhere of the evil deeds of these marauders, who had only a
few weeks before fallen upon a tribe, slain the men, and driven off
the women, children, and cattle, and were said to be again on the
war-path in search of new booty. Our assurance that we would
shortly free their district, as well as the districts of all the tribes with
whom we had contracted or expected to contract alliance, from this
scourge, was received by the Wa-Duruma with great incredulity;
for the Sultan of Zanzibar himself had failed to prevent the Masai
from extending their raids and levying contributions even as far as
Mombasa and Pangani. Nevertheless, our promise spread rapidly
far and near.

On the morning of the fourth day of our journey, just as we were preparing to enter upon the desert, we learnt from some natives, who hurried by breathless with alarm and anxiety, that a strong body of Masai had in the night made a large capture of slaves and cattle, and were now on their way to attack us. Thereupon we altered our arrangements. As the position we occupied was a good one, we left our baggage and the drivers in camp, and got ourselves ready for action. The guns were mounted and horsed, and the rockets prepared; the former were placed in the middle, and the latter in the two wings of the long line into which we formed ourselves. This was the work of scarcely ten minutes, and in less than another quarter of an hour we saw about six hundred Masai approaching at a rapid pace. We let them come on unmolested until they were about 1,100 yards off. Then the trumpets brayed, and our whole line galloped briskly to meet them. The Masai stopped short when they saw the strange sight of a line of cavalry bearing down upon them. We slackened our pace and went on slowly until we were a little over a hundred yards from them. Then we halted, and Johnston, who is tolerably fluent in the Masai dialect, rode a few steps farther and asked them in a loud voice what they wanted. There was a short consultation among the Masai, and then one of them came forward and asked whether we would pay tribute or fight. 'Is this *your* country,' was the rejoinder, 'that you demand tribute? We pay tribute to no one; we have gifts for our friends, and deadly weapons for our foes. Whether the Masai will be our friends we shall see when we visit their country. But we have already formed an alliance with the Wa-Duruma, and therefore we allow no one to rob them. Give back the prisoners and the booty and go home to your kraals, else we shall be obliged to use against you our weapons and our medicines (magic)—which we should be sorry to do, for we wish to contract alliance with you also.'

This last statement was evidently taken to be a sign of weakness, for the Masai, who at first seemed to be a little alarmed, shook their spears threateningly, and with loud shouts set themselves again in motion towards us. Our trumpets brayed again, and while we horsemen sprang forwards the guns and rockets opened fire—not upon the foe, among whose close masses they would have wrought execution as terrible as it would have been unnecessary—but away over their heads. The Masai stayed for only one volley. When the guns thundered, the rockets, hissing and crackling, swept over their heads, and, above all, the strange creatures with four feet and two heads rushed upon them, they turned in an instant and fled away howling. Our artillery sent another volley after them, to increase their panic, if possible; while the horsemen busied themselves taking prisoners and getting possession of the slaves and children, who were now visible in the distance.

In less than half an hour we had forty-three prisoners, and the whole of the booty was in our possession. We should not have succeeded so completely in freeing the Duruma women and children had these not been fettered in such a way as to make it impossible for them to run quickly. For when these poor creatures saw and heard the fighting and the noise, they made desperate attempts to follow the fleeing Masai. The children behaved more sensibly, for, though they were much alarmed by the firing and the rockets, they gave us and our dogs—which performed excellent service in this affair—little difficulty in driving them into our camp.

The captured Masai were fine daring-looking fellows, and maintained a considerable degree of self-composure in spite of their intense alarm and of their expectation of immediate execution. Fortunately there was among them their *leitunu*, or chief and absolute leader of the party—a bronze Apollo standing 6 ft. 6 in. high. He looked as if he would like to thrust his *sime*, or short sword, into his own breast when the Wa-Duruma, who had begun to collect about us, ventured to mock at him and his people and to shout aloud for their death. Johnston most emphatically refused this demand. Speaking loudly enough for the prisoners to hear, he explained that the Masai were to become our allies; we had simply punished them for the wrong they had done. Did they—the Duruma—imagine that we needed their help, or the help of anyone, to slay the Masai if we wished to slay them? Had they not seen that we fired into the air, when a few well-aimed shots from our mighty machines would have sufficed to tear all the Masai in pieces? Then, in order to show the Duruma—but still more the Masai—the truth of these words, which had been listened to with shuddering and without the slightest trace of scepticism, Johnston directed a full volley of all our guns and rockets upon a dilapidated straw-thatched round hut about 1,100 yards off. The hut was completely smashed, and at once burst into flames—a spectacle which made a most powerful impression upon the savages.

'Now go,' said Johnston to the Wa-Duruma, pretending not to notice how intently our prisoners listened and looked on, 'and take your women, children, and cattle, which we have set free, and leave the Masai in peace. We will see to it that they do not trouble you in future. But do not forget that in a few weeks the Masai also will be our allies.'

The Wa-Duruma obeyed, but they did not quite know what to make of this business. When they were gone away, Johnston ordered their weapons to be given back to the captive Masai, whom he commanded to go away, telling them that in at most two weeks' time he expected to visit Lytokitok, the south-eastern frontier district of Masailand; and that it was in order to inform them of this that he had had them brought before him. But instead of at once taking advantage of this permission to go away, the *el-moran* (as the Masai warriors are called) lingered where they were; and at last Mdango, their *leitunu*, stepped forward and explained that it would be certain death for such a small band of Masai, separated from their own people, to seek to get home through Durumaland in its present agitated condition; and if they must die, they would esteem it a greater honour to die by the hand of so mighty a white *leibon* (magician) than to be slain by the cowardly Wa-Duruma or Wa-Teita. As it was our intention to visit their country very soon, we willingly permitted them to accompany us.

Johnston's face beamed with delight at this auspicious beginning; but towards the Masai he maintained a demeanour of absolute calm, and declared in a dignified tone that what they asked was a great favour, and one of which their previous behaviour had shown them to be so little worthy that before he could give them a definite answer he must hold a *shauri* (council) of his people. Leaving them standing where they were, he called aside some twenty of us who were on horseback near him, and told us the substance of the conversation. 'Of course, we will accede to the request of the *leitunu*, who, judging from the large number of *el-moran* that follow him, must be one of their most influential men. If he is completely won over, he will bring over his countrymen with him. So now I will inform him of the result of our council.'

'Listen,' said he, turning to Mdango; 'we have decided to accede to your request, for your brethren in Lytokitok shall not be able to say that we have exposed you to a dishonourable death. But as we have directed our weapons against you, though without shedding of blood, our customs forbid us to admit you as guests to our camp and our table before you have fully atoned for the outrage by which you have displeased us. This atonement will have been made when each of you has contracted blood-brotherhood with him who took you prisoner. Will you do this, and will you honourably keep your word?'

The *el-moran* very readily assented to this. Hereupon another council was held among ourselves, and this was followed by the fraternisation—according to the peculiar customs of the Masai—of the forty-three prisoners with their captors; and we thereby gained forty-three allies who—as Johnston assured us—would be hewed in pieces before they would allow any harm to happen to us if they could prevent it.

By this time it was nine o'clock, and, as the day promised to be glowing hot, we had no desire to set foot upon the burning Duruma desert until the sun was below the horizon. We therefore retired to our camp, which had not been left by the sumpter beasts, and then we prepared our midday meal. In honour of our bloodless victory, we prepared an unusually sumptuous repast of flesh and milk—the only food of the Masai *el-moran*—followed by an enormous bowl of rum, honey, lemons, and hot water, which was heartily relished by our people, but which threw the Masai into a state of ecstasy. The ecstasy knew no bounds when, the punch being drunk, the forty-three blood-brethren were severally adorned with red breeches as a tribute of friendship. The *leitunu* himself received an extra gift in the form of a gold-embroidered scarlet mantle.

The Duruma desert, which we entered about five o'clock, is quite uninhabited, and during the dry months has the bad repute of being almost absolutely without water. Now, however, immediately after the rainy season, we found a sufficient quantity of tolerably good water in the many ground-fissures and well-like natural pits, often two or three yards deep. But we suffered so much from the heat before sunset, that we sacrificed our night-rest in making a forced march to Taro, a good-sized pool formed by the collected rain-water. We reached this towards morning, and rested here for half a day— that is, we did not start again until the evening, husbanding our strength for the worst part of the way, which was yet to come. From this point the water-holes became less frequent, and the landscape particularly cheerless—monotonous stony expanses alternating with hideous thorn-thickets. Yet both men and beasts held out bravely through those three miserable days, and on the 12th of May we reached in good condition, though wetted to the skin by a sudden and unexpected downpour of rain, the charming country of the Wa-Teita on the fine Ndara range of hills.

We here experienced for the first time the ravishing splendour of the equatorial highlands. The Ndara range reaches a height of 5,000 feet and is covered from summit to base with a luxuriant vegetation; a number of silvery brooks and streams murmur and roar down its sides to the valleys; and the view from favourably situated points is most charming. As we rested here a whole day, most of us used the opportunity to make excursions through the marvellous scenery, being most courteously guided about by several Englishmen who had settled here for missionary and business purposes. I could not penetrate so far as I wished into the tangle of delicious shadowy valleys and hills which surrounded us, because I had to arrange for the provisioning of the caravan both in Teita and for the desert districts between Teita and the Kilimanjaro. But my more fortunate companions scaled the neighbouring heights, spent the night either on or just below the summits, refreshed themselves with the cool mountain air, and came back intoxicated with all the beauty they had enjoyed. Even at the foot of the Teita hills it was scarcely less charming. The bath under one of the splashing waterfalls, fanned by the mild air and odours of evening, would ever have been one of the pleasantest recollections of my life, if Africa had not offered me still more glorious natural scenes.

We spent the 14th and 15th in leisurely marches through this paradise, in which a rich booty in giraffes and various kinds of antelopes fell to our huntsmen. Everywhere we concluded friendly alliances with the tribes and their chiefs, and sealed our alliances with presents. During the two following days we worked our way through the uninhabited—but therefore the richer in game—desert of Taveta, which in fact is not so bad as its reputation; and on the afternoon of the 17th we approached the cool forests of the foothills of the Kilima, where a strange surprise was in store for us.

When we were a few miles from Taveta and—as is customary

in Africa—had announced the arrival of our caravan by a salvo
from our guns, Johnston and I, riding at the head of the train,
saw a man galloping towards us with loose rein, in whom we at
once recognised the leader of our advance-guard, Engineer Demestre.
The haste with which he galloped towards us at first gave us some
anxiety; but his smiling face soon showed us that it was no ill-luck
which brought him to us. He signalled to me from a distance, and
cried as he checked his horse in front of us : ' Your sister and Miss
Fox are in Taveta.'

Both Johnston and I must have made most absurd grimaces at
this unexpected announcement, for Demestre broke out into uproar-
ious laughter, in which at last we joined. Then he told us that, on
the previous evening, when he and his party arrived at Taveta, the
two ladies had accosted him in the streets as unconcernedly as if it
were a casual meeting at home, had altogether ignored the slight
they had received, and, when asked, had told him in an indifferent
tone that they had travelled hither from Aden, whence they started
on the 30th of April—therefore while we were waiting at Mombasa
—to Zanzibar, whence, after a short stay, they went to Pangani and,
taking the route by Mkumbara and the Jipé lake, reached Taveta
on the 14th of May. They were accompanied by their servant and
friend, Sam—a worthy old negro who was Miss Fox's constant
attendant—and four elephants upon which they rode, to the boundless astonishment of the negroes. They were quite comfortable in
Taveta. ' Miss Clara sends greetings, and bids me tell you that she
longs to press you to her sisterly heart.'

When I saw that Demestre was not joking I put spurs to my
horse, and in a few minutes found myself in a shady, bowery woodland road which led from the open country into Taveta. Soon after
I saw the two ladies, one of whom ran towards me with outstretched
arms and, almost before I had touched the ground, warmly embraced
me, she weeping aloud the while. After the first storm of emotion
was over, I tried to get from my sister a fuller account of her appearance here among the savages ; but I failed, for as often as the good
creature began her story it was interrupted by her tears and her
expressions of joy at seeing me again, as well as by thoughts of all
the dangers from which I—heedless boy!—had been preserved by
nothing but my good luck. In the meantime Miss Fox had come up
to us. She returned my greeting with a slight tinge of sarcasm, but

none the less cordially ; and I at length learned from her all that I wished to know.

I found that the two, at their very first meeting, had come to an understanding and decided upon the principal features of their plot, reserving the arrangement of details until we had left Europe. My sister had found in Miss Fox the energy and the possession of the requisite pecuniary means for the independent undertaking of an expedition, against the will of the men ; and Miss Fox had found in my sister the companion and elder protectress, without whom even she would have shrunk from such a bold enterprise. As Miss Fox was exactly informed of all our plans, she was able to copy them in her own arrangements. She procured what she needed from the manufacturers and brokers from whom we got our provisions, articles of barter, and travelling necessaries. Like us, she substituted sumpter beasts for *pagazis* ; only, in order to be original in at least one point, she chose elephants instead of horses, camels, or asses. She inferred that, as elephants—though hitherto untamed—abounded in all the districts to which we were going, Indian elephants would thrive well throughout Equatorial Africa. A business friend of her late father's in Calcutta bought for her four fine specimens of these pachyderms, and sent them with eight experienced keepers and attendants to Aden, whence she took them with her to Zanzibar. Here several guides and interpreters were hired ; and, in order not to come into collision with us too near the coast, she chose the route by Pangani. The curiosity of the natives was here and there a little troublesome ; but, thanks mainly to the courteous attentions of the German agents stationed in Mkumbana, Membe, and Taveta, the expedition had not met with the slightest mishap. On their arrival at Taveta they had at once dismissed their Swahili, and intended to join our expedition with the elephants and Indians—unless we insisted on leaving them behind us alone in Taveta.

What was to be done under such circumstances ? It followed as a matter of course that the two Amazons must henceforth form a part of our expedition; and, to tell the truth, I know not how to be angry with either my sister or Miss Fox for their persistency. The worst dangers might be considered as averted by the affair with the Masai in Duruma ; the difficulties of the journey were, as the result showed, no more than women could easily brave. Therefore I gave myself up without anxiety to the joy of the unexpected reunion. I was gratified to note also that the other members of the expedition welcomed this addition to our numbers. So the elephants with their fair burdens—for it may be added in passing that my sister, notwithstanding her thirty-eight years, still retains her good looks—had their place assigned to them in our caravan.

We bade farewell to our Masai friends outside Taveta. They were commissioned to inform their countrymen that we should reach the frontier of Lytokitok in eight or ten days, and that it was our intention to go through the whole of Masailand in order to find a locality suitable for our permanent settlement. This settlement of ours would be in the highest degree profitable to the race in whose neighbourhood we should build our dwellings, as we should make such race rich and invincible by any of their foes. We should force no one to receive us and give us land, although we possessed —as they were convinced—sufficient power to do so; and many thousands of our brethren were only awaiting a message from us to come and join us. If, however, a free passage were not peaceably granted to us through any territory, we knew how to force it. We finally made our blood-brethren solemnly engage to bring as many tribes as possible into alliance with us, especially those who dwelt on the route to the Naivasha lake, our route to the Kenia mountain; and we parted with mutual expressions of good will. They had shown themselves most agreeable fellows, and as parting mementos we gave them a number of what in their eyes were very valuable presents for their beloved ones—the so-called ' Dittos '—such as brass wire, brass bracelets and rings with imitation stones, hand-mirrors, strings of glass pearls, cotton articles, and ribbons. These gifts, which in Europe had not cost 20*l.* altogether, were—as we afterwards had occasion to prove—worth among the Masai as much as a hundred fat oxen ; and the *el-moran* were struck dumb with our generosity. But in their eyes Johnston's final gift was beyond all price -- a cavalry sabre with iron sheath and a good Solingen blade for each of the departing heroes. To give ocular demonstration of the quality of these weapons, Johnston got a Belgian, skilled in such feats, to cut through at one stroke the strongest of the Masai spears, the head of which was nearly five inches broad. He then showed to the astonished warriors the still undamaged sword-blade. ' So do our *simes* cut,' he said, ' when used in righteous battle ; but beware of drawing them in pillage or murder, for they will then shatter in your hands as glass and bring evil upon your heads.' We then gave them a friendly salute, and they were soon out of sight.

We stayed in Taveta five days to give our animals rest after their trying marches, and to refresh ourselves with the indescribable charms of this country, which surpassed in pleasantness and tropical splendour, as well as in the grandeur of the mountain-ranges, anything we had hitherto seen. We wished also, with the assistance of the German agents settled here and in the neighbouring Moshi, to complete our equipment for the rest of the journey. These gentlemen, and not less the friendly natives, readily gave us information as to what wares were then in special demand in Masailand ; and as we happened to have very few of a kind of blue pearls just then fashionable among the Dittos, and not a single piece of a sort of cotton cloth prized as a great novelty, we bought in Taveta several beast-loads of these valuables.

In our excursions from Taveta we saw for the first time the Kilimanjaro mountain in all its overpowering majesty. Rising abruptly more than 13,000 feet above the surrounding high land, this double-peaked giant reaches an altitude of 19,000 feet above the sea, and bears upon its broad massive back a stretch of snow with which in impressiveness neither the glaciers of our European Alps nor, in a certain sense, those of the Andes and the Himalayas, can compare. For nowhere else upon our earth does nature present such a strong and sudden contrast between the most luxuriant and exuberant tropical vegetation and the horrid chilling waste of broken precipices and eternal ice as here in Equatorial Africa. The flora and fauna at the foot of the Himalayas, for example, are scarcely less gorgeous than in the wooded and well-watered country around Taveta ; but while the snow-covered peaks of the mountain-range of Central Asia rise hundreds of miles away from the foot of the mountains, and it is therefore not possible to enjoy the two kinds of scenery together, heightened by contrast, here one can, from under the shade of a wild banana or mango-palm, count with a good telescope the unfathomable glacier-crevasses—so palpably near is the world of eternal ice to that of eternal summer. And what a summer !—a summer that preserves its richest treasures of beauty and fruitfulness without relaxing our nerves by its hot breath. These shady yet cheerful forests, these

crystal streams leaping everywhere through the flower-perfumed
land, these balmy airs which almost uninterruptedly float down
from the near icefields, and on their way through the mountain-
gorges and higher valleys get laden with the spicy breath of
flowers,—all this must be seen and enjoyed in order to know what
Taveta is.

This favoured land produces a superabundance of material
enjoyments of a tangible kind. Fat cattle, sheep and goats, poultry,
dainty fishes from the Jipé lake and the Lumi river, specially dainty
game of a thousand kinds from the banks of the smaller mountain-
streams which flow down the sides of the Kilimanjaro, satisfy the
most insatiable longing for flesh food. The vegetable kingdom
pours forth not less lavishly from its horn of plenty a supply of
almost all the wild and cultivated fruits and garden-produce of the
tropics. At the same time everything is so cheap that the most
extravagant glutton could not exceed a daily consumption costing
more than a penny or two, even should the courteous and hospitable
Wa-Taveta accept payment at all—which, however, they seldom
did from us. It is true that the fame of our heroic deeds against
the Masai had gone before us, and particularly the assurance that
we had delivered Taveta from these unwelcome guests, who, it is
true, had hitherto been kept away on every attack by the impenetrable forest fastnesses of Kilima, but whose neighbourhood was
nevertheless very troublesome. Besides, our hands were ever open
to the men of Taveta, and still more generously to the women.
European goods of all kinds, articles of clothing, primitive ornaments, and especially a selection of photographs and Munich
coloured picture-sheets, won the hearts of our black hosts, so that
when, on the morning of the 23rd of May, we at last set out on our
way, we were as sorry to leave this splendid woodland district as
the Wa-Taveta were to lose us. These good simple-minded men
accompanied us over their frontier; and many of the by no means
ill-looking Taveta girls, who had lost their hearts to their white or
their Swahili guests, shed bitter tears, and told their woe preferably
to our two ladies, who fortunately did not understand a word of
these effusive demonstrations of the Tavetan female heart. Prudery
is an unknown thing in Equatorial Africa; and the Taveta fair
ones would have been as little able to understand why anyone
should think it wrong to open one's heart to a guest as their white

sisters would have been to conceive of the possibility of talking freely and in all innocence of such matters without giving the least offence to friends and relatives.

CHAPTER IV

THERE are two routes from Taveta to Masailand, one leading westward past Kilima through the territory of the Wa-Kwafi, the other along the eastern slopes of the mountain through the lands occupied by the various tribes of the Wa-Chaga.

Both routes pass through fertile and pleasant country; but we chose the latter, because just then the Wa-Kwafi were at war with the Masai, and we wished to avoid getting mixed up with any affair that did not concern us. Moreover, we preferred to have dealings with the quiet and pacific Wa-Chaga rather than with the swaggering Wa-Kwafi. By short day-marches we went on past the wildly romantic Chala lake, shut in by dark perpendicular rocks, through the wooded hillsides of Rombo and over the tableland of Useri. On our way we crossed three considerable streams which unite to form the Tzavo river. We also came upon numberless springs which sent their water down from Kilima in all directions to irrigate the park-like meadows and the well-cultivated fields of the natives. All along our route we exchanged gifts and contracted alliances of friendship. At times the chase was engaged in, furnishing us with a great number of antelopes, zebras, giraffes, and rhinoceroses.

On the 28th of May we reached the frontier of Lytokitok, the south-eastern boundary of Masailand. As we crossed the Rongei stream we met our friend Mdango, accompanied by a large number of his warriors. His report was gratifying. He had given his message, not only to the elders and warriors of his own tribe, but to all the tribes from Lytokitok to the frontiers of Kapté, and had invited them to a great *shauri* at the Minyenye hill, half a day's march from the frontier in the direction of the Useri. The invitation had been numerously accepted by both *el-morun* and *el-moran*—i.e. married men and warriors—the latter attending to the number of above 3,000 men; and two days before they had been in consultation from morning until evening. The result was the

D

unanimous resolve to permit us to pass through ; but they had not yet agreed whether to insist upon the payment of the customary *hongo*, or tribute, exacted from trade-caravans, or to await our spontaneous liberality. Indeed, difficulties still stood in the way of a permanent alliance of friendship with us, and it was mainly the majority of the *el-moran* who wanted to treat us as strangers passing through Masailand were generally treated—that is, to exhibit towards us a violent, arrogant, and extortionate demeanour. They refused to believe in our great power, since we had not killed even one Masai warrior, but had sent home in good condition all who had fought against us, except sixteen—who had, however, been killed by the Wa-Duruma and the Wa-Teita, and not by us. This party advanced the opinion that Mdango and his men had fled from us out of childish alarm, which assertion nearly led to a sanguinary encounter between the deeply incensed accused and their accusers. Since, however, even the latter admitted that we must be very good fellows, inasmuch as we had in no way abused our victory, they were, as already stated, not disinclined graciously to permit our passage through their country. And since Mdango consoled himself with the reflection that we could best dispose of the braggarts who laughed at him, he had restrained himself, and told the other party they had better meet us and try to frighten us ; he and his would remain neutral notwithstanding the blood-brotherhood he had contracted with us, but he would have nothing to do with compelling us to pay tribute. All his six hundred warriors would adhere to him, and nearly as many *el-moran* from other tribes ; the married men—the *el-morun*—were, almost without exception, favourable to us. Thus stood affairs, and we had to prepare ourselves to meet, in a few hours, some 2,000 *el-moran*, to whom we must either pay heavy tribute or play the same game as we had played with him and his in Duruma. Moreover, he gave us plainly to understand that a few sharp shots from the cannons, or, still better, a few rockets, would not be amiss.

Johnston rejected this counsel of revenge, which was unwor of a blood-brother of white men, and pacified him by promising tha the boasters should be thoroughly shamed, and that the laughers in Masailand should be those of Mdango's party. Thereupon Johnstor very quietly made his preparations. The sumpter beasts and thei drivers occupied the well-fenced camp prepared by our advance guard; we whites, on the contrary, placed ourselves conspicuously in the shade of some large isolated sycamores, with our saddled horses a few yards behind us, where were also the limbered-up guns and rocket-battery. Even the four elephants, which Johnston had accustomed to fire in Taveta, had a *rôle* assigned to them in this burlesque, and they were therefore sent with their attendants to feed in the shade of a small wood close at hand. When all this was arranged, we settled down quietly to our cooking, and did not allow ourselves to be disturbed when the first band of *el-moran* became visible. Our apparent indifference perplexed them, and while still a mile and a quarter from us they held a consultation. Then a deputation of ten of their young warriors approached, the rest of the band awaiting their companions who had not yet appeared. The messengers addressed us with great dignity, and, after they had been referred to Johnston as our *leitunu*, asked us what we wanted.

'An unmolested passage through your country, and friendship with you,' was the answer.

Would we pay tribute?

'Our brother Mdango has told you that for our friends we have rich presents, but these presents are given voluntarily or for services rendered. We have weapons for our foes, but tribute for no one.'

The *el-moran* replied with dignity, but haughtily, that it was not the custom of the country to allow travellers to pass through as they pleased; we must either pay what was demanded, or fight.

'Friends, consider well what you are doing. We do not wish to fight, but to keep the peace and become your brethren. Go back to your kraals, and be careful not to molest us. Tell this to your young warriors. If you go away, we will take that as an indication of your friendly disposition, and there shall no harm come to you. But if you come beyond that bush' (here Johnston pointed to a small wood, a little over two hundred yards away from our camp) 'we shall look upon it as an attack. I have spoken.'

The *el-moran* went away with as much quiet dignity as they had exhibited when they approached us. The number in sight had meantime increased to nearly 2,000 men, who were arranged in tolerably good military order. When they received our answer, they raised a not unmusical war-cry and, extending their lances, hurried forward with a quick step. We sat still by the side of our cooking-

vessels as if the affair did not concern us, until the foremost of the
el-moran had reached the specified bush. Johnston then caused
the signal to be blown ; quick as lightning we were in the saddle,
and, with the elephants in our midst, we galloped towards the *el-
moran*, whilst a quick fire with blank-cartridge opened upon them
and our artillery began to play. The effect was not less drastic than
it had been in the case of the followers of Mdango. The arrogant
assailants beat a noisy retreat, and—an unheard-of disgrace for
fighting *el-moran*—many of them let fall their lances and shields
in the panic. The whole body of them fled until they were completely out of our view ; but we went back to our cooking-utensils,
where we found Mdango's followers and adherents, who had been
inactive spectators of the scene, convulsed with laughter. We invited them within our fenced camp, where we loaded each man with
presents. First Mdango was rewarded for his diplomatic services
with a bright-coloured gold-embroidered robe of honour (where,
in speaking of presents, 'gold' is mentioned—which the Central
African neither knows nor values—spurious metal must be understood), a silver watch, a white-metal knife, fork, and spoon, and
several tin plates. The using of the last-named articles must have
been very difficult to him at first ; but it ought to be stated that his
watch continued to go well, and on special occasions he made use of
his knife and fork with a great deal of dignity.

Other Masai notables were honoured with choice presents, though
not so extravagantly as the much-envied Mdango. All the *el-
moran* received—besides strings of pearls and kerchiefs for their
girls—the much-coveted red breeches ; each married man a coloured
mantle ; and every woman, married or single, who honoured our
camp with a visit was made glad by gifts of pictures, pearls, and all
kinds of bronze and glass knickknacks. It took about fifty of us
several hours to distribute these presents. It was difficult to keep
order in this surging mass of excited and chattering men and women.
It was almost sunset before the last of the Masai men left our camp,
whilst the prettiest of the girls and women showed no inclination to
return to their household gods.

Under the pretence of doing honour to our new friends, but
really in order to show that, when necessary, our weapons could strike
as well as make a noise, we ordered a grand parade for the next
forenoon. At this there were present, not merely our adherents, but

also most of our assailants of yesterday. The latter were shy and
confused, like whipped children; but they were attracted both by
curiosity and by the hope of yet winning the favour of the magnanimous *mussungus* (whites). After manœuvring for about half an
hour, we gave a platoon fire with ball-cartridge at a fixed target;
and then one of our sharpshooters smashed ten eggs thrown up in
rapid succession—a feat which won enthusiastic applause from the
el-moran. Even the ringleaders of yesterday's opponents, when
this first part of the play was over, declared that it would be madness to fight with such antagonists; they saw clearly that we could
have blown them all into the air yesterday in ten minutes. The
artillery portion of the spectacle produced a still greater effect.
About a mile and a quarter from our camp Johnston had improvised
several good-sized block-houses of heavy timber covered with brush-
wood and dry grass, and had placed in them a quantity of explosives.
These structures, which were really of a substantial character, were
now subjected to a fire of grenades and rockets; and it can be
readily imagined that the ascending flames, the crackling of the
falling timbers, and the explosion of the enclosed fireworks, would
strongly impress the Masai. But the terrible fascination reached
its climax when Johnston brought into play a mine and an electric
communication which had been prepared during the night, and by
means of which a hut stored with fireworks was sent into the air.
The Masai were now convinced that a movement of our hands was
sufficient alone to blow into the air any enemies, however numerous
they might be; and from that time to offer violent resistance to us
appeared to them as useless as to offer it to supernatural powers.

When we saw that they were thus sufficiently prepared, we
proceeded to conclude our alliance of peace and friendship. First
of all, however, Johnston announced to the abashed and silently
retreating victims of yesterday's sham fight that we whites had for-
given them, that in the solemn act now beginning we wished to
look upon none but contented faces, and that therefore they were
to have presents given them. When this had been announced,
Johnston required the kraals—seventeen from Lytokitok and four
from Kapté were represented—each to nominate the *leitunu* and
leigonani of its *el-moran* and two of its *el-moran* to draw up the
contract with us. The choice of these was soon finished, and an
hour later the deliberations—in which on our side only Johnston,

myself, and six officers took part—were opened by all sorts of ceremonies. First there were several speeches, in which on our side were set forth the advantages which the Masai would derive from our settling in their midst or on their frontiers; and on the side of the Masai orators assurances of admiration and affection for their white friends played the principal *rôle*. Then Johnston laid the several points of the contract before them, as follows :

1. The Masai shall preserve unbroken peace and friendship towards us and our allies, who are the inhabitants of Duruma, Teita, Taveta, Chala, and Useri.

2. The Masai shall on no pretence whatever demand *hongo* (tribute) from any caravan conducted by white men ; but promise on the contrary to assist by all means in their power the progress of such caravans, particularly in furnishing them, as far as their supplies allow, with provisions at a fair price.

3. The Masai shall, when required by us at any time, place at our disposal any number of *el-moran* to act as escort or sentinels, yielding military obedience to us during the period of their service with us.

4. In return we bind ourselves to recognise the Masai as our friends, to protect them in their rights, and to aid them against foreign attacks.

5. The *el-moran* of all the tribes in alliance with us shall receive every man yearly two pair of good cotton trousers and fifty strings of glass pearls to be chosen by themselves, or, if they wish, other articles of like value. The *el-morun* shall receive every man a cotton mantle ; the *leilunus* and *leigonanis* trousers, pearls, and mantle.

6. The *el-moran* who shall be called out for active service among us shall every one receive, besides full rations in flesh and milk, a daily payment of five strings of pearls, or their value.

These conditions, which were received by the Masai present with signs of undisguised satisfaction, were confirmed with great solemnity by the symbolic ceremony of blood-fraternisation between the contracting parties. As the multitude, who stood looking on at a respectful distance, greeted the conditions, when read to them, with loud shouts of joy, we knew that the public opinion of Lytokitok and of a portion of Kapté was completely won.

We told our new allies that it was our intention to pass Matumbato and Kapté on our way to the Naivasha lake, to admit to the alliance as many as possible of the Masai tribes dwelling on our route, and then proceed to the Kenia either by Kikuyu or by Lykipia. To facilitate our entering into friendly relations with the tribes through whose territories we should pass, we asked for a company of fifty *el-moran* to precede us under the leadership of our friend Mdango, who had risen very high in the estimation of his countrymen. Our request was granted, and Mdango felt no little flattered by the choice which had fallen on him. The fifty *el-moran* whom we asked for grew to be above five hundred, for the younger warriors contended among themselves for the honour of serving us. The Masai advised us not to take the route by Kikuyu. The Wa-Kikuyu are not a Masai tribe, but belong to quite a different race, and have from time immemorial been at feud with the Masai. They were described to us as at once treacherous, cowardly, and cruel, as people without truthfulness and fidelity, and with whom an honourable alliance was impossible. But as we had already learnt, in our civilised home, how much reliance is to be placed on the opinions held of each other by antagonistic nations, the above description produced no effect upon our minds beyond that of convincing us that the Wa-Kikuyu and the Masai were hereditary foes. That we were correct in our scepticism the result showed. Mdango was informed that we should adhere to our original purpose. He was to precede us by forced marches, if possible to the frontiers of Lykipia, then turn and await us on the east shore of the Naivasha lake, where, in three weeks' time, we hoped to hold the great *shauri* with the Masai tribes which he would then have got together and won over to our wishes. As to the Wa-Kikuyu who occupied the territory to the east of Naivasha, we ourselves would arrange with them.

Mdango left next morning, while we remained until the 1st of June at Miveruni, on the north side of the Kilimanjaro. The news of what had happened had reached the neighbouring Useri, whose inhabitants—hitherto living in constant feud with the Masai—now came in great numbers, under the leadership of their Sultan, to visit us, and to be convinced of the truth of what they had heard. They brought gifts for both ourselves and the Masai, the gifts for the latter being tokens of their pleasure at the ending of their feud. We received fifty cows and fifty bulls; the Masai half the number. This gift suggested to the Masai elders the idea of sending messengers with greetings from us, and with assurances of peace henceforth, to the Chaga, Wa-Taveta, Wa-Teita, and Wa-Duruma; which embassy, as we learnt afterwards, returned six weeks later so richly rewarded that the inhabitants of Lytokitok gained more in presents than they had ever gained in booty by their raids. And as these presents were repeated annually, though not to so great an amount, the peace was in this respect alone a very good stroke of business for our new friends. But the tribes which had formerly suffered from the Masai when on the war-path profited still more from the peace, for they were henceforth able to pasture their cattle in security and to till their fields, whilst previously just the most fertile districts had been left untilled through dread of the Masai.

As we were abundantly supplied with flesh and milk (for the Masai had given us presents in return in the shape of fine cattle), we begged the Sultan of Useri—who, of course, was not left unrewarded for his friendliness—to hold his presents in his own keeping until we needed them. We intended to use the cattle he offered us for the great caravans that would follow. For the same purpose, we also left in charge of our Masai friends in Miveruni three hundred and sixty head of cattle which we had not used of their presents. We were not dependent upon our cattle for meat, as the chase supplied us with an incredible abundance of the choicest dainties. For instance, in three hours I shot six antelopes of different kinds, two zebras, and one rhinoceros; and as our camp contained many far better sportsmen than I am, it may be imagined how easy a matter it was to provision us. In fact, though unnecessary slaughter was avoided as much as possible, and our better sportsmen tried their skill upon only the game that was very rare or very difficult to bring down, we could not ourselves consume the booty brought home, but every day presented carcases of game to our guest-friends. In particular, we shot rhinoceroses, with which the country swarmed, solely for the use of our blacks, who were passionately fond of certain portions of those animals, whilst no portion is palatable to Europeans except in extreme need. When we were on the march it was often necessary to kill these animals, because they—the only wild animals that do it in Central Africa— have the inconvenient habit of attacking and breaking through the caravans when they discover their neighbourhood by means of the wind. This happened almost daily during the whole of our journey, though only once a serious result followed, when a driver was badly wounded and an ass was tossed and gored. But the inconvenience caused by these attacks was always considerable, and we thought it better to shoot the mischievous uncouth fellows rather than allow them an opportunity of running down a man or a beast.

We had hitherto seen only isolated footprints of elephants, but on the northern declivities of the Kilimanjaro we found elephants in great numbers, though not in such enormous herds as we were to meet with later in the Kenia districts. They were the noble game to which the more fastidious of our sportsmen confined their attentions, without, however, achieving any great success; for the elephants here were both shy and fierce, having evidently been closely hunted by the ivory-seekers. It was necessary to exercise extreme caution; and thus it was that only three of our best and most venturesome hunters succeeded in killing one each, the flesh of which was handed over to the blacks, whilst the small quantity of ivory found its way into our treasury. *A propos* of hunting, it may be mentioned here that the lions, which were met with everywhere on our journey in great numbers, sometimes in companies of as many as fifteen individuals, afforded the least dangerous and generally the least successful sport. The lion of Equatorial Africa is a very different animal from his North African congener. He equals him in size and probably in strength, but in the presence of man he is shyer and even timid. These lions will not attack even a child; in fact, the natives chase them fearlessly with their insignificant weapons when the lions fall upon their herds. All the many lions upon which our huntsmen came made off quickly, and, even if wounded, showed fight only when their retreat was cut off; in short, they are cowards in every respect. The reason for this is to be sought in the great abundance of their prey. As the table is always furnished for the ' king of beasts,' and he need not run any danger or put forth any great effort in order to satisfy his wants, he carefully avoids every creature that appears seriously to threaten his safety. The buffalo, which is certainly the most dangerous of all African wild beasts, is attacked by lions only when the buffalo is alone and the lions are many in company.

At four in the morning of the 1st of June we left Miveruni. A march of several hours placed the last of the woodland belts of the Kilima foot-hills behind us, and we entered upon the bare plains of the Ngiri desert. The road through these and past the Limgerining hills by the high plateau of Matumbato offered little that was note-worthy. On the 6th of June we reached the hills of Kapté, along whose western declivities we passed at a height of from 4,000 to 5,500 feet above the sea. On our left, beneath us, were the monotonous plains of Dogilani, stretching farther than the eye could reach, and on our right the Kapté hills, rising to a height of nearly 10,000 feet, their sides showing mostly rich, grassy, park-like land, and their summits clothed with dark forests. Numerous streamlets, here and there forming picturesque waterfalls, fell noisily down, uniting in the Dogilani country into larger streams, which, as far as the eye could follow them, all took their course westward to fall into the Victoria Nyanza, the largest of all the great lakes of Central Africa. All the tribes on our way received us as old friends, even those with whom we had not previously contracted alliance. They had all heard the wonderful story of the white men who wished to settle amongst them, and who were at once so mighty and so generous. Mdango's invitation to the *shauri* at the Naivasha lake had everywhere been gladly received; multitudes were already on their way, and others joined us or promised to follow. There was no mention at all of *hongo* ; in short, our game was won in all parts of the country.

On the 12th we reached the confines of the Kikuyu country, along which our further route to the Naivasha led. The evil reports of the knavish, hateful character of this people were repeated to us in a yet stronger form by the Kapté Masai, their immediate neighbours. But we had in the meantime received from another source a very different representation. Our two ladies had with them an Andorobbo girl whom they had taken into their service in Taveta. The Andorobbo are a race of hunters who, without settled residence, are to be met with throughout the whole of the enormous region between the Victoria Nyanza and the Zanzibar coast. Sakemba—as the girl of eighteen was called—belonged to a tribe of this race that hunted elephants in the districts at the foot of the Kenia to the north of Kikuyu. She had been stolen two years before by the Masai, who had sold her to a Swahili caravan, with which she had gone to Taveta. The girl had an invincible longing for her home—a rare thing among these races ; and as it was known that my sister and Miss Ellen were awaiting a caravan that was going on to the Kenia, the girl appealed to them to buy her from her master and take her back to her home, where her relatives would gladly pay the cost in elephants' teeth. Touched by the importunity of the girl, Clara and Miss Fox bought her of her master, gave her her liberty, and engaged to take her with them. The girl was very intelligent, and was well-informed concerning the affairs of her native country. She had heard in Miveruni what evil reports the Masai gave of the Wa-Kikuyu, and she took the first opportunity of assuring her protectresses that the case was not nearly so bad as it was made to appear. The Masai and the Wa-Kikuyu were old foes, and, as they consequently did each other all the harm they could, they ascribed every conceivable vice to each other. It was true that the Wa-Kikuyu would rather fight in ambush than in the open field, and they certainly were not so brave as the Masai; but they were treacherous and cruel only to their enemies, while those who had won their confidence could as safely rely upon them as upon the members of any other nation. The Andorobbo would much rather have dealings with the Wa-Kikuyu than with the Masai, because the former were much more peaceable and less overbearing than the latter. Our direct route to the Kenia lay through Kikuyu, whilst the route through Lykipia would have taken at least six days longer on account of the *détour* we should have to make around the Aberdare range of hills.

As we had no reason to question the trustworthiness of this report, the last—and to us most important—part of which was confirmed by a glance at the map, we resolved at any rate to attempt the route through Kikuyu. Therefore, whilst the greater part of the expedition continued to pursue, under Johnston's guidance, the northerly route to the Naivasha lake, I with fifty men and a quantity of baggage went easterly by the frontier place, Ngongo-a-Bagas. My intention was to take with me merely Sakemba as one acquainted with the country and the people, and to leave the two ladies in Johnston's care until my return. But my sister declared that she would not leave me on any account; and as the Andorobbo girl belonged to the women and not to me, and moreover asserted that there would be absolutely no danger for the women, since it had been from time immemorial an unbroken custom for the Masai and the Wa-Kikuyu to respect each other's women in time of war—an assurance which was confirmed on all hands, even by the Masai themselves—my sister and Miss Ellen became members of our party.

As soon as we entered the territory of Kikuyu we found ourselves in luxuriant shady forests, which however could by no means be said to be 'impenetrable,' but were rather remarkable for being in very many places cut through by broad passages, which had the appearance of having been made by some skilful gardener for the convenience and recreation of pleasure-seekers. These ways were not perfectly straight, but as a rule they went in a certain definite direction. In breadth they varied from three to twenty feet; at places they broadened out into considerable clearings which, like the narrower ways, were clothed with a very fine and close short grass, and were deliciously shady and cool. The origin of these ways was, and is, an enigma to me. On each side of them there was underwood between the stems of the tall trees. At places this underwood was very thick, and we could plainly see that dark figures followed us on both sides, watching all our movements, and evidently not quite sure as to what our intentions were. The fact that we came from the hostile Masailand might have excited mistrust, for we proceeded in this way a couple of hours without an actual meeting between ourselves and any of our unknown escort.

An end had to be put to this, for some unforeseen accident might lead to a misunderstanding followed by hostilities. So I asked Sakemba if she dared to go alone among the Wa-Kikuyu. 'Why not?' asked she. 'It would be as safe as for me to go into the hut of my parents.' I therefore ordered a halt, and the Andorobbo girl went fearlessly towards the bushes where she knew the Wa-Kikuyu to be, and at once disappeared. In half an hour she returned accompanied by several Wa-Kikuyu women, who were sent to test the truth of Sakemba's story—that is, to see whether we were, with the exception of a few drivers, all whites, and whether—which would be the most certain proof of our pacific intentions—there were really two white women among us. Uncertain rumours about us had already reached the ears of the Wa-Kikuyu; but, as these reports had come through the hostile Masai, the Wa-Kikuyu had not known how much to believe. But the deputation of women opened up friendly relations between us; a few lavishly bestowed trinkets soon won us the hearts and the confidence of the black fair ones. Our visitors did not waste time in returning to the men, but signalled and called the latter to come to them, with the result that we were immediately surrounded by hundreds of admiring and astonished Wa-Kikuyu.

I went among them, accompanied only by an interpreter, and asked where their sultan and elders were. Sultan had they none, was the answer—they were independent men; their elders were present among them. 'Then let us at once hold a *shauri*, for I have something of importance to tell you.' No African can resist a request to hold a *shauri*; so we immediately sat down in a circle, and I was able to make known my wishes. First, I told them of our victory over the Masai, and how we had forced them to preserve peace with us and with all our allies. I also told them of our subsequent generosity. I then assured them that we also wished to have the Wa-Kikuyu as our allies, which would result in peace between them and the Masai, and would bring great benefit to them from us. We asked for nothing, however, in return but a friendly reception and an unmolested passage through their territory. If they refused, we would force them to grant it, as we did the Masai. ' Look here '—I took a repeating-rifle in my hand—' this thing hits at any distance; ' and I gave it to one of our best marksmen and pointed to a vulture which sat upon a tree a little more than three hundred yards off. The shot was heard, and the vulture fell down mortally wounded. The Wa-Kikuyu showed signs of being about to run away, although they had occasionally heard the reports of guns in their conflicts with Swahili caravans. What frightened them was not the noise, but the certainty of the aim. However, they were soon reassured, and I went on : ' We not only always hit with our weapons, but we can shoot without cessation.' I had this assertion demonstrated to them by a rapid succession of ten shots ; and again my hearers were seized with a horrible fright. ' We have fifty such things here, a hundred and fifty more among the Masai, and many many thousands where we come from. Besides, we carry with us the most dangerous medicines—all to be used only against those who attack us. But we have costly presents for those who are friendly towards us.' Then I ordered to be opened a bale of various wares which had been specially packed for such an occasion, and I said : ' This belongs to you, that you may remember the hour in which you saw us for the first time. No one shall say, " I sat with the white men and held *shauri* with them, and my hands remained empty." If you wish to know how liberally we deal with those who become our allies, go and ask the Masai.'

The effect of this address, and still more of the openly displayed presents, left nothing to be desired. The distribution of the presents gave rise to a tremendous scramble among our future friends ; but when this was over—fortunately without any serious mischief— we were overwhelmed with extravagant asseverations of affection and zealous service. First we were invited to honour with our presence their huts, so ingeniously concealed in the forest thickets, an invitation which we readily accepted. We were careful, however, to take up our quarters in a commanding position, and to keep ourselves well together. I also directed that several of our people should, without attracting attention, keep constant watch. I left the baggage in charge of four gigantic mastiffs which we had brought with us. The former part of these precautions proved to be quite unnecessary; no one harboured any evil design against us, and the anxious timidity which the Wa-Kikuyu at first so manifestly showed quickly yielded to the most complete confidence, in which change of attitude, it may be incidentally remarked, the women led the way. On the other hand, it proved to be extremely advisable to keep watch over the baggage. Desperate cries of ' Murder ! ' and ' Help ! '- were soon heard from a Wa-Kikuyu boy, who, thinking our baggage was unwatched, had crept near it with a knife, but was very cleverly fixed by one of the mastiffs. We released him, frightened nearly to death, but otherwise quite unhurt, out of the clutches of the powerful animal; and we were troubled by no further attempt upon our baggage.

The next morning we asked our hosts to accompany us a few days' march further into the interior of the country in the direction of the Kenia, and to invite as many of their associated tribes as they could communicate with in so short a time to meet us in a *shauri*, since we desired to contract with them a firm alliance. This was readily promised, and so for two days we were accompanied by several hundred Wa-Kikuyu through the magnificent forest, in which the flora vied with the fauna in beauty and multiplicity of species. The Wa-Kikuyu entertained us in a truly extravagant manner, without accepting payment for anything. We were literally overloaded with milk, honey, butter, all kinds of flesh and fowl, *mtama* cakes, bananas, sweet potatoes, yams, and a great choice of very delicious fruits. We wondered whence this inexhaustible abundance, particularly of wild fruits, came; for in the forest clearings which we had passed through pasturage and agriculture were evidently only subordinate industries. At the end of the second day's march, however, the riddle was solved ; for when we had reached the considerable river called the Guaso Amboni, which falls into the Indian Ocean, we found spreading out before us farther than the eye could reach a high plateau which, so far as we could see, had the character of an open park-land, bearing, especially where it touched the forest we had just left, all the indications of a very highly developed agriculture. Here was evidently the source of the Kikuyu's inexhaustible corn supply. Far in the northern horizon we saw a large blue mountain-range, at least 50 or 60 miles distant, which our guides and Sakemba said was the Kenia range. They assured us that from where we were there could be seen in clear weather the snowy peak of the principal mountain ; but at that time it was hidden by clouds.

Here, then, lay before us the goal of our wanderings, and powerful emotion seized us all as we, though only at a great distance, for the first time looked upon our future home. The Kenia peak, however, remained wrapped in clouds during the two days of our stay on the eastern outskirts of the Kikuyu forest. We made our halt in a charming grove of gigantic bread-fruit trees, where the Wa-Kikuyu placed their huts gratuitously at our disposal. The place is called Semba, and had been selected as the meeting-place of the great *shauri*. We found a great number of natives already assembled there ; and on the next day everything was arranged and confirmed between us to our mutual satisfaction. Thus we were able to start on our return march on the 16th of June. We did not go over the Ngongo, but followed a tributary of the Amboni to its source—more than 7,000 feet above the sea—and then dropped abruptly down from the edge of the Kikuyu tableland and went direct to the Naivasha, which we reached on the evening of the 19th. We were somewhat exhausted, but otherwise in good condition and in excellent spirits. We had discovered that we should be able to reach the Kenia a good week earlier than would have been possible by the originally chosen route through Lykipia.

The Naivasha is a beautiful lake in the midst of picturesque ranges of hills, the highest points of which reach 6,500 feet. The lake has a superficies of about thirty square miles, and its characteristic feature is a fabulous wealth in feathered game of all kinds. Here Johnston had made all the necessary preparations for the great feast of peace and joy which we purposed to give the Masai. The news that they had henceforth to reckon the Wa-Kikuyu also among our friends was received by the *el-moran* with mixed feelings; but they submitted to the arrangement without murmuring, and at the feast, in which fifty of the principal men among the Wa-Kikuyu who had accompanied us took part, the new friendship between the two races was more firmly established.

The feast consisted of a two days' great carousing, at which we provided enormous quantities of flesh, baked food, fruits, and punch for not less than 6,000 guests, without reckoning women and children. The chief feature consisted of some splendid fireworks. During these two days 150 fat young bulls, 260 antelopes of various kinds, 25 giraffes, innumerable feathered game, and an enormous quantity of vegetables were consumed. The punch was brewed in 100 vessels, each holding above six gallons, and each filled on the average four times. Nevertheless, this colossal hospitality—apart from the fireworks—cost us nothing at all. The cattle were presents, and indeed were a part of the number brought to us by numerous tribes as tokens of grateful esteem; the game we had, of course, not bought, but shot; and the vegetables were here, on the borders of Kikuyu, so cheap that the price may be regarded as merely nominal. As to the punch, the chief ingredient, rum—fortunately not a home production in Masailand and Kikuyuland—our experts had made on the spot, without touching the nearly exhausted supply we had brought with us. For among our other machinery there was a still. This was unpacked, wild-growing sugar-cane was to be had in abundance, and hence we had rum in plenty. Care was taken that the process was not so watched by the natives as to be learnt by them, for we did not wish to introduce among our neighbours that curse of negroland, the rum-bottle. The hot punch which we served out to them did not contain more than one part of rum to ten of water ; yet nearly three hundred gallons of this noble spirit had to be used in the improvised bowls during the two days of the feast. The jubilation, particularly during the letting-off of the fireworks, was indescribable ; and when finally, after silence had been obtained by flourish of trumpets, we had it proclaimed by strong-voiced heralds that the nation of the Masai were invited by us to be our guests at the same place every year on the 19th and 20th of June, the people nearly tore us to pieces out of pure delight.

The 21st of June was devoted to rest after the fatigues of the feast, and to the arrangement of the baggage ; on the 22nd the march to Kikuyu was begun. To avoid taking the sumpter beasts over the steep acclivities of the hills that skirted the Naivasha valley, we turned back towards Ngongo-a-Bagas, which we reached on the 24th. Here we decided to establish an express communication with the sea, in order that the news of our arrival at our goal, which we expected to reach in a few days, might be carried as quickly as possible to Mombasa, and thence to the committee of the International Free Society. From Mombasa to Ngongo our engineers had measured 500 miles ; we had done the distance in 38 days—from May 5 to June 12—of which, however, only 27 were real marching days. We calculated that our Arab horses, if put to the strain for only one day, could easily cover more than 60 miles in the day, and that therefore the whole distance could be covered in eight stages of a day each. Therefore sixteen of our best riders, with twenty-four of the best-winded racers, were ordered back. These couriers were directed to distribute themselves in twos at distances of about sixty miles—where the roads were bad a little less, and where they were good a little more. As baggage, besides their weapons and ammunition, they were furnished with merely so much of European necessaries and of articles for barter on the way as could be easily carried by the eight supernumerary horses, which were at the same time to serve as a reserve. For the rest we could safely rely upon their being received with open arms and hospitably entertained by the natives they might meet with along the route we had taken. A similar service of couriers was established between Ngongo and the Kenia ; as this latter distance was about 120 miles it was covered by two stages. Thus there was a total of ten stages, and it was anticipated that news from Kenia would reach Mombasa in ten days—an anticipation which proved to be correct.

The march through the forest-land of Kikuyu, which was entered on the 25th, was marked by no noteworthy incident. When, early on the morning of the 27th, we reached the open, we found ourselves at first in a thick fog, which was inconvenient to us Caucasians merely

E

in so far as it hid the view from us; but our Swahili people, who had never before experienced a temperature of 53° Fahr. in connection with a damp atmosphere, had their teeth set chattering. To the northerners, and particularly to the mountaineers among us, there was something suggestive of home in the rolling masses of fog permeated with the balmy odours of the trees and shrubs. About eight A.M. there suddenly sprang up a light warm breeze from the north; the fog broke with magical rapidity, and before us lay, in the brilliant sunshine, a landscape, the overpowering grandeur of which mocks description. Behind us and on our left was the marvellous forest which we had not long since left; right in front of us was a gently sloping stretch of country in which emerald meadows alternated with dark banana-groves and small patches of waving corn. The ground was everywhere covered with brilliant flowers, whose sweet perfume was wafted towards us in rich abundance by the genial breeze. Here and there were scattered small groups of tall palms, some gigantic wide-spreading fig-trees, planes, and sycamores; and numerous herds of different kinds of wild animals gave life to the scene. Here frolicked a troop of zebras; there grazed quietly some giraffes and delicate antelopes; on the left two uncouth rhinoceroses chased each other, grunting; about 1,100 yards from us a score of elephants were making their way towards the forest; and at a greater distance still some hundreds of buffaloes were trotting towards the same goal.

This splendid country stretched out of sight towards the east and the south-east, traversed by the broad silver band of the Guaso Amboni, which, some five miles off, and perhaps at a level of above 300 feet below where we were standing, flowed towards the east, and, so far as we could see, received at least a dozen small tributaries from sources on both of the enclosing slopes. The tributaries springing from the Kikuyu forest on the southern side—on which we were—are the smaller; those from the northern side are incomparably more copious, for their source is the Kenia range. This giant among the mountains of Africa, which covers an area of nearly 800 square miles and rises to a height of nearly 20,000 feet, now—despite the 50 miles between us and that—showed itself to our intoxicated gaze as an enormous icefield with two crystalline peaks sharply projected against the dark firmament.

Even the Swahili, who are generally indifferent to the beauties of nature, broke out into deafening shouts of delight; but we whites stood in speechless rapture, silently pressed each other's hands, and not a few furtively brushed a tear from the eye. The Land of Promise lay before us, more beautiful, grander, than we had dared to dream—the cradle of a happy future for us and, if our hopes and wishes were not vain, for the latest generations of mankind.

From thence onward it was as if our feet and the feet of our beasts had wings. The pure invigorating air of this beautiful table-land, freshened by the winds from the Kenia, the pleasant road over the soft short grass, and the sumptuous and easily obtained provisions, enabled us to make our daily marches longer than we had yet done. On the evening of the 27th we crossed the eastern boundary of Kikuyu, where we had to lay in large stores of provisions, because we then entered a district where the only population consisted of a few nomadic Andorobbo. As far as we could see, the country resembled a garden, but man had not yet taken possession of this paradise. The 28th and the greater part of the 29th found us marching through flowery meadows and picturesque little woodlands, and crossing murmuring brooks and streams of considerable size; but the only living things we met with were giraffes, elephants, rhino-ceroses, buffaloes, zebras, antelopes, and ostriches, with hippopota-muses and flamingoes on the river banks. Most of these creatures were so tame that they scarcely got out of our way, and several over-bold zebras accompanied us for some distance, neighing and capering as they went along. On the afternoon of the 29th we entered the thick highland forest, which stretched before us farther than we could see, and through the dense underwood of which the axe of our pioneers had to cut us a way. The ground had been gradually ascending for two days—that is, ever since we had left the Amboni—and it now became steeper; we had reached the foot of the Kenia mountain. The forest zone proved to be of comparatively small breadth, and on the morning of the 30th we emerged from it again into open undulating park-land. When we had scaled one of the heights in front of us, there lay before us, almost within reach of our hands, the Kenia in all the icy magnificence of its glacier-world.

We had reached our goal!

CHAPTER V

IT was eight weeks since we had left Mombasa, a shorter time than
had ever been taken by any caravan in Equatorial Africa to cover a
distance of more than 600 miles. During the whole time we had
all been, with unimportant exceptions, in good health. There had
been seven cases of fever among us whites, caused by the chills that
followed sudden storms of rain ; the fever in all these cases disappeared again in from two to eight days, and left no evil results.
Twice a number of cases of colic occurred among both whites and
blacks, on both occasions resulting simply from gastronomic excesses,
first in Teita and then at the Naivasha lake ; and these were also
cured, without evil results, by the use of tartar emetic. These
sanitary conditions, exceptionally favourable for African journeys,
even in the healthy highlands, were the result of the judicious marching arrangements, and, particularly among us whites, of the care taken
to provide for all the customary requirements of civilised men. Tea,
coffee, cocoa, meat extract, cognac to use with bad water, light wine
for the evening meals, tobacco, and cigars, were always abundantly
within reach ; our mackintoshes and waterproof boots while marching, and the waterproof tents in camp, protected us from the wet—
the chief source of fever ; and we were assisted to bear our lesser
privations and inconveniences by our zeal for our task, and not least
by the fine balmy air which, from Teita onwards, we almost always
breathed. Our saddle-horses and sumpter beasts also were, by the
nourishing feed and the judicious treatment which they received,
enabled to bear well the heavy labours of the march.

I cannot forbear expressing the opinion that the heavy losses of
other caravans, which sometimes lose all their beasts in a few days,
are to be ascribed less to the climate or to the—in the lowlands,
certainly very troublesome—insect pests, than to the utter inexperi-
ence of the Swahili in the treatment of animals. Had we relied
merely upon our blacks, we should have left most of our beasts, and
certainly all our horses, on the road to feed the vultures and hyenas.
The horses would never have been allowed to cool before they
drank, they never would have been properly groomed, if we had not

continually insisted upon these things being done, and given a good example by attending to our saddle-horses ourselves. That the ' white gentleman ' attended to his horse's wants before he attended to his own wrought such an effect upon the Swahili that at last their care for their beasts developed into a kind of tenderness. The consequence was that during the whole journey we lost only one camel, three horses, and five asses—and of these last only two died of disease, the other three having been killed by wild beasts. Of the dogs, we lost three by wild beasts—one by a rhinoceros, and two by buffaloes.

From the moment of our arrival at the Kenia, the conduct of the expedition devolved into my hands. My first care on the next morning was to despatch to our friends in Europe my detailed journal of the events which had already happened, together with a brief closing report. In the latter I stated that we could undertake to have everything ready for the reception of many thousands of our brethren by the next harvest—that is, according to the African calendar, by the end of October. We could also undertake to get finished a road suitable for slow-going vehicles from Mombasa to Kenia by the end of September at the latest, with draught oxen in sufficient number. I asked the managers of the Society, on their part, to have a sufficient number of suitable waggons constructed in good time; and I, on my part, engaged that, from and after the first of October, any number of duly announced immigrant members should be conveyed to their new home safely and with as little inconvenience as was possible under the circumstances. In conclusion, I asked them to send at once several hundredweight of different kinds of goods, accompanied by a new troop of vigorous young members.

The two couriers with this despatch—the couriers had always to ride in twos—started before dawn on the 1st of July; punctually on the 10th the despatch was in Mombasa, on the 11th at Zanzibar; on the same day the committee received my report by telegraph from our agents in Zanzibar, and the journal, which went by mailship, they received twenty days later. On the evening of the 11th the reply reached Zanzibar; and on the 22nd I was myself able to read to my deeply affected brethren these first tidings from our distant friends. The message was very brief: ' Thanks for the joyful news; membership more than 10,000; waggons, for ten persons

and twenty hundredweight load each, ordered as per request, will
begin to reach Mombasa by the end of September ; 260 horsemen,
with 300 sumpter beasts, and 800 cwt. of goods start end of July.
Send news as often as possible.' I had already anticipated the
wish expressed in the last sentence, for not less than five further
despatches had been sent off between the 6th and the 21st of
July. What they contained will be best learnt from the following
narrative of our experiences and our labours ; and from this time
forward a distinction has to be made between the work of preparing
the new home on the Kenia and the arrangements necessary for
keeping up and improving our communication with the coast.

On the evening of the last day of June we had pitched our camp
on the bank of a considerable stream, the largest we had yet seen. Its
breadth is from thirty to forty yards, and its depth from one to three
yards. The water is clear and cool, but its current is strikingly
sluggish. It flows from north-west to south-east, through a trough-
like plateau about eighteen miles long, which bends, crescent-
shaped, round the foot-hills of the Kenia. The greatest breadth
of this plateau in the middle is nearly nine miles, whilst it narrows
at the west end to less than a mile, and at the east end to two miles
and a half. This trough-like area of about 100 square miles consists
entirely of rich grass-land, with numerous small groves of palms,
bananas, and sycamores. It is bounded on the south by the grassy
hills which we had crossed over, on the west by abrupt rocky walls,
on the north partly by dark forest-hills, and partly by barren lofty
rocks which hide from view the main part of the Kenia lying behind
them. On the east, between the hills to the south and the rocks to
the north, there is an opening through which the stream finds its
outlet by a waterfall of above 300 feet, and the thunder and
plashing of which were audible at the great distance at which we
were. This river, which was later found to be the upper course
of the Dana, entering the Indian Ocean on the Witu coast, enters
our plateau by a narrow gate of rocks through which we were not
at first able to pass. From the north, down the declivities of the
foot-hills of the Kenia, four larger and many smaller streams hurry
to the Dana, and in their course through their rocky basins form a
number of more or less picturesque cascades. The height of this
large park-like plateau above the sea-level, measured at its lowest
point— the stream-bed—is nearly 6,000 feet.

Whilst we were engaged in the detailed examination of this lofty plateau, I sent out several expeditions, whose duty it was to penetrate as far as possible into the Kenia range, in order to find elevated points from which to make exact observations of the form and character of the district lying around us. For though the country immediately about us charmed us so much, yet I would not definitively decide to lay the foundation-stone of our first settlement until I had obtained at least a superficial view of the whole region of the Kenia. The information which Sakemba was able to give us was but little, and insufficient. We were therefore much delighted when eight natives, whom we recognised as Andorobbo, showed themselves before our camp. They had seen our camp-fires on the previous night, and now wished to see who we were. Sakemba, who went out to them, quickly inspired them with confidence, and we now had the best guides we could have wished for. With Sakemba's help we soon informed them of our first purpose—namely, to send out eight different expeditions, each under the guidance of an Andorobbo. The first expedition returned on the evening of the same day, and the last at the end of a week, and all with tolerably exhaustive reports.

Not one of the expeditions had got near the summit of the Kenia. Nevertheless, grand views had been obtained from various easily accessible points of the main body of the mountain, some of them at an altitude of above 16,000 feet. It had been found that the side of the Kenia best adapted to the rearing of stock and to agriculture was that by which we had approached it. To the eastward and northward were large stretches of what appeared to be very fertile land; but that on the east was very monotonous, and lacked the not merely picturesque, but also practically advantageous, diversity of open country and forest, hill and plain, which we found in the south. On the north the country was too damp; and on the west there spread out an endless extent of forest broken by only a small quantity of open ground. It might all be converted into most productive cultivated land at a later date; but, at the outset, soil that was ready for use was naturally to be preferred. The inner portions of the mountain district before us were filled with wooded hills and rocks traversed by numberless valleys and gorges. These foot-hills reached on all sides close to the abruptly rising central mass of the Kenia; only in the south-west, about three miles from the western end of our plateau, did the foot-hills retire to make room for an extensive open valley-basin, in the middle of which was a lake, the outflow from which was the Dana. Our experts estimated the superficies of this valley at nearly sixty square miles; and all agreed that it was very fertile, and that its situation made it a veritable miracle of beauty. The best way into this valley was through the gorge by which the Dana flowed; but, so long as we were without suitable boats, we were obliged to enter the valley not directly from our plateau, but by a circuitous route through a small valley to the south.

I received this report on the morning of the 3rd of July. Next day, without waiting for the return of two of the expeditions which were still absent, I started for this much-lauded lake and valley. The indicated route, which proved to be, in fact, a very practicable one, led from our camp to the western end of the plateau, then bending towards the south and skirting a small, rocky, wooded hill, it entered a narrow valley leading in a northerly direction. This valley opened into the Dana gorge, which is here neither so narrow nor so impassable as at its opening into the plateau. Following this gorge upwards, in an hour we found ourselves suddenly standing in the sought-for valley.

The view was perfectly indescribable. Imagine an amphitheatre of almost geometrical regularity, about eleven miles long by seven miles and a half broad, the semicircle bounded by a series of gently rising wooded hills from 300 to 500 feet high, with a background formed by the abrupt and rugged precipices and cloud-piercing snowy summit of the Kenia. This majestic amphitheatre is occupied on the side nearest to the Kenia by a clear deep-blue lake; on the other side by a flowery park-land and meadows. The whole suggests an arena in which a grand piece, that may be called 'The Cascades of the Kenia Glaciers,' is being performed to an auditory consisting of innumerable elephants, giraffes, zebras, and antelopes. At an inaccessible height above, numberless veins of water, kissed by the dazzling sunlight, spring from the blue-green shimmering crevasses. Foaming and sparkling—now shattered into vapour reflecting all the hues of the rainbow, now forming sheets of polished whiteness – they rush downwards with ever-increasing mass and tumult, until at length they are all united into one great torrent which, with a thundering roar plainly audible in a favourable wind six miles away, hurries from its glacier home towards the precipitous rocks. There the whole colossal mass of water—which a few miles off forms the Dana river—falls perpendicularly down from a height of 1,640 feet, so dashed into vapour-dust as to form a great rainbow-cloud. The stream suddenly disappears in mid-air, and the eye seeks in vain to track its course against the background of dark glistening cliffs until, more than 1,600 feet below, the masses of falling vapour are again collected into flowing water, thence, with the noise and foam of many smaller cascades, to reach the lake by circuitous routes.

Speechless with delight, we gazed long at this unparalleled natural miracle, whose grandeur and beauty words cannot describe. The eye eagerly took in the flood of light and glittering colour, and the ear the noise of the water pealing down from a fabulous height; the breast greedily inhaled as a cordial the odorous air which was wafted through this enchanted valley. The woman who was with us —Ellen Fox—was the first to find words. Like a prophetess in an ecstasy, she looked long at the play of the water; then, suddenly, as a stronger breath of wind completely dissipated the vaporous veil of the waterfall, which just before had formed a waving, sabre-like, shimmering band, she cried, 'Behold, the flaming sword of the archangel, guarding the gate of Paradise, has vanished at our approach! Let us call this place Eden!'

The name Eden was unanimously adopted. That this valley must be our future place of abode was at once decided by all of us. A more careful examination showed its superficies to be over sixty-two square miles. Allowing thirteen miles for the elliptical lake stretching out under the Kenia cliffs, and fifteen miles for the woods which clothed the heights around the valley, there remained above thirty miles of open park-land surrounding the lake, except where the Kenia cliffs touched the water, stretching in narrow strips to the Kenia on the north-east, and broadening on the other sides to from 1,100 yards to four miles. The glacier-water forming the Dana entered the valley on the north-west, and left it on the south-east. The water, which was not so cold when it entered the lake as might have been expected, rapidly acquired a higher temperature in the lake; on hot days the lake rose to 75° Fahr. Other streams fall into the lake, some of them from the Kenia cliffs, and others from the various hills which surround the valley. We counted not less than eleven such streams, among them a hot one with a temperature of 125° Fahr.

Naturally we had not been idle during the four days which preceded our discovery of Eden Vale. On the 1st of July, a few hours after the couriers with the first despatches, the expeditions appointed to establish regular communication with Mombasa were sent off. There were two such expeditions : one, under Demestre and three other engineers, had to construct the road ; and the other, under Johnston, had to procure the draught oxen—of which it was estimated about 5,000 would be required—and to arrange for the provisioning of the whole distance. To the first expedition were allotted twenty of our members and two hundred of our Swahili men, with a train of fifty draught beasts ; with Johnston went merely ten of ourselves, twenty draught beasts, and ten sheep-dogs. How these expeditions accomplished their tasks shall be told later.

I had now sent away altogether 53 of our own people, 200 Swahili men, and 131 saddle and draught beasts, besides having lost nine of the latter by death during the journey. I had, therefore, now with me at the Kenia 149 whites, 80 Swahili, and 475 beasts, besides the dogs and the elephants. In addition to the above, we were offered the services of several hundred of the Wa-Kikuyu, who had followed us. Of these latter I retained 150 of the most capable ; the others, in charge of five of ourselves, I sent back at once to their home, with the commission to purchase and send on to the Kenia 300 strong draught oxen, 150 cows, 400 oxen for slaughter, and several thousand hundred-weight of various kinds of corn and food. Having attended to these things, I allotted and gave out to the most suitable hands the many different kinds of work which had first to be done. One of our workmen had charge of the forge and smithy, another the saw-mill, with, of course, the requisite assistance. A special section was told off for the tree-felling, and another section had to get ready and complete the agricultural implements. One of the engineers who remained at the Kenia was appointed, with one hundred blacks under him, to construct the requisite means of communication in the settlement—particularly to build bridges over the Dana.

On the 5th of July we shifted our settlement to Eden Vale. The ground was exactly measured, and on the shores of the lake the future town was marked out, with its streets, open spaces, public buildings, and places of recreation. In this projected town we allowed space for 25,000 family houses, each with a considerable garden ; and this covered thirteen square miles. Outside of the building area—which could be afterwards enlarged at pleasure— 2,500 acres were selected for temporary cultivation, and irrigated with a network of small canals; as soon as possible it was to be fenced in to protect it against the incursions of the numberless wild animals that swarmed around it, as well as from our domestic animals which, though shut up at night in a strong pen, were allowed during the day, when they were not in use, to pasture in the open country under the care of some of the Swahili men and the dogs.

In the meantime, the saw-mill, which had been set up in the Dana plateau, hard by the river, and had for its motive-power one of the rapid streams that came down from the hills, had begun its work. The first timber which it cut up was used in the construction of two large flat boats, in which the transportation of the building timber up the river to the Eden lake was at once begun. A few weeks later, on the shores of the lake, there had arisen forty spacious wooden buildings, into which we whites removed from the confined camp-tents we had previously occupied. The negroes preferred to remain in the grass huts which they had made for themselves in the shelter of a little wood. By this time the cattle were also furnished with their pen, which was high and strong enough to offer an insurmountable obstacle to any invasion by quadrupeds. In this pen there was room for about two thousand beasts, and it was, moreover, provided with a covered space for protection against rain.

By the 9th of July, our smiths, wheelwrights, and carpenters had converted ten of the ploughshares we had brought with us into ploughs, and by the same date the first consignment of cattle had come in from Kikuyu—120 oxen and 50 cows, together with 200 sheep and a large quantity of poultry. Ploughing was at once attempted, under the direction of our agriculturists. The Kikuyu oxen struggled a little against the yoke, and at first they could not be made to keep in the furrow; but in three days we were able to work them with ease in teams of eight to a plough. This expenditure of force was necessary, as the black fat soil, matted by the thick virgin turf, was extremely difficult to break up. At first it was necessary to have a driver to every pair of oxen, and the furrows were not so straight as if ploughed by long-domesticated oxen; but at any rate the ground was broken up, and in a comparatively short time the beasts got accustomed to their work and went through it most satisfactorily. On the 15th of July a fresh arrival of oxen brought fifteen more ploughs into use; and again on the 20th. By the end of the month, with these forty ploughs, some 750 acres had been broken up. This was at once harrowed and prepared for the seed. It was then sown with what seed-corn we had brought with us—chiefly wheat and barley—supplemented to the extent of about three-fourths by African wheat and *mtama* corn. The ground was then rolled again, and the work was finished in the second half of August. The whole of the cultivated area was then hedged in, and we cheerfully greeted the beginning of the shorter rainy season.

In the meantime a garden—provisionally of about twenty-five acres—had been laid out, a little farther from the precincts of the town than the arable land; for whilst the latter could easily be removed farther away as the town increased, it was necessary to find for the garden as permanent a site as possible—one therefore that lay outside of the range of the growth of the town. As we had among us no less than eighteen skilled gardeners, and as these had as much assistance as they required from the Swahili and Wa-Kikuyu, the twenty-five acres were in a few months planted with the choicest kinds of fruits and berries, vegetables, flowers—in short, with all kinds of useful and ornamental plants which we had brought from our old homes, had collected on our way, or had met with in the neighbourhoods in which we had settled. The garden also was covered with a network of irrigating canals, and enclosed against unwelcome intruders by a high and strong fence.

Against accidental inroads of monkeys there was no other protection than the vigilance of our dogs and the guns of the gardeners. A war of annihilation was therefore begun against the monkeys of the whole district, of which there were untold legions in the woods that girdled Eden Vale and in some small groves in the vale itself. While we shot other animals only when we needed their flesh, the monkeys were destroyed wherever they showed themselves in the neighbourhood of Eden Vale; and very soon the cunning creatures began carefully to avoid the inhospitable valley, whilst outside of it they retained their former daring. Several other animals were also excluded from the general law of mercy, and that even more rigorously than the monkeys, which were proscribed only within the boundaries of the valley. These animals were leopards and lions, against which we organised, whenever we had time, serious hunting expeditions. After a few months these animals entirely disappeared from the whole district ; and subsequently they almost voluntarily forsook all the districts into which we penetrated with our weapons and with our noisy activity. They have room enough elsewhere, and hold it to be unnecessary to expose their skin to the bullets of white men. On the other hand, we did not molest the hyenas ; the harm which they now and then did by the theft of a sheep was more than compensated for by their usefulness as devourers of carrion. They are shy, cowardly beasts, which do not readily attack anything that is alive ; but in the character of unwearied sanitary police they scour field and forest for dead animals. In the list of beasts not to be spared stood at first the hippopotamuses, which haunted the Eden lake and the Dana in large herds. We should have had nothing to object to in these uncouth brutes if they had not molested our boats and behaved aggressively towards our bathers. But, after our shells had somewhat lessened their number, and in particular after certain uncommonly daring old fellows had been disposed of, the rest acquired respect for us and kept at a distance whenever they saw a man ; we then relaxed our severity, and for the time contented ourselves with keeping them out of Eden Vale. But of course we showed no mercy to the numberless crocodiles that infested the lake and the river. We attacked these with bullet and spear, with hook and poison, day and night, in every conceivable way ; for we were anxious that our women and children, when they came, should be able to bathe in the refreshing waters without endangering their precious limbs. As the district which these animals frequented was in the present case a very circumscribed one—fresh individuals could come neither down from the Kenia nor over the waterfall at the end of the great plateau— we soon succeeded in so thinning their numbers that only a few examples were left, the destruction of which we handed over to our Andorobbo huntsmen, whom we furnished with weapons for this purpose, and to whom we offered a large premium for every crocodile slain in the Eden lake or in the Dana above the waterfall. As a fact, before the arrival of the first caravan of immigrants, the last crocodile had disappeared from Eden Vale and from the basin of the Dana.

Agriculture, gardening, and the chase had not absorbed all the strength at our disposal. We were at the same time busy constructing a number of practicable roads round the lake, along the river-bank to the east end of the plateau, and a number of branches from this main road to different parts of our district. It must not be imagined that these roads were works of art—they were merely fieldways, which, however, made it possible to carry about considerable loads without the expenditure of an enormous amount of force. In three places the Dana was bridged over for vehicular traffic, and in two others for foot traffic. Only in two places was much work required—at the end of the gorge through which the Dana passed from Eden Vale into the great plateau, and at a place where the Kenia cliffs touched the lake. At these places several cubic yards of rock had to be blown away, in order to make room for a road.

As in the meanwhile neither wheelwrights nor smiths had been standing still, when the roads were ready there were also ready for use upon them a number of stout waggons and barrows.

The construction of the flour-mill demanded a greater expenditure of labour. The mill was fixed on the upper course of the Dana, 1,100 yards above the entrance of the river into the Eden lake, and was furnished with ten complete sets of machinery. The site was chosen because just above there was a strong rapid, while below the Dana flowed calmly with a very trifling fall until it reached the great cataract. Thus we had, through the whole of the provisionally occupied district, a splendid waterway to the mill, and yet for the mill we could take advantage of the rapid flow of the upper Dana. We had brought from Europe the more complicated and delicate parts of this mill; but the wheels, shafts, and the ten mill-stones we manufactured ourselves. This mill—which was provisionally constructed of wood only—was ready by the end of September, thanks to the additional assistance of the two instalments of members which had reached us in the early part of the same month.

I have already mentioned that, as soon as we had reached the Kenia, I asked our committee for fresh supplies and a fresh body of

pioneers; and that the committee had informed me that at the
end of July there would start an expedition of 260 horsemen
and 800 cwt. of goods upon 300 beasts. This expedition reached
Mombasa on the 16th of August. Then it divided into two groups :
one group, containing the most adventurous 145 horsemen, started
at once on the 18th of August with fifty very lightly loaded led-
horses—the whole of the 300 sumpter beasts were horses—without
taking with them a single native except an interpreter. They relied
upon the assistance of those of our men who were constructing the
roads, and of the population friendly to us; but they were at the
same time resolved to bear without murmuring any deprivations
and fatigue that might await them. A forced ride of twenty days,
with only a one day's rest at Taveta, brought these brave fellows
among us on the 9th of September. Five horses had died, seven
others had to be left behind knocked up; they themselves, however,
all reached us, except one who had broken his leg in a fall, and was
left in good hands in Miveruni, somewhat exhausted, but otherwise
in good condition. The newly arrived joined us heartily in our
work two days after. The 115 others reached us ten days later,
with 250 sumpter horses and 100 Swahili drivers. The greater part
of the goods they had given to Johnston on the way, who met with
them at Useri, where he had been eagerly awaiting them. The
articles brought to us at the Kenia—in all something over 300 cwt.
—contained a quantity of tools and machinery ; these, and especially the considerable addition of workmen, contributed in no small
degree to expedite our various works.

The flour-mill was—as has been stated—ready by the end of
September. It at once found abundant employment. It is true
that our harvest was not yet gathered in; but we had been
gradually purchasing different kinds of grain—to the amount of
10,000 cwt.—of the Wa-Kikuyu, and had stored it near the lake
in granaries, for which the saw-mill had supplied the building
material. All this grain was ground by the end of October ; and,
even if our harvest had failed, the first few thousands of those who
were coming would not have had to suffer hunger.

But our harvest did not fail. A few weeks after the beginning
of the hot season—which begins in October—the fertile soil, which
had been continuously kept moist by our system of irrigation,
blessed us with a crop that mocked all European conceptions.

Every grain sowed yielded on an average a hundred and twenty fold. Our 750 acres yielded 42,000 cwt. of different kinds of grain, for each haulm ended, not in single lean ears, but in thick heavy bunches of ears—our European wheat and barley not less than the African kinds. We had fortunately made ample preparation for the work of the harvest. Before the end of August a machine-factory had been erected a few hundred yards above the flour-mill. Water-power was used, and the work of manufacture began at once. Partly of materials brought with us, but mainly of materials prepared by ourselves, we had constructed several reaping-machines and two threshing-machines, worked by horse-power.

Our factories were able to produce these machines because our geologists had discovered, among other valuable mineral treasures, iron and coal in our district. The coal lay in one of the foot-hills of the Kenia, on the Dana plateau, nearly two miles from the river; the iron in one of the foot-hills which the Dana in its upper course had cut through, a mile and a quarter above Eden Vale. The coal was moderately good anthracite, and the iron ore was a rich forty-per-cent. ferro-manganese. A smelting and refining furnace, as well as an iron-works, were at once put up near the source of the iron; they were of a primitive and provisional character, but they sufficed to supply us with serviceable cast and wrought iron, and thus to make us at once independent of the supplies brought from Europe. We now possessed a small but independent iron industry, and this enabled us to gather in and work up within a few weeks the un-expectedly rich harvest.

A further use which we immediately made of our increased powers of production was to put up two new saw-mills and a brewery. The saw-mills were needed to supply material for the shelter of the con-tinually increasing stream of fresh arrivals; and the brewery was intended to serve as a means of agreeably surprising the new-comers with a welcome draught of a familiar beverage with which most of them would be sorry to dispense. As soon as the barley was cut and threshed, it was malted. Our gardeners had grown hops of very acceptable quality on the sides of the Kenia foot-hills; and soon a cool cellar, made by utilising some natural caverns, was filled with casks of the noble drink.

By the end of October we were able to contemplate our four months' labours with a restful satisfaction. Six hundred neat block-houses awaited as many families; 50,000 cwt. of corn and flour, copious supplies of cattle for slaughter and draught, building material and tools, were ready for the food, shelter, and equipment of many thousands of members. The garden had been not less successfully cultivated, and its dainty gifts were already beginning to be enjoyed. Our own garden-produce did not, as yet, suffice to cover our anticipated requirements; but it continued to be supplemented by a brisk barter trade with the Wa-Kikuyu. For these natives we had established a regular weekly market in Eden Vale, which several hundreds of them attended, bringing with them their goods upon ox-carts, the use of which we had introduced among them and had made possible by means of the roads our engineers had constructed through their country. Since we had set up our iron-works, the Wa-Kikuyu came to us principally for iron either in a raw condition or made up into tools. For this they at first bartered cattle and vegetables; afterwards, when we no longer needed these things, they offered mainly ivory, of which we had already acquired 138 tons, partly through our trade with the Wa-Kikuyu and the Andorobbo, and partly as the fruits of our own hunting. For ivory is as cheap here as blackberries; the Wa-Kikuyu and the Andorobbo are glad to buy our wrought iron for double its weight in the material which is so valuable in the West. An iron implement, whether hammer, nail, or knife, is exchanged for from ten to twenty times its weight in ivory. Thus almost the whole cost of our expedition was already covered by our ivory—the cattle and provisions, the implements and machinery, not to speak of the land, being thrown in gratis.

CHAPTER VI

WHILST we at the Kenia were thus busily preparing a comfortable home for our brethren who were expected from the Old World, our colleagues, under the direction of Demestre and Johnston, were working not less successfully on the tasks allotted to them.

Demestre had nothing to do with the construction of roads within the Kenia district; his work began with the great forests that girdled this district. The execution of the work from thence to the boundary between Kikuyu and Masailand, at Ngongo, he

F

deputed to the engineer Frank, an American; the second section, from Ngongo to Masimani in Masailand, midway between Ngongo and Taveta, was allotted to the engineer Möllendorf, a German; the third section, from Masimani to Taveta, to Lermanoff, a Russian, as his name shows; the last and most difficult section, from Taveta to Mombasa, including two of the worst deserts, Demestre reserved to himself. To each of the four sections five whites were appointed. His 200 Swahili, strengthened by double that number of Wa-Kikuyu hired on the march through their land, Demestre divided between the first two sections, allotting 50 Swahili and 300 Wa-Kikuyu to the first in Kikuyuland, and 150 Swahili and 100 Wa-Kikuyu to the second in Masailand. The third section was organised from Taveta. Lermanoff and a companion rode thither from Kenia, by making use of our courier-stages, in six days. He engaged 100 Swahili men in Taveta—where Swahili caravans are always to be met with—and 250 natives in Useri and Chaga. In the meantime his four colleagues had arrived and brought with them the pack-horses allotted to his—as to each—section; and the work from Taveta to Useri was begun on the 15th of July. Demestre also made use of the courier-stages, and rode, with no other breaks than night-rests, first to Teita, where he hired 400 Wa-Teita, whom he at once set to work, under the direction of one of his colleagues, upon the road between Teita and Taveta. He then hastened on to Mombasa, and by the 20th of July he was able to put 500 people of the coast upon the most difficult part of the work—the road from Mombasa to Teita.

The work to be done in all cases was threefold. First, in the places where there was a deficiency of water—of which places there were several in the lower sections, particularly in the deserts of Duruma, Teita, and Ngiri—wells had to be dug and, where there was no spring-water, cisterns made capacious enough to supply water sufficient not merely for the workmen during the construction of the road, but afterwards for the men and cattle of the caravans that passed that way. As there occur in Equatorial Africa at all seasons of the year heavy storms of rain, which in the so-called hot season are only much less frequent than in the so-called rainy season, there was no danger that large cisterns draining the rain-water from a sufficiently wide area would be exhausted even in the hot months; but the cisterns had to be protected from the direct rays of the sun as well as from impurities. The former was effected by providing the cisterns with covering and shelter; the second by making the rain-water filter through layers, several yards thick, of sand and gravel. The natural water-holes, which are found in all deserts, but which dry up in times of protracted drought, indicated the spots where it would be most practicable to construct cisterns, for such spots were naturally the lowest points. The larger of these water-holes needed only to be deepened, the evaporation of the water guarded against, and the cisterns surrounded by the above-mentioned natural filter, and the work was then finished. Of these in the different sections twenty-five were dug, with a depth of from nine to sixteen yards and a diameter of from two to nine yards. Of ordinary wells with spring-water thirty-nine were made. Each of these artificial supplies of water was placed under the protection of a watchman.

In the second place, there was the road-making itself. In general, the route which the expedition had taken from Mombasa to the Kenia was chosen, and merely freed from obstacles and widened to twice its original width where it led through bush. But at certain places, particularly where steep heights had to be traversed, it was necessary to look for a fresh and less hilly track. That several bridges had to be built scarcely need be mentioned.

The third part of the work consisted in the erection of primitive houses of shelter, at suitable places, for both men and cattle. Accommodation for several hundred men, pens for cattle, and storehouses for provisions, were constructed at sixty-five stations, at distances varying from seven to twelve miles.

These works were all completed between Mombasa and Teita by the end of September, and in all the other sections fourteen days later. The workmen, however, were not discharged, as a part of them were required for guarding and maintaining the road and buildings, and another part found occupation in the transport service on the newly made highway. The cost of construction for the whole by no means small undertaking was 14,500*l*., half of which went in wages and half in rations; the material used in the work cost nothing.

By this time Johnston had completed the purchase of the draught-beasts required for the transport service, and had organised the commissariat of the caravans. His Masai friends procured for him in a few weeks the originally ordered 5,000 head of cattle ; and as every despatch from the committee of the Free Society reported a larger and larger number of members on their way to the settlement, our order was increased to 9,000, exclusive of the 750 head of cattle, the unused remnant of our presents which we had left behind us in Useri and Masailand. As the committee had reason to anticipate that by the end of October the number of members intending at once to join the colony would reach 20,000, they had enlarged their orders for waggons to 1,000, and announced that fact to us in the course of September. Therefore, as every waggon —which weighed 14 cwt., and would carry ten persons, with 20 cwt. of luggage—would require four yoke of oxen, the total number of draught-oxen needed would be 8,000, in addition to a reserve of 200 head, and 1,550 oxen and cows for slaughter. Johnston received this message on the southern frontier of Masailand, and, as there was not time to return, he had to complete his provisioning in the districts of Kilima and Teita. Nevertheless he succeeded in collecting the full number of cattle and distributing them along the sixty-five stages between Mombasa and the Kenia without materially raising prices by his purchases in these favoured districts. He bought 8,500 oxen and 500 cows, and the cost—including the travelling expenses and wages of the buyers and drivers—amounted to no more than 3,650l.—that is, the goods which we bartered for them had cost us this amount. Each head of cattle cost on the average a little over eight shillings, half of which represented incidental expenses, the bare selling price being less than four shillings a head.

Johnston so arranged the transport service that every day twenty-five waggons left Mombasa, and at every one of the sixty-five stations found fresh draught-oxen ready. Arrived at Eden Vale, the waggons had to return to Mombasa in the same manner. By this simple and practical arrangement, all the waggons were kept constantly in motion between Mombasa and the Kenia, whilst the draught-oxen merely moved to and fro in fixed teams between neighbouring stations. In this way 250 persons could be conveyed every day, and to convey 20,000 —the total number of members reported by the committee—would require eighty days, unless some of them made the journey on horseback.

The waggons constructed in England, America, and Germany

arrived punctually at Mombasa. They were in every respect models
of skilful construction, solidly and yet, in proportion to their size,
lightly built, affording many conveniences without sacrificing simplicity. Each one accommodated ten persons with sitting space in
the day and with good sleeping space at night. By a very simple
alteration of the seats, room could be made for ten persons—four
above and six beneath. Strong springs made the riding easy, a
movable leathern covering gave shelter from rain or sun, and the
mattrasses which served as beds at night were by day so buckled
on the under-side of the leathern covering as to afford double protection against the heat of the sun. Accommodation for the baggage
was provided in a similarly practical manner.

The first ship, with 900 members, arrived on the 30th of September. This ship, like all that followed, was the property of the
Society. Anticipating that the stream of emigrants would not soon
cease, would probably continue to increase, and desirous to keep the
transportation of the emigrants as much as possible in their hands,
the Society had bought twelve large, swift-sailing steamships, aver-
aging 3,500 tons burden, and had had them adapted to their purpose. They could do this without overstraining their resources;
for, though the 940,000*l.* which these twelve steamers cost exceeded
the amount actually in hand, the Society could safely reckon that
the deficit would soon be made good by the contributions of new
members, to accommodate whom the vessels and all the other provisions were intended. In fact, by the middle of September the
number of members exceeded 20,000, and the property of the
Society had grown to 750,000*l.* Of this amount, however, 150,000*l.*
had been spent independently of the purchase of the ships, and a
similar amount would in the immediate future be required for the
general purposes of the Society; thus less than half of the cost of
the ships was in hand and available for payment. But the sellers
readily gave the Society credit, and handed over the vessels without
delay, even before any money was paid. They risked nothing by
this, for the Society's executive were fully justified in calculating that
the future income from new members would be at least 100,000*l.* a
month, while the Society's property was quite worth all the money
they had hitherto spent upon it.

The chief thing, however, was that people were getting to
have more and more faith in the success of the Society's under-

taking, and to look upon that undertaking as representative of the great commonwealth of the future. Several governments already offered their assistance to the committee, who accepted those offers only so far as they afforded a moral support. A number of scientific and other public associations took a most lively interest in the aims of the Society. For example, the Geographical Societies of London and Rome gave, the one 4,000*l.* and the other 50,000 lires, merely stipulating in return that a periodical report should be sent to them of all the scientifically interesting experiences of the Society. That the business world should also interest themselves in the Society's doings is not surprising. For the vessels which had been bought the Society made an immediate payment of forty per cent., and undertook to pay the remainder within three years. The whole was, however, paid off before the end of the second year.

The ships thus bought were employed to convey the emigrant members from Trieste to Mombasa. As each vessel carried from 900 to 1,000 passengers, while the waggons could convey 250 persons daily from Mombasa to the settlement, it was necessary that two ships should reach Mombasa per week; it being assumed that a part of the emigrants would prefer to travel from Mombasa on horseback. And as the average length of a voyage to Mombasa and back was thirty-five days, the twelve vessels were sufficient to maintain a continuous service, with an occasional extra voyage for the transport of goods, particularly of horses. There was no distinction of class on board the vessels of the Society; no fee was taken from anyone, either for transport or for board during the whole voyage, and everyone was therefore obliged to be content with the same kind of accommodation, which certainly was not deficient in comfort. On deck were large dining-rooms and rooms for social intercourse; below deck was a small sleeping-cabin for each family, comfortably fitted up and admirably ventilated. The members were received on board in the order in which they had entered the Society, the earlier members thus having the priority. Of course it was optional for any member to make the voyage on any ship not belonging to the Society, without losing his place in the list of claimants when he arrived at Mombasa.

At Mombasa everyone was at liberty to continue his journey either on horseback or in a waggon. The horsemen might either accompany the caravans or ride in advance in such stages as they pleased, only the horses must be changed regularly at the sixty-five stations, provision being made for a sufficient supply of horses. The travellers in waggons had, moreover, the option of going on night and day uninterruptedly, pausing only to effect the necessary changes of oxen ; or of travelling more deliberately, halting as long as they pleased at the midday or the night stations. In the former case they could, in favourable weather, reach Eden Vale in fourteen days, or even less ; in the latter case twenty days or more would be spent on the journey.

All the arrangements were perfectly carried out. There was no hitch anywhere. The commissariat left nothing to be desired. An escort of ten Masai, which Johnston had organised for each station, kept guard against wild beasts during the night journeys, and had to serve as auxiliaries in any difficulty ; while four commissioners sent from among our members, and located respectively at Teita, Taveta, Miveruni, and Ngongo, superintended the whole. The natives greeted the first train of waggons with jubilant astonishment, but received all with the greatest friendliness and helpfulness. Particularly the Wa-Taveta, the Sultan of Useri, and the Masai tribes did not fail to overwhelm our travellers with proofs of their respect and love for the white brethren who had ' settled on the great mountain.'

The first new arrivals—among them our beloved master— entered Eden Valley on the 14th of October ; they were followed by an uninterrupted series of fresh companies. But, before the story of this new era in the history of our undertaking is told, a brief account must be given of what had been taking place at the Kenia.

As early as August, a numerous deputation of Masai tribes from Lykipia—the country to the north-west of the Kenia—and from the districts between the Naivasha and the Baringo lakes, arrived at Eden Vale offering friendship, and asking to be admitted into the alliance between us and the other Masai. This very affecting request was made with evident consciousness of its importance, and the granting of it certainly placed us under new and heavy obligations. Yet I granted it without a moment's hesitation, and my act received the approval of all the members. For the pacification of the most quarrelsome and unquestionably the bravest of all the tribes of the equatorial zone was not too dearly bought by the sacrifice of a few thousand pounds sterling per annum. We now had a satisfactory guarantee that civilisation would gradually develop in these regions, which had hitherto been cursed by incessant feuds and pillage ; that we should be able so to educate the black and brown natives that they would become more and more useful associates in our great work; and that, in proportion as we taught them to create prosperity and luxury for themselves, we should be increasing the sources of our own prosperity. So I addressed to the brown warriors a flattering panegyric, declared myself touched by the friendly sentiments they had expressed, and promised with all speed to send an embassy to them in order to conclude the treaty of alliance and to do them honour. They were sent away richly laden with presents; and they on their part had not come empty-handed, for they brought with them a hundred choice beasts, and two hundred fat-tailed sheep. Johnston, whom I at once informed of the incident, undertook the fulfilment of the promise I had given. I have already stated that for this purpose he provided himself with a full supply of the necessary goods from the baggage of the expedition which he met with in September on its way to the Kenia. When his task in the road-stages was finished, he started, about the beginning of October, for the Naivasha lake, and went thence through the extensive and, for the most part, exceedingly fertile high plateau—6,000 feet above the sea—which, bounded by hills from 3,300 to 6,600 feet higher, contains the elevated lakes of Masailand—namely, not only the Naivasha lake, the marvellous Elmeteita lake, and the salt lake of Nakuro, but also a series of smaller basins. On the 20th of October he reached the Baringo lake, on the northern limit of Masailand, a lake that covers 77 square miles in a depression of the land not more than 2,500 feet above the sea. Thence, in a westerly direction, he went over ground, rising again, past the grand Thomson Falls, through the wooded and well-watered Lykipia, and in the second week of November he reached us at the Kenia, having on the way contracted alliance with all the Masai tribes through whose lands he had passed, as well as with the ' Njemps ' at the Baringo lake.

In the next place an account has to be given of the successful attempts made, at the instigation of our two ladies, to tame several of the wild animals indigenous to the Kenia. The idea was originated by Miss Fox, who in the first instance wished merely to provide pleasure for the women and children of the expected new arrivals. Miss Fox won over my sister, a great friend to animals,

to this idea ; and so they hired several Andorobbo and Wa-Kikuyu
to capture monkeys and parrots, of which in Eden Vale there were
several very charming species. The attempts to tame these creatures
were successful beyond expectation—so much so that after a few
weeks the captives, when let loose, voluntarily followed their mistresses. This excited the ambition of both of the ladies, and the
Andorobbo were commissioned to capture some specimens of a particularly pretty species of antelope, which our naturalists decided to
be a variety of the tufted antelope (*Cephalophus rufilatus*), which is
almost peculiar to Western Africa. This attempt was also successful. It is true that the old animals proved to be so shy and intractable that they were at last allowed to go free ; but several young
ones became attached to their guardians with surprising rapidity, and
followed them like dogs. These antelopes are not larger than a
medium-sized sheep, and the young ones in particular look exceedingly pretty with their red tufts, and disport themselves like frisky
kids. Miss Ellen and my sister soon had about them a whole
menagerie of antelopes, monkeys, and parrots, trained to perform
all sorts of tricks for the delectation of the children who were
expected.

Thus matters stood when one of the elephant-keepers whom
Miss Ellen had brought with her to the Kenia, and who had given
up all thoughts of returning to their home, ventured to ask his
' mistress '—for the Indians could not accustom themselves to the
idea that they were perfectly independent men—whether she would
not like an elephant-baby also as a pet ? Receiving an affirmative
answer, he undertook to capture one or more, if he were allowed to
go with the four elephants and their keepers into the woods for a
few days. As Miss Ellen had allowed her elephants to be employed
in the building operations, where these interesting colossi were of
invaluable service, and as the work could not be interrupted for the
sake of a plaything, she told the Indian that she would forego her
wish, or at least would wait until the elephants could be more easily
spared from the work. The Indian went away, but the idea that
his beloved mistress should be deprived of anything that would—as
he had at once perceived—have given her great pleasure, roused
him out of his customary fatalistic indolence. He brooded over the
matter for a couple of days, and on the third he appeared with the
proposal to make good the loss of time occasioned by the temporary

absence of the four elephants by capturing, with the aid of the other Cornaks, not only a young elephant, but also several old elephants, and training them for work. 'But African elephants cannot be trained like the Indian ones,' objected Miss Ellen. The Indian ventured to question this, and his seven colleagues were all of his opinion. Elephants were elephants; they would like to see an animal with a trunk that they could not tame in a few weeks if he only got into their hands. 'If it is really so, why have you not said so before; for you must have seen what good use can be made of elephants here?' asked the American, and received for answer merely a laconic 'Because you have not asked us.'

Miss Ellen did not know what to do. The idea of furnishing the colony of Eden Vale with herds of tame elephants—for if these animals could be tamed, there might as well be thousands as one— did not allow her to rest. On the other hand, she remembered to have read, in her natural-history studies, that African elephants were untameable. We all, when she asked us, were obliged to affirm that there were no tame elephants anywhere in Africa. She thought over this problem until she began to grow melancholy; evidently she was anxious that a trial should be made. But the Indians insisted upon the impossibility of capturing wild elephants without the assistance of the tame ones; and she shrank the more from using the latter in a doubtful attempt at a time when work urgently required doing, because the tame elephants were her own property, and therefore the decision depended entirely upon herself. Just then our zoologist, Signor Michaele Faënze, returned from a long excursion to the central mass of the Kenia; and when Miss Fox took him into her confidence, he at once sided with the Indians. He admitted that, as a matter of fact, there were no tame African elephants; but he maintained that this was simply because the Africans had forgotten how to make the noble beast serviceable to man. The reason did not lie in the character of the African elephant, for in the days of the Romans trained elephants were as well known in Africa as in Asia. They should let the Indians make an attempt; if the latter understood their business they would succeed as well in Africa as in India.

And so it turned out. The eight Cornaks with their four elephants went into the neighbouring forests; and when, as soon happened, they had found a herd of wild elephants, they did with them exactly as they had learnt to do at home. The tame elephants were sent without their attendants into the midst of the herd of wild ones, by whom they were at first greeted with some signs of surprise, but were ultimately received into companionship. The crafty animals then fixed their attention upon the leader of the herd, the strongest and handsomest bull, caressed him, whisked the flies off him, but in the meantime bound, with some strong cord they had taken with them, one of his legs to a stout tree. Having done this, they uttered their cry of alarm—a sharp trumpet-like sound—and ran off as if they had discovered some danger. On this signal, the Indians rushed forward with loud cries and the firing of guns, and thus caused the whole herd to rush off after the tame elephants. The poor prisoner, of course, could not run off with the rest, desperately as he strained at the ropes ; and the Indians allowed him to stamp and trumpet, without for a while troubling themselves about him. Their next care was to follow the track of the escaped herd. In the course of an hour they had again crept up to it, to find that in the meantime the four tame elephants had repeated the same trick with a new victim, which was also fettered and then left in the same manner. In the course of the day three more elephants shared the same fate ; and by that time the herd appeared to have grown suspicious, for their betrayers returned alone to their keepers.

Now first was a visit paid to the five captives, among whom was a female with a yearling about the size of a half-grown calf. The tame elephants went straight to the captives straining at the ropes, and bound their fore-feet tightly together. This was not done without furious resistance on the part of the betrayed beasts ; but this resistance was overcome in a most brutal way by strokes of the trunk and by bites. Thereupon the merciless captors busied themselves removing from within their victims' reach everything that is pleasant to an elephant's palate—grass, bushes, and tree-twigs ; and what their trunks could not do they enabled the keepers to do with axe and hatchet by dragging the captives down upon their sides.

When night came, all five captives were securely bound and deprived of every possibility of getting food. They were watched, however, to secure them from being attacked by lions or leopards. The next morning the tame elephants again visited their captive brethren one after the other, helped the fallen ones to get up—which was not effected without a good deal of thrashing and pushing—and then again left them to their fate.

This went on for three days ; the poor captives suffered from hunger and thirst, and received barbarous blows from their treacherous brethren whenever the latter came near them. By the fourth day they had become so weak and subdued that they no longer roared, but pitifully moaned when their tormentors approached, which nevertheless fell upon them fiercely with trunk and teeth. Now a rescuing angel appeared to them, in human form. An Indian, with threatening actions and several noisy blows, drove the captors from their victim, and offered to the latter a vessel of water. If the wild elephant, struck with astonishment, took time to survey the situation, the tragi-comedy was over—the beast was tamed. For, in this case, he would, after a little hesitation, accept the proffered drink, and then a little food ; he could afterwards be fed and watered without danger, and, under the escort of the tame elephants, led home for further training. If, on the contrary, the sight of the man maddened him—as was the case with three out of the five— the thrashing-and-hunger treatment had to be continued until the elephant began to understand that release from his situation could be afforded only by the terrible biped.

At last all the captives submitted to their fate. The only danger in this process consists in the necessity, on the part of the hunter, of relying upon the accuracy of his judgment concerning the captive's character when he first approaches him. It is true that the tame elephants stand by observant and ready to help ; but as a single thrust of the tusk of an enraged animal may be fatal, the business requires a great deal of courage and presence of mind. However, the Indians asserted that anyone only partially accustomed to the ways of elephants could tell with certainty from the look of the animal what he meant to do ; it was therefore necessary merely to take the precaution not to get very close to a captive elephant before reading in his eye submission to the inevitable, and then there was nothing to fear.

After an absence of six days, the expedition returned with the five captives, which were certainly not yet trained and serviceable for work, but were so far tame that they quietly allowed themselves

to be shut up, fed, watered, and taught. In the course of another
fortnight they were ready for use in all kinds of work, particularly
when they had one of the veterans by their side. Miss Ellen had
a double triumph : she possessed a charming baby elephant, which
was certainly a little too clumsy for a lap-dog, but was nevertheless
as droll a creature as could be, and soon made itself the acknowledged favourite of all Eden Vale ; and she had besides opened out
for the Society an inexhaustible source of very valuable motive
power, of which no one would have thought but for her.

From that time forth we actively carried on the capture of
elephants, so that in a little while the elephant was the chief
draught-beast in the Kenia, and could be employed wherever heavy
weights had to be removed to short distances or to places inaccessible to waggons.

This successful experiment with the elephants suggested to us
the taming of other animals, for purposes, not merely of pleasure,
but of utility. The first attempt was made upon the zebra, and
was successful. Though the old animals were useless, the foals,
when captured quite young, were tolerably tractable and not particularly shy ; and in the second generation our tame zebras were
not distinguishable from the best mules, except in colour. Ostriches
and giraffes came next in the order of our domestic animals ; but
our trainers achieved their greatest triumph in taming the African
buffalo. This is the most vicious, uncontrollable, and dangerous of
all African beasts ; and yet it was so thoroughly domesticated that
in the course of years it completely supplanted the common ox as
a draught-beast. The bulls that had grown up in a wild condition
were, and remained, perfect devils ; but the captured cows could
be so thoroughly domesticated that they would eat out of their attendants' hands, and the buffaloes bred in a state of domestication
exhibited exactly the same character as the ordinary domestic cattle.
The bulls, especially when old, continued to be somewhat unre-
liable ; but the cows and oxen, on the other hand, were as gentle
and docile as any ruminant could be. They were never valued
among us as milch kine—for, though their milk was rich, it was
not great in quantity—but they were incomparable as draught-
beasts. They were higher by half a foot than the largest domestic
cattle ; they measured two feet across the shoulders, and their
horns were too thick at the base to be spanned by two hands. No

load was too heavy for these gigantic beasts; two buffaloes would keep up their steady pace with a load that would soon have disabled four ordinary oxen. They bore hunger, thirst, heat, and rain better than their long-domesticated kindred ; in short, they proved themselves invaluable in a country where good roads were not everywhere to be found.

The third incident——— But this really concerns only me personally, and belongs to this narrative merely so far as it relates to the mode of life and the social conditions of Eden Vale. It will therefore be best if I next tell how we lived, what our habits were, and how we worked in the new home, before the arrival of the main body of our brethren.

CHAPTER VII

The colonists in Eden Vale looked upon me—the Society's plenipotentiary, who had organised our expedition to the Kenia and procured the necessary means—as their president in the full sense of the word : I might have commanded and I should have been obeyed. But, on the other hand, I acted not only in harmony with my own inclination, but also according to the evident intention of the committee, when I assumed merely the position of president of an association of men who had power to manage their own affairs. Whenever it was possible, I consulted my colleagues previous to making any arrangements, and acted in accordance with the will of the majority; and only in the most urgent cases, or when orders had to be given to persons who were absent, did I act independently. The distribution of the work to different groups was made by arrangement between all the members concerned, and the superintendents of the several branches of work were elected by their special colleagues. Though in all essential matters the views and proposals of myself and of those more particularly in my confidence were always carried out (so that if in what I have written I had, for brevity's sake, said ' I arranged,' ' I designed,' it would have been essentially correct}, yet this was due entirely to the fact that my confidants were the intellectual leaders of the colony, and the others voluntarily subordinated themselves to them. Moreover, we all knew that the present was only a provisional arrangement. In the meanwhile, no one worked for himself; all that we produced belonged not to the producer, not even to the whole of the producers, but to the undertaking upon the common property of which we were, in return, all living. In a word, the Free Society which we wished to found was not yet founded—it was in process of forming; and for the time we were, in reference to it, nothing more than persons employed according to the old custom, and differed from ordinary wage-carners simply in the fact that it was left to ourselves to decide what we should keep for our own maintenance and what we should set apart as the employer's share of the gains. If any evil-intentioned colleague had compelled me to do so, I not only had the right, but was resolved, to assume the attitude of the 'plenipotentiary.' That I was able to avoid doing this contributed no little to heighten the mutual pleasure we all experienced, and very materially facilitated the transition to the ultimate form of our organisation; but this did not alter the fact that our life and work, both on the journey and at the Kenia, were carried on under the social forms of the old system.

During this period the hours of work, whether of overseer or simple workman, white or negro, at Eden Vale were alike for all—from 5 A.M. to 10 A.M. and from 4 P.M. to 6 P.M.; only in the harvest-time were one or two hours added. All work ceased on Sundays.

The order of the day was as follows: We rose about 4 A.M. and took a bath in Eden Lake, where several bathing-houses had been constructed. The washing and repairing of clothes was attended to—under the superintendence of a member who was an expert in such matters—by a band of Swahili, to whom this work was allotted as their sole duty. We wore every day the clothes which had been cleansed on the previous day, and which were brought to the owner in the course of the day to be ready for him in the morning. After the toilet came the breakfast, the preparation of which, as well as of all the other meals, was also the special duty of a particular band of Swahili. In initiating them into the mysteries of French cookery my sister was of great service. This first breakfast consisted, according to individual taste, of tea, chocolate, coffee—black or *au lait*—milk, or some kind of soup; to these might be added, according to choice, butter, cheese, honey, eggs, cold meat, with some kind of bread or cake. After this first breakfast came work until 8, followed by a second breakfast, consisting

of some kind of substantial hot food—omelets, fish, or roast meat
—with bread, also cheese and fruits; the drinks were either the
delicious spring-water of our hills, or the very refreshing and
agreeable banana-wine made by the natives. Fifteen or twenty
minutes were usually spent over this breakfast, and work followed
until 10 A.M. Then came the long midday rest, when most of us,
particularly in the hotter months, took a second bath in the lake,
followed by private recreation, reading, conversation, or games. As
a rule, the heat in this part of the day was great; in the hot season
the thermometer frequently measured 95° Fahr. in the shade. It
is true that the heat out of doors was prevented from becoming un-
endurable by cool breezes, which, in fine weather, blew regularly
between 11 A.M. and 5 P.M. from the Kenia, and these breezes were
the stronger the hotter the day; but it was most agreeable and
most conducive to health to spend the midday hours under cover.
At 1 P.M. the principal meal was taken, consisting of soup, a course
of meat or fish with vegetables, sweet pastry, and fruit of many
kinds, with banana-wine or, when our brewery had been set to
work, beer. The meal over, some would sleep for half an hour, and
the rest of the time would be filled up with conversation, reading,
and games. When the fiercest heat was over, the two hours of
afternoon work would be gone through. After this a few indulged
in a third and hasty bath. At 7 P.M. a meal similar to the first
breakfast was taken, out of doors if it did not rain, and in larg
companies. It should be stated that, with reference to the meals
and to all other means of refreshment, everyone could choose what
and how much he pleased. It was only in the matter of alcoholic
drinks that there was any restriction, and that for easily understoc
reasons. Later, when everyone acted for himself, even in this
matter there was perfect liberty; but so long as we were under the
then existing obligations to the Society it was necessary to observe
restrictions for the sake of the negroes.

The evenings were generally devoted to music. We had some
very skilful musicians, an excellent orchestra of wind and string
instruments numbering forty-five performers, and a fine choir; and
these performed whenever the weather permitted. The air would
grow cool two or three hours after sunset; on some nights the
thermometer would measure over 70° Fahr., but it occasionally sank
to less than 60° Fahr., so that the night-rest was always refreshing.

Sundays were given up to recreation and instruction : excursions into the adjoining woods, hunting expeditions, concerts, public lectures, addresses, &c.

The block-houses in which we dwelt were intended to serve each family as a future—though merely provisional—home. Each stood in a garden of 1,200 square yards ; and with its six rooms—living-room, kitchen, and four bedrooms—covered 150 square yards. At this time each such house was occupied by four of us; to the two women and Sakemba—the latter had been visited by her parents and their family, and had induced them to put up their grass hut in Eden Vale—a separate house was of course allotted.

This last arrangement, however, did not please my sister at all. During the journey she had yielded to the necessity of being separated from me, the darling ward given into her charge by our sainted mother. Arrived at Eden Vale, she expected to resume her old rights of guardianship and domestic superintendence ; but she found herself prevented from carrying out her wishes by her duty towards a second, who in the meantime had become a favourite with her—namely, Miss Fox. She could not possibly leave this young woman alone among so many men ; but as little could she bring us both into the same house, though in her eyes we were mere children. What would her friends in Paris have said to that ? I spent all my leisure time in the women's house, whither I was un-consciously more and more strongly attracted, not less by the young American's conversation—which was a piquant mixture of animated controversy and unaffected chatter—than by her harp-playing and her clear alto voice. But this did not satisfy sister Clara, who at last hit upon the plan of marrying us. Our common ' foolishness '—that is, our social ideas—made us, she thought, mutually suitable ; and though, in her opinion, we should make a pair entirely lacking in sound domestic common sense, *she* was there to think and act for both of us.

Having once conceived this purpose, she, as a prudent and discreet person who rightly foresaw that in this matter she could not expect implicit obedience from either Miss Fox or myself, placed us under close observation. Though she was peculiarly lacking in personal experience in matters of love, yet, by means merely of that delicate sensibility peculiar to woman, she made the startling discovery that we were already over head and ears in love with each other. At first she was so astonished at this discovery that she would not believe her own eyes. But the thing was too clear to make mistake possible. We two lovers had ourselves not the re- motest suspicion of our condition ; but to anyone who knew Miss Fox so well as several months of unbroken companionship with the open-hearted and ingenuous young American had enabled my sister to do, there could be no difficulty in understanding what was the matter when a young woman, who had hitherto lived only for her ideals, freedom and justice, whose idol had been humanity, but who had shown no interest in any individual man apart from the ideas to which he devoted himself, was thrown into confusion as often as she heard the footsteps of a certain man, and in her confidential intercourse with my sister, instead of talking of the grandeur of our principles, preferred to talk of the excellences of him who in Eden Vale was the leading exponent of those principles. As to my own feelings, sister Clara knew too well that hitherto woman had interested me merely on account of her position in human society not to feel as if scales had fallen from her eyes when one day, after long and devotedly watching Miss Fox as she was busying herself about something, I broke out with the words, ' Is not every move- ment of that girl music ? '

So my sister took us each aside and told us we must marry. But she met with a check from both of us. On hearing of the proposal, Miss Ellen, though she became alternately crimson and pale, at once exclaimed that she would rather die than marry me. ' Would not those arrogant men who deny us women any sense of the ideal, any capacity for real effort, and look upon us as the slaves of our egoistic impulses—would they not triumphantly assert that my pretended enthusiasm for our social undertaking was merely passion for a man ; that it was not for the sake of an idea, but for the sake of a man, that I had run off to Equatorial Africa ? No— I don't love your brother—I shall never love, still less marry ! ' This heroic apostrophe was, however, followed by a flood of tears, which, when sister Clara wished to interpret them in my favour, were declared to be signs of emotion at the offensive suspicion. I re- ceived the proposal in a similar way. When Clara hinted to me that I was in love with Miss Fox, I laughed at her heartily, and declared that what she took to be symptoms of my passion were merely signs of psychological interest in a woman who was capable of a genuine enthusiasm for abstract ideas.

But a motherly sister who has once conceived the purpose of getting her brother—and her female friend as well—married, is not so easily driven from the field : at least, not when she has such good and manifold grounds to adhere to her intention. As she could not gain her end in a direct way, she tried a circuitous one—-not a new one, but one often tried : she made us both jealous. She told each of us in confidence that she had given up her ' stupid plan,' as the other party was no longer free. As she slily added to me that she had devised her project merely to be able to come into my house with my young wife and to resume her motherly care over me, and as this was evidently the truth, I also gave credence to the invention that Ellen had left a betrothed lover in America, who was about to appear in Eden Vale. ' Only think, Ellen never made this confession until I approached her with my plan of getting her married.! It is very lucky that you, my boy, care nothing for the sly little creature ; it would have been a pretty business if you had set your heart upon Ellen ! '

I declared myself perfectly satisfied with this turn of affairs ; but at the same time I felt as if a knife had pierced my heart. Suddenly my love stood clear and distinct before my mind's eye—a glowing boundless passion, such as he only can feel whose heart has remained six-and-twenty years untouched. It seemed to me an unalterable certainty that, though I might still live and struggle, I could never more enjoy life and life's battles ! But was my fate so certain and inevitable ? Was it not possible to drive from the field this lover who had exposed his betrothed to all the dangers of an adventurous journey, to all the temptations of her unprotected condition, and who was now about to appear and snatch the bliss from my Eden ? Was it at all conceivable that Ellen—this Ellen—such as I had known her for months, would love such a wretched fellow ? Away to her, to learn the truth at any price !

I rushed over to the neighbouring house. There in the meantime my sister had been telling a similar tale to Ellen. She had, she said to Ellen, conceived the idea of making us man and wife ; and therefore, in the hope that my wooing would overcome her

(Ellen's) resistance, she had also told me of her plan ; and when I hesitated she had urged it more strongly, until at last I had confessed that, unknown to her, I had become betrothed in Europe. The bride would reach Eden Vale with the next party that arrived. . . . Clara had got so far when my appearance interrupted the story.

Deadly pale, Ellen turned towards me. She tried to speak, but her voice failed her. My half-sad, half-angry inquiry after the American betrothed first gave her speech. In a moment she found the key to the situation—that I loved her, and that my sister had deceived us both. What followed can be easily imagined. Thus it came to pass that Ellen was my betrothed when Dr. Strahl arrived at Eden Vale ; and this is the third incident which I was about to narrate above.

Whether the joy with which I for the first time pressed to my heart the woman of my love was greater than that with which I welcomed the friend of my soul, the idol of my intellect, to the earthly paradise to which he had shown us the way—this I cannot venture to decide.

When, in the eyes of my revered friend, as he looked upon our new home and the strongly pulsing joyous life that already filled it, I saw tears of joy, and in those tears a sure guarantee of immediate success, I was not seized with such an extravagant delight—almost more than the breast which felt it for the first time could bear—as I felt a few days before when my beloved revealed to me the secret of her heart. But when my hair shall have grown white and my back shall be bent with years, and the recollection of those lover's kisses may no longer drive my blood so feverishly through my veins as to-day, yet the thought of the hour in which, hand in hand with my friend, I experienced the proud pure joy of having accomplished the first and most difficult step towards the redemption of our suffering disinherited brethren out of the tortures of many thousands of years of bondage—the thought of that hour will never lose its bliss-inspiring power as long as I am among the living.

Long, long stood the master on the heights above Eden Vale, eagerly taking in every detail of the charming picture. Then, turning to us standing around him, he asked if we had given a name to the country that stretched out before us on all sides, and which was to be our home. When I said that we had not, and added that to him, who had given words to the idea that had led us hither, also belonged the office of finding a word for the country in which that idea was to be realised, he cried out: 'Freedom will find its birthplace in this country; FREELAND we will name it.'

BOOK II

CHAPTER VIII

WE now resume the thread of our narrative where Ney's journal left off.

With the President there had arrived in Eden Vale three members of the executive committee; five others followed a few days after with the first waggon-caravan from Mombasa; so that, including Ney, Johnston, and Demestre (the last of whom had been co-opted at the suggestion of the two former), twelve were now in Freeland. As the committee at that time consisted of fifteen members, there still remained three at a distance, of whom one was in London, another at Trieste, and the third at Mombasa, at which places they were for the present to act as the committee's authorised agents in the foreign affairs of the Society. Their duty was to receive fresh members, to collect and provisionally to have charge of the funds, and to superintend the emigrations to Eden Vale.

Their instructions respecting applications for membership were to receive every applicant who was not a relapsed criminal, and who could read and write. The former condition needs no justification. We had an unqualified confidence in the ennobling influence of our social reforms, because those reforms removed the motive that impelled to most vices; we were perfectly satisfied that Freeland would produce no criminals, and would even, if it were not beyond the bounds of possibility, wean from vice those who had been previously made criminals by misery and ignorance; but we wished, in the beginning, to avoid being swamped by bad elements, and, in view of the excusable attempts of certain States to rid themselves in some way or another of their relapsed criminals, we were compelled to exercise caution.

It may seem a greater hardship that the perfectly illiterate were excluded. But this was a necessary requirement of our programme. We wished to transfer the right of the absolute free self-control of the individual to the domain of labour from that of the relation of servitude which had existed for thousands of years. We wished to transform the worker who had been dependent upon his employer for his bread into the independent producer acting at his own risk in free association with free colleagues. It follows, as a matter of course, that in this our work we could use only such workers as were raised above at least the lowest stage of brutality and ignorance. That we thus excluded the most miserable of the miserable, is true; but, apart from the fact that generally the ignorant man lacks a clear consciousness of his misfortune and degradation, and his sufferings are therefore, as a rule, rather of a physical than of a moral nature, we could not allow ourselves to be so led astray by pity as to endanger the success of our work. The ignorant man *must* be under authority; and as it was not our purpose to educate our members gradually to become free producers, but to introduce them immediately to a system of free production, we were compelled to protect ourselves against ignorance as well as against crime.

Should it, on the other hand, be contended that ability to read and write is of itself by no means a sufficient evidence of the possession of that degree of culture and intelligence which must be presupposed in men who are to exercise control over their own work, the answer is that for such a purpose a very high degree of intelligence is certainly requisite, yet not in all, but only in a relatively not large number of the workers, who thus organise themselves, whilst the majority need not possess more than that moderate amount of mental capacity and mental training which is enough to enable them to look after their own interests. When a hundred or a thousand workers unite to work for their common profit and at their common risk, it is not every one of them that can or need have the abilities requisite to organise and superintend this common production—it is merely necessary that a very few possess this higher degree of intelligence; whilst it is enough for the majority that they are able rightly to judge what ought to be and is the result of the production in common, and what characteristics those must possess in whose hands the guardianship of the common interest is placed. But just here is the knowledge of letters absolutely indispensable, for it is the printed word alone which makes man and his judgment independent of the accidental influences of immediate surroundings and first opens his mind to instruction. It will later on be seen in how large a measure the most comprehensive publicity of all the proceedings connected with this productive activity—a publicity possible only through writing and print—contributed to the success of our work.

Of course these two conditions which applicants for membership had to satisfy had from the beginning been insisted upon by the committee, and the second condition at first very strictly so. It had been found, however, that the intellectual level of most of the applicants was surprisingly high. In the main, from among the class of manual labourers it was only the *élite* who in any numbers interested themselves in our undertaking ; and as, when the membership had gone beyond 20,000, a slight leaven of ignorance could not be very dangerous, the committee contented itself with requiring that the application should be made in the applicant's own handwriting.

The number of applicants—women and children are always reckoned in—continued to increase, particularly after the publication of the first report of the settlement of the colony at the Kenia. When the committee—with the exception of the delegates left behind—embarked at Trieste, the rate of increase of members had reached 1,200 weekly ; three months later it had risen to 1,800 weekly. The European agents had to register the new members— as had previously been done with the old members—carefully, according to sex, age, and calling, and at every opportunity to despatch the lists to Freeland ; they had also to organise and superintend the transport to Mombasa, which in all cases was gratuitous ; and they were authorised to pay all necessary expenses, in case of need even to buy new ships, subject to subsequent examination and approval of the accounts. It was also the duty of the agents to advise and help the members when they were preparing for the journey ; and they had authority to give material assistance to needy comrades. The members' contributions showed a tendency to increase similar to that of the number of members. It was evident that the interest in and the understanding of the character of our undertaking grew not merely among the working classes, but also among the wealthy ; the weekly addition to the funds increased from 20,000*l.* at the end of September to 30,000*l.* at the end of December. These funds, after payment of the expenses incurred by the agents, were under the control of the committee, whose executive organ, however, in this respect also, for the payment of debts incurred outside of Freeland, were the delegates who had been left behind.

On the 20th of October the committee held its first sitting in Eden Vale, for the purpose of drawing up such rules as were required to regulate the constitution of the free associations that were henceforth to be responsible for all production in Freeland. Hitherto the sittings of the committee had been so far public that every member of the Society had access to them, and this was to continue to be the case; but a provisional regulation was now adopted by which the audience might take part in the proceedings, though simply as consultative members. This regulation was to be in force until the press could perform its news-spreading and controlling functions. At the same time it was found that, whilst the committee had long been unanimous in holding that the Society's programme—that is, the organisation of production upon the basis of absolute individual independence on the one hand, and the securing to every worker the full and undiminished produce of his work on the other hand—should be carried out as soon as the committee had reached the new home, a part of the members of the Society still wished to continue the provisional organisation for at least a few months. In favour of this it was alleged that the executive knew best what were the needs as well as the capabilities of the gradually assembling community; the colonists should be allowed time to become accustomed to their new conditions and to acquire confidence in themselves; the committee had hitherto exhibited so much discretion in all their measures, that it was their duty to keep for some time longer the absolute direction of affairs in their own hands. It was particularly the members who had just arrived in Eden Vale who exhibited this dread of immediate and absolute independence. They thought they should not be able at once to act wisely for themselves; it would be cruel to pitch them as it were head-over-heels into the water, forcing upon them the alternative of swimming or sinking, when they themselves did not know whether they could swim or not. Ney, as the director of the works at the Kenia, was especially importuned by these faint-hearted ones to manage their affairs for them, and not to force upon them an independence for which they did not yet feel themselves qualified.

The committee were prepared for this demand, and had no difficulty in dispelling the fears thus expressed. In the first place, the timid members were made to understand that to continue production as the common undertaking of the whole community after the Society, as such, had settled in Freeland, would be sheer Communism. The 200 pioneers of the first expedition, and the 260 of the second, were simply functionaries appointed by the Society, whose relation to the Society was not altered in the least by the fact that they were at the Kenia, while the committee were in Europe. The pioneers were well aware of this before they left the Old World. But the case was different with all who now came to the settlement. Those who came now were not the officials, but the members of the Society; they did not come to do something at the bidding of the Society, but to work on their own account on the basis of the Society's principles of organisation. We had therefore no further right to utilise the first comers for the benefit of those who came after them. Even if we had such a right, it would be a fatal mistake to exercise it. For those that came now were no longer the carefully selected small band with whom we formerly had to do, but persons who, though influenced by one great common idea, were yet a thoroughly heterogeneous crowd accidentally thrown together, whom it would be a very dangerous experiment to entrust with an anti-egoistic system of production. The first 460 were — at least, in their character of workers—mainly men of one mould, similar in their capacities and in their requirements; the few leaders found ready obedience because no one questioned their intellectual superiority, and chiefly because every one who took part in the two expeditions was, as it were, pledged beforehand to obedience. The new-comers, on the contrary, were persons of very various capacities, and still more diverse in their requirements : there were among them women and old persons, fathers with numerous children. There might also be among them —and this was the greatest danger—ambitious persons, to whom one could not assign the right place because their capacities would not be known, and who would certainly refuse to obey.

Thus, Communism would most probably in a very short time

produce universal dissatisfaction, and that would lead to chaos.
Consequently we had as little power as we had right to introduce it.
But we had not the least occasion to do so. Why should not that
take place at once which must take place sooner or later—namely,
the organisation of free labour, with all the profits taken by the
workers themselves? Because there was not yet enough human
material for the organisation of all the branches of industry? What
necessity was there to organise all branches at once; and, on the other
hand, what certainty was there that it would be possible or useful
to do so in the course of several weeks or months? To take an
example : there were several weavers among us, for whom at present
there were no companions, and who therefore were not in a position
to start their industry with reasonable hopes of success. What was
there to prevent these weavers, in the meantime, from engaging in
some other occupation; and who would guarantee that a little later
on there would be weavers enough to set up a factory ; and that,
should such a factory be set up, the conditions of the settlement
would be such as to make weaving sufficiently profitable to justify
the carrying of it on? And while it was admitted that there would
be at first more such torsos -- such insufficient fragments—of future
branches of industry than there would be later on, this inconvenience was more than counterbalanced by the fact that it was easier
to begin a new organisation among a small than among a large
number of men. In every respect it appeared advisable at once
to organise production upon the basis of free individual action. Of
course it did not follow that the committee did not possess, not merely
the right, but also the duty, of making all the provision in its power
to facilitate and promote the work of organisation. They would not
confine themselves to the work of smoothing the way for the members of the Society, but would utilise their knowledge and experience in pointing out to the members the best way. They would
assume no compelling authority, but claimed to be the best —
because the best-informed—advisers of the members. Further,
there was no doubt that the whole of the hitherto acquired property, whether derived from the contributions of the members or
created in Freeland, since it belonged to the whole community and
not to the individual members, was at the disposal of the committee, and that the committee would make a legitimate use of this
its responsibility. The members might therefore rest assured that

no one should be left uncared for or exposed to blind accident. The
committee would act as advisers and helpers to anyone who wished
for their advice and help, not only now, but at any time. In truth,
what the committee purposed to do—conformably to the Society's
programme—differed from the above-mentioned demands in only
two points. The committee offered their advice, whilst they were
asked to command and to allow no scope to other and probably, in
many points, better counsel ; and they offered both advice and help
in the interest of each separate individual, whilst they were asked
to act in the interest of the whole community alone.

These explanations gave general satisfaction, and afterwards,
when those detailed regulations had been decided upon which were
partly in contemplation and partly already in operation for the
establishment of the new forms of organisation, the last remnant of
fear and hesitation vanished.

The fundamental feature of the plan of organisation adopted was
unlimited publicity in connection with equally unlimited freedom of
movement. Everyone in Freeland must always know what products were for the time being in greater or less demand, and in what
branch of production for the time being there was a greater or less
profit to be made. To the same extent must everyone in Freeland
always have the right and the power—so far as his capabilities and
his skill permitted—to apply himself to those branches of production which for the time being yield the largest revenue, and to this
end all the means of production and all the seats of production
must be available to everyone. The measures required, therefore,
must first of all have regard to these two points. A careful statistical report had to register comprehensively and—which is the
chief point—with as much promptitude as possible every movement
of production on the one hand and of consumption on the other, as
well as to give universal publicity to the movement of prices of all
products. In view of the great practical importance of this system
of public advertisement, care would have to be taken to exclude
deception or unintentional errors—a problem which, as what follows
will show, was solved in the most perfect yet simple manner.

And in order that the knowledge thus made common to everyone
may be actually and profitably made use of by everyone—which is
possible only when everyone is placed in a position to apply his
capabilities to those among the branches of labour in which he is

skilled, and which for the time being yield the highest revenue—provision must be made that everyone shall always be able to obtain possession of the requisite means of production. Of these means of production there are two classes—the powers of nature and capital. Without these means of production, the most exact information as to which are the branches of labour whose products are in greatest demand, and which, therefore, yield the highest profits, would be of as little use as the most perfect skill in such branches of production. A man can utilise his power to labour only when he has command both of the materials and forces supplied by nature, and of the appropriate instruments and machines ; and if he is to compete with his fellow-workers he must possess both classes of the means of production as fully and as completely as they. In order to grow wheat, a man must not only have land at his command, but he must have land that is equally good for growing wheat as is the land of the other wheat-growers, otherwise he will labour with less profit and possibly with actual loss. And possession of the most fertile land will not make the work possible, or at any rate equally profitable, unless the worker possesses the requisite agricultural implements, or if he possesses them in a less degree than his competitors.

Then as to capital : the Free Society undertook to place it at the disposal of everyone who wished for it, and that without interest, on condition that it was reimbursed out of the proceeds of production within a period the length of which was to be determined by the nature of the proposed investment. As the instruments of labour and the other capitalistic aids to labour could be provided to any amount and of any quality, one part of the problem was thereby solved.

The case was different with the natural powers, as representative of which we will take the land with which those powers are bound up. No one has produced the land, therefore no one has a claim of ownership upon it, and everyone has a right to use it. But not merely has no one produced the land, no one can produce it ; the land, therefore, exists in a limited quantity, and, moreover, the existing land is not all of the same quality. Now, in spite of all this, how is it possible to satisfy everyone's claim not merely to land, but to produce-bearing land ?

In order to make this clear, the third and, in reality, most fundamental predicate of economic justice must be expounded. When every worker is promised the undiminished produce of his own labour, it is necessarily assumed that the worker himself is the sole and exclusive producer of the whole of this produce. But this he was, by no means, according to the old economic system. The worker as such produced only a part of the product, while another part was produced by the employer, whether he was landowner, capitalist, or undertaker. Without the organising disciplinary influence of the latter the toil of the worker would have been fruitless, or at least much less fruitful; formerly the worker supplied merely the power, while the organising mind was supplied by the employer.

It is not implied by this that the more intellectual element in the work of production was formerly to be found exclusively or necessarily on the side of the employer: the technicians and directors who superintend the great productive establishments belong essentially to the wage-earners; and it will be readily admitted that in many cases the higher intelligence is to be found not in the employers, but in the workers. Nevertheless, in all cases where a number of workers have had to be brought together and accustomed to work in common, this work of organising has been the business of the employer. Hitherto the worker has been able to produce for himself only in isolation; whenever a number had to be brought together, in one enterprise, a ' master ' has been necessary, a master who with the whip—which may be made either of thongs or of the paragraphs in a set of factory regulations - has kept the rebellious together, and *therefore*—not because of his higher intelligence - has swept the profits into his own pocket, leaving to the workers, whether they belonged to the proletariat or to the so-called intelligent classes, only so much as sufficed to sustain them. Hitherto the workers have made no attempt to unite their productive labours without a master, as free, self-competent men, and not as servants. The employment of those powerful instruments and contrivances which science and invention have placed in the hands of men, and which so indefinitely multiply the profits of human activity, presupposes the united action of many; and hitherto this united action has been taken only hand in hand with servitude. The productive associations of a Schulze-Delitzsch and others have effected no change in the real character of servitude; they have merely altered the name of the masters. In these associations there are still the employers and the workers; to the former belongs the profit, the

latter receive stall and manger like the biped beasts of burden of
the single employer or of the joint-stock societies whose shareholders
do not happen to be workers. In order that labour may be free
and self-controlling, the workers must combine as such, and not as
small capitalists ; they must not have over them any employer of
any land or any name, not even an employer consisting of an association of themselves. They must organise themselves as workers,
and only as such ; for only as such have they a claim to the full
produce of their labour. This organisation of work without the
slightest remnant of the old servile relationship to an employer of
some kind or other, is the fundamental problem of social emancipation : if this problem be successfully solved, everything else will
follow of itself.

But this organisation was not nearly so difficult as it appears
to be at first sight. The committee started from the principle that
the right forms of the organisation of free labour were best found
through the free co-operation of all those who shared in this organisation. No special difficulties were discovered in this. The questions which had to be dealt with were of the simplest nature. For
example: in order to set up an iron-works, it was not at all necessary
that the workers should all understand the whole mechanism of
the manufacture of iron. Two things only were necessary—first,
that the men should know what sort of persons they ought to set
at the head of their factory ; and, secondly, that on the one hand
they should give those persons sufficient authority properly to
control the work, and, on the other hand, they should reserve to
themselves sufficient authority to hold the reins of their undertaking in their own hands. Doubtless, very serious mistakes might
be made in the organisation of the managing as well as of the
overlooking organs—there might be a serious misproportion in the
powers conferred. But the previously mentioned unlimited publicity
of all productive operations, which on other grounds also would be
demanded in the interest of the commonwealth, materially lightened
the task of the associations of workers ; and as all the members of
each such productive association had in this decisive point exactly
the same interests, and their whole attention was always directed
to these interests, they learnt with remarkable speed to correct the
mistakes they had made, so that after a few months the new
apparatus worked tolerably well, and in a remarkably short time

reached a high degree of perfection. From the beginning there
was nothing left to desire in the industry and diligence of all the
associates—a fact which might have been anticipated in view of the
full play given to self-interest as well as of the incessant mutual
encouragement and control of men who had equal rights and were
equally interested.

The committee therefore drew up a ' Model Statute ' for the use
of the associations, not at all anticipating that it would really be
preserved as a model, but merely for the sake of making a beginning
and of providing a formula which the associations might use as the
skeleton of the schemes of organisation that their experience would
enable them to devise. As a matter of fact this ' Model Statute,'
which was at first accepted almost unaltered by all the associations,
was in less than twelve months so much altered and enlarged that
little more than the leading principles of its original form remained.
These, however, were the following:

1. Admission into every association is free to everyone, whether
a member of any other association or not; and any member can
leave any association at any time.

2. Every member has a claim upon such a share of the net
profits of the association as is proportionate to the amount of work
he has contributed.

3. Every member's contribution of work shall be measured by
the number of hours he has worked ; the older members receiving
more than those who have joined the association later, in the proportion of a premium of x per cent. for every year of seniority.
Also, a premium can be contracted for, in the way of free association,
for skilled labour.

4. The labour contribution of superintendents or directors shall,
according to a voluntary arrangement with every individual concerned, be reckoned as equal to a certain number of hours of work
per day.

5. The profits of the association shall be calculated at the end of
every year of business. and, after deducting the repayment of capital
and the taxes paid to the Freeland commonwealth, divided. During
each year the members shall receive, for every hour of work or of
reckoned work, advances equal to x per cent. of the net profits of
the previous year.

6. The members shall, in case of the dissolution or liquidation of

an association, be liable for the contracted loan in equal proportions; which liability, so far as regards the still outstanding
amount, attaches also to newly entering members. When a member leaves, his liability for the already contracted loan shall not
cease. This liability for the debts of the association shall, in case
of dissolution or liquidation, be in proportion to the claim of the
liable member upon the existing property.

7. The highest authority of the association is the general meeting, in which every member possesses an equal active and passive
vote. The general meeting carries its motions by a simple majority
of votes; a majority of three-fourths is required for the alteration
of statutes, dissolution, or liquidation.

8. The general meeting exercises its rights either directly as
such, or through its elected functionaries, who are responsible to it.

9. The management of the business of the association is placed
in the hands of a directorate of x members, elected for x years
by the general meeting, but their appointment can be at any time
rescinded. The subordinate business functionaries are nominated
by the directorate; but the fixing of the salaries—measured in
hours of work—of these functionaries is the business of the general
assembly on the proposition of the directorate.

10. The general meeting annually elects a council of inspection
consisting of x members, to inspect the books and take note of the
manner in which the business is conducted, and to furnish periodical
reports.

It will strike the reader at once that only with reference to the
possible dissolution of an association (section 6) is there a mention
of what should apparently be regarded as the principal thing—
namely, of the ' property ' of the associations and of the claims of
the members upon this property. The reason of this is that any
' property ' of the association, in the ordinary sense, does not exist.
The members, it is true, possess the right of usufruct of the
existing productive capital; but as they always share this right
with every newly entering member, and are themselves bound to the
association by nothing except their interest in the profits of their
labour, so there can be no property-interest in the association so
long as they are carrying on their work. And, in fact, that which
everyone can use cannot constitute property, however useful it may be.
There are no proprietors—merely usufructuaries of the association's

H

capital. And should it be thought that this is in contradiction
to the obligation to reimburse the loaned productive capital of the
associations, it ought not to be overlooked that even this repayment
of capital—except in the already mentioned case of a liquidation—
is done by the members merely in their capacity of usufructuaries
of the means of production. As the reimbursed capital is derived
from the profits, and these are divided among the members in proportion to each one's contribution of work, every member contri-
butes to the reimbursement in proportion to the amount of work he
does. And when the subject is looked at more closely it will be
seen that the repayments are ultimately derived from the consumers
of the commodities produced by the associations; they form, of
course, a part of the cost of production, and must necessarily be
covered by the price of the product. That this shall take place
fully and universally is ensured with infallible certainty by the free
mobilisation of labour. A production in which these repayments
were not completely covered by the price of the commodities produced would fail to attract labour until the diminished supply of
the commodities had produced the requisite rise in price. When
the repayments have all been made, this part of the cost of production ceases; the association capital may be regarded as amortised,
and the prices of the commodities produced sink—again under the
influence of the free mobilisation of labour; so that the members
of the association individually profit as little by the employment of
burdenless capital as they suffered before by the liquidation of their
burden. Profit and loss are always distributed—still thanks to the
mobilisation of labour—equally among all the workers of Freeland.

Thus it is seen that, in consequence of this simple and infallibly
operative arrangement, productive capital is, strictly speaking, as
ownerless as the land; it belongs to everyone, and therefore to no
one. The community of producers supplies it and employs it, and
it does both in exact proportion to the amount of work contributed
by each individual; and payment for the expenditure is made by the
community of consumers—again by each one in exact proportion to
the consumption of each individual.

That an absolute and universally uniform level of profits should
result from this absolutely free mobility of labour neither was expected, nor has it been attained. Often the inequality is not discovered until the balance-sheets are drawn up, and therefore cannot

until then be removed by the ebb and flow of labour. But, besides this, there is an important and continuous difference of gains—a difference which it is impossible to equalise, and which has its intrinsic foundation in the difference in the amount of effort and inconvenience involved in engaging in the different branches of labour. Certainly it is not the same in Freeland as in other parts of the world, where only too often the burden of labour is in inverse ratio to its profitableness; with us difficult, burdensome, unpleasant kinds of labour must without exception obtain larger gains than the easier and more agreeable—so far as the latter do not demand special skill—otherwise everyone would at once forsake the former and apply themselves to the latter. Moreover, the premium allowed to the older members in section 3—which varies in different associations from one to three per cent. for each year, and therefore, in cases of long-continued labour, amounts to a very respectable sum, and is intended to attach the proved veteran of labour to the undertaking—prevents an absolute equalisation of gains even in associations of exactly similar constitution.

Section 5 of the statutes requires a brief explanation. In the first year, the calculation of the advances to be made to the association members could not, of course, be based upon the net profits of the previous year, and the committee therefore suggested a fixed sum of one shilling per hour. This strikingly high rate will perhaps excite surprise, particularly in view of the scale of prices that prevailed at the Kenia; and it may reasonably be asked whence the committee derived the courage to hope for such a high rate of profits as would justify the payment of such an advance. But this valuation was not recklessly made, it was in truth the expression of extreme prudence. The results of the associated productive labour hitherto in operation had actually been much more favourable. The corn industry, for example, had yielded a gross return of a little over 41,000 cwt. of different cereals for a total expenditure of 44,500 hours of labour. The average price of these cereals in Eden Vale at that time was not quite 3s. per cwt., as we had grown more than we needed, and the export through Mombasa yielded only 3s. on account of the still very primitive means of transport. We had therefore, in round figures, agricultural produce worth 6,000l. The cost of producing this was: materials 400l., amortisation of invested capital (implements

H 2

and cattle) 300*l.*; so that 5,300*l.* remained as net profit. As a tax
to cover all those expenses which, in accordance with our programme,
had to be incurred by the commonwealth, and which will be spoken
of further on, not less than thirty-five per cent. was set aside. Thus a
round sum of 3,400*l.* remained as disposable profit. Divided by
the 44,500 hours of labour, this gave 1*s.* 6*d.* for each hour. This
was also approximately the average profit of the other kinds of production, so far as it was possible to assess it in the absence of a
general market at the Kenia. Thus it could be assumed with the
utmost confidence that, had we been able to control the prices of all
commodities by means of supply and demand, there would either
have been paid, or might have been assessed, at least a price equivalent to that which produced the agricultural profit. For we could
at once have produced – as far as our supply of labour went—and
disposed of cereal crops valued at 3*s.* per cwt. at Eden Vale; therefore, in the period of work through which we had already passed
everyone was able to earn at least 1*s.* 6*d.* by one hour's labour.
But, as will presently be seen, we were entering upon the next
period of work with much improved means; therefore, apart from
unforeseen contingencies, the productiveness of our labour must
very considerably increase, so that, in granting an advance of one
shilling for each hour of labour, we calculated that we were advancing scarcely the half of the actual earnings—an assumption that
was fully borne out by the result. In later seasons it became the
practice of most associations to make the advance as much as ninety
per cent. of the net profits of the previous year.

As to the salaries of the directorate, these were from the beginning very different in different associations. Where no extraordinary
knowledge and no special talent were necessary, the overseers were
content to have their superintendence valued at the price of from
eight to ten hours of work per diem. There were directors who
received as much as the value of twenty-four hours of work per
diem, and in the very first year this amounted to an income of
about 850*l.* The functionaries of a lower grade received, as a rule,
the value of from eight to ten hours of work per diem. In most
cases the controlling council of inspection received no extra remu-
neration for their duties.

The credit granted to the associations in the first year of work
reached an average amount of 145*l.* per head of the participating

workers; and if it be asked whence we derived the funds to meet the requirements of the total number of our members, the answer is, from the members themselves. And the reference here is not merely to those voluntary contributions paid by the members on their joining the International Free Society, for these contributions were in the first instance devoted to the transport service between Trieste and Freeland, and would not have sufficed to supply our associations with capital if they had all been devoted to that purpose. The credit required in the course of the first year rose to nearly two million pounds sterling, while the voluntary contributions up to that date did not much exceed one million and a-half. The principal means which enabled us to meet the requirements of our members were supplied us, on the one hand by the Society's property in disposable materials, and on the other hand by the members' tax.

It should be mentioned here that, for the first year, the committee reserved to itself the right of deciding the amount and the order of granting the credit given. This, though merely negative, interference with the industrial relations of the associations was not in harmony with the principle of the producers' right of unconditioned self-control ; but was so far unavoidable, inasmuch as our commonwealth had not yet actually attained to that high degree of productiveness of labour which is the assumed result of the perfect realisation of all the fundamental principles of that commonwealth. Later, when we were more fully furnished with the best means of production which technical progress placed within our reach, and we were consequently no longer occupied in provisionally completing and improving what already existed, there could never be any question whether the surplus of the current production would suffice to meet the heaviest fresh claims for capital that could arise. It was different at the beginning, when the need for capital was unlimited, and the means of supplying that need as yet undeveloped. The Free Commonwealth could not offer more than it could supply, and it had therefore to reserve to itself a right of selection from among the investments that applied for credit. Thanks to the thorough solidarity of interests created by the free mobility of labour, this could happen without even temporarily affecting the essential material interests of the producers by giving some a dangerous advantage over others. For if, as was scarcely to be avoided, certain productions were helped or hindered by the giving or withholding of credit, this was immediately and naturally followed by such a shifting of labour as at once restored the equilibrium of profits.

But this interference during the first year extended only to the controlling of the amount and order of granting the credit asked for, and not to the way in which it was used. In this respect, from the very beginning the principle of the producers' responsibility was carried out to the fullest extent. As it was necessary for the producers to be successful in order to repay the capital taken up, so it was their business to see that care was taken to make a profitable use of such capital. It is true that—as has been already stated—the consumers ultimately bear the cost of production; but they do this, of course, only when and in so far as the processes employed in production have been useful and necessary. If an association should procure unnecessary or defective machinery, it would be impossible for it to transfer to the purchasers of its commodities the losses thus occasioned; the association would not have increased, but diminished, its gains by such investments. It can therefore be left to the self-interest of those who are concerned in the associations to guard against such a waste of capital.

We now come to the question how it is possible to guarantee the equal right of everyone to equally fertile land. This problem also is solvable in the simplest manner by the free mobility of labour involved in the principle of free association. As everywhere else in the world, there was in Freeland richer and poorer land; but as more workers were attracted to the better land than to the worse, and as, according to a well-known economic law, a greater expenditure of labour upon an equal extent of land is followed by *relatively diminishing* returns, so the individual worker obtained no higher net profit per hour of labour on the best land than upon the worst land which could be cultivated at all.

On the Dana plateau, for example, by the expenditure of 32 hours of labour 48 cwt. of wheat could be produced per acre; in Eden Vale the same expenditure of labour would produce merely 36 cwt. Therefore, as the cwt. of wheat was worth 3s. 1½d., and 1½d. was sufficient to cover all expenses, the land association in the Dana plateau had at the end of the year a return of 4s. 6d. for every hour of work, and, after deduction of tax and repayment of capital,

2*s*. 9*d*. for division among the members. The members of the Eden Vale association, on the other hand, had only 2*s*. per hour of labour to divide among the members; and as careful investigation proved that this difference was due neither to accidental uncongeniality of the weather nor to a less amount of labour, but to the character of the soil, the consequence was that in the next year the newly arrived agriculturists preferred the better land of the Dana plateau. There was now an average expenditure of 42 hours of labour to the acre in the Dana plateau, but in Eden Vale only 24; yet in the former place the additional 10 hours of labour did not yield the 1½ cwt. per hour, as was the case when the expenditure of labour was only 32 hours, but merely a scant 3 qrs.; that is, the returns did not rise from 48 cwt. to 63 cwt., but merely to 55 cwt.—sank therefore to 1·34 cwt. per hour of labour. The consequence was that the returns, notwithstanding the considerable increase in the price of grain due to the improved means of communication, rose merely to 5*s*., of which 3*s*. per hour of labour was available for division among the members. In Eden Vale, on the other hand, the gross returns were lessened merely 3 cwt. by the withdrawal of eight hours of labour per acre; the produce therefore now was 33 cwt. for 24 hours of labour, or 1·37 cwt. per hour of labour. The Eden Vale association therefore numbered a trifle more than that of Dana; and as Eden Vale was a more desirable place of residence, and had more conveniences than the Dana plateau, the stream of agriculturists flowed back to Eden Vale until, after two other harvests, there remained a difference of profit of about five per cent. in favour of the Dana plateau, and this advantage, with slight variations, continued permanently.

But just as the principle of the solidarity of interests brought about by the mobility of labour placed him who used the actually worse land in the enjoyment of the advantages of the better land, so everyone, whatever branch of production he might be connected with, participated in all the various kinds of advantages of the best land; and, on the other hand, every cultivator of the soil, like every other producer, derived profit from all the increased productiveness of labour, in whatsoever branch of labour in our commonwealth it might arise, just as if he were himself immediately concerned in it. *All* means of production are common property; the use which any one of us may make of this common property does not depend upon the accident of possession, nor upon the superintending care of an all-controlling communistic authority, but solely upon the capacity and industry of each individual.

CHAPTER IX

As already stated, the fundamental condition of the successful working of the simple organisation described above was the completest publicity of all industrial proceedings. The organisation was in truth merely a mode of removing all those hindrances that stand in the way of the free realisation of the individual will guided by a wise self-interest. So much the more necessary was it to give right direction to this sovereign will, and to offer to self-interest every assistance towards obtaining a correct and speedy grasp of its real advantage.

— No business secrets whatever! That was at once the fundamental law of Eden Vale. In the other parts of the world, where the struggle for existence finds its consummation not merely in exploiting and enslaving one another, but over and above this in a mutual industrial annihilation — where, in consequence of the universal over-production due to under-consumption, competition is synonymous with robbing each other of customers — there, in the Old World, to disclose the secrets of trade would be tantamount to sacrificing a position acquired with much trouble and cunning. Where an immense majority of men possess no right to the increasing returns of production, but, not troubling themselves about the productiveness of labour, must be content with 'wages '—that is, with what is necessary for their subsistence—there can be no sufficient demand for the total produce of highly productive labour. The few wealthy cannot possibly consume the constantly growing surplus, and their endeavour to capitalise such surplus—that is, to convert it into instruments of labour—is defeated by the impossibility of employing the means of a production the products of which cannot be consumed. In the exploiting world, therefore, there prevails a constant disproportion between productive power and consumption, between supply and demand ; and the natural consequence is that the disposal of the products gives rise to a constant and relentless struggle between the various producers. The principal care of the exploiting producers is not to produce as much and as well as possible, but to acquire a market for as large as possible a quantity of their own commodities; and as, in view of the disproportion above explained, such a market can be acquired and retained only at the expense of other producers, there necessarily exists a permanent and irreconcilable conflict of interest. It is different among us. We can always be sure of a sale, for with us no more can be produced than is used, since the total produce belongs to the worker, and the consumption, the satisfaction of real requirements, is the exclusive motive of labour. Among us, therefore, the disclosure of the sources of trade can rob no one of his customers, since any customers whom he may happen to lose must necessarily be replaced by others.

On the other hand, what reason has the producer in the world outside to communicate his experiences to others? Can those others make any use of the knowledge they would thus acquire, except to do him injury? And can he use any such information when communicated to him, except to the injury of others? Does he allow others to participate in his business when his is the more profitable, or does another let him do so with the business of that other when the case is reversed? If the demand for the commodities of a producer increases, the labour market is open to him, where he can find servants enough ready to work without inquiring about his profits so long as they receive their ' wages.' Thus, elsewhere in the world, not even are the consumers interested in the publication of trade practices, which publication, moreover, as has already been said, would be a matter of impossibility. Quite different is this among us in Freeland. We allow everyone to participate in our trade advantages, and we can therefore participate in the trade advantages of everyone else ; and we are compelled to publish these advantages because, in the absence of a market of labourers who have neither will nor interest of their own, this publicity is the only way of attracting labour when the demand for any commodities increases.

And—which is the principal thing—whilst elsewhere no one has an interest in the increase of production by others, among us every one is most intensely interested in seeing everyone produce as easily and as well as possible. For the classical phrase of the solidarity of all economic interests has among us become a truth ; but elsewhere it is nothing more than one of those numerous self-deceptions of which the political economy of the exploiting world is composed. Where the old system of industry prevails, *universal* increase of production of wealth is a chimera. Where consumption by the masses cannot increase, there cannot production and wealth increase, but can be only shifted, can only change place and owner; in proportion as the production of one person increases must that of some one else diminish, unless consumption increases, which, where the masses are excluded from enjoying the increasing returns of labour, can happen only accidentally, and by no means step by step with the increasing power of productiveness of labour. With us in Freeland, on the contrary, where production—in view of the necessary growth of the power of consumption in exactly the same proportion can and does increase indefinitely so far as our facilities and arts permit, with us it is the supreme and most absolute interest of the community to see that everyone's labour is employed wherever it can earn the highest returns; and there is no one who is not profited when the labour of all is thus employed to the completest extent possible. The individuals or the individual associations which, by virtue of our organisation, are compelled to share an accidentally acquired advantage with another, certainly suffer a loss of gain by this circumstance looked at by itself; but infinitely greater is the general advantage derived from the fact that the same thing occurs everywhere, that productiveness is constantly increasing, and their own advantage therefore compels the occurrence of the same everywhere. To how undreamt-of high a degree this is the case will be abundantly shown by the subsequent history of Freeland.

It remains now to say something of the measures adopted to ensure the most extensive publicity of industrial proceedings. We start from the principle that the community has to concern itself with the affairs of the individual as little as possible in the way of hindering or commanding, but, on the other hand, as much as possible in the way of guiding and instructing. Everyone may act as he pleases, so far as he does not infringe upon the rights of others; but, however he acts, what he does must be open to everyone. Since he here has to do not with industrial opponents, but only with industrial rivals, who all have an interest in stimulating him as much as possible, this publicity is to his own advantage. In conformity with this principle, when a new member was admitted by the out-

side agents, his industrial specialty was stated, and the report sent
as quickly as possible to the committee. This was not done out of
idle curiosity, nor from a desire to exercise a police oversight;
rather these data were published for the use and advantage of the
productive associations as well as of the new members themselves.
The consequence was that, as a rule, the new members on their
arrival at the Kenia found suitable work-places prepared for them,
such as would enable them at once to utilise their working capacity
to the best advantage. No one forced them to-accommodate themselves to these arrangements made without their co-operation, but
as these arrangements served their advantage in the best conceivable
way, they—with a few isolated exceptions—accepted them with the
greatest pleasure.

The second and most important subject of publication were the
trade reports of the producers, of the associations as well as of the
comparatively few isolated producers. Of the former, as being by
far the more important and by their very nature compelled to adopt
a careful system of bookkeeping, a great deal was required—in fact
the full disclosure of all their proceedings. Gross returns, expenses,
net returns, purchases and sales, amount of labour, disposal of the
net returns,—all must be published in detail, and, according to the
character of the respective data, either yearly, or at shorter intervals
—the amount of labour, for example, weekly. In the case of the
isolated producers, it sufficed to publish such details as would be
disclosed by the regulation about to be described.

The buying and selling of all conceivable products and articles
of merchandise in Freeland was carried on in large halls and warehouses, which were under the management of the community. No
one was forbidden to buy and sell where he pleased, but these
public magazines offered such enormous advantages that everyone
who did not wish to suffer loss made use of them. No fee was
charged for storing or manipulation, as it was quite immaterial, in
a country where everyone consumed in proportion to his production,
whether the fees were levied upon the consumers as such, or upon
the same persons in their character as producers in the form of a
minimal tax. What was saved by the simplification of the accounts
remained as a pure gain. Further, an elaborate system of warranty
was connected with these warehouses. Since the warehouse officials
were at the same time the channel through which purchases were

made, they were always accurately informed as to the condition of the market, and could generally appraise the warehoused goods at their full value. The sales took place partly in the way of public auction, and partly at prices fixed by the producers; and here also no commission was charged to either seller or buyer.

The supreme authority in Freeland was at the same time the banker of the whole population. Not merely every association, but every individual, had his account in the books of the central bank, which undertook the receipts and the disbursements from the millions of pounds which at a later date many of the associations had to receive and pay, both at home and abroad, down to the individual's share of profits on labour and his outlay on clothes and food. A 'clearing system,' which really included everything, made these numberless debit and credit operations possible with scarcely any employment of actual money, but simply by additions to and subtractions from the accounts in the books. No one paid cash, but gave cheques on his account at the central bank, which gave him credit for his earnings, debited his spendings to him, and gave him every month a statement of his account. Naturally the loans granted by the commonwealth as capital for production, mentioned in the previous chapter, appeared in the books of the bank. In this way the bank was informed of the minutest detail of every business transaction throughout the whole country. It not only knew where and at what price the producers purchased their machinery and raw material and where they sold their productions, but it knew also the housekeeping account, the income and cost of living of every family. Even the retail trade could not escape the omniscience of this control. Most of the articles of food and many other necessaries were supplied by the respective associations to their customers at their houses. All this the bank could check to a farthing, for both purchases and sales went through the books of this institution. The accounts of the bank had to agree with the statements of the statistical bureau, and thus all these revelations possessed an absolutely certain basis, and were not merely the results of an approximate valuation. Even if anyone had wished to do so, it would have been simply impracticable to conceal or to falsify anything.

This comprehensive and automatically secured transparency of the whole of the productive and business relations afforded to the

tax assessed in Freeland a perfectly reliable basis. The principle
was that the public expenditure of the community should be covered
by a contribution from each individual exactly in proportion to his
net income; and as in Freeland there was no source of income
except labour, and the income from this was exactly known, there
was not the slightest difficulty in apportioning the tax. The ap-
portionment of the tax was very simply made as soon as the
income existed, and that through the medium of the bank; and
this was done not merely in the case of the associations, but also
of the few isolated producers. In fact, by means of its bank the
community had everyone's income in hand sooner than the earners
themselves; and it was merely necessary to debit the earners with
the amount and the tax was paid. Hence in Freeland the tax
was regarded not as a deduction from net income, but as an outlay
deducted from the gross product, just like the trade expenses. In
spite of its high amount, no one looked upon it as a burden, because everyone knew that the greater part of it would flow back to
him or to his, and every farthing of it would be devoted to purposes of exclusively public utility, which would immediately benefit
him. It was therefore quite correct to recognise no difference
whatever between productive outlay by the commonwealth and the
more private outlay of the associations and individuals, and accordingly to designate the former not as ' taxes,' but as ' general
expenditure.'

This general expenditure, however, was very high. In the first
year it amounted to thirty-five per cent. of the net profits, and it never
sunk below thirty per cent., though the income on which the tax was
levied increased enormously. For the tax which the community in
Freeland had imposed upon themselves for the very purpose of
making this increase of wealth possible was so comprehensive in
its objects as to make a most colossal amount necessary.

One of its objects was to create the capital required for the purposes of production. But it was only at first that the whole of this
had to be met out of the current tax, as afterwards the repayment
of the loans partly met the new demands.

A constantly increasing item of expenditure was the cost of
education, which swallowed up a sum of which no one outside of
Freeland can have any conception.

The means of communication also involved an expenditure

that rose to enormous dimensions, and the same has to be said of public buildings.

But the chief item of expenditure in the Freeland budget was under the head of 'Maintenance,' which included the claims of those who, on account of incapacity for work or because they were by our principles released from the obligation of working, had a right to a competence from the public funds. To these belonged all women, all children, all men over sixty years of age, and of course all sick persons and invalids. The allowances to these different classes were so high that not merely urgent necessities, but also such higher daily needs as were commensurate with the general wealth in Freeland for the time being, could be met. With this view the allowances had to be so calculated that they should rise parallel with the income of the working part of the population; the amounts, therefore, were not fixed sums, but varied according to the average income. The average net profit which fell to the individual from all the productive labour in the country, and which increased year by year, was the unit of maintenance. Of this unit every single woman or widow—unless she was a teacher or a nurse, and received payment for her labour—was allotted thirty per cent.; if she married, her allowance sank to fifteen per cent.; the first three children in every household were allowed five per cent. each. Parentless orphans were publicly supported at an average cost of twelve per cent. of the maintenance unit. Men over sixty years and sick persons and invalids received forty per cent.

It may at once be remarked that it would startle those unaccustomed to Freeland ideas to hear the amounts of these allowances. In the first year the maintenance unit reached 160*l.*; therefore an unmarried woman or a widow received 48*l.*; a married woman 24*l.*; a family with three children and a wife 48*l.*; an old man or invalid 64*l.*, which, in view of the prices that then prevailed among us, was more than most European States give as pensions to the highest functionaries or to their widows and orphans. For a cwt. of fine flour cost, in that first year at the Kenia, 7*s.*, a fat ox 12*s.*; butter, honey, the most delicious fruits, were to be had at corresponding prices. Lodgings cost not more at most than 2*l.* a year. In brief, with her 48*l.* a single woman could live among us in the enjoyment of many luxuries, and need not deny herself to any material extent of those conveniences and enjoyments which at that time were obtainable at all in Eden Vale. And afterwards, when prices in Freeland were somewhat higher, the profits of labour, and consequently the percentage of the maintenance allowance, quickly rose to a much greater extent, so that the purchasing power of the allowance constantly became more pronounced. But this was the intention of the people of Freeland. Why? In the proper place this subject will be again referred to, and then will in particular be explained why the women, without exception, receive a maintenance allowance, and why teaching and nursing are the only occupations of women that are mentioned. Here we merely state that it naturally required a constantly increasing tax to cover all these expenses.

Considerable items of expenditure were to be found under the heads, 'Statistics,' 'Warehouses,' and 'Bank'; but the relative cost of these branches of the executive—notwithstanding their great absolute growth—fell so rapidly in comparison with the taxable income, that in a few years it had sunk to a minimal percentage of the total expenditure.

On the other hand, the departments of justice, police, military, and finance, which in other countries swallow up nine-tenths of the total budget, cost nothing in Freeland. We had no judges, no police organisation, our tax flowed in spontaneously, and soldiers we knew not. Yet there was no theft, no robbery, no murders among us; the payment of the tax was never in arrears; and, as will be shown later on, we were by no means defenceless. Our stores of weapons and ammunition, as well as our subsidies to the warlike Masai, might be reckoned as a surrogate for a military budget. As to the lack of a magistracy, we were such arrant barbarians that we did not even consider a civil or a criminal code necessary, nor did we at that time possess a written constitution. The committee, still in possession of the absolute authority committed to it at the Hague, contented itself with laying all its measures before public meetings and asking for the assent of the members, which was unanimously given. For the settlement of misunderstandings that might arise among the members, arbitrators were chosen—at the recommendation of the committee—who should individually and orally, to the best of their knowledge, give their judgment, and from them appeal was allowed to the Board of Arbitrators; but they had as good as nothing to do. Against vices and their dangerous results to the community, we did not exercise any right of *punishment*, but only a right of *protection*; and we esteemed *reformation* the best and most effectual means of protection. Since men with a normal mental and moral character, in a community in which all the just interests of every member are equally recognised, cannot possibly come into violent collision with the rights of others, we considered casual criminals as mentally or morally diseased persons, whose treatment it was the business of the community to provide for. They were therefore, in proportion to their dangerousness to the community, placed under surveillance or in custody, and subjected to suitable treatment as long as seemed, in the judgment of competent professional men, advisable in the interest of the public safety. Professional men in the above sense, however, were not the justices of the peace, who merely had to decide *whether* the accused individual should undergo the reforming treatment, but medical men specially chosen for this purpose. The man who was under surveillance or in custody had the right of appealing to the united Board of Medical Men and Justices of the Peace, and publicly to plead his case before them, if he thought that he had been injured by the action of the medical man set over him.

The appointment of the officers for public buildings, means of communication, statistics, warehouses, central bank, education, &c., was vested provisionally in the committee. The salaries were reckoned in hour-equivalents, like those of the functionaries of the associations; and these salaries ranged from 1,200 to 5,000 labour hours per annum, which in the first year amounted to from 150*l.* to 600*l.* The agents in London, Trieste, and Mombasa were each paid 800*l.* per annum. These agents remained only two years at their foreign posts, and then had a claim to corresponding positions in Freeland. To each of its own members the committee gave a salary of 5,000 hour-equivalents.

Each member of the committee was president of one of the twelve branches into which the whole of the public administration of Freeland was provisionally divided. These branches were:

1. The Presidency.
2. Maintenance.
3. Education.
4. Art and science.

5. Statistics.
6. Roads and means of communication.
7. Post—including later the telegraph.
8. Foreign affairs.
9. Warehouses.
10. Central bank.
11. Public undertakings.
12. Sanitation and administration of justice.

These are, in general outlines, the principles upon which in the beginning Freeland was organised and administered. They stood the test of experience in all respects most satisfactorily. The formation of the associations was effected without the slightest delay. As the majority of the members who successively arrived were unknown to each other, it was necessary in filling the more responsible positions provisionally to follow the recommendations of the committee; in most cases, therefore, provisional appointments were made which could be afterwards replaced by definitive ones. The already mentioned kinds of productive labour—agriculture, gardening, pasturage, millering, saw-mills, beer-brewing, coal-mining, and iron-working—were considerably enlarged and materially improved by the increase of labour which daily arrived with the Mombasa caravans. A great number of new industries were immediately added. One of the first—most of the material of which was imported and only needed completing—was a printing-office, with two cylinder machines and five other machines; and from this office issued a daily journal. Then came in quick succession a machine-factory, a glass-works, a brickyard, an oil-mill, a chemical-works, a sewing and shoe factory, a carpenter's shop, and an ice-factory. On the first day of the new year the first small screw steamboat was launched for towing service in the Eden lake and the Dana river. This was at short intervals followed by other and larger steamers for goods and passengers, all constructed by the ship-building association, which, on account of its excellent services, increased with extraordinary rapidity.

At the same time the committee employed a not inconsiderable part of the newly arriving strength in public works; and the workers thus employed had naturally to be paid at a rate corresponding to the average height of the general labour-profit, and even at a higher rate when specially trying work was required. These public works

I

were, in the first instance, the provisional house-accommodation for the newly arriving members. It was arranged that every family should be furnished with a separate house, whilst for those who were single several large hotels were built. The family houses were of different sizes, containing from four to ten dwelling-rooms, and each house had a garden of above 10,000 square feet. Every new-comer could find a house that was convenient to him as to size and situation, and might pay for it either at once or by instalments. Not fewer than 1,500 such houses had to be got ready per month ; they were strongly built of double layers of thick planks, and the average cost was about 8*l*. 10*s*, per room. For the use of hotel rooms, sixpence per week per room was sufficient to cover the amortisation of the capital and the expenses of management.

Together with the dwelling-houses, the building of schools was taken in hand ; and as it was anticipated that for some time from 1,000 to 1,200 fresh school-children would arrive per month, it was necessary to make provision to secure a continuous increase of accommodation. These schools, as well as the private houses, were of course erected, some in Eden Vale and some on the Dana plateau, and were only of a provisional character, but light, airy, and commodious. It was also necessary to secure a timely supply of teachers, a task the accomplishment of which the committee connected with another scarcely less important question. There was in Freeland a great disproportion in the comparative number of the sexes, particularly of young men and young marriageable women. Of the 460 pioneers who had reached the Kenia between June and September, very few had either wives or betrothed in the old home ; and among the later arrivals there was a preponderance of young unmarried men. It was not to be expected that the immediate future would bring an adequate number of young unmarried women unless some special means were adopted ; but this forced celibacy could not continue without danger of unpleasant social developments in a community that aimed at uniting absolute freedom with the strictest morality. In Taveta and Masailand, a few isolated cases of intrigue with native girls and wives had occurred. At the Kenia, our young people had, without exception, resisted the enticements of the ugly Wa-Kikuyu women ; but our young people could not permanently be required to exercise a self-denial which, particularly in this luxurious country, would be contrary to nature.

It was therefore necessary to attract to Freeland young women who would be a real gain not only to the men whom they married, but also to the country that received them. We had merely to make the state of affairs known in Europe and America, and to announce that women who remained single were in Freeland supported by the State, and we should very soon have had no reason to complain of a lack of women. But whether we should have been pleased with those whom such an announcement might bring, is another question. We preferred, therefore, to instruct our representatives in the old home to engage women-teachers for Freeland. The salary—180*l.* for the first year—was attractive, and we had a choice of numberless candidates. It was therefore to no one's injury if these highly cultured women, most of whom were young, gave up their teaching vocation not long after they reached Freeland and consented to make some wooer happy. The vacated place was at once filled by a new teacher, who quite as quickly made room for a fresh successor.

In this way, for several years Freeland witnessed a constant influx of quickly marrying women-teachers, though our representatives had no instructions to make their choice of the candidates for our teacherships depend in any way upon the suitability of such persons as candidates for matrimony. Our announcement in the leading newspapers of the old home was seriously meant and taken. 'Well-qualified cultured women-teachers wanted. Salary 180*l.* for the first year; more afterwards.' Elderly women who seemed suitable for teachers were sometimes appointed; but young, sprightly women are in the nature of things better fitted than old and enfeebled ones to educate children, and thus we obtained what we needed without exhibiting the least partiality. Later, this announcement was no longer needed; for it gradually became known, especially in England, France, and Germany, that young women-teachers found in Freeland charming opportunities of becoming wives; so that the permanent preponderance of men among the general immigrants was continually balanced by this influx of women-teachers.

The next problem to which special attention was given during this first year of the new government was that of the post. The courier-service between Eden Vale and Mombasa no longer sufficed to meet the demands of the increased intercourse. The mails had grown to be larger in quantity than could be transported in saddle-bags, and they had to be more quickly carried. It was most desirable that letters and despatches should pass between Mombasa and Freeland at a more rapid rate than a little over sixty miles a day, which had hitherto been the maximum. With this in view, the road to Mombasa was thoroughly repaired. It should be remembered that this road had not been ' constructed ' in the Western sense of the term, but was mainly in the condition in which nature had left it, nothing having been done but to remove wood that stood in the way, fill up holes, and build bridges. As the so-called dry season extends from September to February, very little rain had yet fallen ; nevertheless our heavy waggons, which were daily passing to and fro, had in places, where the ground was soft, made deep ruts ; and it was to be expected that the long rainy season beginning in March would completely stop the traffic in some places if the road was not seen to in time. Demestre, the head of the department for road construction, therefore engaged 2,000 Swahili, Wa-Kikuyu, and Wa-Teita in order at once to repair the worst places, and afterwards to improve the whole of the road.

In the meantime, our general postmaster, Ferroni, had organised a threefold transport and post service. For ordinary goods a luggage-service was established, running uninterruptedly day and night, the oxen-teams being still retained. The old waggons, carrying both passengers and luggage, had been obliged to halt longer at certain stations in the day than at others, for the meal-times ; and, apart from this, they were often delayed on the way by the travellers. The new luggage-waggons stayed nowhere longer than was necessary to give time to change the oxen and the attendants, and thus gained an average of four hours a day, so that under favourable conditions they could reach Eden Vale in twelve days. Of course passengers were not taken. A second kind of service was arranged for express goods, and here elephants were the motive power. Mrs. Ellen Ney's Indians, assisted by several of our own people, who had been initiated into the secrets of the catching and taming of these pachyderms, had trained several hundred of these animals. Thirty-five elephants were placed at stages between Eden Vale and Mombasa, and upon their backs from ten to twelve hundredweight of the most various kinds of goods were daily carried in both directions. This elephant-post covered the 600 miles and odd between the coast and Eden Vale in seven or eight days. For the third and fastest service mounted couriers were employed; only there were twenty-two instead of only ten relays, and sixty-five fresh horses were used, so that, with an average speed of over eleven miles an hour, the whole journey was made in two days and a-half. They carried merely despatches and letters; but from Mombasa they also carried a packet of European and American newspapers for our Eden Vale newspaper. (All newspapers sent to private persons were carried by the elephant-post.) A few months later, our representative in Mombasa effected an arrangement between the Sultan of Zanzibar and the English and the German governments, in accordance with which a telegraph-line was constructed between Mombasa and Zanzibar at the common cost of the contracting parties. This very' soon made it possible for us to communicate with and receive answers from all parts of the civilised world in five or six days; and our newspaper was able every Wednesday—its publishing day—to report what had happened three days before in London or New York, Paris or Berlin, Vienna or Rome, St. Petersburg or Constantinople. For passengers, besides the oxen-waggons, which, on account of their greater comfort, were retained for the use of women and children, there were express-waggons drawn by horses, which made the journey in ten days.

For the rest, the mode of life at the Kenia had meanwhile altered but little, with the exception of the fact that Eden Vale, which before the arrival of the first waggon-caravan was only a large village, in the course of a few months grew to be a considerable town of more than 20,000 inhabitants. On the Dana plateau, where at first there were only a few huts, two large villages had sprung up—one at the east end near the great waterfall, and inhabited by the workers in several factories; the other nearer to Eden Vale, and the home of an agricultural colony. A very noticeable air of untroubled joyousness and unmistakable comfort was common to all the inhabitants of Freeland. The manner of life was still very primitive, in harmony with the provisional character of the houses and the dress; on the other hand, as to meat and drink there was abundance, even luxury. The meals were in the main still arranged as they had been at first by the earliest comers; only the women had soon invented a number of fresh and ingenious modes of utilising the many delicate products of the country. The list of æsthetic and intellectual enjoyments within reach had not been considerably enlarged. The journal; a library founded by the Education Bureau, and daily enriched by newly arriving chests of books, so that by the New Year it contained 18,000 volumes, which did not by any means meet the demand for reading, particularly during the hot midday hours; several new singing and orchestral societies; reading or debating circles; and two dozen pianos—these were all that had been added to the original stock of means of recreation. But there was frequent hunting in the splendid woods; and excursions to the more accessible points of view were the order of the day. In short, the Freelanders endeavoured to make life as pleasant as possible with such a temporarily small variation in the programme of pleasures and intellectual recreation. In spite of all drawbacks, happiness and content reigned in every house.

With respect also to the hours of labour, the system originally adopted was on the whole retained. The men worked for the most part between 5 and 10 A.M. and between 4 and 6 P.M.; the women, assisted by natives, took care of the home and of the children when they were not at school. Yet no one felt bound to observe these hours—everyone worked when and as long as he pleased; and several associations, the work of which would not well bear the interruption of meal-times, introduced a system of relays which ensured the presence of a few hands at work during the hot hours. But as no one could be compelled to work during those hours, it became customary to pay for the more burdensome midday work a higher rate than for the ordinary work, and this had the effect of bringing the requisite number of volunteers. The same held good for the night work that was necessary in certain establishments.

CHAPTER X

At the end of our first year of residence at the Kenia, Freeland possessed a population of 95,000 souls, of whom 27,000 were men belonging to 218 associations and engaged in eighty-seven different kinds of work. In the last harvest—there are here two harvests in the year, one in October after the short rainy season, and the other in June after the long rainy season—36,000 acres had yielded nearly 2,000,000 cwt. of grain, representing in value the sum of 300,000*l.*, and giving to the 10,800 workers an average profit of nearly 2*s.* 6*d.* for every hour of labour. But it must not be supposed that all these workers spent their whole time in agricultural pursuits; except during sowing and harvest a great many agriculturists found profitable employment for the labour which would have been superfluous in the fields in the neighbouring industrial establishments. The average profit of all the industries was a little higher than that of agriculture; and as it was usual to work about forty hours a week, the average weekly earnings of an ordinary worker of moderate application were 5*l.* 5*s.*

Next to agriculture, the iron-works and machine-factories gave employment to the greatest number; in fact, if we take not the temporary employment of a large number of men, but the total number of labour-hours devoted to the work, as our measure, then these latter industries employed much more labour than agriculture. And this is not to be wondered at, for all the associations needed machinery in order to carry on their work to the best advantage. In other countries, where the wages of labour and the profit of labour are fundamentally different things, there is a fundamental distinction between the profitableness of a business and the theoretical perfection of the machinery used in it. In order to be theoretically useful a machine must simply save labour—that is, the labour required for producing and working the machine must be less than that which is saved by using it. The steam-plough, for example, is a theoretically good and useful machine if the manufacture of it, together with the production of the coal consumed by it, swallows up less human labour than on the other hand is saved by ploughing with steam instead of with horses or cattle. But the actual profitableness of a machine is quite another thing—out of Freeland, we mean, of course. In order to be profitable, the steam-plough must save, not labour, but value or money—that is, it must cost less than the labour which it has saved would have cost. But elsewhere in the world it by no means follows that it costs less because the amount of labour saved is greater than that consumed by the manufacture of the steam-plough and the production of the coal it uses. For whilst the labour which the improved plough saves receives merely its ' wages,' with the bought plough and the bought coal there have to be paid for not only the labour required in producing them, but also three items of ' gain '—namely, ground-rent, interest, and undertaker's salary. Thus it may happen that the steam-plough, between its first use and its being worn out, saves a million hours of labour, whilst in its construction and in the total quantity of coal it has required, it may have consumed merely 100,000 hours of labour ; and yet it may be very unprofit-able—that is, it may involve very great loss to those who, relying upon the certainty of such an enormous saving of labour, should buy and use it. For the million hours of labour saved mean no more than a million hours of *wages* saved ; therefore, for example, 10,000*l.*, if the wages are merely 1*l.* for a hundred hours of labour. For the construction of the plough and for the means of driving it 100,000 hours of labour are required, which alone certainly will have cost 1,000*l.* But then the rent which the owners of the iron-pits and the coal-mines charge, and the interest for the invested capital, must be paid, and finally the profits of the iron-manufacturer and the coal-producer. All this may, under certain circumstances, amount to more than the difference of 9,000*l.* between cost of labour in the two cases respectively ; and when that is the case the Western employer loses money by buying a machine which saves a thousand per cent. of his labour. With us the case is quite different : the living labour which the steam-plough spares *us* is hour for hour exactly as valuable as the labour-time which has been bestowed upon the plough and has been transformed into commodities ; for in Freeland there is no distinction between the profit of labour and the wages of labour, and in Freeland, therefore, every theoretically useful—that is, every really labour-saving—machine is at the same time, and of necessity, profitable. This is the reason why in Free-land the manufacture of machines is necessarily of such enormous and constantly increasing importance. One half of our people are engaged in the manufacture of ingenious mechanical implements, moved by steam, electricity, water, compressed or rarefied air, by means of which the other half multiply their powers of production a hundredfold ; and it follows as a natural consequence that among us the employment of machinery has developed a many-sidedness and a perfectness of which those who are outside the limits of our country have no conception.

The most important manufacture taken in hand before the end

of this first year was that of steam-ploughs and—worked provisionally by animal labour—seed-drills and reaping-machines sufficient
for the cultivation of the 64,000 acres which were to be brought
under the plough for the October harvest. We calculated that, by
the initial expenditure of 3,500,000 hours of labour, we should save
at least 3,000,000 hours of labour yearly. In other parts of the
world that would have been a great misfortune for the workers who
would thus have been rendered superfluous, while the community
would not have profited at all. We, on the contrary, were able to
find excellent employment for the labour thus saved, which could
be utilised in producing things that would elevate and refine, and
for which the increased productiveness of labour had created a
demand.

A second work, which had to be carried out during the next
year, was the improvement of the means of communication by deep-
ening the bed of the Dana from the flour-mill above the Eden lake
to the great waterfall on the Dana plateau, and by the construction
of a railway across the Dana plateau. With this were to be connected rope-lines on several of the Kenia foot-hills for the use of the
miners and the foresters.

That all the existing industries were enlarged, and a great
number of new ones started, will be taken for granted. It should
be mentioned that only such factories were erected in Eden Vale or
on the upper course of the Dana as would pollute neither the air nor
the water; the less cleanly manufactures were located at the east
end of the Dana plateau, close upon or even below the waterfall.
Later, means were found of preventing any pollution whatever of
the water by industrial refuse.

The town of Eden Vale had grown to contain 48,000 souls and
covered more than six square miles, with its small houses and
gardens, and its numerous large, though still primitively constructed, wooden public buildings. The herds of cattle, and the
horses, asses, camels, elephants, and the newly imported swine—all
of which had increased to an enormous extent—were for the main
part transferred to the Dana plateau, while the wild animals were
excluded by a strong stockade drawn round the heights that encircled
Eden Vale.

We were driven to this last somewhat costly measure by an
ncident which fortunately passed off without serious consequences,

but which showed the necessity of being protected against marauding animals. The noise of the town had for months made the wild animals which once abounded in Eden Vale avoid our immediate neighbourhood. But in the surrounding woods and copses there were still considerable numbers of antelopes, zebras, giraffes, buffaloes, and rhinoceroses; the elephants alone had completely disappeared. One fine evening, just before sunset, an enterprising old rhinoceros bull approached the town, and, enraged by some dogs— of which we had imported a good number, besides those that were descended from the dogs we brought with us—made his way into one of the principal streets of the town. This street led to a little grove which was a favourite playground for children, especially in the evening, and which was full of children when the savage brute suddenly appeared among them. The children were in charge of several women-teachers, who, as well as the children, lost their heads at sight of the monster, which was snorting and puffing like a steam-engine. Teachers and children fled together, chased by the rhinoceros, which, singling out a little fugitive, tossed her like a feather into the air. Seeing one of the teachers, who had fallen in her fright, lying motionless on the ground, the rhinoceros chose her as his next victim, and was within a few steps of her when the dogs, which had so far contented themselves with barking, now fell in a body upon the beast as if they recognised the danger of the women and children, and, by biting its ears and other tender parts, drew its fury upon themselves. The struggle was an unequal one, and in a few moments the rhinoceros had slain two of the brave dogs and severely wounded three others; but the rest persisted in their attack, and thus gave the children and their attendants time to save themselves. The little girl who had been tossed was merely frightened, and found safety in one of the houses near by. The rhinoceros, when he had put several more of the dogs *hors de combat*, trotted off, and was soon out of sight of the men who had hastened to the rescue with all kinds of weapons.

Such a scene could not be allowed to be repeated. The next day it was resolved to surround Eden Vale with a fence, and the work was at once begun. As the Kenia rocks formed a secure defence on one side, it was necessary only to construct a semicircular barrier. On the ridge of the surrounding heights, with timber obtained on the spot, a barrier five feet high was constructed, strong enough to

resist the attacks of any wild beast, and extending about twenty
miles. This protection was intended simply to keep out rhinoceroses,
elephants, and buffaloes; antelopes, zebras, even giraffes and such
like, if they had a fancy for leaping the barrier, could do no harm.
Nor did we need any protection against beasts of prey—lions and
leopards—for these had for months entirely left the neighbourhood.
When this barrier was completed, except for a distance of about 220
yards, we had a great hunt, by which all the wild beasts that were
still in the valley were driven to this opening and then chased out.
The chain of hunters was so close that we had every reason to be
sure that not an animal was left behind. Two rhinoceroses and a
buffalo made an attempt to break the chain, but were shot down.
The opening in the barrier was then closed up, and there was no
longer any wild quadruped worth mentioning in the whole of Eden
Vale.

On the other hand, the groves and woods within the barrier
became increasingly populous with tame antelopes of all kinds, which
were accustomed to return to their owners in the evening. Very
soon there was not a family—particularly with children—in Eden
Vale which did not possess one or more tame antelopes, monkeys,
or parrots; and elephant cubs, under two years of age, wandered by
dozens in the streets and in the public places, the pampered pets
of the children, who were remarkably attached to these little probos-
cidians. An elephant cub is never better pleased than when he has as
many children as he can carry upon his back, and he will even neglect
his meals in order to have a frolic with his two-legged comrades.

At the beginning of the second year our European agents
informed us that the rate of increase of members had assumed very
large proportions. The notices of Freeland which had been published in the journals—correspondents of some of the principal
European and American journals had visited us—had naturally very
powerfully quickened the desire to emigrate; and if all the indications did not deceive us, we had to expect, during the second year
of our residence at the Kenia, an influx of at least twice, probably
thrice, as many as had come during the first year. Provision had,
therefore, to be made for the requisite means of transport. As many
of the more wealthy new members paid for passages in ships belonging to foreign companies, instead of waiting to take their turn in our
own ships, the most urgent part of the work was that of increasing

the means of transport from Mombasa. A thousand new waggons were therefore purchased as speedily as possible, together with the requisite number of draught-cattle; and they were set to work in the order of purchase from March onwards. At the same time our London agent bought first six, and shortly afterwards four more, steamships of from 4,000 to 10,000 tons burden, and adapted them to our requirements so that each ship could carry from 1,000 to 3,000 passengers. By means of these new steamships the traffic through Trieste was increased; the largest ships took passengers from thence as the most favourably situated point of departure for the whole of the middle of Europe. Twice a week, also, a ship went from Marseilles, and once a month another from San Francisco across the Pacific Ocean. After a third set of a thousand waggons had been ordered to provide for emergencies, we thought we had made adequate provision for the transport of immigrants during the second year.

So stood affairs when Demestre approached the committee with the declaration that our primitive method of transport from Mombasa could not possibly suffice to meet the requirements of the strong permanent tide of immigration which promised to set in. We must at once think about constructing a railway between Eden Vale and the coast. The cost would be covered by the immigrants alone, and the incalculable advantage that would accrue to the whole of our industry would be clear profit. When he spoke of the covering of the cost by the immigrants he did not mean to propose that they should pay for travelling on the railway. The fare, however high it were fixed, would not suffice to cover the cost; and he did not propose to levy any direct payment for transport by rail, any more than had been done for transport by waggon. What he referred to was the saving of time. The waggons did the journey on an average in fourteen days, and after the fatigues of the journey the immigrants needed a rest of several days before they were ready for work. By rail the 600 miles and odd could comfortably be done in twenty-four hours; there would thus be an average saving of twelve labour-days. When it was considered that, among the 250,000 or 300,000 immigrants who might be expected to arrive yearly for some time to come, there would be between 70,000 and 80,000 persons able to work, the railway would mean a gain for them of from 800,000 to 1,000,000 labour-days. At present the average daily earnings amounted to 15s., and the 800,000 labour-days therefore represented a total value of 600,000l. But before the railway was finished the average value of labour in Freeland would probably have doubled ; and when he said that the railway would in the first year of its working yield to the immigrants at least a million pounds sterling he was certainly within the mark. Every year would this gain increase in proportion to the increased productiveness of labour in Freeland.

On the other side was the cost of construction of the line ; he would not speak of the cost of working, for, though there was no doubt that it would be less than the cost of working the transport services hitherto in operation, yet the saving might be left out of sight as not worth mentioning. The cost of constructing a railway to the coast could not be definitely calculated, particularly as the route was not yet decided upon. Whether the route of our caravan-road should be, with slight alterations, retained ; whether another route to Mombasa should be chosen ; or whether the coast should be reached at quite another point, nobody could say at present, when only one of the routes had been surveyed at all, and that only very imperfectly. But on the supposition that no better route could be found than the old one, or that this should be ultimately chosen on technical grounds, he could positively assert that the railway could not possibly cost nearly so much as the savings of the immigrants would amount to in the course of a few years. And, in consequence of the way in which labour was organised in Freeland, every increase in the produce of labour was converted into immediate gain to the whole community.

We should therefore proceed at once to construct the railway, even if it were merely to the advantage of the immigrants. That it was not merely to their advantage, however, was self-evident, since the profit which the community would derive from the cheapening and facilitating of the goods traffic would be infinitely greater—so great that it could not be even approximately calculated. He merely wished to throw a few rays of light upon the economic result of the railway. Assuming that the line would be completed in three years, we should then have a population of about a million, and there was no doubt that when we had sufficient means of transport we should be able easily to produce ten million hundredweight of grain for export. Such a quantity of grain at the Kenia then represented

one and a-half million pounds sterling. If the cost of transport
sank from five or six shillings per cwt., the current price—independently of the fact that a greater quantity could not then be
conveyed—to one shilling, or at most eighteen-pence, which might
be looked upon as the maximum railway freight for 600 miles, then
the value of the above quantity of grain would be raised to a round
two million pounds sterling. In short, he was firmly convinced
that the railway, even at the highest probable cost, must fully pay
for itself in three or four years at the latest. He therefore proposed
that they should at once send out several expeditions of skilled
engineers to find the most suitable route for the future line. They
should not proceed too cautiously, for even a considerable difference
in cost would be preferable to loss of time.

Everything that Demestre urged in support of his project was
so just and clear that it was unanimously adopted without debate;
in fact, everyone secretly wondered why he had not himself
thought of it long before. The only thing to do now, therefore, was
to trace the route of the future railway. In the first place, there
was the old route through Kikuyu into Masailand, thence to the
east of Kilimanjaro, past Taveta and Teita, to Mombasa. A second
and possibly more favourable route was thought of, which led also
southwards, and reached the coast at Mombasa, but took a direction
two degrees further east, through Kikuyu, into the country of the
Ukumbani, and thence followed the valley of the Athi river to
Teita. This track might probably shorten the distance by more
than a hundred miles. The third, the shortest route to the ocean,
led directly east, following the Dana, through the Galla lands, to
the Witu coast; here eventually nearly half the distance might be
saved, for we were but about 280 miles from the coast in a straight
line.

It was decided that these three routes should be examined as
carefully as would be possible in the course of a few months; for
the beginning of the construction of the line was not to be delayed
more than half a year. Demestre was appointed to examine the
old route, with which he was already well acquainted. Two other
skilful engineers were sent to the Athi and the Dana respectively,
each accompanied, as was Demestre, by a staff of not less qualified
colleagues. But these two latter expeditions, having to explore
utterly unknown districts, inhabited by probably hostile tribes, had

to be well armed. They were each 300 strong, and, besides a sufficient number of repeating-rifles, they took with them several war elephants, some cannons, and some rockets. All these expeditions were accompanied by a small band of naturalists, geologists in particular. They started in the beginning of May, and they were instructed to return, if possible, in August, before the short rainy season.

Whilst our attention was fixed principally upon the east in making provision for the enormous influx expected from Europe and America, an unexpected complication was brought about in the west by means of our allies, the Masai. In order to find a new field for their love of adventure, which they could no longer bring into play against the Swahili, Wa-Duruma, Wa-Teita, Wa-Taveta, and Wa-Kikuyu, whom we had made their allies, the Masai fell upon the Nangi and Kavirondo, who live west of Lake Baringo, and drove off a large number of their cattle. But when the patience of these large tribes was exhausted, they forgot for a time their mutual animosities, turned the tables upon the Masai, and overran their country. In this war the Masai suffered a great deal, for their opponents, though not equal to them in bravery, far surpassed them in numbers. If the Masai had but got together in time, they might have easily collected in their own country an army equal to the 18,000 Kavirondo and Nangi who took the field against them; but they were thrown into confusion by the unexpected attack, got together a poor 7,000 *el-moran*, and suffered utter defeat in two sanguinary engagements. More than a thousand of their warriors fell, and the swarms of the victors poured continuously over the whole country between the Lakes Baringo and Naivasha, sweeping all the Masai before them, and getting an immense booty in women, children, and cattle. This was at the beginning of May; and the Masai, who knew not how to escape from their exasperated foes except by our aid, sent couriers who reached the Kenia with their petitions for help on the 10th of the month.

This help was of course at once granted. On the day after the messengers reached us, 500 of our horsemen, with the still available cannons and rockets, and with twenty-four elephants, started in forced marches for the Naivasha, where the Masai, favoured by the character of the country, thought they could hold out for a time.

Our men reached their destination on the 16th, just after our allies had met with another reverse and were scarcely able to hold out another day. Johnston, who led our little army, scarcely waited to refresh his horses before he sent word to the Kavirondo and the Nangi that they were to cease hostilities at once; he was come, not as their enemy, but as arbitrator. If they would not accept his mediation, he would at once attack them; but he warned them beforehand that successful resistance to his weapons and to those of his people was impossible. Naturally, this threat had no effect upon the victorious blacks. It is true they had already heard all sorts of vague rumours about the mysterious white strangers; and the elephants and horses, which they now saw, though at a distance, were not likely to please them. But their own great numbers, in comparison with the small body of our men, and chiefly their previous successes, encouraged them, after their elders had held a short *shauri*, to send a defiant answer. Let Johnston attack them; they would 'eat him up' as they meant to eat up the whole of Masailand.

Johnston anticipated such an answer, and had made the necessary preparations. As soon as he had received the challenge he caused his men to mount at once, told the Masai not to join in the fight at all, and then he attacked the Kavirondo and Nangi. This time he did not rely upon the effect of blank-cartridges, not because an entirely bloodless battle would scarcely have satisfied the Masai's longing for revenge, but because he wished to end the whole war at a single stroke. He therefore allowed his men to approach within 550 yards of the blacks, who kept their ground; and then, whilst the horsemen charged the enemy's centre, he directed several sharp volleys from the cannons and rockets against them. Naturally, the whole order of battle was at once broken up in wild flight, though not many men fell. Those who fled westward Johnston allowed to escape; but the main body of the enemy, who tried to get away along the banks of the Naivasha to the north, were cut off by 400 of our men, whilst he kept with the other hundred between the blacks and the Masai, principally for the purpose of preventing the latter from falling upon the conquered. Our 400 horsemen, who made a wide circle round the fugitives, much as sheep-dogs do around a scattering flock of sheep, soon brought the Kavirondo and Nangi to a stand, who, when they found themselves completely surrounded, threw down their weapons and begged for mercy. Johnston ordered them to send their elders to him, as he did not intend to do them any further harm, but merely wished to bring about peace between them and the Masai.

As might be supposed, the peace negotiations were brief, for Johnston did not require anything unjust from the conquered, who were completely at his mercy. They were to give up all their prisoners and booty; and, after they had taken an oath to keep the peace with us and the Masai, they should remain unmolested. In the meantime, however, until the prisoners and the booty had been given up—for only a part of both had fallen into our hands, the Kavirondo having sent off the greater part to their own country several days before—they were to remain upon one of the Naivasha islands as our prisoners. Those who thus remained numbered more than 10,000, and included some of the chief men of their nation. The Kavirondo and Nangi accepted these terms; in the course of the afternoon and night they were ferried across to one of the neighbouring islands, and twelve of their number were sent home to bring back the booty.

Johnston, having caused the Masai leaders to be brought before him, administered to them a very severe reprimand. Did they think that we should continue to be friends with thieves and robbers? Had he not told them that the swords which we had given to their *leitunus* would snap asunder like glass if drawn in an unrighteous cause? And in the war with the Kavirondo and Nangi were not the Masai in the wrong? 'We have saved you from the just punishment with which you were threatened, for the alliance which we had contracted still stood good when you were defeated; but we dissolve that alliance! I stay here until the Kavirondo and Nangi have brought back their booty, which shall be handed over to you in its entirety; but, after that, do not expect anything more from us. We can live in friendship with only peaceable honourable people. Henceforth the Kavirondo and Nangi are our friends; woe to you in the future if you ever break the peace; our anger will shatter you as the lightning shatters the sycamore-tree!'

The Masai were completely cowed. This unlooked-for dissolution of a friendship which had for a year past been their chief pride, and which had just been their salvation in extremity, was more than they were able to bear. But Johnston preserved a

K

severe attitude towards them, and finally insisted upon their leaving his camp. When the *leitunus* and *leigonanis* returned to their people with the terrible news that their friendship with the white brethren was at an end there were exhibited the most extravagant signs of distress. The whole camp of the Masai rushed over to ours; but Johnston ordered them to be told that, weaponless though they were, he would fire upon them if they dared to come near. This was repeated several times during the next few days. The Masai sent messengers throughout the whole country, called together the wisest of their elders, and again and again endeavoured to induce Johnston to treat with them ; but he remained inexorable, had his camp entrenched, and threatened to shoot every Masai who attempted to enter it.

In ten days the Kavirondo and Nangi messengers returned with the prisoners and the cattle. Johnston now bade the Masai elders appear before him that he might hand over to them what he had won for them in battle. The Masai came, and took advantage of the opportunity of making their last attempt to appease the terrible white man. Johnston might keep all that he—not they—had recovered ; they were willing to regard the loss they had suffered as the just punishment of their crime ; they were ready to do yet more if he would but forgive them and give them his friendship again. It was to this point that Johnston had wished to bring these people, whom he knew right well. He showed himself touched by their appeal, but said that he could grant nothing without the knowledge and consent of the other leaders in Eden Vale. He would report to the great council the repentance of the Masai people ; and it was for the council to decide what was to be done. On the 19th and 20th of June, the days appointed for the commemoration of the alliance with us, they were to come with their fellow-countrymen to the place of rendezvous on the south shore of Naivasha lake ; there should they receive an answer.

It is unnecessary to say that Johnston's threats were not seriously meant. The alliance with the Masai was of too much importance to us for us to wish it dissolved. But Johnston had been instructed by the committee to use every means to restrain the Masai from plundering in the future and to induce them to keep the peace with all their neighbours. And the committee were well aware that extreme measures were necessary to attain these ends, for to convert the Masai into a peaceable people meant nothing less than to divest them of their characteristic peculiarities. They are in truth a purely military nation. War is their peculiar business—their organisation and habits of life all have reference to war. They differ from all their neighbours, being ethnographically distinct, for they are not negroes, but a bronze-coloured Hamitic race evidently related to the original inhabitants of Egypt. They carry on no industry, even their cattle-breeding being in the hands of their captured slaves; while they themselves are in youth exclusively warriors, and in age dignified idlers. The warriors, the *el-moran*, live apart and unmarried—though by no means in celibacy—in separate kraals; the older married men—the *el-morun*—also live in separate villages. They buy their weapons of the Andorobbo who live among them; and the small amount of corn which the married men and their wives consume—for the *el-moran* eat only milk and flesh—they buy of neighbouring foreign tribes. Their morals are exceptionally loose, for the warriors live in unrestrained fellowship with the unmarried girls—the Dittos; and the married women allow themselves all conceivable liberties, without any interference on the part of their husbands. Notwithstanding all this, these dissolute plundering carls form the finest nation of the whole district east of the Victoria Nyanza—brave, strong, ingenuous, intelligent, and, when they are once won, trustworthy. To convert them into industrious and moral men would be a grand work and would make our new home, in which we could not go far without coming into collision with them, truly habitable to us.

But it was very difficult to accomplish this. Their military organisation had to be broken up, their immorality suppressed, their prejudice against labour overcome. That this was by no means impossible was proved by many past examples. The Wa-Kwafi, living to the south and west of them, as well as the Njemps on the Baringo lake, are either of pure Masai extraction or have much Masai blood in their veins; yet they practise agriculture and know nothing of the *el-moran* and Ditto abuse. But the change had been effected among these by the agency of extreme want. It was only those Masai tribes who were completely vanquished by other Masai and robbed of all their cattle that were dispersed among agricultural negro tribes, whose customs they had to adopt, while they unfortunately gave up their good characteristics

K 2

along with their bad ones. Johnston's task now was to see if it were not possible by rational compulsion to effect such a change in them as in other instances had been effected by want. How he prosecuted his attempt we have seen.

When Johnston released the Kavirondo and Nangi prisoners, he invited them to send, on the 19th, as numerous an embassy as possible of their elders to Naivasha, where we would confirm the newly formed alliance and seal it with rich presents. He left the whole of his army at Naivasha, partly to cover the retreat of the discharged prisoners, and partly to watch the booty (the Masai still hesitated to take back the booty, and even forbade their captured wives and children to leave our camp), while he himself, accompanied by only a few horsemen, hastened to Eden Vale, there to get further instructions. The proposal which he laid before the committee was that everything should now be demanded from the Masai—the iron could be forged if struck when it was hot ; and as conditions of the renewal of friendship he suggested the following three points : dissolution of the *el-moran* kraals, emancipation of all slaves whatever, formation of agricultural associations. Of course we were not to be content with the statement of these demands, but must ourselves take in hand the work of carrying them out. Particularly would it be necessary to assist the Masai in the organisation of the agricultural associations, to furnish them with suitable agricultural implements, and to give them instruction in rational agriculture. Finally, and chiefly, was it necessary to win over the *el-moran* by employing them in relays as soldiers for us. The ideal of these brown braves was the routine of a military life. The alliance with the Kavirondo and Nangi might lead to hostile complications with Uganda, the country adjoining Kavirondo, when we could very well make use of a Masai militia, and thus accomplish two ends at once—viz. the complete pacification and civilisation of Masailand, and assistance against Uganda, the great raiding State on the Victoria Nyanza, with which sooner or later we must necessarily come into collision.

The committee adopted these suggestions after a short deliberation. Five hundred fresh volunteers (as a matter of course, all our expeditions consisted of volunteers) from among our agriculturists were placed under Johnston's orders, as agricultural teachers for the Masai ; whilst a part of the five hundred men already at

Naivasha were selected to superintend the military training of the *el-moran*. Further, Johnston received for his work the whole of the ploughs which had been thrown out of use in Freeland by the introduction of steam-machinery. There were not less than 3,000 of these ploughs, as well as a corresponding number of harrows and other agricultural implements. With these were also granted 6,000 oxen accustomed to the plough, as well as supplies of seeds, &c. The committee at once telegraphed to Europe for 10,000 breechloaders and a million cartridges, with 10,000 sidearms, which were supplied cheaply by the Austrian Government out of the stock of disused Werndl rifles, and could reach Naivasha by the end of June. Five complete field-batteries and eight rocket-batteries were at the same time ordered in Europe ; these, however, were not for the Masai militia, but for our own use in any future contingencies. An English firm promised to deliver two weeks later 10,000 very picturesque and strikingly designed complete uniforms, of which, moreover, our Eden Vale sewing-factory speedily got ready several hundred made of our large stores of brightly coloured woollen goods, so that the *el-moran* were able to see, on the 19th and 20th of June, the splendours in store for them.

Thus furnished, Johnston left Eden Vale on the 12th of June, and reached the shore of the Naivasha on the 16th, leaving his caravan of goods a few days' march behind him. The elders and *leitunus* of all the Masai tribes, as well as the ambassadors of the Kavirondo and Nangi, already awaited him. The negotiations with the latter were soon ended : the conditions of alliance were again discussed, rich presents exchanged (the Kavirondo had brought several thousand head of cattle for their magnanimous victors), and on this side nothing further stood in the way of the approaching covenant-feast. We had thus secured trustworthy friends as far as the Victoria Nyanza, a great part of the shore of which was in the hands of the Kavirondo ; in return for which, it is true, we had undertaken—what we did not for a moment overlook—the heavy responsibility of protecting the Kavirondo against all foes, even against the powerful Uganda.

The Masai, on the other hand, were at first greatly troubled by the conditions demanded of them. Johnston's eloquence, however, soon convinced them that their acceptance of these conditions was not merely unavoidable, but would be very profitable to themselves.

He overcame their prejudice against labour by showing them that an occupation to which we powerful and rich white men were glad to devote ourselves could be neither degrading nor burdensome. They were not to suppose that we intended them to grub about in the earth, like the barbarous negroes, with wretched spades; the hard work would be done by oxen; they need only walk behind the implements, which were already on the way ready to be distributed among them. A few hours' light work a day for a few months in the year would suffice to make them richer than they had ever been made by the labour of their slaves. Even the *el-moran* were won over without very much difficulty by the promise that, if they would only work a little in turns, they should now be trained to become invincible warriors like ourselves, and should receive fine clothing and yet finer weapons. And when at last the endless caravan with the oxen and the agricultural implements arrived; when the wonderful celerity with which the ploughs cut through the ground was demonstrated; and when Johnston dressed up a chosen band of *el-moran* in the baggy red hose and shirts, the green jackets, and the dandyish plumed hats, with rifle, bayonet, and cartridge-box,· and made them march out as models of the future soldiery, the resignation which had hitherto been felt gave way to unrestrained jubilation. The Masai had originally yielded out of fear of our anger, and more still of the danger lest our friendship to the surrounding tribes might lead to the unconditional deliverance of the Masai into the hands of their hereditary foes. The numerous embassies which had appeared from all points of the compass (for the Wa-Kikuyu, Wa-Taveta, Wa-Teita, and Wa-Duruma —even the Wa-Kwafi and Swahili tribes—had sent representatives laden with rich presents to take part in the Naivasha festival) were significant reminders to them. But now they accepted our terms with joy, and were not a little proud of being able to show to the others that they were still the first in our favour.

And as the Masai, when they have made any engagement, are honourably ambitious—unlike the negroes—to keep it, the carrying out of the stipulations was a comparatively easy and speedy matter. A hasty census, which we made for several purposes, showed that there were some 180,000 souls in the twelve Masai tribes scattered over a district of nearly 20,000 square miles, from Lykipia in the extreme north to Kilimanjaro in the south. The country, although dry and sterile in the south-west, is exuberantly fertile in the east and north, and—particularly around the numerous ranges of hills, which rise to a height of 15,000 feet—equals in beauty the Teita, Kilima, and Kenia districts, and could well support a population a hundred times as large as the present one; but the perpetual wars and the licentiousness of the people have hitherto limited the increase of the population. Among the 180,000 were about 54,000 men capable of labour, the *el-moran* being included in that number. We handed over to the Masai 12,000 yoke-oxen, in exchange for which we received the same number of oxen for fattening. Our 500 agricultural instructors now looked out for the most suitable arable ground for their pupils, whom they organised into 280 associations similar to ours, without a right of property in the soil and with the amount of labour as the sole measure of the distribution of produce. The instructors taught them the use of the implements; and were able, two months later, to report to Eden Vale, with considerable satisfaction, that above 50,000 acres had been sown with all kinds of field-produce. The harvest proved to be abundantly sufficient not only to cover all the needs of the Masai, but also to secure to their white teachers, both agricultural and military, the payment then customary in Freeland.

While in this way, on the one hand, the agricultural associations were set to work, on the other hand some 300 military instructors initiated relays of 6,500 *el-moran* into the mysteries of the European art of war. The 26,000 Masai warriors were divided into four companies, each of which was put into uniform and exercised for a year. The rifles remained our property, the uniforms became the property of the Masai warriors, but could be worn only when the owners were on duty. There was no pay for peace duty—rather, as above mentioned, the Masai defrayed the cost of their military training out of the proceeds of their agriculture.

The agricultural as well as the military instructors made themselves useful in other ways, by imparting to their pupils all kinds of skill and knowledge. There were no specially learned men among them, but they opened up a new world to the Masai, exercised a refining and ennobling influence upon their habits and morals, and in a surprisingly short time made tolerably civilised men of them. The Masai, on their part, enjoyed their new lives very much. They were well aware that their altered condition made them the object of all their neighbours' envy, whilst they were still more highly respected than before. And, what was the main thing—at the beginning at least—they enjoyed their new wealth and their increased honour without finding their labour at all painful to those needs. For in this fortunate country it required very little labour expended in a rational way to get from the fruitful soil the little that was there looked upon as extraordinary wealth. He who twice a year spent a few weeks in sowing and harvesting could for the rest of the year indulge in the still favourite luxury of *dolce far niente.* In later years, when the needs of the Masai had been largely multiplied by their growing culture, more labour was required to satisfy those needs; but in the meantime our pupils had got rid of their former laziness; and it may be confidently asserted that not one of them ever regretted that we had imposed our civilisation upon his nation. On the contrary, the example of the Masai stimulated the neighbouring peoples; and, in the course of the following years, the most diverse tribes voluntarily came to us with the request that we would do with them as we had done with the Masai. The suppression of property in the soil among those negro races who—unlike the Masai and most of the other peoples of Equatorial Africa—possessed such an institution in a developed form, in no case presented any great difficulty : the land was voluntarily either given up or redeemed. Nowhere was property in land able to assert itself along with labour organised according to our principles.

CHAPTER XI

THE meeting of the International Free Society at the Hague had, as the reader will remember, conferred full executive power upon the committee for the period of two years. This period expired on the 20th of October, when the Society would have to give itself a new and definitive constitution, and the powers hitherto exercised by the committee would have to be taken over by an administrative body freely elected by the people of Freeland. On the 15th of September, therefore, the committee called together a constituent assembly ; and, as the inhabitants were too numerous all to meet together for consultation, they divided the country into 500 sections, according to the number of the inhabitants, and directed each section to elect a deputy. The committee declared this representative assembly to be the provisional source of sovereign authority, and required it to make arrangements for the future, leaving it to decide whether it would empower the committee to continue to exercise its executive functions until a constitution had been agreed upon, or would at once entrust the administration of Freeland to some new authority. After a short debate, the assembly not only decided unanimously to adopt the former course, but also charged the committee with the task of preparing a draft constitution. As such a draft had already been prepared in view of contingencies, the committee at once accepted the duty imposed upon it. Dr. Strahl, in the name of the committee, laid the draft constitution ' upon the table of the House.' The assembly ordered it to be printed, and three days after proceeded to discuss it. As the proposed fundamental law and detailed regulations were extremely simple, the debate was not very long-winded ; and, on the 2nd of October, the laws and regulations were declared to be unanimously approved, and the new constitution was put in force.

The fundamental laws were thus expressed :

1. Every inhabitant of Freeland has an equal and inalienable claim upon the whole of the land, and upon the means of production accumulated by the community.

2. Women, children, old men, and men incapable of work, have a right to a competent maintenance, fairly proportionate to the level of the average wealth of the community.

3. No one can be hindered from the active exercise of his own free individual will, so long as he does not infringe upon the rights of others.

4. Public affairs are to be administered as shall be determined by all the adult (above twenty years of age) inhabitants of Freeland, without distinction of sex, who shall all possess an equal active and passive right of vote and of election in all matters that affect the commonwealth.

5. Both the legislative and the executive authority shall be divided into departments, and in such a manner that the whole of the electors shall choose special representatives for the principal public departments, who shall give their decisions apart and watch over the action of the administrative boards of the respective departments.

In these five points is contained the whole substance of the

public law of Freeland; everything else is merely the natural consequence or the more detailed expression of these points. Thus the
principles upon which the associations were based—the right of the
worker to the profit, the division of the profit in proportion to the
amount of work contributed, and freedom of contract in view of
special efficiency of labour—are naturally and necessarily implied in
the first and third fundamental laws. As the whole of the means of
labour were accessible to everyone, no one could be compelled to
forego the profit of his own labour; and as no one could be forced
to place his higher capabilities at the disposal of others, these
higher capabilities—so far as they were needed in the guidance and
direction of production—must find adequate recompense in the way
of freedom of contract.

With reference to the right of maintenance given to women,
children, old men, and men incapable of working, by the second
section, it may be remarked that this was regarded, in the spirit of
our principles, as a corollary from the truth that the wealth of the
civilised man is not the product of his own individual capabilities,
but is the result of the intellectual labour of numberless previous
generations, *whose bequest belongs as much to the weak and helpless
as to the strong and capable.* All that we enjoy we owe in an infinitely small degree to our own intelligence and strength; thrown upon
these as our only resources, we should be poor savages vegetating in
the deepest, most brutish misery; it is to the rich inheritance received
from our ancestors that we owe ninety-nine per cent. of our enjoyments. If this is so—and no sane person has ever questioned it—then
all our brothers and sisters have a right to share in the common heritage. That this heritage would be unproductive without the labour of
us who are strong is true, and it would be unfair—nay, foolish and
impracticable—for our weaker brethren to claim an *equal* share.
But they have a right to claim a fraternal participation—not merely
a charitable one, but one based upon their right of inheritance—in
the rich profits won from the common heritage, even though it be
by *our* labour solely. They stand towards us in the relation, not
of mendicant strangers, but of co-heirs and members of our family.
And of us, the stronger inheritors of a clearly proved title, every
member of the common family demands the unreserved recognition
of this good title. For we cannot prosper if we dishonour and condemn to want and shame those who are our equals. A healthy

egoism forbids us to allow misery and its offspring—the vices—to harbour anywhere among our fellows. Free, and 'of noble birth,' a king and lord of this planet, must everyone be whose mother is a daughter of man, else will his want grow to be a spreading ulcer which will consume even us—the strong ones.

So much as to the right of maintenance in general. As to the provision for women in particular, it was considered that woman was unfitted by her physical and psychical characteristics for an active struggle for existence ; but was destined, on the one hand, to the function of propagating the human race, and, on the other hand, to that of beautifying and refining life. So long as we all, or at least the immense majority of us, were painfully engaged in the unceasing and miserable struggle to obtain the barest necessities of animal life, no regard could be paid to the weakness and nobility of woman ; her weakness, like that of every other weak one, could not become a title to tender care, but became inevitably an incitement to tyranny ; the nobility of woman was dishonoured, as was all purely human and genuine nobility. For unnumbered centuries woman was a slave and a purchasable instrument of lust, and the much-vaunted civilisation of the last few centuries has brought no real improvement. Even among the so-called cultured nations of the present day, woman remained without legal rights, and, what is worse, she was left, in order to obtain subsistence, to sell herself to the first man she met who would undertake to provide and 'care for' her for the sake of her attractions. This prostitution, sanctioned by law and custom, is in its effects more disastrous than that other, which stands forth undisguised and is distinguished from the former only in the fact that here the shameful bargain is made not for life, but only for years, weeks, hours. It is common to both that the sweetest, most sacred treasure of humanity, woman's heart, is made the subject of vulgar huckstering, a means of buying a livelihood ; and worse than the prostitution of the streets is that of the marriage for a livelihood sanctioned by law and custom, because under its pestilential poison-breath not only the dignity and happiness of the living, but the sap and strength of future generations are blasted and destroyed. As love, that sacred instinct which should lead the wife into the arms of the husband, united with whom she might bequeath to the next generation its worthiest members, had become the only means of gain within her reach

woman was compelled to dishonour herself, and in herself to dishonour the future of the race.

Happiness and dignity, as well as the future salvation of humanity, equally demanded that woman should be delivered from the
dishonourable necessity of seeing in her husband a provider, in
marriage the only refuge from material need. But neither should
woman be consigned to common labour. This would be in equal
measure prejudicial both to the happiness of the living and to the
character and vigour of future generations. It is as useless as it is
injurious to wish to establish the equality of woman by allowing her
to compete with man in earning her bread—useless, because such a
permission, of which advantage could be taken only in exceptional
cases, would afford no help to the female sex as a whole; injurious,
because woman cannot compete with man and yet be true to her
nobler and tenderer duties. And those duties do not lie in the
kitchen and the wardrobe, but in the cultivation of the beautiful in
the adult generation on the one hand, and of the intellectual and
physical development of the young on the other. Therefore, in the
interests not only of herself, but also of man, and in particular of
the future race, woman must be altogether withdrawn from the
struggle for the necessaries of life; she must be no wheel in the
bread-earning machinery, she must be a jewel in the heart of
humanity. Only one kind of 'work' is appropriate to woman—that
of the education of children and, at most, the care of the sick and
infirm. In the school and by the sick-bed can womanly tenderness
and care find a suitable apprenticeship for the duties of the future
home, and in such work may the single woman earn wages so far
as she wishes to do so. At the same time, our principles secured
perfect liberty to woman. She was not forbidden to engage in any
occupation, and isolated instances have occurred of women doing so,
particularly in intellectual callings, but public opinion in Freeland
approved of this only in exceptional cases—that is, when special
gifts justified such action; and it was our women chiefly who
upheld this public opinion.

The fact that the maintenance allowance for women was fixed at
one-fourth less than that for men—and the constituent assembly confirmed not only the principle, but the proposed ratio of the different
maintenance allowances—was not the expression of any lower estimate of the *claim* of woman, but was due simply to the consideration

that the *requirements* of woman are less than those of man. We acted upon the calculation that a woman with her thirty per cent. of the average labour-earnings of a Freeland producer was as well provided for as a maintenance-receiving man with his forty per cent.; and experience fully verified this calculation.

Not only had the single woman or the widow a right to a maintenance, but the married woman also had a similar right, though only to one-half the amount. This right was based upon the principle that even the wife ought not to be thrown upon the husband for maintenance and made dependent upon him. As in housekeeping the woman's activity is partly called forth by her own personal needs, it was right that some of the burden of maintenance should be taken from the husband, and only a part of it left as a common charge to both. With the birth of children, the family burden is afresh increased, and, as this is specially connected with the wife, we increase her maintenance allowance until it reaches again the full allowance of a single woman—that is, thirty per cent. The allowances would be as follows:

A childless family	15 per cent.
A family with one child	20 „
„ „ two children	25 „
„ „ three or more children	30 „
A working widow with a child	5 „
„ „ „ two children	10 „
„ „ „ three or more children	15 „
An independent woman	30 „
„ „ „ with a child	35 „
„ „ „ with two children	40 „
„ „ „ with three or more children	45 „

Just as the women's and children's maintenance-claims accumulated according to circumstances, so was it with those claims and the claims of men unable to work, and old men. The maximum that could be drawn for maintenance was not less than seventy per cent. of the average income, and this happened in the cases—which were certainly rare—in which a married man who had a claim had three or more children under age.

The fourth fundamental principle—the extension of the franchise to adult women—calls for no special comment. It need only be remarked that this law included the negroes residing in Freeland.

This was conditioned, of course, by the exclusion from the exercise of political rights of all who were unable to read and write—an exclusion which was automatically secured by requiring all votes to be given in the voter's own handwriting. We took considerable pains not only to teach our negroes reading and writing, but also to give them other kinds of knowledge ; and as our efforts were in general followed by good results, our black brethren gradually participated in all our rights.

A more detailed explanation is, however, required by the fifth section of the fundamental laws, according to which the community exercised their control over all public affairs not through *one*, but through several co-ordinated administrative boards, elected separately by the community. To this regulation the administrative authorities of Freeland owed their astonishing special knowledge of details, and the public life of Freeland its equally unexampled quiet and the absence of any deeply felt, angry party passions. In the States of Europe and America, only the executive consists of men who are chosen—or are supposed to be thus chosen -on account of their special knowledge and qualification for the branches of the public service at the head of which they respectively stand. Even this is subject to very important limitations ; in fact, with respect to the parliamentary constitutions of Europe and America, it can be truthfully asserted that those who are placed at the head of the different branches of the administration only too often know very little about the weighty affairs which they have to superintend. The assemblies from which and by whose choice parliamentary ministers are placed in office are, as a rule, altogether incapable of choosing qualified men, for the reason that frequently there are none such in their midst. It does not follow from this that parliamentary orators and politicians by profession do not generally understand the duties of their office better than those favourites of power and of blind fortune who hold the helm in non-parliamentary countries ; but experts they are not, and cannot be. Yet, as has been said, the organs of the executive at least *ought* to be such, and by a current fiction they are held to be such ; and a man who specially distinguishes himself in any department thereby earns a claim—though a subordinate one—to receive further employment in that department of the public service. For the legislative bodies outside of Freeland, on the other hand, special knowledge is not even theoretically a qualification. The men who make laws and control the administration of them, need, in theory, to have not the least knowledge of the matters to which these laws refer. The support of the electors is usually quite independent of the amount of such knowledge possessed by the representatives, who are chosen not as men of special knowledge, but as men of 'sound understanding.'

But this is followed by a twofold evil. In the first place, it converts the public service into a private game of football, in which the players are Ignorance and Incapacity. The words of Oxenstiern, ' You know not, my son, with how little understanding the world is governed,' are true in a far higher degree than is generally imagined. The average level of capacity and special knowledge in many of the branches of public service in the so-called civilised world is far below that to be found in the private business of the same countries. In the second place, this centralised organisation of the public administration, with an absence of persons of special qualification, converts party spirit into an angry and bitter struggle in which everything is risked, and the decision depends very rarely upon practical considerations, but almost always upon already accepted political opinions. Incessant conflict, continuous passionate excitement, are therefore the second consequence of this preposterous system.

An improvement is, however, simply impossible so long as the present social system remains in force. For, so long as this is the case, the public welfare is better looked after by ignorant persons who act independently of professional knowledge than it would be if professional men had power to further the interests of their own professions at the expense of the general public. For the interests of specialists under an exploiting system of society are not merely sometimes, but generally, opposed to those of the great mass of the people. Imagine a European or American State in which the manufacturers exercised legislative and executive control over manufactures, agriculturists over agriculture, railway shareholders over the means of transport, and so forth—the specialist representatives of each separate interest making and administering the laws that particularly concerned their own profession ! As under the exploiting system of society the struggle for existence is directed towards a mutual suppression and supplanting, so must the consequences of such a ' constitution ' as we have just supposed be positively dreadful. In those cases which are grouped together under the heading of ' political corruption,' where isolated interests have succeeded in imposing their will upon the community, the shamelessness of the exploitage has exceeded all bounds.

But it is different in Freeland. With us no separate interest is antagonistic to or not in perfect harmony with the common interest. Producers, for example, who in Freeland conceive the idea of increasing their gains by laying an impost upon imports, must be idiotic. For, to compel the consumers to pay more for their manu- factures would not help them, since the influx of labour would at once bring down their gains again to the average level. On the other hand, to make it more difficult for other producers to produce would certainly injure themselves, for the average level of gain— above which their own cannot permanently rise—would be thereby lowered. And exactly the same holds good for all our different interests. In consequence of the arrangement whereby every interest is open to everyone, and no one has either the right or the might to reserve any advantage to himself alone, we are fortunately able to entrust the decision of all questions affecting material interest to those who are the most directly interested—therefore, to those who possess the most special knowledge. Not merely do the legislature and the executive thereby acquire in the highest degree a specialist character, but there disappears from public life that passionate prepossession which elsewhere is the characteristic note of party politics. As a well-understood public interest and sound reason decide in all matters, we have no occasion to become heated. At our elections our aim is not 'to get in one of our party,' but the only thing about which opinions may differ is which of the candidates happens to be the most experienced, the most apt for the post. And as, in consequence of the organisation of our whole body of labour, the capabilities of each one among us must in time be discovered, mistakes in this determining point in our public life are scarcely possible.

As the constituent assembly retained the twelvefold division of the governing authority, there were henceforth in Freeland, besides the twelve different executive boards—which in their sphere of action were to some extent analogous to the ministries of Western nations—twelve different consultative, determining, and supervising assemblies, elected by the whole people, in place of the single parliament of the Western nations. These twelve assemblies

were elected by the whole of the electors, each elector having the
right to give an equal vote in all the elections ; but the distribution
of the constituencies was different, and the election for each of the
twelve representative bodies took place separately. Some of these
elections—those, namely, for the affairs of the chief executive and
finance, for maintenance, for education, for art and science, for
sanitation and justice—took place according to residence ; the
elections in the other cases according to calling. For the latter
purpose, the whole of the inhabitants of Freeland were divided,
according to their callings, into larger or smaller constituencies,
each of which elected one or more deputies in proportion to its
numbers. Of those callings which had but few followers, several of
the more nearly allied were united into one constituency. Membership of the respective constituencies depended upon the will of the
elector—that is, every elector could get his or her name entered in
the list of any calling with which he or she preferred to vote, and
thus exercise the right of voting for the representative body elected
by the members of that calling.

The highest officers in the twelve branches of the executive were
appointed by the twelve representative bodies ; the appointment of
the other officers was the business of the chiefs of the executive.
In all the more important matters all these had to consult together
beforehand upon the measures that were to be laid before the
representative bodies.

The discussions of the different representative bodies, as a rule,
took place apart, and generally in sessions held at different periods.
Several of the bodies sat permanently, others met merely for a
few days once a year. The numerical strength of these specialist
parliaments was different : the smallest—that for statistics —consisted of no more than thirty members, the four largest of a hundred
and twenty members each. When matters which interested equally
several different representative bodies had to be discussed, the bodies
thus interested sat together. Disputes as to the competency of the
different bodies were impossible, as the mere wish expressed by any
representative body to take part in the debates of another sufficed to
make the subject under consideration a common one.

The natural result of this organisation was that every inhabitant
of Freeland confined his attention to those public affairs which he
understood, or thought he understood. In each branch of the

L

administration he gave his vote to that candidate who in his opinion was the best qualified for a seat in that branch of the administration. And this, again, had as a consequence a fact to Western ideas altogether incredible—namely, that every branch of the public administration was in the hands of the most expert specialists, and the best qualified men in all Freeland. Very soon there was developed a highly remarkable kind of political honour, altogether different from anything known in Western nations. Among the latter, it is held to be a point of honour to stick to one's party unconditionally through thick and thin, to support it by vote and influence whether one understands the particular matter in question or not. The political honour of a citizen of Freeland demands of him yet more positively that he devote his attention and his energy to public affairs; but public opinion condemns him severely if—from whatever motive—he concerns himself with matters which he plainly does not understand. Thus it is strictly required that the elector should have some professional knowledge of that branch of the administration into which he throws the weight of his vote. The elections, therefore, are in very good hands; attempts to influence the electors by fallacious representations or by promises would, even if they were to be made, prove resultless. There is no elector who would vote in the elections of the whole twelve representative bodies. The women, in particular, with very few exceptions, refrain from voting in the elections in which the separate callings are specially concerned; on the other hand, they take a lively interest in the elections in which the electors vote according to residence; and in the elections for the board of education their votes turn the scale. Their passive franchise also comes into play, and in the representative bodies that have charge of maintenance, of art and science, of sanitation and justice, women frequently sit; and in that which has charge of education there are always several women. They never take part in the executive. By way of completing this description, it may be mentioned that the elected deputies are paid for their work at the rate of an equivalent of eight labour-hours for each day that they sit.

After the constituent assembly had passed the constitution it dissolved itself, and the election of the twelve representative bodies was at once proceeded with. Punctually on the 20th of October these bodies met, and the committee handed its authority over into their hands. The members of the committee were all re-elected as heads of the different branches of the administration, except four who declined to take office afresh. The government of Freeland was now definitively constituted.

In the meantime, the three expeditions sent to discover the best route for a railway to the coast had returned. The expedition which had been surveying the shortest route—that through the Dana valley to the Witu coast—had met with no exceptional difficulty as to the land, and the expectation that this, by far the shortest, would prove to be also technically preferable had been verified. Nor in any other respect had any serious difficulty been encountered within about 125 miles from Kenia. But from thence to the coast the Galla tribes offered to the expedition such a stubborn and vicious opposition that the hostilities had not ceased at the end of two months, and several conflicts had taken place, in which the Galla tribes had always been severely punished; but this did not prevent the expedition from having to carry out its thoroughly peaceful mission in perpetual readiness to fight. A railway through that region would have had to be preceded by a formal campaign for the pacification or expulsion of the Galla tribes, and could then have been constructed only in the midst of a permanent preparedness for war. This route had therefore, provisionally at least, to be rejected.

There were not less weighty reasons against the route over Ukumbani along the Athi river. Along the river-valley the road could have been made without special technical difficulty, but, particularly on the second half of it, the route lay through unhealthy swamps and jungles, which could not immediately be brought under cultivation. And if a route were chosen which would leave the valley proper and pass among the adjoining hills, the technical conditions would not be more favourable, nor the estimated cost less, than a line along the third route following the old road to Mombasa. This third route was therefore unanimously fixed upon. It had in its favour the important circumstance that it passed through friendly districts, which at no very distant future would most probably be settled by Freeland colonists. That it was the longest and the most expensive of the three could not, therefore, prevent us from giving it the preference, unless the difference in cost proved to be too great —which, as the event showed, was not the case.

The work was begun forthwith. Powerful and novel machines

of all kinds were, in the meantime, constructed in great number by
our Freeland machine-factories, and, furnished with these, 5,000
Freeland and 8,000 negro workers began the work at eighteen different points, not including the eleven longer and the thirty-two
shorter tunnels—with a total length of twenty-four miles—each
of which formed a separate part of the work. The rails, of the best
Bessemer metal, were partly made by ourselves, and were partly
—those for the distance between Mombasa and Taveta—brought
from Europe. Two years after the turning of the first sod the part
between Eden Vale and Ngongo was ready for traffic; three months
later the part between Mombasa and Taveta; and nine months later
still the middle portion between Ngongo and Taveta. Thus exactly
five years after our pioneers had first set foot in Freeland, the first
locomotive, which the day before had seen the waves of the Indian
Ocean breaking upon the shore at Mombasa, greeted the glaciers of
the Kenia with its shrill whistle.

That this extensive work could be completed in so short a time
and with so little expenditure of labour we owed to our machinery;
which also enabled us to keep the cost within comparatively moderate
limits, despite the fact that we had necessarily to pay our workers at
a rate at which no railway constructors were ever paid before. Our
Freeland railway constructors, who had at once formed themselves
into a number of associations, earned in the first year 22s. a day
each, and in the third year 28s. a day, though they worked only seven
hours a day. Notwithstanding this, the whole 672 miles, most of it
tolerably difficult work through hills, cost only 9,500,000l., or a little
over 14,000l. per mile. Our 13,000 workers did more with their
magnificent labour-sparing machines than 100,000 ordinary workers
could have done with pick and barrow; and the employment of this
colossal 'capital'—valued at 4,000,000l.—was profitable because
labour was paid at so high a rate.

As a matter of course, a telegraph was laid between Eden Vale
and Mombasa together with this double-railed railway.

Whilst these works were in progress and the incessantly growing population of Freeland was brought into closer connection with
the old home, important changes had been brought about in our
relations with our native African neighbours—changes in part
pacific, in part warlike, and which exercised a not less important
influence upon the course of development of our commonwealth.

In the first place, the Masai of Lykipia and the lake districts between Naivasha and Baringo, had, at their own initiative and at their own cost, though under the direction of some of our engineers, constructed a good waggon-road, 236 miles long, through their whole district from the Naivasha lake northwards, and then eastwards through Lykipia as far as Eden Vale. They declared that their honour and their pride were offended by having to pass through a foreign district when they wished to visit us, the only practicable road having been one through the country of the Wa-Kikuyu. So strong was their desire to be in immediate touch with our district that, when a part of the hired Wa-Taveta road-makers, on account of some misunderstanding, left them in the lurch, the Masai themselves took their places, and, taking turns to the number of 3,000, they carried on the work with an energy which no cne could have supposed to be possible in a people who not long before had been so averse to labour. We decided to reward this proof of strong attachment and of great capacity by an equally striking act of recognition. When the Masai road was finished, and a deputation of the elders and leaders of all the tribes made a jubilant and triumphant entry by it into Eden Vale, we received them with great honour, and gave them presents for the whole Masai people which were worth about as much as the new road had cost. In addition, the 6,500 Werndl rifles, which had hitherto been only lent to the Masai, and 2,000 horses were given them as their own property in token of our friendship and respect. It goes without saying that the weapons were received by this still martial people with great enthusiasm. And the horses were almost more valuable still in their eyes ; for riding was the one among all our arts which the Masai most admired, and among all our possessions which they esteemed most highly were our horses. But we had hitherto been very frugal with our horses, and we had given away only a few to individual natives in Masailand and Taveta in recognition of special services. Tho number of horses in Freeland had, partly by breeding, but mainly by continuous systematic importation, increased during the first two years to 26,000 ; but we expected at first to make more use of horses than was afterwards found to be necessary, and that was the reason why this noble animal, which we had been the first to establish in Equatorial Africa, was still a much-admired rarity everywhere outside of Freeland, particularly in Masailand, where the horse was regarded as the ideal of martial valour.

In the second place, it should be mentioned that the civilisation of the Masai, as well as of the other tribes in alliance with us, made rapid progress. The *el-moran*, when once they had become accustomed to light work, and had given up their inactive camp-life, allowed themselves to be induced by us to enter early upon the married state. Our women succeeded in uprooting the Ditto abuse. Several of the ladies, with Mrs. Ney at their head, undertook a tour through Masailand, and offered to every Masai girl who made a solemn promise of chastity until marriage, admission into a Freeland family for a year, and instruction in our manners, customs, and various forms of skilled labour. So great was the number who accepted this offer, that they could not all be received into Freeland at once, but had to be divided into three yearly groups. Yet even those who could not be immediately received were decorated with the insignia of their new honour—a complete dress after the Freeland pattern, their barbarian wire neck-bands, leg-chains, and ear-stretchers, as well as their coating of grease, being discarded—and they were solemnly pronounced to be ' friends of the white women.' So permanent was the influence of this distinction upon the Masai girls, who had not given up their ambition along with their licentious habits, that not one of them proved to be unworthy of the friendship of the virtuous white ladies. The Masai youth were so zealous in their efforts to win the favour of the girls who were thus distinguished, that the latter were all very soon married. That at the end of the year there was an eager competition for the girls who were returning home is as much a matter of course as that those who in the meantime had married, even if they had had children, had not forfeited their right to a residence in Freeland—a circumstance that led to not a few embarrassments. The ultimate result was that in a very short time the once so licentious Masailand was changed into a model country of good morals. The hitherto prevalent polygamy died out, and several hundred good schools arose in different parts of the country, which in that way made gigantic strides towards complete civilisation.

In the meantime, in the north-west, among our Kavirondo friends on the north shore of the Victoria Nyanza, events of another kind were preparing. The Kavirondo, a very numerous and peaceable agricultural and pastoral tribe, touched Uganda, where, during recent years, there had been many internal struggles and revolutions. Unlike the other peoples whom we have become acquainted with, and who lived in independent, loosely connected, small tribes under freely elected chiefs with little influence, the Wangwana (the name of the inhabitants of Uganda) have been for centuries united into a great despotically governed State under a *kabaka* or emperor. Their kingdom, whose original part stretches along the north bank of the Victoria Nyanza, has been of varying dimensions, according as the fierce policy of conquest of the *kabaka* for the time being was more or less successful ; but Uganda has always been a scourge to all its neighbours, who have suffered from the ceaseless raids, extortions, and cruelties of the Wangwana. Broad and fertile stretches of country became desert under this plague ; and as for many years the *kabaka* had been able, by means of Arab dealers, to get possession of a few thousand (though very miserable) guns, and a few cannons (with which latter he had certainly not been able to effect much for want of suitable ammunition), the dread of the cruel robber State grew very great. Just at the time of our arrival at the Kenia there was an epoch of temporary calm, because the Wangwana were too much occupied with their own internal quarrels to pay much attention to their neighbours. After the death of the last *kabaka* his numerous sons terribly devastated the country by their ferocious struggles for the rule, until in the previous year one of the rivals who was named Suna (after an ancestor renowned both for his cruelty and for his conquests) had got rid of most of his brothers by treachery. The power was thenceforward concentrated more and more in the hands of this *kabaka*, and the raids and extortions among the neighbouring tribes at once recommenced. Suna's anger was directed particularly against the Kavirondo, because these had allowed one of his brothers, who had fled to them, to escape, instead of having delivered him up. Repeatedly had several thousand Wangwana fallen upon the Kavirondo, carried off men and cattle, burnt villages, cut down the bananas, destroyed the harvests, and thus inflicted inhuman cruelty. In their necessity the Kavirondo appealed to the northern Masai tribes for help. They had heard that we had supplied the Masai with guns and horses ; and they now begged the Masai to send a troop of warriors with European equipments to guard their Uganda frontier. As payment, they promised to give to every Masai warrior who came to their aid a liberal maintenance and an ox monthly, and to every horseman two oxen.

Less on account of this offer than to gratify their love of adventure, the Masai, having first consulted us in Freeland, consented. We saw no sufficient reason to keep them from rendering this assistance, although we were by no means so certain as to the result as were our neighbours, who considered themselves invincible now they were in possession of their new weapons. We offered to place several experienced white leaders at the head of the troops they sent to Kavirondo ; but as we saw that our martial friends looked upon this as a sign of distrust and were a little displeased at the offer, we simply warned them to be cautious, and particularly not to be wasteful of the ammunition they took with them.

At first everything went well. Wherever the Wangwana marauders showed themselves they were sent home with bleeding heads, even when they appeared in large numbers ; and after a few months it seemed almost as if these severe lessons had induced the Wangwana to leave the Kavirondo alone in future, for a long time passed without any further raids. But suddenly, when we were busy getting in our October harvest, there reached us the startling news of a dreadful catastrophe which had befallen our Masai friends in Kavirondo. The *kabaka* Suna had only taken time to prepare for an annihilating blow. While the former raids had been made by bodies of only a few thousand men, this time Suna had collected 30,000, of whom 5,000 bore muskets; and, placing himself at their head, he had with these fallen upon the Kavirondo and Masai unexpectedly. He surprised a frontier-camp of 900 Masai with 300 horses when they were asleep, and cut them to pieces before they had time to recover from their surprise. The Masai thus not only lost more than a third of their number, but the remainder of them were divided into two independent parts, for the surprised camp was in the middle of the cordon. But, instead of hastily retreating and waiting until the remaining force had been able to unite before taking the offensive, one of the Masai leaders, as soon as he had hurriedly got some 500 men together, was led by his rage at the overthrow of so many of his comrades to make a foolhardy attack upon the enormously over-numbering force of the enemy; he thereby fell into an ambush, and, after having too rashly shot away all his cartridges, was, together with his men, so fearfully cut down that, after a most heroic resistance, only a very few escaped. Our friend Mdango, who now took the command, was able to collect only 1,100 or 1,200 Masai on the other wing ; and with these he succeeded in making a tolerably orderly retreat into the interior of Kavirondo, being but little molested by Suna, whose eye was kept mainly fixed upon collecting the colossal booty.

Our ultimatum was despatched to Suna on the very day on which we received this sad news. We told the Masai, who offered to send the whole body of their warriors against Uganda, that 1,000 men, in addition to the 1,200 at present in Kavirondo, would be sufficient. We placed these 2,200 Masai under our Freeland officers, chose from among ourselves 900 volunteers, including 500 horsemen, and added twelve cannons and sixteen rockets, together with thirty elephants. On the 24th of October Johnston, the leader of this campaign, started for Kavirondo along the Masai road.

There he found, around the camp of the *el-moran*—now, when it was too late, very carefully entrenched and guarded—unnumbered thousands of Kavirondo and Nangi, armed with spear and bow. These he sent home as a useless crowd. On the 10th of November he crossed the Uganda frontier ; six days later Suna was totally overthrown in a brief engagement near the Ripon falls, his host of 110,000 men scattered to the winds, and he himself, with a few thousand of his bodyguard armed with muskets and officered by Arabs from the coast, taken prisoner.

On the second day after the fight our men occupied Rubaga, the capital of Uganda. Thither came in rapid succession all the chief men of the country, promising unconditional submission and ready to agree to any terms we might offer. But Johnston offered to receive them into the great alliance between us and the other native nations—an offer which the Wangwana naturally accepted with the greatest joy. The conditions laid upon them were: emancipation of all slaves, peaceful admission of Freeland colonists and teachers, and reparation for all the injury they had done to the Kavirondo and the Masai. In this last respect the Wangwana people suffered nothing, for the countless herds of cattle belonging to their *kabaka* which had fallen into our hands as booty amply sufficed to re-place what had been stolen from the Kavirondo and as indemnity for the slain Kavirondo and Masai warriors. Suna himself was carried away as prisoner, and interned on the banks of the Naivasha lake.

The subsequent pacific relations were uninterrupted except by an isolated attempt at resistance by the Arabs that had been left in the country; but this was promptly and vigorously put down by the Wangwana themselves without any need of our intervention. What contributed largely to inspire respect in the breasts of the Wangwana were a military road which the Kavirondo and Nangi constructed from the Victoria Nyanza to the Masai road on the Baringo lake, and a Masai colony of 3,000 *el-moran* on the Kavirondo and Uganda frontier. But on the whole, after the battle at the Ripon falls, the mere sound of our name was sufficient to secure peace and quiet in this part also of the interior of Equatorial Africa. All round the Victoria Nyanza, whose shores from time immemorial had been the theatre of savage, merciless fighting, humane sentiments and habits gradually prevailed; and as a consequence a considerable degree of material prosperity was developed with comparative rapidity among what had previously been the wildest tribes.

Even apart from its size, the Victoria Nyanza is the most important among the enormous lakes of Central Africa. It covers an area of more than 20,000 square miles, and is therefore, with the exception of the Caspian, the Sea of Aral, and the group of large lakes in North America, the largest piece of inland water in the world. It is larger than the whole of the kingdom of Bavaria, and its depth is proportionate to its size, for the plummet in places does not touch the ground until it has sunk 250 fathoms; it lies 4,400 feet above the sea-level—more than 650 feet above the Brocken, the highest hill in Middle Germany. This lake is nearly encircled by ranges of hills which rise from 1,500 to 5,000 feet above its surface; so that the climate of the immediately contiguous country, which is healthy without exception and quite free from swamp, is everywhere temperate, and in some districts positively Arcadian. And this magnificent, picturesque, and in many places highly romantic lake is the basin source of the sacred Nile, which, leaving it at the extreme northern end by the Ripon falls, flows thence to the Albert Nyanza, which is 1,500 feet lower, and thence continues its course as the White Nile.

Two months after we had established ourselves in Kavirondo and

Uganda a screw steamer of 500 tons burden was ploughing the sea-like waves of the Victoria Nyanza, and before the end of the next year our lake flotilla consisted of five ships. These were well received everywhere on the coast, and the brisk commerce created by them proved to be one of the most effective of civilising agencies. The fertility of the lands surrounding this splendid lake is positively unbounded. A few hundred square yards of well-watered ground are sufficient to supply the needs of a large family ; and when we had once instructed the natives in the use of agricultural implements, the abundance of the choicest field and garden produce was unexampled. But the growth of higher needs, particularly among the tribes that dwelt on the western shores of the lake, remained for a long time remarkably behind the improvement in the means of production. These simple tribes produced more than sufficient to supply their wants, almost without any expenditure of labour, and often out of mere curiosity to see the results of the improved implements which had been furnished to them. As they had no conception of property in land, and the non-utilisable over-production could not, therefore, with them—as would unquestionably have happened elsewhere—beget misery among the masses, here for years together the fable of the Castle of Indolence became a reality. The idea of property was almost lost, the necessities of life became valueless, everyone could take as much of them as he wished to have ; strangers travelling through found everywhere a well-spread table ; in short, the Golden Age seemed about to come to the Victoria Nyanza. This absolute lack of a sense of higher needs, however, proved to be a check to further progress, and we took pains —not altogether without regret—so far to disturb this paradisiacal condition as to endeavour to excite in the tribes a taste for what they had not got. Our endeavours succeeded, but the success was long in coming. With the advent of more strongly felt needs a higher morality and intellectual culture at once took root in this corner of the earth.

CHAPTER XII

ONE of the principal tasks of the Freeland government, and one in which, as a rule, the ministries for art and science and for public works co-operated, was the thorough investigation and survey of

our new home: first of the narrower district of the Kenia, and
then of the neighbouring regions with which we were continually
coming into closer relationship. The orographic and hydrographic
systems of the whole country were determined; the soil and the
climate were minutely examined. In doing this, both the higher
scientific standpoint and that of prosaic utility were kept in view.
For scientific purposes there was constructed an accurate map of
the whole of the Masai and Kikuyu territories, showing most of the
geographical details. All the more prominent eminences were
measured and ascended, the Kenia not excepted.

The view from the Kenia is magnificent above measure ; but,
apart from the mountain itself and its glaciers, it offers little variety.
In a circle, as far as the eye can reach, spreads a most fertile country,
intersected by numerous watercourses, which nowhere, except in a
great trough-like basin of about 1,900 square miles in extent in the
north-west, give rise to swamps. The most striking feature of the
whole region is the tableland falling away in a number of terraces,
and broken by the shoulders of massive hills. The foot-hills proper
of the Kenia begin with the highest terrace, where they form a
girdle of varying breadth and height around the central mass of the
mountain, which rises with a steep abrupt outline. This central
mass, at a height of from 16,000 to 18,000 feet, bears a number of
gigantic glacier-fields, from the midst of which the peak rises
abruptly, flanked at some distance by a yet steeper, but small,
horn.

A very different character marks the next in importance of the
mountain-formations that belong to the district of Freeland—namely,
the Aberdare range, about forty-five miles west of the Kenia, and
stretching from north to south a distance of more than sixty miles,
with an average breadth of twelve and a-half miles. The highest peak
of this chain reaches nearly 15,000 feet above the sea ; and while the
Kenia everywhere bears an impress of grandeur, a ravishing loveliness
is the great characteristic of the Aberdare landscapes. It is true that
here also are not wanting colossal hills that produce an overwhelming impression, but the chief peculiarity is the charming variety of
romantic billowy-outlined hills, intermingled with broad valleys,
covered in part with luxuriant but not too dense forests, in part
spreading out into emerald flowery pastures everywhere watered
by numberless crystal-clear brooks and rivers, lakes and pools,

This mountain-district of nearly 800 square miles resembles a magnificent park, from whose eminences the mighty snow-sea of the Kenia is visible to the east, and the emerald-and-sapphire sheen of the great Masai lakes—Naivasha, El-Meteita, and Nakuro—to the west. And this marvellously lovely landscape, which combines all the charms of Switzerland and India, bears in the bosom of its hills immense mineral treasures. Here, and not at the Kenia, as our geologists soon discovered, was the future seat of the Freeland industry, particularly of the metallurgic industry. Beds of coal which in extent and quality at least equalled the best of England, magnetite containing from fifty to seventy per cent. of iron, copper, lead, bismuth, antimony, sulphur in rich veins, a large bed of rock-salt on the western declivity just above the salt lake of Nakuro, and a number of other mineral treasures, were discovered in rapid succession, and the most accessible of them were at once taken advantage of. In particular, the newly opened copper-mines had a heavy demand made upon their resources when the telegraph was laid to the coast ; the demand was still heavier as electricity became more and more largely used as a motive force.

For great changes had meantime taken place at the Kenia. Newcomers continued to arrive in greater and greater numbers. At the close of the fourth year the population of Freeland had risen to 780,000 souls. A great part of Eden Vale had become a city of villas, which covered forty square miles and contained 58,000 dwelling-houses, whose 270,000 occupants devoted themselves to gardening, industrial, or intellectual pursuits. The population of the Dana plateau had risen to 140,000, who, besides cultivating what land was still available there for agriculture, gave by far the greater part of their attention to various kinds of industries. The main part of the agriculture had been transferred to a plain some 650 feet lower down, beyond the zone of forest. This lower plateau extended, with occasional breaks, round the whole of the mountain, and offered in its 3,000 square miles of fertile soil abundant agricultural ground for the immediate future.

Here some 240,000 acres were at first brought under the plough after they had—like all the cultivated ground in Freeland—been protected against the visits of wild animals by a strong timber fence. The smaller game, which could not be kept away from the seed by fencing, had respect for the dogs, of which many were bred and trained to keep watch at the fences as well as to guard the cattle. This protection was amply sufficient to keep away all the creatures that would have meddled with the seed, except the monkeys, some of which had occasionally to be shot when, in their nocturnal raids, they refused to be frightened away by the furious barking of the four-footed guardians.

Steam was still provisionally employed as motive power in agriculture; but provision was being made on a very large scale to substitute electric for steam force. The motive power for the electric dynamos was derived from the Dana river where, after being supplemented by two large streams from the hills just below the great waterfall, it was broken into a series of strong rapids and cataracts as it hurried down to the lower land. These rapids and cataracts were at the lower end of the tableland which, as indicative of the use we made of it, we named Cornland. It was these rapids and smaller cataracts, and not the great waterfall of 300 feet, that were utilised for agricultural purposes. These afforded a total fall of 870 feet; and, as the river here already had a great body of water, it was possible, by a well-arranged combination of turbines and electro-motors, to obtain a total force of from 500,000 to 600,000 horse-power. This was far more than could be required for the cultivation of the whole of Cornland even in the intensest manner. The provision made for the next year was calculated at 40,000 horse-power. Well-isolated strong copper wires were to convey the force generated by twenty gigantic turbines in two hundred dynamos to its several destinations, where it had to perform all the labours of agriculture, from ploughing to the threshing, dressing, and transport of the corn. · For a network of electrical railways was also a part of this system of agricultural mechanism.

The great Dana cataract, with what was calculated to be a force of 124,000 horse-power, was utilised for the purposes of electric lighting in Eden Vale and in the town on the Dana plateau. For the time being, for the public lighting it sufficed to erect 5,000 contact-lamps a little more than 100 feet high, and each having a lighting power of 2,000 candles. These used up a force of 12,000 horse-power. For lighting dwelling-houses and isolated or night-working factories, 420,000 incandescent-lamps were employed. This required a force of 40,000 horse-power; so that the great cataract had to supply a force of 52,000 horse-power to the electro-

motors. This was employed during the day as the motive power
of a net of railways, with a total length of a little over 200 miles,
which traversed the principal streets and roads in the Dana plateau
and Eden Vale. In the evening and at night, when the electricity
was used for lighting purposes, the railways had to be worked by
dynamos of several thousand horse-power. In this way altogether
nearly two-fifths of the available force was called into requisition at
the close of the fifth year ; the remaining three-fifths remained for
the time unemployed, and formed a reserve for future needs.

The fourth and fifth years of Freeland were also marked by the
construction of a net of canals and aqueducts, both for Eden Vale
and for the Dana plateau. The canals served merely to carry the
storm-water into the Dana ; whilst the refuse-water and the sewage
were carried away in cast-iron pipes by means of a system of pneu-
matic exhaust-tubes, and then disinfected and utilised as manure.
The aqueducts were connected with the best springs in the upper hills,
and possessed a provisional capacity of supplying 22,000,000 gallons
daily, and were used for supplying a number of public wells, as well
as all the private houses. By the addition of fresh sources this
supply was in a short period doubled and trebled. At the same
time all the streets were macadamised ; so that the cleanliness and
health of the young towns were duly cared for in all respects.

The board of education had made no less vigorous efforts. A
public opinion had grown up that the youth of Freeland, without
distinction of sex and without reference to future callings, ought to
enjoy an education which, with the exception of the knowledge of
Greek and Latin, should correspond to that obtainable, for example,
in the six first classes in a German gymnasium. Accordingly, boys
and girls were to attend school from the age of six to that of sixteen
years, and, after acquiring the elements, were to be taught grammar,
the history of literature, general history, the history of civilisation,
physics, natural history, geometry, and algebra.

Not less importance was attached to physical education than to
intellectual and moral. Indeed, it was a principle in Freeland that
physical education should have precedence, since a healthy,
harmoniously developed mind presupposed a healthy harmoniously
developed body. Moreover, in the cultivation of the intellect less
stress was laid upon the accumulation of knowledge than upon the
stimulation of the young mind to independent thought; therefore

nothing was more anxiously and carefully avoided than over-pressure
of mental work. No child was to be engaged in mental work—home
preparation included—longer than at most six hours a day; hence
the hours of teaching of any mental subject were limited to three a
day, whilst two other school hours were devoted daily to physical
exercises—gymnastics, running, dancing, swimming, riding; and
for boys, in addition, fencing, wrestling, and shooting. A further
principle in Freeland education was that the children should not
be *forced* into activity any more than the adults. We held that a
properly directed logical system of education, not confined to the
use of a too limited range of means, could scarcely fail to bring the
pliable mind of childhood to a voluntary and eager fulfilment of
reasonably allotted duties. And experience justified our opinion.
Our mode of instruction had to be such as would make school exceedingly attractive ; but, when this had been achieved, our boys and
girls learnt in half the time as much, and that as thoroughly, as the
physically and intellectually maltreated European boys and girls of
the same age. For health's sake, the teaching was carried on out
of doors as much as possible. With this in view, the schools were
built either in large gardens or on the border of the forest, and the
lessons in natural history were regularly, and other lessons frequently,
given in connection with excursions into the neighbourhood. Consequently our school children presented a different appearance from
that we had been accustomed to see in our old home, and especially
in its great cities. Rosy faces and figures full of robust health,
vigour, and the joy of living, self-reliance, and strong intelligence
were betrayed by every mien and every movement. Thus were
our children equipped for entering upon the serious duties of
life.

Naturally such a system of instruction demanded a very
numerous and highly gifted staff of teachers. In Freeland there
was on an average one teacher to every fifteen scholars, and the
best intelligence in the land was secured for the teaching profession
by the payment of high salaries. For the first four classes, which
were taught chiefly by young women—single or widowed—the
salaries ranged from 1,400 to 1,800 labour-hour equivalents ; for the
other six classes from 1,800 to 2,400. In the fifth year of the
settlement these salaries, reckoned in money, amounted to from
350*l.* to 600*l.*

But even such a demand for high intelligence Freeland was determined to meet out of its own resources. In the third year, therefore, a high school was founded, in which all those branches of knowledge were taught which in Europe can be learnt at the universities, academies, and technical colleges. All the faculties were endowed with a liberality of which those outside of Freeland can have scarcely any conception. Our observatories, laboratories, and museums had command of almost unlimited means, and no stipend was too high to attract and retain a brilliant teacher. The same held good of the technical, and not less of the agricultural and commercial, professorial chairs and apparatus for teaching in our high school. The instruction in all faculties was absolutely untrammelled, and, like that in the lower schools, gratuitous. In the fifth year of the settlement the high school had 7,500 students, the number of its chairs was 215; its annual budget reached as high as 2,500,000*l.*, and was rapidly increasing.

The means for all this enormous outlay was furnished in rich abundance by the tax levied on the total income of all producers; for this income grew amazingly under the double influence of the increasing population and the increasing productiveness of labour. When the railway to the coast was finished and its results had begun to make themselves felt, the value of the average profit of a labour-hour quickly rose to 6*s.*; and as at this time, the end of the fifth year in Freeland, 280,000 workers were productively engaged for an average of six hours a day—that is, for 1,800 hours in the year—the total value of the profit of labour that year in Freeland amounted to 280,000 × 1,800 × 6*s.*—that is, to a round sum of 150,000,000*l.* Of this the commonwealth reserved thirty-five per cent. as tax—that is, in round figures, 52,500,000*l.*; and this was the source from which, after meeting the claims for the maintenance allowances—which certainly absorbed more than half—all the expenses it was held desirable to indulge in were defrayed.

In fact, the growth of revenue was so certain and had reached such large proportions that, at the end of the fifth year, the executive resolved to place before the representative bodies, meeting together for the purpose, two measures of great importance : first, to make the granting of credits to the associations independent of the central authority ; and, secondly, to return the free contributions

M

of the members who had already joined, and in future to accept no such contributions.

For the reasons given in the eighth chapter, the amount and order of the loans for productive purposes had hitherto been dependent upon the decision of the central authority. The stock of capitalistic aids to labour, and consequently the productive means of the community, had now, however, reached such a stage as to make any limit to the right of free and independent decision by the workers themselves quite unnecessary. The associations might ask for whatever they thought would be useful to themselves, the capital of the country being considered equal to any demands that could be reasonably anticipated. And this confidence in the resources of Freeland proved to be well grounded. It is true that twice, in the years that immediately followed this resolution, it happened that, in consequence of unexpectedly large demands for capital, the portion of the public revenue used for that purpose considerably exceeded the normal proportion; but, thanks to the constant increase in all the profits of production, this was borne without the slightest inconvenience. Later, the reserves in the hands of the commonwealth sufficed to remove even this element of fluctuation from the relations between the demand for capital and the public revenue.

On the other hand, this resolution called forth a remarkable attempt to swindle the commonwealth by means of the absolute freedom with which loans were granted. In America a syndicate of speculative 'men of business' was formed for the purpose of exploiting the simple-minded credulity of us 'stupid Freelanders.' Their plan was to draw as large a sum as possible from our central bank under the pretence of requiring it to found an association. Forty-six of the cleverest and most unscrupulous Yankees joined in this campaign against our pockets. What they meant to do, and how far they succeeded, can be best shown by giving the narrative written by their leader, who is at present the honoured manager of the great saltworks on the Nakuro lake:

'After we had arrived in Eden Vale, we decided to try the ground before we proceeded to execute our design. We noticed, to our great satisfaction, that the mistrust of the Freelanders would give us very little trouble. The hotel in which we put up supplied us with everything on credit, and no one took the trouble to ask who we were. When I remarked to the host in a paternal tone that it was a very careless procedure to keep a pump indiscriminately free to any stroller who might come along, the host—I mean the director of the Eden Vale Hotel Association—laughed and said there was no fear of anyone's running away, for no one, whoever he might be, ever thought of leaving Freeland. " So far, so good," thought I ; but I asked further what the Hotel Association would do if a guest *could* not pay ? "Nonsense," said the director; "here everyone can pay as soon as he begins to work." " And if he can't work ? " "Then he gets a maintenance allowance from the commonwealth." " And if he won't work ? " The man smiled, slapped me on the shoulder, and said, " Won't work won't last long here, you may rely upon it. Besides, if one who has sound limbs *will* be lazy—well, he still gets bed and board among us. So don't trouble yourself about paying your score ; you may pay when you can and will."

'He made a curious impression upon us, this director. We said nothing, but resolved to sound these Freelanders further. We went into the great warehouses to get clothes, linen, &c., on credit. It succeeded admirably. The salesmen—they were clerks, as we found—asked for a draft on the central bank ; and when we replied that we had no account there as yet, they said it did not matter—it would be sufficient if we gave a written statement of the amount of our purchases, and the bank, when we had an account there, would honour it. It was the same everywhere. Mackay or Gould cannot get credit in New York more readily than we did in Freeland.

'After a few days, we began to take steps towards establishing our association. As I have said, we had at first no fear of exciting distrust. But it was inconvenient that the Freeland constitution insisted upon publicity in connection with every act, date, and circumstance connected with business. We knew that we had nothing to fear from police or courts of justice ; but what should we do if the Freeland public were to acquire a taste for the proposed association and wish to join it ? Naturally we could not admit outsiders as partners, but must keep the thing to ourselves, otherwise our plan would be spoilt. We tried to find out if there were any means of limiting the number of participators in our scheme. We minutely questioned well-informed Freelanders upon the subject. We complained of the abominable injustice of being compelled to share with everybody the benefit of the splendid "idea" which we had conceived, to reveal our business secrets, and so forth. But it was all of no use. The Freelanders remained callous upon this point. They told us that no one would force us to reveal our secrets if we were willing to work them out with our own resources; but if we needed Freeland land and Freeland capital, then of course all Freeland must know what we wanted to do. "And if our business can employ only a small number of workers—if, for example, the goods that we wish to make, though they yield a great profit, yet have a very limited market—must we also in such a case let everybody come in ?" "In such a case," was the answer, "Freeland workers will not be so stupid as to force themselves upon you in great numbers." "Good!" cried I, with dissembled anger; "but if more should come in than are needed ?" The people had an answer even to this; for they said that those workers that were not needed would withdraw, or, if they remained, they would have to work fewer hours, or work in turns, or do something of that sort; opportunity of making profitable use of spare time was never lacking in Freeland.

'What was to be done? We should be obliged to give our plans such a character as to prevent the Freeland workers from having any wish to share in them. But this must not be done too clumsily, as the people would after all smell a rat, or perhaps join us out of pure philanthropy, in order to save us from the consequences of our folly. We ultimately decided to set up a needle-factory. Such a factory would be obviously—in the then condition of trade—unprofitable, but the scheme was not so absolutely romantic as to bring the inquisitive about our necks. We therefore organised ourselves, and had the satisfaction of having no partners except a couple of simpletons who, for some reason or other, fancied that needle-making was a good business; and it was not very difficult to get rid of these two. The next thing was to fix the amount of capital to be required for the business—that is, the amount of credit we should ask for at the central bank. We should very naturally have preferred to ask at once for a million pounds sterling; but that we could not do, as we should have to state what we needed the money for, and a needle-factory for forty-eight workers could not possibly have swallowed up so much without bringing upon us a whole legion of investigating critics in the form of working partners. So we limited our demand to 180,000*l*., and even this amount excited some surprise; but we explained our demand by asserting that the new machines which we intended to use were very dear.

'But now came the main anxiety. How were we to get this 180,000*l*., or the greater part of it, into our pockets? Our people had elected me director of the first "Eden Vale Needle-factory Association," and, as such, I went the next day into the bank to open our account there and to obtain all the necessary information. The cashier assured me that all payments authorised by me should be at once made; but when I asked for a "small advance" of a few thousand pounds, he asked in astonishment what was to be done with it. "We must pay our small debts." "Unnecessary," was his answer; "all debts are discharged here through the bank." "Yes, but what are my people and I to live upon in the mean time, until our factory begins to work?" I asked with some heat. "Upon your work in other undertakings, or upon your savings, if you have any. Besides, you cannot fail to get credit; but we, the central bank, give merely productive credit—we cannot advance to you what you consume."

'There we were with nothing but our credit for 180,000*l*., and we began to perceive that it was not so easy to carry off the money. Certainly we could build and give orders for what we pleased. But what good would it do us to spend money upon useless things?

'The worst was that we should have to begin to work in earnest if we would not after all excite a general distrust; so we joined different undertakings. But we would not admit that we were beaten, and after mature reflection I hit upon the following as the only possible method of carrying out the swindle we had planned. The central bank was the channel through which all purchases and sales were made, but, as I soon detected, did not interfere in the least with the buyer or the person who ordered goods in the choice of such goods as he might think suitable. We had, therefore, the right to order the machinery for our needle-factory of any manufacturers we pleased in Europe or America, and the central bank would pay for it. We, therefore, merely had to act in conjunction with some European or American firm of swindlers, and share the profits with them, in order to carry off a rich booty.

' At the same time, it occurred to me that it would be infinitely
stupid to make use of such a method. It was quite plain that very
little was to be gained in that way ; but, even if it had been possible
for each of us to embezzle a fortune, I had lost all desire to leave
Freeland. The chances were that I should be a loser by leaving.
I was a novice at honest work, and any special exertion was not
then to my taste. Yet I had earned as much as 12s. a day, and
that is 180l. a year, with which one can live as well here as with
twice as much in America or England. Even if I continued to work
in the same way, merely enough to keep off *ennui*, my income
would very soon increase. In the worst case, I could live upon my
earnings here as well as 400l. or 500l. would enable me to live
elsewhere ; and there was not the slightest prospect of being able to
steal so much. The result was that I declined to go away. Firstly,
because I was very happy here ; intercourse with decent men was
becoming more and more pleasant and attractive to the scoundrel,
which I then was ; and then—it struck me as rather comical—I
began to get ashamed of my roguery. Even scoundrels have their
honour. In the other parts of the world, where *everyone* fleeces
his neighbour if he can, I did not think myself worse than the so-
called honest people : the only difference was that I did not adhere
so closely to the law. There, all are engaged in hunting down
their dear neighbours ; that I allowed myself to hunt without my
chart did not trouble my conscience much, especially as I only had
the alternative of hunting or being hunted. But here in Freeland no
one hunted for his neighbour's goods ; here every rogue must confess
himself to be worse than all the rest, and indeed a rascal without
necessity, out of pure delight in rascality. If one only had the spur
of danger which in the outer world clothed this hunting with so
much poetry ! But here there was not a trace of it ! The Freelanders would not even have pursued us if we had bolted with our
embezzled booty ; we might have run off as unmolested as so many
mangy dogs. No ; here I neither would nor could be a rascal. I
called my companions together to tell them that I resigned my
position as director, withdrew altogether from the company, and
meant to devote myself here to honest work. There was not one
who did not agree with me. Some of them were not quite reconciled to work, but they all meant to remain. One specially persistent
fellow asked whether, as we were once more together by ourselves,

and might not be so again, it would not be a smart trick if we were to embezzle a few thousand pounds before we became honest folks; but it did not even need a reference to the individual responsibility of the members of the association for the debts that the association contracted in order to dispose of the proposition of this last adherent to our former rascality. Not only would they all stay here, but they would become honest—these hardened rogues, who a few weeks before were wont to use the words *honest* and *stupid* as synonyms. So it came to pass that the fine plan, in devising which the " smartest fellows " of New England had exhausted their invention, was silently dropped; and, if I am well informed, not one of the forty-six of us has ever uttered a complaint.'

The second proposal brought before the united representatives of Freeland—the repayment of the larger or smaller contributions which most of the members had up to then paid on admission into the Society—involved the disbursement of not less than 43,000,000*l*. The members had always been told that their contributions were not repayable, but were to be a sacrifice towards the attainment of the objects of the Society. Nevertheless, the government of Freeland considered that now, when the new commonwealth no longer needed such a sacrifice, it was only just to dispense with it, both prospectively and retrospectively. The generous benefactors had never based any claim to special recognition or higher honour upon the assistance they had so richly afforded to the poorer members; in fact, most of them had even refused to be recognised as benefactors. Neither was this assistance in any way inconsistent with the principles upon which the new community was founded; on the contrary, it was quite in harmony with those principles that the assistance afforded by the wealthy to the helpless should be regarded as based upon sound rational self-interest. But when the time had come when, as a consequence of this so generously practised rational egoism, the commonwealth was strong enough to dispense with extraneous aids, and to repay what had been already given, it seemed to us just that this should be done.

This proposal was unanimously accepted without debate, and immediately carried into execution. All the contributors received back their contributions—that is, the amounts were placed to their credit in the books of the central bank, and they could dispose of them as they pleased.

With this, the second epoch of the history of Freeland may be regarded as closed. The founding of the commonwealth, which occupied the first epoch, was effected entirely by the voluntary sacrifices of the individual members. In the second period, this aid, though no longer absolutely necessary, was a useful and effective means of promoting the rapid growth of the commonwealth. Henceforth, grown to be a giant, this free commonwealth rejected all aid of whatever kind that did not spring out of its regular resources ; and, recompensing past aid a thousand-fold, it was now the great institution upon whose ever-inexhaustible means the want and misery of every part of the world might with certainty reckon.

BOOK III

CHAPTER XIII

TWENTY years have passed away—twenty-five years since the arrival of our pioneers at the Kenia. The principles by which Freeland has been governed have remained the same, and their results have not changed, except that the intellectual and material culture, and the number and wealth of the inhabitants have grown in a continually increasing ratio. The immigration, by means of fifty-four of the largest ocean steamers of a total of 495,000 tons register, had reached in the twenty-fifth year the figure of 1,152,000 heads. In order to convey into the heart of the continent as quickly as possible this influx to the African coast from all parts of the world, the Freeland system of railways has been either carried to or connected with other lines that reach the ocean at four different points. One line is that which was constructed in the previous epoch between Eden Vale and Mombasa. Four years later, after the pacification of the Galla tribes, the line to the Witu coast through the Dana valley was constructed. Nine years after that, a line—like all the other principal lines in Freeland, double-railed—along the Nile valley from the Victoria Nyanza and the Albert Nyanza, through the equatorial provinces of Egypt, Dongola, the Soudan, and Nubia, was connected with the Egyptian railway system, and thus brought Freeland into railway communication with the Mediterranean. Finally, in the twenty-fourth year, the finishing touch was given to the great Equatorial Trunk Railway, which, starting from Uganda on the Victoria Nyanza, and crossing the Nile where it leaves the Albert Nyanza, reaches the Atlantic Ocean through the valleys of the Aruwhimi and the Congo. Thus we possess two direct railway communications with the Indian Ocean, and one each with the Mediterranean Sea and the Atlantic Ocean.

Naturally, the Mombasa line was largely superseded by the much shorter Dana line; our passenger trains run the 360 miles of the latter in nine hours, while the Mombasa line, despite its shortening by the Athi branch line, cannot be traversed in less than double that time. The distance by rail between Eden Vale and Alexandria is 4,000 miles, the working of which is in our hands from Assuan southward. On account of the slower rate of the trains on the Egyptian portion, the journey consumes six days and a half; nevertheless, this is the most frequented route, because it shortens the total journey by nearly two weeks for all the immigrants who come by the Mediterranean Sea—that is, for all Europeans and most of the Americans. The Grand Equatorial Trunk Line—which, by agreement with the Congo State, was constructed almost entirely at our cost and is worked entirely by us—has a length of above 3,000 miles, and travellers by it from the mouth of the Congo can reach Eden Vale in a little less than four days.

Eden Vale, and the Kenia district generally, have long since ceased to receive the whole influx of immigrants. The densest Freeland population is still to be found on the highlands between the Victoria Nyanza and the Indian Ocean, and the seat of the supreme government is now, as formerly, in Eden Vale; but Freeland has largely extended its boundaries on all sides, particularly on the west. Freeland settlers have spread over the whole of Masailand, Kavirondo, and Uganda, and all round the shores of the Victoria Nyanza, the Mutanzige, and the Albert Nyanza, wherever healthy elevated sites and fruitful soil were to be found. The provisional limits of the territory over which we have spread are formed on the south-east by the pleasant and fertile hill-districts of Teita; on the north by the elevated tracts between the lakes Baringo and Victoria Nyanza and the Galla countries; on the west by the extreme spurs of the Mountains of the Moon, which begin at the Albert lake; and on the south by the hilly districts stretching to the lake Tanganika. This makes an area of about 580,000 square miles. This area is not, however, everywhere covered with a compact Freeland population; but in many places our colonists are scattered among the natives, whom they are everywhere raising to a higher and freer civilisation. The total population of the territory at this time under Freeland influence amounts to 42,000,000 souls, of whom 26,000,000 are whites and 16,000,000 black or brown natives. Of the whites

12,500,000 dwell in the original settlement on the Kenia and the Aberdare range; 1,500,000 are scattered about over the rest of Masailand, on the north declivities of the Kilimanjaro and in Teita; the hills to the west and north of Lake Baringo have a white population of 2,000,000; round the Victoria Nyanza have settled 3,500,000; among the hills between that lake and Lakes Mutanzige and Albert 1,500,000; on the Mountains of the Moon, west of Lake Albert Nyanza, 3,000,000; and finally, to the south, between these two lakes and Lake Tanganika, are scattered 2,000,000.

The products of Freeland industry comprehend almost all the articles required by civilised men; but mechanical industry continues to be the chief branch of production. This production is principally to meet the home demand, though the productive capacity of Freeland has for years materially surpassed that of all the machine-factories in the rest of the world. But Freeland has employment for more machinery than the whole of the rest of the world put together, for the work of its machines takes the place of that of the slaves or the wage-labourers of other countries; and as our 26,000,000 whites— not to reckon the civilised negroes—are all 'employers,' we need very many steel and iron servants to satisfy our needs, which increase step by step with the increase of our skill. Therefore comparatively few of our machines—except certain specialties—go over our frontiers. On the contrary, agriculture is pursued more largely for export than for home consumption; indeed, it can with truth be asserted that the whole of the Freeland corn-produce is available for export, since the surplus of the corn-production of the negroes which reaches our markets is on an average quite sufficient to cover our home demand. In the twenty-fourth year there were 22,000,000 acres of land under the plough, which in the two harvests produced 2,066,000,000 cwt. of grain and other field-produce, worth in round figures 600,000,000*l.* To this quantity of agricultural produce must be added other export goods worth 550,000,000*l.*; so that the total export was worth 1,150,000,000*l.* On the other hand, the chief item of import goods was that of 'books and other printed matter'; and next to this followed works of art and objects of luxury. Of the articles which in other countries make up the chief mass of outside commerce, the Freeland list of imports shows only cotton goods, cotton being grown at home scarcely at all. This item of import reached the

value of 57,000,000*l*. The import of books—newspapers included—
reached in the previous year 138,000,000*l*., considerably more than
all the rest of the world had in that same year paid for books. It
must not be inferred that the demand for books in Freeland is
entirely, or even mainly, covered by the import from without. The
Freeland readers during the same year paid more than twice as
much to their home publishers as to the foreign ones. In fact,
at the date of our writing this, the Freelanders read more than
three times as much as the whole of the reading public outside of
Freeland.

The above figures will show the degree of wealth to which Freeland has attained. In fact, the total value of the productions of the
7,500,000 producers during the last year was nearly seven milliard
pounds sterling (7,000,000,000*l*.) Deducting from that amount two
milliards and a-half to cover the tax for the purposes of the
commonwealth, there remained four milliard and a-half as profit to
be shared among the producers, giving an average of 600*l*. to each
worker. And to produce this we worked only five hours a day on
the average, or 1,500 hours in the year; so that the average net
value of an hour's labour was 8*s*.—little less than the average weekly
wage of the common labourer in many parts of Europe.

Almost all articles of ordinary consumption are very much
cheaper in Freeland than in any other part of the civilised world.
The average price of a cwt. of wheat is 6*s* ; a pound of beef about
2½*d*., a hectolitre (twenty-two gallons) of beer or light wine 10*s*., a
complete suit of good woollen clothing 20*s*. or 30*s*., a horse of splendid
Arab stock 15*l*., a good milch cow 2*l*., &c. A few articles of luxury
imported from abroad are dear—*e.g.* certain wines, and those goods
which must be produced by hand-labour—of which, however, there
are very few. The latter were all imported from abroad, as it would
never occur to a Freelander to compete with foreigners in hand-
labour. For though the harmoniously developed, vigorous, and
intelligent workers of our country surpass two- or three-fold the de-
bilitated servants of Western nations in the strength and training of
their muscles, they cannot compete with hand-labour that is fifty-
or a hundred-fold cheaper than their own. Their superiority begins
when they can oppose their slaves of steel to the foreign ones of
flesh and bone ; with these slaves of steel they can work cheaper
than those of flesh and bone, for the slaves which are set in motion

by steam, electricity, and water are more easily satisfied than even
the wage-labourers of 'free' Europe. These latter need potatoes
to fill their stomach, and a few rags to cover their nakedness;
whilst coal or a stream of water stills the hunger of the former, and
a little grease suffices to keep their joints supple.

This superiority of Freeland in machinery, and that of foreign
countries in hand-labour, merely confirms an old maxim of experience, which is none the less true that it still escapes the
notice of the so-called 'civilised nations.' That only the relatively
rich nations—that is, those whose masses are relatively in the best
condition—very largely employ machinery in production, could not
possibly long escape the most obtuse-minded ; but this undeniable
phenomenon is wrongly explained. It is held that the English or
the American people live in a way more worthy of human nature
than, for example, the Chinese or the Russians, because they are
richer; and that for the same reason—namely, because the requisite capital is more abundant—the English and Americans use
machinery while the Chinese and Russians employ merely human
muscles. This leaves unexplained the principal question, whence
comes this difference in wealth ? and also directly contradicts the
facts that the Chinese and the Russians make no use of the capital
so liberally and cheaply offered to them, and that machine-labour
is unprofitable in their hands as long as their wage-earners are
satisfied with a handful of rice or with half-rotten potatoes and a
drop of spirits. But it is a part of the *credo* of the orthodox
political economy, and is therefore accepted without examination.
Yet he who does not use his eyes merely to shut them to facts, or
his mind merely to harbour obstinately the prejudices which he has
once acquired, must sooner or later see that the wealth of the
nations is nothing else than their possession of the means of production; that this wealth is great or small in proportion as the means
of production are many and great, or few and small ; and that many
or few means of production are needed according as there is a
great or a small use of those things which are created by these
means of production—therefore solely in proportion to the large
or small consumption. Where little is used little can be produced,
and there will therefore be few instruments of production, and the
people *must* remain poor.

Neither can the export trade make any alteration ; for the

things which are exported must be exchanged for other things, whether food, or instruments of labour, or money, or some other commodity, and for that which is imported there must be some use; which, however, is impossible if there is no consumption, for in such a case the imported articles will find as little sale as the things produced at home. Certainly those commodities which are produced by a people who use neither their own productions nor those of other people, may be lent to other nations. But this again depends upon whether foreigners have a use for such a surplus above what is required at home ; and as this is not generally the case, it remains, once for all, that any nation can produce only so much as it has a use for, and the measure of its wealth is therefore the extent of its requirements.

Naturally this applies to only those nations whose civilisation has reached such a stage that the employment of complex instruments of labour is prevented, not by their ignorance, but simply by their social political helplessness. To such nations, however, applies in full the truth that they are poor simply because they *cannot* eat enough to satisfy themselves ; and that the increase of their wealth is conditioned by nothing else than the degree of energy with which the working classes struggle against their misery. The English and the Americans *will* eat meat, and therefore do not allow their wages to sink below the level at which the purchase of meat is possible ; this is the only reason why England and America employ more machinery than China and Russia, where the people are contented with rice or potatoes. But we in Freeland have brought it to pass that our working classes are secure of obtaining the whole profit of their labour, however great that profit may be ; what, therefore, could be more natural than that we should employ as much machinery as our mechanicians can invent ?

Nothing can permanently prevent the operation of this first law of economics. Production exists solely for the sake of consumption, and must therefore—as ought long since to have been seen— depend, both in its amount and in the character of its means, upon the amount of consumption. And if some tricksy Puck were to carry off overnight to some European country all our wealth and all our machinery, without taking to that country our social institutions as well, it is as certain that that country would not be a farthing richer than it was before, as it is that China would not be richer if all the wealth of England and America were carried thither without allowing the Chinese labourers more than boiled rice for food and a loincloth for clothing. Just as in this case the English and American machinery would become mere useless old iron in China, so in the former case would our machinery in Europe or America. And just as the English and the Americans, if their working classes only retained their present habits, would very quickly produce fresh machinery to take the place of that which had been spirited away to China, and would thereby regain their former level of wealth, so it would not be difficult for us to repeat what we have already effected—namely, to place ourselves afresh in possession of all that wealth which corresponds to *our* habits of life. For the social institutions of Freeland are the true and only source of our wealth; that we can *use* our wealth is the *raison d'être* of all our machinery.

Under the name of machinery we here include everything which on the one hand is not a free gift of nature, but the outcome of human effort, and on the other hand is intended to increase the productiveness of human labour. This power has grown to colossal dimensions in Freeland. Our system of railways—the lines above-named are only the four largest, which serve for communication with other countries—has reached a total length of road of about 358,000 miles, of which less than 112,000 miles are main lines, while about 248,000 miles are lines for agricultural and industrial purposes. Our canal system serves mainly for purposes of irrigation and draining, and the total length of its numberless thousands of larger and smaller branches is beyond all calculation, but these canals are navigable for a length of 36,000 miles. Besides the passenger ships already mentioned, there are afloat upon the seas of the world nearly 8,000 of our freight steamers with a total registered tonnage of 14,500,000. On the lakes and rivers of Africa we possess 17,800 larger and smaller steamers with a total register of 5,200,000 tons. The motive power which drives these means of communication and the numberless machines of our agriculture and our factories, our public and private institutions, reaches a total of not less than 245,000,000 horse-power—that is, fully twice the mechanical force employed by the whole of the rest of the world. In Freeland there is brought into use a mechanical force of nearly nine and a-half horse-power per head of the population; and as every registered horse-power is equal to the mechanical force of twelve or thirteen men, the result in labour is the same as if every Freelander without exception had about 120 slaves at his disposal. What wonder that we can live like masters, notwithstanding that servitude is not known in Freeland!

The value of the above enormous investments of all kinds can be calculated to a farthing, because of the wonderful transparency of all our industrial operations. The Freeland commonwealth, as such, has, during the twenty-five years of its existence, disbursed eleven milliards sterling for investment purposes. The disbursement through the medium of associations and of individual workers (the latter in relatively insignificant numbers) has amounted to twenty-three milliards sterling. So that the total investments represent a sum of thirty-four milliards, all highly profitable capital, despite—or rather because of—the fact that it belongs to no one particular owner ; for this very absence of private proprietorship of the total productive capital is the reason why any labour power can avail itself of those means of production by the use of which the highest possible profit can be realised. Every Freelander is joint-possessor of this immense wealth, which amounts—without taking into account the incalculable value of the soil   to 1,300l. per head, or 6,000l. per family. Thus, in these twenty-five years we have all become in a certain sense quite respectable capitalists. This capital does not bear us interest ; but, on the other hand, we owe to it the labour-profit of seven milliards sterling, which gives an average of 270l. per head for the 26,000,000 souls in Freeland.

But, before we describe the Freeland life which has developed itself upon the foundation of this abundance of wealth and energy, it will be necessary to give a brief outline of Freeland history during the last twenty years.

In the former section we had reached the first railway connection with the Indian Ocean on the one hand, and the campaign against Uganda, with the first colonisation of the shores of the Victoria Nyanza, on the other. The attention of our explorers was next directed to the very interesting hill-country north and north-west of Lake Baringo, particularly Elgon, the district on the frontier of Uganda, which rises to an elevation of some 14,000 feet. Here was a large field for future settlement equal to the Kenia and Aberdare ranges in fertility, climate, and beauty of scenery. In variety, the view from the summit of Elgon surpassed anything we had before seen. To the south-west stretched the sea-like expanse of the Victoria

Nyanza, bounded only by the horizon. To the north, forty miles away rose the snow-covered peak of Lekakisera. To the east, the eye ranged over immense stretches of forest-hills, whilst the smiling highlands of Uganda closed the view to the west.

The very evident traces of the former activity of a highly developed civilised people stimulated the spirit of investigation of our archæologists. The great caves which had been noticed by earlier travellers in the foot-hills around the Elgon had every appearance of being of an artificial origin. It was quite as evident that none of the races dwelling within thousands of miles of these caves could have excavated them. They are all in a hard agglomerate, and their capacity varies from about 25,000 to 125.000 cubic yards. Their purpose was as enigmatical as their origin. For the most part they are to be found on steep, scarcely accessible, precipitous mountain-sides, but, without exception, only in a thick layer of breccia or agglomerate interposed between a trachytic and a volcanic stone. At that time they were inhabited by a race of a very low type, subsisting solely upon the chase and pasturage, and who were utterly incapable of making such dwellings, and declared that the caves had existed from the beginning. But who made them, and for what purpose were they originally made? That they were to be found only in one particular stratum naturally gave rise to the supposition that they were made by mining operations. They must have been opened in a past age for some kind of ore or other mineral product, and have been worked with a great expenditure of labour and for a very long period; for the caves are so many and so large that, even with modern appliances, it would have needed thousands of men for many decades to excavate them in the hard agglomerate of sand and pebbles. The excavation had been made, however, not with powder and dynamite, but with chisel and pickaxe; the caves must therefore have been the work of thousands of years. There was only *one* people who could here have expended upon such a work sufficient strength for a sufficient time—the Egyptian. This most ancient civilised people in the world, whose history covers thousands of years, must have excavated these caves; of this there was no doubt among our archæologists.

That in the grey antiquity the Egyptians penetrated to the sources of their holy river (it may be remarked in passing that the Ripon falls, where the Nile flows out of the Victoria Nyanza, are in clear

N

weather very plainly to be seen from the Elgon) has nothing in it
so remarkable, even though modern historical investigation has not
been able to find any trace of it. But wherever the Egyptians
penetrated, and particularly wherever they built, one is accustomed
to find unmistakable traces of their activity. It behoved us, therefore, to search for such traces, and then to discover what the
Pharaohs of the ancient dynasties had sought for here. Our re-
searches were successful as to the first object, but not as to the
second. In two places, unfortunately outside of the entrances to
the caves in question, where atmospheric and perhaps other influences had been destructively at work, there were found conically
pointed basalt prisms, which exhibited unmistakable traces of hiero-
glyphic writing. These inscriptions were no longer legible; and
though our Egyptologists, as well as those of London and Paris,
agreed in thinking that the inscription on one stone distinctly referred to the goddess Hathor, this view is rather the verdict of a
kind of archæological instinct than a conclusion based upon tangible
evidence. That the stones bore Egyptian inscriptions, and had
stood for thousands of years at the entrances to these caves, was plain
enough, even to the eyes of laymen. Parenthetically it may be
remarked that this discovery throws light upon the origin of the
Masai, of whom it has already been said that they were not negroes,
but a bronze-coloured race showing the Hamitic type. Plainly the
Masai are Egyptians, who, in a forgotten past, were cut off from
the rest in the highlands south of the Baringo lake. Their martial
habits would suggest descent from the ancient Egyptian warrior
caste, possibly from those discontented warriors who, twenty-
five centuries ago, in the days of Psammetichus I., migrated to
Ethiopia, when Pharaoh had offended them by the employment of
Greek mercenaries.

But this did not tell what the Egyptians, in honour either of
Hathor or of some other celestial or terrestrial majesty, were
looking for on the Elgon. We spared no pains in seeking further
evidence; both in the caves and in other parts of the agglomerate
in which they were excavated, we diligently looked for something
to throw light upon the subject. But we found nothing, at least
nothing that appeared to be of any special use to the Egyptians,
either in the way of metals or of precious stones. We were finally
compelled to content ourselves with the supposition that some of

the variously coloured stones which were present in the formation in great number and variety were highly valued in the days of the Pharaohs, without the knowledge of the fact having descended to our days. There would be nothing remarkable in this, for neither would it have been the first instance in which men have for thousands of years reckoned as very precious that upon which subsequent generations scarcely deigned to glance, nor do we know enough of the life of the ancient Egyptians to be able positively to assert that every object in the inscriptions and papyrus-rolls means this or that. It is therefore very possible that in many of the Egyptian inscriptions which have come down to us a great deal is told of the stones found here on the Elgon, whilst we, misled by the great value which the narrator ascribes to the said stones, think that some precious stone now highly valued was referred to, and that generations of Egyptian slaves have spent their lives here in cruel toil, in order to procure for their masters an object of luxury which we to-day carelessly kick aside when it accidentally comes in our way.

Let this be as it may, we found nothing of any value in the agglomerate in which the Egyptians had excavated. But, in the immediate neighbourhood of the cave-hills, we found something else : something that men coveted thousands of years ago, as they do to-day, but which, singularly enough, escaped the miners of the Pharaohs, and was not looked for by them on the Elgon—namely, gold, and that in large rich veins. It was accidentally discovered by one of the engineers engaged in the examination of the caves, who, significantly, was at first seized with horror at his discovery. He was an enthusiastic young Spaniard, who had only recently reached Freeland, and he saw in his discovery a great danger for those Freeland principles which were so passionately worshipped by him, and he therefore at first resolved to keep it secret. He reflected, however, that some one else would soon come upon the same trace, and that the evil which he dreaded would become a fact. He therefore decided to confide in those under whom he was acting, and to point out to them the danger that threatened the happiness of Freeland. It was very difficult to make Nunez—as this young enthusiast was named—understand that there would be little hope for the security and permanent vitality of the institutions of Freeland if the richest possible discovery of gold were able to put them in jeopardy, and to convince him that gold-mining was like any other kind of work—that labour would flow to the mines as long as it was possible to earn as much there as in any other branch of production, and the result of his discovery could only be that of slightly raising the average earnings of Freeland labour.

And so it was. Nunez had not erred in his estimate of the productiveness of the mines; the newly opened gold-diggings soon yielded some 12,000,000*l*. a year.

The managers of the central bank utilised this new source of wealth in gold for the establishment of an independent Freeland coinage. Hitherto the English sovereign had been our gold currency, and we had reckoned in English pounds, shillings, and pence. Now a mint was set up in Eden Vale, and the coinage underwent a reform. We retained the sterling pound and the shilling, but we minted our pound nearly one per cent. lighter than the English one, so that it might be exactly equal to twenty-five francs of the French or decimal system of coinage ; the shilling we divided, not into twelve parts, but into a hundred.

Of these Freeland pounds, which in the course of a few years acquired undisputed rank as a cosmopolitan coin, and passed current everywhere, only a comparatively small number circulated in Freeland itself. We needed in our domestic transactions scarcely any cash. All payments were made through the bank, where everyone —our civilised negroes not excepted—had an account, and which possessed branches all over the country. At first the coins were used for paying small amounts, then cheques came into general use for these, and later still it came to be sufficient to write a simple order on the bank. The coinage was therefore almost exclusively needed for foreign use ; in the course of sixteen years the mint has issued some 130,000,000*l*., of which scarcely seven per cent. remained in Freeland, and all except a very small portion of this lies in the bank cellars, where its repose is never disturbed. For with us there are no fluctuations of the *money* market, since there exists scarcely any demand for *money* in Freeland. Gold is our measure of value, and will remain so as long as there is no commodity discovered better fitted to perform this function—that is, exposed to less variation in value—than this metal. The instrument of *transferring* value among us is not money, but paper, ink, and pen. Scarcity and superfluity of gold are therefore in Freeland as meaningless conceptions as would be a scarcity or superfluity of mètres in Europe.

The gold discoveries on the Elgon at any rate contributed toward: hastening the settlement of those splendid highlands lying to the north-west of Lake Baringo. The adjacent Uganda was used as a seat of agriculture, whilst the towns, essentially copies of Eden Vale, whose wooden houses had meanwhile given place to elegant villas of stone and brick, were located on the cooler heights of the wooded hills.

Our pioneers pursued their way ever farther and farther. There was still abundant room in the older settlements ; but the spirit of discovery, together with the fascination of novelty that hung around the distant districts, continually led new bands farther and farther into the 'Dark Continent.' When the shores of the Victoria Nyanza no longer contained anything unknown, our pathfinders penetrated the primitive forests of the hilly districts between Lakes Mutanzige and Albert Nyanza. Here, for the first time, we came into contact with cannibal races, the subjection of whom was no small task and was not accomplished without bloodshed. From the Albert Nyanza, the east shores of which are mostly bare and barren, we obtained an enticing view of the Mountains of the Moon, whose highest point rises above 13,000 feet, and in the cool season frequently shows a cap of snow. Down the picturesque declivities that look towards the lake fall from incredible heights a number of powerful cataracts, giving rise to pleasant inferences as to the nature of the district in which the streams have their source. Naturally they did not long remain unvisited, and the fame of the new marvels of natural beauty found there soon drew hundreds of thousands of settlers thither. There also we came into collision with cannibal races, some of which still carry on their evil practices in secret. From hence our pioneers turned southwards, everywhere making use of the hill-ranges as highways. Six years ago our outposts had reached Lake Tanganika, where they gave preference to the western heights that rise in places 3,000 feet above the level of the lake, which is itself about 5,000 feet above the sea. At present hundreds of thousands of our people are settled on the lovely shores of this the longest, though only the second largest, of the equatorial lakes. Lake Tanganika is not quite half so large as the Victoria Nyanza, and is nowhere too broad for a good eye to see the opposite hills, but its length reaches 360 miles, about three-fourths as long as the Adriatic Sea, and the fastest of the 286 steamers which at this time navigate it at our charge takes nearly twenty-four hours to go from end to end.

We now came more and more into immediate contact with colonies under European influence. In the south and east we touched German and English interests and spheres of influence; in the north-east, more or less directly, French and Italian; in the north Egyptian; in the west the vigorously developing Congo State. Our intercourse was everywhere directed by the best and most accommodating intentions, but a number of questions sprang up which urgently demanded a definitive solution. For instance, the neighbouring colonies found it inconvenient to be in close proximity to Freeland settlements; their population was drawn away by us like iron filings by a magnet. Wherever a Freeland association established itself near a foreign colony, nothing of that colony was left after a little while, except the empty dwellings and the forsaken plantations: the colonists had settled among us and become Freelanders. At the same time, the foreign governments neither could nor wished to do anything, since the interests of their subjects were not damaged; but with respect to the establishment of their power in the countries in question, the foreign governments were necessarily made uncomfortable by the impossibility of asserting themselves in our neighbourhood.

We were also compelled to moot the question, what would happen if Freelanders were to settle in any district belonging to a Western nation? We had hitherto purposely avoided doing this, but ultimately it would be unavoidable. What would happen then? Should we, in possession of the stronger form of civilisation, yield to the weaker and more backward one? Could we do so, even if we were willing? Freeland is not a state in the ordinary sense of the word. Its character does not lie in dominion over a definite territory, but in its social institutions. These institutions are in themselves quite compatible with foreign forms of government, and for the sake of keeping peace with our neighbours we were compelled to try to obtain legal recognition of our institutions, in the first place, in the neighbouring colonial districts.

And not merely upon the continent of Africa, but in other parts of the world also, there came into existence a number of questions between ourselves and various governments, which urgently needed settling. On principle we avoided getting mixed up with any of the political affairs of foreign countries ; but we held it to be our right and our duty to help with our wealth and power our needy brethren, in whatever part of the inhabited world they might live. Freeland money was to be found wherever want had to be relieved and the disinherited and wretched to be aided against exploitage. Our offices and our ships were gratuitously at the service of all who wished to flee to us out of the sorrow of the old system of society ; and we never wearied in our efforts to make the blessings of our institutions more and more accessible to our suffering brethren. All this, as has been said, we considered to be both our duty and our right, and we were not disposed to allow ourselves to be turned aside from the fulfilment of our mission by the protests of foreign Powers. But it became impossible not to perceive that the relations between us and several European and Asiatic governments were getting more and more strained. In the democratic west of Europe, in America, and in Australia, public opinion was too strong in our favour for us to fear any—even passive—resistance to our effort from those countries. But the case was different with several Eastern States. Particularly since our means, and consequently our propagandist activity, had attained the colossal dimensions of the last few years, with a promise of continued growth, it had been here and there seriously asked whether, and by what means, it was possible to keep out Freeland money and to counteract Freeland influence. For a time the governments in question avoided an open breach with us, partly on account of the public opinion which was powerful in our favour even in their countries, and partly on account of the large financial resources which were in our hands. They did not wish to have us as avowed enemies, but they wished to control the influx of Freeland money and the purposes to which it was applied, and to check the emigration to Freeland.

We were not disposed to stand and look upon such attempts with folded arms. The right to spring to the aid of our enslaved fellow-men, or to keep open to them a refuge in Freeland, we were determined to defend to the utmost of our strength ; and no one in Freeland doubted that we were strong enough in case of need to resist any attempts by foreign Powers to limit our activity. But all in Freeland were agreed that every conceivable pacific means must be tried before we appealed to arms. And the difficulty in the way of a bloodless settlement of the quarrel lay in the fact that the Free-landers and the foreigners held opposite views concerning the military strength of Freeland. Whilst we, as has been said, were convinced that we were as strong as any military State in the world—nay, as several of them put together—those very foreign govern-ments with whom we were at variance looked upon us as powerless from a military point of view. We were therefore convinced that a definitive threat by our plenipotentiaries would not be taken seriously, and that on this very account any attempt energetically to maintain our position could produce the requisite effect only by actual war. And a war it was that confirmed our position everywhere abroad, though not with either an European or an Asiatic, but with an African power—a war which, though it had a very indirect bearing upon the subject in question, yet brought this question to a decision.

How this came about will be told in the letters given in the following chapters. These letters were written by Prince Carlo Falieri, a young Italian diplomatist, who has since settled in Free-land, but who at the time to which these letters refer was visiting Eden Vale in his country's service. This correspondence will, at the same time, give a vivid picture of Freeland manners and life in the twenty-fifth year of its history.

CHAPTER XIV

Eden Vale: July 12, ——

AFTER a silence of several months I am writing to you from the chief city in Freeland, where my father and I have already been for some days. What has brought us to the country of social liberty? You know—or perhaps you do not know—that my chiefs at Monte Citorio have for some time not known how to deal with the brown Napoleon of the East Coast of Africa, the Negus John V. of Abyssinia; and that our good friends in London and Paris have experienced the same difficulty. So the cabinets of the three Western Powers have agreed to seek an African remedy for the common African malady. To find this we are here. Lord E—— and Sir W. B—— are sent on the part of England; Madame Charles Delpart and M. Henri de Pons on the part of France; while Italy is represented by Prince Falieri and his son—my littleness. We are commissioned to represent to the Freelanders that it would be to their interest as well as to ours if they allowed their country to be the theatre of war against Abyssinia.

Those of us among Europeans who have possessions on the African coast of the Red Sea and south of the Straits of Bab-el-Mandeb have had much trouble with the Negus. During the late war he kept the allied armies of England, France, and Italy in check ; and, had it not been for the intervention of our Italian fleet, those armies would narrowly have escaped the fate of that Egyptian host which, according to the Bible, was drowned in the Red Sea 3,300 years ago. The Negus—plainly with the aid of certain friends of his in Europe—has utilised the five years' peace (which was not a very creditable one for us) in perfecting his already powerful army and organising it according to the Western pattern. He now possesses 300,000 men armed with weapons of the best and most modern construction, an excellent cavalry of at least 40,000, and an artillery of 106 batteries, which our representatives describe as quite equal to any European troops. What John means to do with an armament so enormously beyond the needs of poor Abyssinia has been rendered plain by the events of the last five years. He wishes to take from us and the English the coast towns on the Red Sea, and from the French their province south of Bab-el-Mandeb. Our coast fortresses and fleet will not be able in the long run to prevent this, unless we can defeat the Abyssinians in the open field. But how are armies, equal to the reorganised Abyssinian forces, to be maintained on those inhospitable coasts ? How can a campaign be carried on, with nothing but the sea at the rear, against an enemy of whose terrible offensive strength we have already had only too good proof? Yet the Negus must be met, cost what it will ; for with the sacrifice of the coast towns the connection with East Asia, and with that part of East Africa which during the last twenty years has become one of the principal seats of commerce, will be lost to all European Powers. We know only too well that John V. has been making the most extensive preparations. To-day his agents in Greece, Dalmatia, and even North America are engaging sailors by thousands, who are evidently intended to man a fleet of war as soon as the possession of the points on the coast makes it possible for the Abyssinians to keep one. Whether he will buy his fleet abroad or build it himself is at present an enigma. If he did the former, it could not possibly escape the knowledge of the Powers threatened by this future fleet ; but none of the great shipwrights of the world have any warships of unknown destination in course of construction. If the Abyssinian fleet is to be built in the Red Sea after the coast has passed into the possession of Abyssinia, why does he want so many sailors at once ? This enigma is by no means calculated to lay our fears as to the ultimate aims of Abyssinia. In short, it has been decided in London, Paris, and Rome to take the bull by the horns, and to begin offensive operations against the East African conqueror. The three cabinets will together furnish an expedition of at least 300,000 men, and immediately after the close of the five years' peace—that is, at the end of September next— attack Abyssinia. But Freeland, and not this time our own coast possessions, is to form the basis of the operations. This will give the allied armies a secure rear for provisioning and retreat ; and our task as diplomatists is to win over the Freeland government to this project. We ask for nothing but passive co-operation—that is, a free passage for our troops. Whether our instructions go so far as to compel this passive assistance in case of need I do not know ; for not I, but merely my father, is initiated into the most secret views of the leaders of our foreign politics ; and though my well-known enthusiasm for this land of Socialists has not prevented our government from appointing me as *attaché* to my father's mission, yet I imagine I shall not be admitted to share the more important secrets of our diplomacy.

Now you know, my friend, *why* we have come to Freeland. If you are curious to know *how* we got here, I must tell you that we came from Brindisi to Alexandria by the 'Uranus,' one of the enormous ships which Freeland keeps afloat upon all seas for the mail and passenger service. With us came 2,800 immigrants to Freeland; and if these find in the new home only one-half of what they promised themselves, Freeland must be a veritable paradise. My father, who at first hesitated to entrust himself to a Freeland steamer which carries all its passengers free of charge and, as is well known, makes no distinction in the treatment of those on board, admitted, when he had been two days on the voyage, that he did not regret having yielded to my entreaty. Our cabins were not too small, were comfortable, and most scrupulously clean ; the cooking and commissariat in general left nothing to be desired ; and—what surprised us most—the intercourse with the very miscellaneous immigrants proved to be by no means disagreeable. Among our 2,300 fellow-voyagers were persons of all classes and conditions, from *savants* to labourers ; but even the latter showed themselves to be so inspired by the consciousness that they were hastening to a new home in which all men stood absolutely on an equality, that not the slightest rowdyism or disturbance was witnessed during the whole voyage.

At Alexandria we took the first express-train to the Soudan, which, however, until it reached Assuan - that is, as long as it was in the hands of Egyptian conductors and drivers—was express in little more than the name. At Assuan we entered a Freeland train ; and we now went on with a punctuality and speed elsewhere to be met with only in England or America. Sleeping, dining, and conversation cars, furnished with every convenience and luxury, took us rapidly up the Nile, the line crossing the giant stream twice before we reached Dongola. It was characteristic that no fare was charged above Assuan. The food and drink consumed in the dining-cars or in the stations had to be paid for—on the ' Uranus ' even the board was given for nothing—but travelling accommodation is provided gratuitously by the Freeland commonwealth, on land as well as at sea.

You will allow me to omit all description of land and people in Egypt and its dependencies. In the last decade, and especially since the completion of the Freeland Nile line, there has been some change for the better ; but on the whole I found the misery of the fellahs still very severe, and only different in degree and not in essence from what has been so often described by travellers in these regions. A picture of a totally different kind presented itself to the eye when we neared the Albert Nyanza and reached Freeland territory. I could scarcely trust my senses when, on awaking on the morning of the fifth day of our railway journey, I looked out of the car and, instead of the previous scenery, I caught sight of endless cultivated fields pleasantly variegated by luxuriant gardens and smiling groves, among which elegant villas, here scattered and there collected into townships, were conspicuous. As the train stopped soon after at a station the name of which was a friendly omen for an Italian—Garibaldi— we saw for the first time some Freelanders in their peculiar dress, as

simple as it is becoming, and, as I at once perceived, thoroughly
suitable to the climate.

This costume is very similar to that of the ancient Greeks ; even
the sandals instead of shoes are not wanting, only they are worn
not on the naked foot, but over stockings. The dresses of the Freeland women are, for the most part, more brightly coloured than
those of the men, which latter, however, do not exhibit the dull and
monotonous tints of the dress of men in the West. In particular,
th' Freeland youths are fond of bright clear colours, the younger
women preferring white with coloured ornaments. The impression
which the Freelanders made upon me was quite a dazzling one.
Full of vigour and health, they moved about with cheerful grace in
the shade of the trees in the station-garden ; they showed such an
aristocratic self-possessed bearing that I thought at first that this
was the rendezvous of the leaders of the best society of the place.
This notion was strengthened when several Freelanders entered
the train, and I discovered, in conversation with them as the train
went on, that their culture fully corresponded to their appearance.
Yet these were but ordinary country people—agriculturists and
gardeners, with their wives, sons, and daughters.

Not less astonishing was the respectability of the negroes scattered among and freely mingling with the whites. Their dress was
still lighter and airier than that of the whites—mostly cotton
garments instead of the woollen clothes worn by the latter ; for the
rest, these natives had the appearance of thoroughly civilised men.
From a conversation which I held with one in the train I found that
their culture had reached a high stage—at any rate, a much higher
one than that of the rural population in most parts of Europe. The
black with whom I conversed spoke a fluent, correct English, had
a Freeland newspaper in his hand, and eagerly read it during the
journey ; and he showed himself to be well acquainted with the
public affairs not only of his own country, but also of Europe. For
instance, he gave expression to the opinion that our difficulties
with Abyssinia had evidently been occasioned by the Russian
government, who necessarily wished to make it difficult for the
Western Powers, and particularly England, to communicate with
India ; and he justified this opinion in a way that revealed as much
knowledge as soundness of judgment.

Towards noon, at the station ' Baker,' we reached the Albert lake, just where the White Nile flows out of it. Here a very agreeable surprise awaited me. You remember David Ney, that young Freeland sculptor with whom we trotted about Rome together last autumn, and to whom I in particular became so much attached because the splendid young fellow charmed me both by his outward appearance and by the nobility of his disposition. What you probably did not know is that, after David left Europe at the close of his art studies in Rome, we corresponded; and he was therefore informed of my intended visit. My friend had taken the trouble to make the thirty hours' journey from Eden Vale, where he lives with his parents—his father is, as you know, a member of the Freeland government—to the Albert Nyanza, had got as far as 'Baker' station, and the first thing I noticed as we entered the station was his friendly, smiling face. He brought to my father and me an invitation from his parents to be their guests while we remained in Eden Vale. 'If you, your grace,' said he to my father, 'will be content with the house and entertainment which a citizen of Freeland can offer you, you will confer a very great favour upon all of us, and particularly upon me, who would thus have the privilege of undisturbed intercourse with your son. The splendour and magnificence to which you are accustomed at home you will certainly miss in our house, which scarcely differs from that of the simplest worker of our country; but this deprivation would be imposed upon you everywhere in Freeland; and I can promise that you shall not want for any real comfort.' To my great satisfaction, after a moment's reflection my father cordially accepted this invitation.

I will not now enlarge upon what I saw during the day and a half's journey from the Albert lake to Eden Vale, as I shall have occasion to refer to it again. Indeed, this my first Freeland letter will swell to far too great a size if I give you only a superficial report of what first interested me here—that is, of the daily life of the Freelanders. Our express flew in mad speed past the cornfields and plantations that clothe the plains of Unyoro and the highlands of Uganda; then ran for several hours along the banks of the billowy Victoria Nyanza, through a lovely country of hill and mountain—the whole like one great garden. Leaving the lake at the Ripon falls, we turned into the wildly romantic mountain district of Elgon, with its countless herds and its rich manufacturing towns, skirted the garden-fringed Lake Baringo, and sped through the Lykipia to the Alpine scenery of the Kenia. Towards nine in the evening of the sixth day of our railway journey we at length reached Eden Vale.

It was a splendid moonlit night when we left the station and entered the town; but brighter than the moon shone the many powerful electric arc-lamps, so that nothing escaped the curious eye. Even if I wished to do it now, I could not describe to you in detail the impression made upon me by this first Freeland town into which I had been. Imagine a fairy garden covering a space of nearly forty square miles, filled with tens of thousands of charming, tastily designed small houses and hundreds of fabulously splendid palaces; add the intoxicating odours of all kinds of flowers and the singing of innumerable nightingales—the latter were imported from Europe and Asia in the early years of the settlement and have multiplied to an incredible extent—and set all this in the framework of a landscape as grand and as picturesque as any part of the world can show; and then, if your fancy is vigorous enough, you may form some mild conception of the delight with which this marvellous city filled me, and fills me still more and more the longer I know it. The streets and open places through which we passed were apparently empty; but David assured us that the shores of the lake were full of life every evening until midnight. In many of the houses which we passed could be heard sounds of mirth and gaiety. On broad airy terraces and in the gardens around them sat or sauntered the inhabitants in larger or smaller groups. The clinking of glasses, music, silvery laughter, fell upon the ear: in short, everything indicated that here the evenings were devoted to the most cheerful sociality.

After a rapid ride of about half an hour, we reached the home of our hosts, near the centre of the town and not far from the lake. The family Ney received us in the most cordial manner; nevertheless their dignified bearing very profoundly impressed even my proud father. The ladies in particular were so much like princesses in disguise that my father at once transformed himself into the inimitable gallant Paladin of chivalry you have known him to be in Rome, London, and Vienna. Father Ney betrayed, at the first glance, the profound thinker accustomed to serious work, but who by no means lacked the mien of agreeable self-possession. Judging

from the fact that he had been six-and-twenty years in the service
of the Freeland commonwealth, he must be at least fifty years old,
but he looks to be scarcely forty. The younger of the sons, Emanuel,
technician by calling, is a complete duplicate of David, though a
little darker and more robust than the latter, who, as you know, is
no weakling. The mother, Ellen by name, an American by birth,
who—thanks, evidently, to David's reports of me—received me with
a truly motherly welcome, must be, judging from the age of her
children, about forty-five, but her youthful freshness gives her the
appearance rather of a sister than a mother of her children. She is
brilliantly beautiful, but is rendered specially charming by the
goodness and nobility of mind impressed upon her features. She
introduced to us three girls between eighteen and twenty years of
age as her daughters, of whom only one—Bertha—resembled her
and her sons. This one, a young copy of the mother, at once
embarrassed me by the indescribable charm of her presence. She
was so little like the others—Leonora and Clementina—that I could
not refrain from remarking upon it to David. 'These two are not
blood-relations to us, but pupil daughters of my mother; what that
means I will tell you by-and-by,' was his answer.

As, despite the comfort of Freeland cars, we were naturally
somewhat exhausted by our six days' railway journey, after a short
conversation with our hosts we begged to be allowed to retire to our
rooms. David acted as our guide. After leaving the spacious
garden-terrace upon which we had hitherto lingered, we passed
through a simple but tastefully arranged drawing-room and a
stately dining-hall which communicated, as I noticed, with a large
room used as a library on the right, and with two smaller rooms
on the left. These latter rooms were, David told us, his parents'
workrooms. We then came into a richly decorated vestibule, from
which stairs led above to the bedrooms. Here David took us into
two bedrooms with a common anteroom.

Then followed a short explanation of the many provisions for the
comfort of the users of the rooms. 'Pressure upon this button
on the right near the door-post,' demonstrated David, 'lights the
electric chandelier; a touch on the button near the bedside-table
lights the wall-lamp over the bed. Here the telephone No. 1 is
for use within the house and for communication with the nearest
watch-room of the Association for Personal Service. A simple

ringing—thus—means that some one is to come hither from the watch-room. All these buttons—they are known by their distinctive borders—here and there about the walls, there by the writing-desk and here by the bed, are connected with this telephone-bell. Thus, whenever you wish to call a member of this association, which always has persons on duty, you need not move either from the arm-chair in which you may be sitting or from the bed on which you are resting. Every telephone and every signal has its number in the watch-room as well as on a list in the vestibule we have just left ; in two minutes at the longest after you have rung, a messenger of the association will have hastened to wait on you.'

' That is a wonderful arrangement,' I remarked, ' which secures for you all the convenience of having a *valet-de-chambre* ready to obey every hint of yours, without being obliged to put up with the trouble which our valets cost us. But this luxury must be very costly, and therefore not commonly enjoyed.'

' The cost is very moderate, just because everybody makes use of this public service,' answered my friend. ' There is one such watch-room with three watchers for every 600 or 800 houses. The attendance is paid for—or rather calculated—according to the length of time during which it is required, and, as is customary with us, the rate of payment is measured by the average value of an hour's work as shown by the accounts published every year by our central bank. In the past year, when an hour's work was worth 8s., we had to pay about 5d. for every three minutes - for that is the unit upon which this association bases its calculation. Those who ring often and keep the association busy have to pay a larger share at the end of the year, and those who ring seldom a smaller share. But in all cases the association must come upon them for its expenses and for the payment of its nine watching members—for the three watchers change morning, noon, and evening. Last year the amount required for each watch-room was in round figures 6,000l. ; and as, for example, the time-bills of the 720 families of our radius amounted to not quite two-thirds of that sum, the remaining 2,000l. had to be assessed in proportion to the use made of the service by each family. Our family makes comparatively little demand upon the service of this association ; we paid, for example, last year 6l. in all - that is, 4l. direct payment for time, and 2l. additional assessment—for we used the service only 203 times during the whole year.'

'Why,' asked my father, 'is there comparatively less use of the service in your house than elsewhere ? '

'Because our household always contains two or three young women, who make it their pleasant duty to give to my parents all that personal attendance which is befitting well-bred cultured women. Those two girls—for a year they have been assisted by my sister—are young Freelanders such as are to be found in every Freeland house whose housewife has a special reputation for intelligence and refined manners; pardon me for classing my mother among these exceptions. Every young woman of Freeland esteems it a special honour and a great privilege to be received into such a house for at least a year, because it is universally acknowledged that nothing refines the intellect and the manners of developing girls more than the most intimate intercourse possible with superior women. As a matter of course such young ladies are regarded and treated exactly as if they were children of the family ; and they render to their adoptive parents the same service as thoughtful and affectionate daughters. Father and mother can scarcely feel a wish which is not divined and gratified.'

'Ah, that is exactly our institution of royal maids of honour,' said my father, smiling.

'Certainly ; but I very much doubt whether your royal pair are so thoroughly, and in particular so tenderly, confided in as my parents always are by these pupil-daughters of my mother. During the past eighteen years—which is the age of this institution in Freeland—not less than twenty-four of these young ladies have passed through our house ; and they all still maintain filial relations with my parents and sisterly ones with us. Those who are at present with us—Leonora and Clementina—you have already seen.'

'You said just now,' said my father, 'that your whole household —four ladies and three gentlemen—during a whole year, called for your ministering spirits by means of this alarum only two hundred times three minutes. You mentioned, besides, the service rendered by those charming young ladies. But who does all that coarser work, which even the spirit of Aladdin's lamp could scarcely get through in 600 minutes, or ten hours, a year in such a house as this ? It seems to me that you have some ten or twelve dwelling-rooms. It is true the floor is of marble, but it must be swept. Everywhere I see heavy carpets—who keeps these clean ? In a word, who does

o

the coarser work in this comfortably furnished house, which one can see at a glance is kept most carefully in order ? '

' The association with whose watch-room I have already made you acquainted. Only we do not need to ring in order to get our regular requirements attended to. The household work is done on the basis of a common tariff without any trouble on our part, and with a punctuality that leaves nothing to be desired. The association possesses duplicates of the house-keys and room-keys of all the houses that it serves. Early in the morning, when we are most of us still asleep, its messengers come noiselessly, take the clothing that has to be cleaned—or rather that has to be exchanged, for we Freelanders never wear the same garment on two successive days— from where they were left the previous evening, put the clean clothes in the proper place, get ready the baths—for in most Free-land houses every member of the family has a separate bath which is daily used, unless a bath in the lake or the river is preferred— clean the outer spaces and some of the rooms, take away the carpets, and disappear before most of us have had any knowledge of their presence. And all this is done in a few minutes. It is almost all done by machinery. Do you see that little apparatus yonder in the corridor ? That is a hydraulic machine brought into action by the turning of that tap there, which places it in connection with the high-pressure service from the Kenia cascades. (In other towns, where a hydraulic pressure of thirty-five atmospheres is not so easily to be had, electric or atmospheric motors are employed.) Here the steel shaft in the hollow in the floor covered with that elegant grating, and there near the ceiling the bronze shaft that might be mistaken for a rod on which to hang mirrors or pictures— these transmit the motion of the hydraulic machine to every room in the house, from the cellar to the rooms under the roof. And there, in that room, are a number of machines whose uses I can scarcely explain to you unless you see them at work. The three or four messengers of the association bring a number of other implements with them, and when these machines are brought into connection with the shafts above or below, and the tap of the water-motor is opened, the room is swept and washed while you can turn round, and the heaviest articles set in their places ; in short, everything is put right silently and with magical rapidity, though human hands could have done it only slowly and with a great deal of disagreeable noise.

'A little later the workers of the association reappear in order to clean the rest of the rooms, to lay the carpets in their places, and prepare everything in the kitchen and the breakfast-room for breakfast. And so these people come and go several times during the day, as often as is agreed upon, in order to see that all is right. Everything is done without being asked for, silently, and with the speed of lightning. Our house belongs to the larger, and our style of living to the better, in Freeland; the association has, therefore, more to do in few houses than in ours; nevertheless, last year, for all these services they charged us for not more than 180 hours, for which, according to the tariff already mentioned, we had to pay 72*l*. I question if any house equal to ours in Europe or America could be kept in a like good condition for double or treble this sum. And instead of having to do with troublesome " domestics," we are served by intelligent, courteous, zealous men of business who are compelled by competition—for we have six such associations in Eden Vale— to do their utmost to satisfy the families that employ them. The members of these associations are " gentlemen " with whom one can very properly sit at the same table, the table which they have themselves just prepared, and neither our two " maids of honour " nor my sister would have the slightest objection to wait upon, among other guests, members of the Association for Personal Services.

'You will soon become acquainted with the gentlemen of the association, for the members that have charge of our house will come immediately to obtain the most exact information as to all your special wishes. You must not grow impatient if *you* have to undergo a somewhat circumstantial examination; it will be for your comfort, and will not be repeated. When you have once been subjected to the association's questions, which leave out nothing however trivial, it will never, so long as you are in Freeland, happen to you to find the wrong garments brought you, or your bath a degree too hot or too cold, or your bed not properly prepared, or any of those little items of neglect and carelessness on the absence of which domestic happiness in no small degree depends.

'That is enough about the Association for Rendering Personal Services. I can now go on with my explanation of our domestic arrangements. This other telephone has the same use as the telephone in Europe, with this difference, that here everyone possesses his own telephone. That screw there opens the cold-air service, which brings into every room artificially cooled and slightly ozonised air, should the heat become unpleasant; and as this sometimes happens even at night—as when in the hot months a nocturnal storm rises—the screw is placed near the bed.'

I give you all these details because I think they will interest you as showing how marvellously well these Freelanders have understood how to substitute their 'iron slaves' for our house slaves. I will merely add that the Association for Rendering Personal Services satisfied even my father's very comprehensive demands. He declares that he never found better attendance at the Bristol Hotel in Paris.

Not to weary you, I will spare you any description of the first and second breakfast on the next day, and will only make your mouth water by describing the principal meal, taken about six o'clock in the evening. But first I must introduce you to two other members of the Ney family with whom we became acquainted in the course of our second day. These are David's aunt Clara, his father's sister, and her husband, Professor Noria, both originals of a very special kind. Aunt Clara, at heart an ardent Freelander, has a passion for incessantly arguing about the equality which here prevails, in which ' truly high-toned' sentiments and manners cannot possibly permanently exist. But woe to anyone who would venture to agree with her in this. In spite of her sixty years, she is still a resolute lively woman, with a very respectable remnant of what was once great beauty. Nineteen years ago she married the professor, first because in him she found an indefatigable antagonist in her attacks upon Freeland, and next because he realised in a very high degree her ideal of manly ' distinction.' For Professor Noria is passionately fond of studying heraldry, has all kinds of chivalrous and courtly ceremonials, from the days of King Nimrod down to the present, at his fingers' ends, but has always been too proud to degrade his knowledge by selling it for filthy lucre. Being an enthusiast in the cause of equality and freedom he came to Freeland, where for a few hours at morn and eve he works at gardening, and thereby comfortably supports himself and his wife—children they have none ; but through the day he labours at his great heraldic work, which, if it is ever finished, is to prove to the world that all the ills it has hitherto suffered can be explained by the facts expressed in heraldry.

But now for our dinner. David admitted, when I questioned him, that in honour of us a fifth course was added to the customary four. But the charm of the meal consisted, not in the number, but in the superiority of the dishes, and not less in the absence of the attendants, who, not belonging to the society at table, necessarily are a disturbing element. I may say, without exaggeration, that I have seldom seen a meal so excellently prepared, and never one consisting of such choice material. The flesh of young oxen fattened upon the aromatic pastures of the higher hills and of the tame antelopes cannot be matched anywhere else ; the vegetables throw the choicest specimens of a Paris Exhibition in the shade ; but the special pride of Freeland is the choiceness and multiplicity of its fruits. And now for the mysterious mode of serving. A cupboard in the wall of the dining-room yielded an apparently inexhaustible series of eatables. First Miss Bertha fetched from this cupboard a tureen, which she had to lift carefully by its ivory handles, and which when uncovered was found to contain a delicious soup. Then from another compartment of the same cupboard was brought a fish as cold as if it had just come from the ice. Then followed, from yet another compartment, a hot ragout, followed by a hot joint, with many vegetables and a salad. Next came ices, with pastry, fruits, cheese. The meal was ended with black coffee made in the presence of the guests, and choice cigars, both, like the beer and the wine, of Freeland growth and manufacture. There was no attendance visible during the meal; the three charming girls fetched everything either out of the mysterious cupboard or from a side-table.

Mrs. Ney now became the cicerone. ' This wall-cupboard,' she explained, ' is one-half ice-cellar—that is, it is cooled by cold air passing through it ; the other half is a kind of hearth—that is, it is furnished with an electrical heating apparatus. Between the two compartments, and divided from them by non-conducting walls, is a neutral space at the ordinary temperature. The cupboard has also the peculiarity of opening on two sides—here into the dining-room, and outside into the corridor. Whilst we were at table the Food Association brought in quick succession the dishes which had been ordered, in part quite ready, in part—as, e.g., the roast meat and the vegetables—prepared but not cooked. The food that was ready was placed in the respective compartments of the cupboard from the corridor ; a member of the association cooked the meat and

vegetables in a kitchen at the back of the house, furnished also with
electrical cooking apparatus. This is not the usual order; when we
are alone the cooking is as a rule done in the cupboard, and attended
to by my daughters. It takes but a little time, and the smell of
the cooking is never perceptible, as the cupboard is both hearth
and ice-cellar in one, and therefore possesses the character of a good
ventilator. Washing the dishes, &c., is the business of the association, as is also attendance at table if it is required.'

Coffee was taken out-of-doors on one of the terraces, where the
ladies sang to the harp and the piano. Meantime Mr. Ney told us
the family relationships of the two pupil-daughters. Leonora is
the child of an agriculturist in Lykipia, Clementina the daughter of
one of his heads of departments. The latter information surprised
us. ' Why,' I asked, ' do these ladies forsake the parental houses,
which must be highly respectable ones? ' Mr. Ney explained that
it was not a respectable house that the pupil-daughters sought, but
simply the cultured, intellectual housewife. The husband may be
ever so famous and learned, but if the housewife is only an ordinary
character, no pupil-daughters will ever cross the threshold. The
institution was intended to afford girls the benefit of a higher
example, of an ennobling womanly intercourse, and not the splendour
of richer external surroundings ; which, it may be remarked, had no
application to the prevailing circumstances in Freeland, as, generally
speaking, all families here live on the same footing. Clementina's
mother is a brave woman with a good heart, but after all only a
good practical housekeeper, ' therefore,' said he, with a sparkle in his
eye, ' she begged my Ellen, who is reckoned among the noblest
women in this country which is so rich in fine women, to take her
Clementina for a couple of years as a favour.'

I must now conclude for to-day, for I am tired; but I have a
great deal more to tell you of my experiences both inside and outside
of the house of the Neys.

─────────

CHAPTER XV

Eden Vale : July 18, ──.

To-day I take up again the report of our experiences here, which I
began a week ago. You will readily imagine that my father and I
were both full of curiosity to see the town. Guessing this, Mr. Ney

next morning invited us to join him and his son on a tour round Eden Vale. The carriage was already waiting. It was a light and elegant vehicle with steel wheels like those of a velocipede, and with two seats each comfortably accommodating two persons. As we, in response to David's signal, exhibited some hesitation and made no effort to get into the vehicle, David perceived that we missed—the horses! He explained to us that in Freeland, and particularly in the towns, the use of animals to draw vehicles was for many reasons given up in favour of mechanical power, which was safer, cleaner, and also cheaper. This vehicle was a kind of *draisine*, and the driver, whose place is on the right side of the front seat, has nothing to do but to press lightly downwards upon a small lever at his right hand, in order to set the machine in motion, the speed depending upon the strength of the pressure. The upward motion of the lever slacks the speed or brings the vehicle to a standstill; while a turning to right or left is effected by a corresponding rotary motion of the same lever. The motive power is neither steam nor electricity, but the elasticity of a spiral spring, which is not inseparably attached to the vehicle, but can be inserted or removed at will.

'The cylindrical box, a little over half a yard long and about eight inches deep, here over the front axle,' demonstrated my friend, ' contains the spiral spring. Before being used the spring is wound up and that very tightly—an operation which is effected by steam-engines in the workshops of the Association for Transport, the energy present in the steam being thus converted into the energy of the tension of the spring. The power thus laid up in the spring is transferred to the axle by a very simple mechanism, and is sufficient to make the wheel revolve ten thousand times even if the vehicle is tolerably heavily loaded ; and as the wheel has a circumference of about six feet and a half, the spring will carry the vehicle a distance of about twelve miles and a half. The speed depends, on the one hand, upon the load in the vehicle, and on the other hand upon the amount of pressure upon the regulating lever. The maximum speed attained by these ordinary *draisines*, on a good road and with a moderate load, is two and a half revolutions—that is, about thirteen feet—in the second, or a little over eleven miles an hour. But we have what are called racing carriages with which we can attain nearly twice that speed. The force of the spring is

exhausted when the wheel has made ten thousand revolutions, which
in slow travelling occurs in from one and a quarter to one and a half
hours. On longer or more rapid journeys provision must therefore be
made for sufficient reserve force, and this is done in various ways.
One can take with him one or more springs ready wound up, for carrying which surplus boxes are attached to the back of the vehicle.
When the spring is wound up and the escapement secured, it will retain its energy for years. But as every spring weighs at least nearly
eighty pounds, this mode of providing reserve power has its limits.
Besides, the changing of the springs is no little trouble. As a rule, a
second method is preferred. The Transport Association has a number
of station-houses for other purposes, on all the more frequented roads.
These stations are indicated by flags, and travellers in the *draisines*
can halt at these and get their springs changed. Every station always
has on hand a number of wound-up springs ; and so travellers can
journey about at any time without let or hindrance, particularly if
they are prudent enough to furnish themselves with a reserve spring
for emergencies. Such stations exist not merely in and around Eden
Vale, but in and around all the towns in Freeland as well as on all
the more frequented country roads.   And as the different associations carrying on the same industry all over the country were shrewd
enough to adopt the same measure for all their springs, it is possible
to travel through the whole of Freeland certain of finding everywhere a relay of springs.   But if one would be absolutely sure, he
can bespeak the necessary springs for any specified route through
the agency of his own association ; and in this case nothing would
prevent him from leaving the highways and taking the less frequented byways so far as they are not too rough and steep—a contingency which, in view of the perfect development of the Freeland
system of roads, is not to be feared except among the most remote
mountain-paths.   In this way, two years ago, our family went
through the whole of the Aberdare and Baringo districts, travelling
a distance of above a thousand miles, and doing the whole journey
most comfortably in a fortnight.'

    At last, with a shake of the head, we consented to get into the
automatic carriage. My father sat in front with Mr. Ney, and
David and I behind ; a pressure by Ney upon the lever, and the
machine noiselessly moved off towards the Eden lake. The banks
of this lake—except on the north-western side, where quays

for the merchant traffic stretch for more than three miles—are bordered by a fourfold avenue of palm-trees, and are laid out in marble steps reaching down to the water, except where occupied by piers covered with lines of rails. At these piers the passengers are landed from the steamers which navigate the lake in all directions, but which, in order not to pollute the balmy air, are provided with perfectly effective smoke-consuming apparatus. Even the discordant shriek of the steam-whistle has been superseded in Freeland. For the Eden lake is only incidentally a seat of traffic; its chief character is that of an enormous piece of water for pleasure and ornament. A large portion of the shore is taken up by the luxuriously furnished bathing-establishments which stretch far out into the lake and are frequented by thousands at all times in the day. These baths are for the most part surrounded by shady groves, and near them are to be found the theatres, opera-houses, and concert-halls of Eden Vale, to the number of sixteen, which we on this occasion saw only on the outside. Our hosts told us that the lake looked most charming by moonlight or under the electric light, and that therefore we would visit it in the course of a few evenings.

We then turned away from the lake, and went to the heights which rose in a half-crescent form around Eden Vale. Here we perceived at once, even at a distance of nearly two miles, a gigantic building which must constantly excite the admiration of even those who are accustomed to it, and which fairly bewildered us strangers. It is as unparalleled in size as it is incomparable in the proportions and harmonious perfection of all its parts. It gives at once the impression of overpowering majesty and of fairy-like loveliness. This wonderful structure is the National Palace of Freeland, and was finished five years ago. It is the seat of the twelve supreme Boards of Administration and the twelve Representative Bodies. It is built entirely of white and yellow marble, surpasses the Vatican in the area it covers, and its airy cupolas are higher than the dome of St. Peter's. That it could be built for 9,500,000*l.* is explained only by the fact that all the builders as well as all the best artists of the country pressed to be employed in some way in its erection. And—so David told me—the motive that prompted the artists and builders to do this was not patriotism, but pure enthusiasm for art. Freeland is rich enough to pay any price for its National

Palace, and no one had a thought of lessening the cost of the building; but the peculiar and impressive beauty of the work as seen in the design had fascinated all artists. David described the feverish excitement with which the commissioners appointed to decide upon the designs sent in announced that a plan had been presented, by a hitherto unknown young architect, which was beyond description; that a new era had been opened in architecture, a new style of architecture invented which in nobility of form rivalled the best Grecian, and in grandeur the most massive Egyptian monuments. And all who saw the design shared in this enthusiasm. The competitors—there were not less than eighty-four, for there had already been a great deal of beautiful building in Eden Vale—without exception withdrew their designs and paid voluntary homage to the new star that had risen in the firmament of art.

We were loth to turn away and look at any other buildings. Not until we had three times been round the National Palace did we consent to leave it. I will spare you the catalogue of the numberless handsome buildings which we hurriedly passed by; I will only say that I was quite bewildered by the number and magnificence of the public buildings devoted to different scientific and artistic purposes. The academies, museums, laboratories, institutions for experiment and research, &c., seemed endless; and one could see at a glance that they were all endowed with extravagant munificence. I must confine myself to a description of the largest of the three public libraries of Eden Vale, the interior of which we were invited to inspect. I was at once struck with the great number of visitors, and next with the fact that only a part of the magnificent rooms were devoted exclusively to reading, other rooms being filled with guests who were enjoying ices or coffee, or with readers of both sexes who were smoking, or again with people talking and laughing. 'It seems,' said I to Mr. Ney, 'that in Freeland the libraries are also *cafés* and conversation *salons*.' He admitted this, and asked if I supposed that the number of serious readers was affected by this arrangement. As I hesitated to answer, he told me that at first a considerable party in Freeland saw in this combination of reading with recreative intercourse a desecration of science. But all opposition was given up when it was seen that the possibility of alternating study with cheerful conversation very largely increased the number of readers. Of course the Association for Providing

Refreshments—for this, and not the library executive, provide the refreshments—was not allowed to enter a certain number of reading-rooms, and in certain of the rooms where refreshments and smoking were allowed talking was forbidden. Thus people visited the library either to study, to amuse themselves with a book, or to converse with acquaintances, according to their mood. The magnificent airy rooms, particularly those with large verandahs communicating with the central pillared court laid out with flower-beds and shrubs, formed, even in the heat of mid-day, a pleasant rendezvous ; so that in the public life of Eden Vale the libraries played somewhat the same *rôle* as the Agora in that of ancient Athens or the Forum in that of ancient Rome. At times there were as many as 5,000 persons of both sexes assembled in this building : at least, our host assured us, as many as that might be found in the two smaller libraries at the northern and western ends of the city; and anyone who cared to take the trouble to examine the eighty-two rooms of the building would probably find that quite one half of those present made a considerable use of the 980,000 volumes which the institution already possessed.

After we had passed numberless public buildings, the purposes of some of which I could scarcely understand, as our ' civilised ' Europe possesses nothing like them—I mention, as an example, merely the Institute for Animal Breeding Experiments, the work of which is, by experiment and observation, to establish what influence heredity, mode of life, and food exercise upon the development of the human organism—it occurred to me that we had not passed a hospital. As I was curious to see how the world-renowned Freeland benevolence, which for years past had richly furnished half the hospitals of the world with means, dealt with the sick poor in its own country, I asked David to take me to at least one hospital. ' I can show you a hospital as little as I can a prison or a barracks, in Eden Vale, for the very simple reason that we do not possess one in all Freeland,' was his answer.

' The absence of prisons and barracks I can understand ; we knew that you Freelanders can manage without criminal laws or a military administration ; but—so I thought—sickness must exist here : that has nothing to do with your social institutions ! '

' Your last sentence I cannot unconditionally assent to,' said Mr. Ney, joining in our conversation. ' Even diseases have decreased under the influence of our social institutions. It is true they have not disappeared—we have sick in Freeland—but no poor sick, for we have no poor at all, either sick or sound. Therefore we do not possess those reservoirs of the diseased poor which in other countries are called "hospitals." We certainly have institutions in which sick persons can, at good prices, procure special and careful treatment, and they are largely patronised, particularly in cases requiring surgical operations; but they are private institutions, and they resemble both in their constitution and their management your most respectable sanatoria for "distinguished patients." '

I was satisfied with this explanation so far; but now another doubt suggested itself. Without public hospitals there could be no proper medical study, I thought; and anatomy in particular could not be studied without the corpses of the poor for dissecting purposes. But Mr. Ney removed this doubt by assuring me that the so-called clinical practice of Freeland medical men was in many respects far superior to that of the West, and even anatomical studies did not suffer at all. It had become the practice, both in Eden Vale and in all Freeland university towns, for medical students in their third year to assist practising physicians, whom, with the permission of the patients and under pledge of behaving discreetly, they accompanied in their visits to the sick, of course only in twos, or at most in threes, if the patient required the assistance of several persons. As all the physicians approved of this practice, which secured to them very valuable gratuitous assistance of various kinds, and as the patients also for the same reason profited much by it, the people rapidly became accustomed to it. In difficult cases these assistants were a great boon to the sick, to whom they ministered with indefatigable care, and whose kindness in allowing them to be present they thus repaid by their skilful attention. When you reflect that in Freeland only *one* commodity is dear and scarce, the labour of man, it can easily be estimated how valuable, as a rule, such assistance is both to the physician and to the patient. And in this way on the average the young medical men learn more than is learnt by hospital practice. They do not see so many sick persons, but those whom they do see they see and treat more fully and more considerately. As a layman, he—Mr. Ney—could not perhaps give sufficiently exhaustive proof of the fact, but he knew that men who had been trained in hospitals admitted that physicians educated as they were in Freeland became better diagnosticians than hospital students. As to anatomical studies, he said, in the first place, that preparations and models afforded—certainly very expensive—substitutes for many school dissections, and in numerous instances were to be preferred; and, in the next place, that the scarcity of subjects for dissection was by no means so extreme in Freeland as I seemed to think. It was true there were no poor who, against their own will and that of their friends, could be subjected to the dissecting-knife; but on this very account there was to be found here no such foolish prejudice against dissection as was elsewhere entertained by even the so-called cultured classes. The medical faculty received great numbers of subjects; and it could scarcely be a detriment to study that the students were compelled to treat these subjects with more respect, and to restore them in a short time to their surviving friends for cremation.

David further told me that in Freeland the physician is not paid by the patient, but is a public official, as is also the apothecary. The study of medicine is nevertheless as free in the universities here as any other study, and no one is prevented from practising as a physician because he may not have undergone an examination or passed through a university. This is the inevitable consequence of the principles of the commonwealth. On the other hand, however, the commonwealth exercises the right of entrusting the care of health and sanitation to certain paid officials, as in every other kind of public service. These appointments are made, according to the public needs, by the head of the Education Department, who, like all other heads of departments, is responsible to his own representative board—or parliament of experts, as we may call it. It is the practice for the professors to propose the candidates, who, of course, undergo many severe examinations before they are proposed. Anyone who fails to get proposed *may* practise medicine, but as the public knows that the most skilful are always chosen with the utmost conscientiousness conceivable, this liberty to practise is of no value. Anyone who thus fails to get proposed, and has neither the energy nor the patience to attempt to wipe off his disgrace at the next opportunity, simply hangs his medical vocation on a nail and turns to some other occupation. The elected physicians are not allowed to receive any payment whatever from their patients. At first their salary is moderate, scarcely more than the average earnings of a worker—that is, 1,800 hour-equivalents per annum; but it is increased gradually, as in the cases of the other officials, and the higher sanitary officials are taken from among the physicians. As the payments are controlled by the departmental parliament, and as this is elected by the persons who in one way or another are interested in this branch of the government, the best possible provision is made to prevent the physicians from assuming an unbecoming attitude towards their patients. No one is obliged to call in any one particular physician. The physicians live in different parts of each town, as conveniently distributed as possible; but everyone calls in the physician he likes best; and as physicians are naturally elected as far as possible upon the Representative Board for Sanitation—whose sittings, it may be remarked in passing, are generally very short—the number of votes which the representatives receive is the best evidence of their relative popularity. It goes without saying that foreign physicians also, if they are men of good repute and do not object, have the same right as the Freeland physicians to submit their qualifications to the proposing body of professors. It should be added that in the larger towns, besides the ordinary physicians and surgeons, specialists are also appointed for certain specific diseases.

We had now been in our carriage for four hours, and were tired of riding, as was natural, notwithstanding the easy motion and comfort of the vehicle. The Neys proposed that we should send the carriage home and return on foot, to which we assented. We left the carriage at one of the stations of the Transport Association, and walked under the shady alleys with which every street in Eden Vale is bordered. We now had leisure to examine more closely the elegant private houses, which, while they all showed the Eden Vale style of architecture—half-Moorish half-Grecian in its character—were for the rest alike neither in size nor in embellishment. The most conspicuous charm of these villas consists in their wonderfully lovely gardens, with their choice trees, their surpassingly beautiful flowers, the white marble statuary, the fountains, and the many tame animals—especially monkeys, parrots, brightly coloured finches, and all sorts of song-birds—which were sporting about in them among merrily shouting children. We were astonished at the extraordinary cleanness of the streets; and the chief reason of this was said to be that, since the invention of automatic carriages, no draught animals kicked up dust or dropped filth in the streets of Freeland towns.

'Are there no horses here?' I asked; and I was told that there were a great number, and of the noblest breed; but they were used only for riding outside of the town, among the neighbouring meadows, groves, and woods.

'But that must be a very expensive luxury here,' I said. 'The horse itself and its keep may be cheap enough; but, as human labour is the dearest thing in Freeland, I cannot understand how any Freeland income can support the cost of a groom. Or do such servants receive exceptionally low wages here?'

'The last would be scarcely possible among us,' answered Mr. Ney, smiling; 'for who would be willing to act as groom in Freeland? We are obliged to give those who attend to horses the same average payment as other workers; and if, for the seven saddle-horses which I keep in the stables of the Transport Association, I had to pay for servants after the scale of Western lands, the cost would be more than the whole of my income. But the riddle is easily solved: the work in the stables is done by means of machinery, so that on an average one man is enough for every fifty horses. You shake your heads incredulously! But when you have seen in how few minutes a horse can be groomed and made to look as bright as a mirror by our enormous cylindrical brushes set in rotation by mechanism; in how short a time our scouring-machines and water-service can cleanse the largest stable of dung and all sorts of filth; and how the fodder is automatically supplied to the animals, you will not only understand how it is that we can keep horses cheaply, but you will also perceive that in Freeland even the " stable-men " are cultured gentlemen, as deserving of respect and as much respected as everybody else.'

Conversing thus we reached home, where a hearty luncheon was taken, and some matters of business attended to. After the dinner described in my last, our hosts and we went again to the lake, and visited first the large opera-house, where, on that day, the work of a Freeland composer was given. This piece was not new to us, for it is one of the many Freeland compositions which have been well received and are often performed in other countries. But we were astonished at the peculiar—yet common to all Freeland theatres— arrangement of the auditorium. The seats rise in an amphitheatre to a considerable height; and the roof rests upon columns, between which the outer air passes freely. As many as ten thousand persons can find abundant room in the larger of these theatres, without an accumulation of vitiated air or any excessive heat.

The performance was excellent, the appointments in every respect brilliant; yet the price—which was not varied by any difference of rank—was ridiculously low according to Western notions. A seat cost sixpence—that is in the large opera-house; the other theatres are considerably cheaper. The undertakers are in all cases the urban communes, and the performers, as well as the managers, act as communal officials. The theatres are all conducted on the economic principle that the cost and maintenance of the building fall upon the communal budget; and the door-money has to cover merely the hire of the performers and the stage expenses.

I learnt from David that Eden Vale possessed, besides the grand opera, also a dramatic opera, and four theatres, as well as three concert-halls, in which every evening orchestral and chamber music and choruses are to be heard. But as a Freeland specialty he mentioned five different theatres for instruction, in which astronomical, archæological, geological, palæontological, physical, historical, geographical, natural history—in short, all conceivable scientific lectures were delivered, illustrated by the most comprehensive display of plastic representative art. The lectures are written by the most talented specialists, delivered by the most eloquent orators, and placed on the stage by the most skilful engineers and decorators. This kind of theatre is the most frequented; as a rule, the existing accommodation is not sufficient, hence the commune is building two new lecture-houses, which will be opened in the course of a few months. The grandeur of these presentations—as I learnt for myself the next evening—is really astounding; and though the young generally compose the greater part of the audience, adults also attend in large numbers.

When we left the theatre, the Neys engaged one of the gondolas which an association keeps there in readiness, and which is propelled by a screw worked by an elastic spring; and we steered out into the lake. The lake was lit up as brilliantly as if it were day, by elevated electric lights, with reflectors all round the shore. We had that evening the special pleasure of hearing a new cantata by Walter, the most renowned composer of Freeland, performed for the first time by the members of the Eden Vale Choral Society. This society, which generally chooses the Eden lake as the scene of its weekly performances, makes use on such occasions of a number of splendid barges, the cost of whose—often positively fairylike—appointments is defrayed by the voluntary contributions of its members and admirers.

Was it the influence of the very peculiar scenery, or was it the beauty of the composition itself?—certainly the effect which this cantata produced upon me was overwhelming. On the way home I confessed to David that I had never before been so struck with what I might call the transcendental power of music as during the performance on the lake. I seemed to hear the World-spirit speaking to my soul in those notes; and I seemed to understand what was said, but not to be able to translate it into ordinary Italian or English. At the same time I expressed my astonishment that so young a community as that of Freeland should have produced not merely notable works in all branches of art, but in two—architecture and music—works equal to the best examples of all times.

Mrs. Ney was of opinion that this was simply a necessary consequence of the general tendency of the Freeland spirit. Where the enjoyment of life and leisure co-exist the arts must flourish, since the latter are merely products of wealth and noble leisure. And it could be easily explained how it was that architecture and music were the first of the arts to develop. Architecture necessarily and at once received a strong stimulus from the needs of a commonwealth of a novel and comprehensive character; and in the case of Freeland the influence of the grand yet charming nature of the country was unmistakable. On the other hand, music is the earliest of all forms of art—that to which the genius of man first turns itself whenever a new era of artistic creation is introduced by new modes of feeling and thinking.

'From the circumstance that your greatest master has to-day given the public a gratuitous first performance of his new composition, one might almost conclude that in this country the composers, or at any rate some of them, are also public officials. Is it so?' asked my father.

Mr. Ney said it was not so, and added that composers, poets, authors, and creative artists in general, when they produced anything of value, could with certainty reckon upon making a very good

P

income from the sale of their works. As all Freeland families spent large sums in purchasing books, journals, musical compositions, and works of art of all kinds, the conditions of the art-world could not be correctly measured by Western standards. The artistic productions sold during the previous year had realised 800,000,000*l*. Of this sum, however, the greater part represented the cost of reproductions, particularly in the case of printed works ; yet the author of an only tolerably popular composition, book, or essay was sure of a very considerable profit. Editions numbering hundreds of thousands were here not at all remarkable ; and editions of millions were by no means rare. For instance, Walter had hitherto composed in all six larger and eighteen smaller works, and for the sale of them the Musical Publishing Association had, up to the end of the last year, paid him 21,000*l*. In fact, it could be positively asserted that an author of any kind, who produced only *one* exceptionally good work, could live very comfortably upon the proceeds of its sale. It had even happened that the public libraries had bought 50,000 copies of a single book. Freeland possesses 3,050 such institutions, and the larger of them are sometimes compelled to keep many hundred copies of books which are much sought after. When the interest of the reading public diminishes, the libraries withdraw a part of these copies, and there are yearly large auctions of such withdrawn books, without, however, diminishing the sales of the publishing associations. Moreover, the authors of Freeland are continuously and profitably kept busy by thousands of journals of all conceivable kinds which, so far as they offer what is of value, have a colossal sale. Capable architects, sculptors, painters can always reckon upon brilliant successes, for the demand for good and original plans and beautiful statues and pictures is always greater than the supply. The *grand* art, it is true, finds employment only in public works, but here, as we have seen, it finds it on a most magnificent and most profitable scale. In Freeland they attach extraordinary importance to the cultivation of the beautiful and the noble ; they hold the grand art to be one of the most effectual means of ethical culture ; and as the community is rich enough to pay for everything that it thinks desirable, the public outlay for monumental buildings and their adornment finds its limits only in the capacities of the creative artists. And the happy organisation of the departments which have these things in charge has—hitherto at any rate—preserved the Freelanders from serious blunders. Not everything that has been produced at the public cost is worthy of being accepted as perfect—many works of art thus produced have been thrown into the shade by better ones; but even those subsequently surpassed creations were at the time of their production the best which the existing art could produce, and to ask for more would be unjust. And I could not avoid perceiving that the population of Freeland are not merely proud of their public expenditure in art, but that they thoroughly enjoy what they pay for; and in this respect they are comparable to the ancient Athenians, of whom we are told that, with solitary exceptions, they all had an intense appreciation of the marvellous productions of their great masters.

'With such a universal taste for the beautiful among your people,' said my father to Mrs. Ney, 'I am surprised that so little attention is given to the adornment of the most beautiful embellishment of Freeland—its queenly women. Certainly their dress is shapely, and I have nowhere noticed such a correct taste in the choice of the most becoming forms and colours; but of actual ornaments one sees none at all. Here and there a gold fastener in the hair, here and there a gold or silver brooch on the dress—that is all; precious stones and pearls seem to be avoided by the ladies here. What is the reason of this?'

'The reason is,' answered Mrs. Ney, ' that the sole motive which makes ornaments so sought after among other nations is absent from us in Freeland. Vanity is native here also, among both men and women; but it does not find any satisfaction in the display of so-called "valuables," things whose only superiority consists in their being dear. Do you really believe that it is the *beauty* of the diamond which leads so many of our pitiable sisters in other parts of the world to stake happiness and honour in order to get possession of such glittering little bits of stone? Why does the woman who has sold herself for a genuine stone thrust aside as unworthy of notice the imitation stone which in reality she cannot distinguish from the real one? And do you doubt that the real diamond would itself be degraded to the rank of a valueless piece of crystal which no "lady of taste" would ever glance at, if it by any means lost its high price? Ornaments do not please, therefore, because they are beautiful, but because they are dear. They flatter vanity not by

their brilliancy, but by giving to the owner of them the consciousness of possessing in these scarcely visible trifles the extract of so
many human lives. " See, here on my neck I wear a talisman for
which hundreds of slaves have had to put forth their best energies
for years, and the power of which could lay even you, who look
upon the pretty trifle with such reverent admiration, as a slave at
my feet, obedient to all my whims ! Look at me : I am more than
you ; I am the heiress who can squander upon a trifling toy what
you vainly crave to appease your hunger." That is what the
diamond-necklace proclaims to all the world ; and *that is why* its
possessor has betrayed and made miserable perhaps both herself and
others, merely to be able to throw it as her own around her neck.
For note well that ornaments adorn only those to whom they belong ; it is mean to wear borrowed ornaments—it is held to be im-
proper ; and rightly so, for borrowed ornaments lie—they are a crown
which gives to her who wears it the semblance of a power which in
reality does not belong to her.

' The power of which ornaments are the legitimate expression—
the power over the lives and the bodies of others—does not exist in
Freeland. Anyone possessing a diamond worth, for example, 600*l.*,
would here have at his disposal a year's income from one person's
labour ; but to buy such a diamond and to wear it because it represented that value would, in view of our institutions, be to
make oneself ridiculous ; for he who did it would simply be investing in that way the profits of *his own labour*. Value for value
must he give to anyone whose labour he would buy for himself
with his stone ; and, instead of reverent admiration, he would
only excite compassion for having renounced better pleasures, or
for having put forth profitless efforts, in order to acquire a paltry
bit of stone. It would be as if the owner of the diamond announced to the world : " See, whilst you have been enjoying
yourselves or taking your ease, I have been stinting myself and
toiling in order to gain this toy ! " In everybody's eyes he would
appear not the more powerful, but the more foolish : the stone,
whose fascination lies purely in the supposition that its owner belongs to the masters of the earth who have power over the labour
of others, and *therefore* can amuse themselves by locking up the
product of so much sweating toil in useless trinkets—the stone can
no longer have any attraction for him. He who buys such a stone

in Freeland is like a man who should set his heart upon possessing a crown which was no longer the symbol of authority.'

'Then you do not admit that ornaments have any real adorning power? You deny that pearls or diamonds add materially to the charms of a beautiful person?' asked my father in reply.

'That I do, certainly,' was the answer. 'Not that I dispute their decorative effect altogether; only I assert that they do not produce the same and, as a rule, not so good an effect as can be produced by other means. But, in general, the toy, which has no essential appropriateness to the human body, does not adorn, but, in ninety-nine cases out of a hundred, rather disfigures, its proud possessor. That in other parts of the world a lady decked with diamonds pleases you gentlemen better than one decked with flowers is due to the same cause that makes you—though you may be staunch Republicans—see more beauty in a queen than in her rivals, though at the bar of an impartial æsthetics the latter would be judged the more beautiful. A certain something, a peculiar witchery, surrounds her—the witchery (excuse the word) of servility; this it is, and not your æsthetic judgment, which cheats you into believing that the diamond lends a higher charm than the rose-wreath. Let the rose become the symbol of authority to be worn only by queens, and you would without any doubt find that roses were the adornment best fitted to reveal true majesty.'

'But the precious metals'—thus I interposed—'are not so completely abjured in Freeland as precious stones and pearls. Is there no inconsistency here?'

'I think not,' answered Mrs. Ney. 'We make use of any material in proportion to its beauty and suitability. If we find gems or pearls really useful for decorative purposes, and sufficiently beautiful when thus used to compensate in their æsthetic attractiveness for their cost, we make use of them without hesitation. But that does not apply to jewels as personal ornaments: the natural rose is, under all circumstances, a better adornment than its imitation in rubies and diamonds. The precious metals, on the other hand, have certain properties—durability, lustre, and extraordinary malleability—which in many cases make it imperative to employ them for decorative purposes. Nevertheless, even their employment is very limited among us. These studs here, and the fillet in my daughter's hair, are not of pure gold, but are made of

an alloy the principal ingredient in which is steel, and which owes
its colour and immunity from rust to gold, without being as costly
as silver. No one wishes to pass off such steel-gold for real gold;
we use this material simply because we think it beautiful and
suitable, and would at once exchange it for another which was
cheaper and yet possessed the same properties. We use pure gold
only exceptionally. Our table-plate, which you perhaps thought to
be silver, is made of an alloy which owes to silver nothing but its
resistance to most of the acids. If you examine the plate more
closely you will see that this silver-alloy differs from pure silver
both in being of a lighter colour and in being less weighty. In
short, we use the noble metals never *because* of, but now and then
in spite of, their costliness.

'I might say that we women of Freeland are vain, because our
desire to please is more pronounced than that of our Western sisters.
We are not content with being beautiful; we wish to appear
beautiful, and the men do all they can to stimulate us in this
endeavour; only I must ask you to make this distinction—we do
not wish to make a show, but to please. Therefore to a Freeland
woman dress and adornment are never ends in themselves, but
means to an end. In Europe a lady of fashion often disfigures
herself in the cruellest manner because she cares less about the
effect produced by her person than about that produced by her
clothes, her adornment; she does not choose the dress that best
brings out her personal charms, but the most costly which her
means will allow her to buy. We act differently. Our own æsthetic
taste preserves us from the folly of allowing a dressmaker to induce
us to wear garments different from those which we think or know
will best bring out the good points of our figure. Besides, we can
always avail ourselves of the advice of artistically cultured men.
No painter of renown would disdain to instruct young women how
to choose their toilette; in fact, special courses of lectures are given
upon this important subject. Naturally there cannot be any uniform fashion among us, since the composition, the draping, and the
colours of the clothing are made to harmonise with the individuality
of the wearer. To dress the slender and the stout, the tall and the
short, the blonde and the brunette, the imposing and the *petite*,
according to the same model would be regarded here as the height
of bad taste. A Freeland woman who wishes to please would think

it quite as ridiculous if anyone advised her to change a mode of dressing or of wearing her hair which she had proved to be becoming to her, merely because she had been seen too often dressed in this style. We cannot imagine that, in order to please, it is best to disfigure oneself in as many ways as possible; but we hold firmly to the belief—and in this we are supported by the men—that the human form should be covered and veiled by clothing, but not distorted and disfigured.'

We gallantly declared that we thoroughly agreed with these principles of the toilette. The truth is, that a stranger in Freeland, accustomed to the eccentricities of Western fashions, at first thinks the artistically designed costumes of the women a little too simple, but he ultimately comes to find a return to the Western caricatures simply intolerable. You will remember that in Rome David assured us that European fashions gave him exactly the same impression as those of the African savages. After being here scarcely a week, I begin to entertain the same opinion.

But I see that I must conclude without having exhausted my matter. Promising to give next time what I have omitted here,

Thine,

————.

CHAPTER XVI

Eden Vale : July 28, ——

I COULD not keep my promise to write again soon, because last week was taken up with a number of excursions which I made with David on horseback, or by means of automatic *draisines*, into the environs of Eden Vale and to the neighbouring town of Dana, and by rail to the shores of the Victoria Nyanza. In this way I have got to know quite a number of Freeland towns, as well as several scattered industrial and agricultural colonies. I have seen the charming places embosomed in shady woods in the Aberdare range, where extensive metallurgical industries are carried on; Naivasha city, the emporium of the leather industry and the export trade in meat, and whose rows of villas reach round the Naivasha lake, stretching a total distance of some forty miles; the settlements among the hills to the north of the Baringo lake, with their numerous troops of noble horses, herds of cattle and swine, flocks of sheep, multitudes of tame elephants, buffaloes, and zebras, their gold and silver mines ; and Ripon, the centre of the mill industry and of the Victoria Nyanza trade. In all the towns I found the arrangements essentially the same as in Eden Vale : electric railways in the principal streets, electric lighting and heating, public libraries, theatres, &c. But what surprised me most was that even the rural settlements, with very few exceptions, were not behind the towns in the matter of comforts and conveniences. Electric railways placed them in connection with the main lines. Wherever five or six villas—for the villa style prevails universally in Free-land—stand together, they have electric lighting and heating ; even the remotest mountain-valleys are not without the telegraph and the telephone ; and no house is without its bath. Wherever a few hundred houses are not too widely scattered a theatre is built for them, in which plays, concerts, and lectures are given in turn. There is everywhere a superfluity of schools ; and if a settler has built his house too far from any neighbours for his children to be able to attend a school near home, the children are sent to the house of a friend, for in Freeland nothing is allowed to stand in the way of the education of the young.

Of course I have not neglected the opportunity of observing the people of Freeland at their work, both in the field and in the factory. And it was here that I first discovered the greatness of Freeland. What I saw everywhere was on an overpoweringly enormous scale. The people of the Western nations can form as faint a notion of the magnitude of the mechanical contrivances, of the incalculable motive force which the powers of nature are here compelled to place at the disposal of man, as they can of the refined, I might almost say aristocratic, comfort which is everywhere associated with labour. No dirty, exhausting manual toil ; the most ingenious apparatus performs for the human worker everything that is really unpleasant ; man has for the most part merely to superintend his never-wearying iron slaves. Nor do these busy servants pain the ears of their masters by their clatter, rattle, and rumbling. I moved among the pounding-mills of Lykipia, which prepare the mineral manure for the local Manure Association by grinding it between stone-crushers with a force of thousands of hundredweights, and there was no unpleasantly loud sound to be heard, and not an atom of dust to be seen. I went through iron-works in which steel hammers, falling with a force of 3,000 tons, were in use. The same quiet prevailed in the well-lit cheerful factory; no soiling of the hands or faces of the workers disturbed the impression that one here had to do with gentlemen who were present merely to superintend the smithy-work of the elements. In the fields I saw ploughing and sowing : again the same appearance of the lord of the creation who, by the pressure of a finger, directed at will the giants Steam and Electricity, and made them go whither and on what errand he thought fit. I was *under* the ground, in the coal-pits and the iron-mines, and there I did not find it different: no dirt, no exhaustive toil for the man who looked on in gentlemanly calm whilst his obedient creatures of steel and iron wrought for him without weariness and without murmuring, asking of him nothing but that he should guide them.

During these same excursions I learnt more about a number of the recreations in which the Freelanders specially indulge. With David I visited the numerous points on the Kenia and the Aberdare mountains from which one obtains the most charming views. To these points every Sunday the young people resort for singing and dancing, and as a rule they are treated to some surprise which the Recreation Committee—a standing institution in every Freeland town—has organised in celebration of some event or other. To me the most surprising was the Ice-Festival on the great skating-pool on the Kenia glacier. Five years before, the united Recreation Committees of Eden Vale, Dana City, and Upper Lykipia had converted a plateau nearly 14,000 feet above the sea, and covering 5,900 acres, into a pool fed by water from the adjoining large icefield. From the end of May until the middle of August there are always at this elevation severe night frosts, which quickly convert the glacier-water of the pool, already near the freezing-point, into a solid floor of ice. After surrounding this magnificent skating-place with luxurious warmable waiting, dressing, and refreshment rooms, and connecting it with the foot of the mountain by means of an inclined railway, the united committees handed over their work to the public for gratuitous use. The large expense of construction was easily defrayed by voluntary contributions, and the cost of maintenance was more than covered by the donations of the numerous visitors. During the whole of the cool season the large ice-pool is covered by skaters, very many of whom are women, not merely from the Kenia district—that is, from a radius of sixty or seventy miles—but also from all parts of Freeland. Even from the shores of the Indian Ocean and of the great lakes men and women who are fond of this healthy amusement come to participate in the brilliant ice-festivals. There is at present a project on foot to build at the skating-place a magnificent hotel, which shall enable the lovers of this graceful and invigorating exercise to spend the night at an elevation of nearly 14,000 feet above the sea. Moreover, the great popularity of the Kenia ice-pool has given occasion to another similar undertaking, which is nearly completed on the Kilimanjaro, at a level 1,640 feet higher than the ice-pool of the Kenia. Another projected ice-pool on the Mountains of the Moon, near the Albert Nyanza, has not yet been begun, as the local committee have not yet found a site sufficiently high and large.

But all these arrangements for recreation did not excite my admiration and astonishment so much as the buoyant and—in the best sense of the word—childlike delight and gladness with which the Freelanders enjoyed not merely their pleasures, but their whole life. One gets the impression everywhere that care is unknown in this country. That ingenuous cheerfulness, which among us in Europe is the enviable privilege of the early years of youth, here sits upon every brow and beams from every eye. Go through any other civilised country you please, you will seldom, I might say never, find an adult upon whose countenance untroubled happiness, buoyant enjoyment of life, are to be read ; with a careful, most often with an anxious, expression of face men hurry or steal past us, and if there is anywhere to be seen a gaiety that is real and not counterfeited it is almost always the gaiety of recklessness. With us it is only the ' poor in spirit ' who are happy ; reflection seems to be given us only that we may ponder upon the want and worry of life. Here for the first time do I find men's faces which bear the stamp of both conscious reflection and untroubled happiness. And this spectacle of universal happy contentedness is to me more exhilarating than all else that there is to be seen here. One breathes more freely and more vigorously ; it is as if I had for the first time escaped from the oppressive atmosphere of a stifling prison into the freedom of nature where the air was pure and balmy.

'Whence do you get all this reflected splendour of sunny joyousness?' I asked David.

'It is the natural result of the serene absence of care which we all enjoy,' was his answer. 'For it is not a mere appearance, it is a reality, that care is unknown in this country, at least that most hideous, most degrading of all care—how to get daily bread.) It is not because we are richer, not even because we are all well-off, but because we—that is, every individual among us—possess the absolute certainty of continuing to be well-off. Here one cannot become poor, for everyone has an inalienable right to his share of the incalculable wealth of the community. To-morrow lies serene and smiling before us; it cannot bring us evil, for the well-being of even the last among us is guaranteed and secured by a power as strong and permanent as the continuance of our race upon this planet—the power of human progress. In this respect we are really like children, whom the shelter and protection of the parental house save from every material care.'

'And are you not afraid,' I interposed, 'that this absence of care will eventually put an end to that upon which you rely—that is, to progress? Hitherto at least want and care have been the strongest incentives to human activity; if these incentives are weakened, if the torturing anxiety about to-morrow ceases, then will progress be slackened, stagnation and then degeneration will follow, and together with the consequent inevitable impoverishment want and care will come again. I must admit that none of this has so far shown itself among you; but this does not remove my fears. For at present you in Freeland are enjoying the fruits of the progress of others. What has been thought out and invented under the pressure of the want and sorrow of unnumbered centuries, what is still being thought out and invented under the pressure of the want and sorrow of untold millions outside the boundaries of your own country—it is all this which makes your present happiness possible. But how will it be when what you are striving after has happened, when the whole human race shall have been converted to your principles? Do you believe that want can completely disappear from off the face of the earth without taking progress with it?'

'We not only believe that,' was his answer, 'but we know it; and everyone who does not allow obsolete prejudices to distort his judgment of facts must agree with us. To struggle for existence is the inexorable command, upon the observance of which nature has made progress—nay, the very being of every living thing—to depend : this we understand better than any other people in the world. But that this struggle must necessarily be prompted by hunger we deny ; and we deny also that it is necessarily a struggle between individuals of the same species. Even we have to struggle for existence ; for what we require does not fall into our lap without effort and labour. Yet not *opposed* but *side by side* do we stand in our struggle ; and it is on this very account that the result is never doubtful to us. When we are referred to the conflict to be found everywhere in the animal world, we can appeal to the fact that man possesses other means of struggling than do his fellow-creatures which stand on a lower level, and can work out his evolution in a different manner. But to plead this would be to resort to a poor and unnecessary subterfuge, for in reality the reverse is the case. Want and material care are—with very rare exceptions—no natural stimulants to fight in the competitive struggle for existence. By far the larger number of animals never suffer lack, never feel any anxiety whatever about the morrow ; and yet from the beginning all things have been subjected to the great and universal law of progress. Very rarely in the animal world is there the struggle of antagonism between members of the same species ; the individuals live together in peace and generally without antagonism, and it is against foes belonging to other species that their weapons are directed. It is against lions and panthers that the gazelle fights for existence by its vigilance and speed, not against its own fellows ; lions and panthers employ their cunning and strength against the gazelle and the buffalo, and not against other lions and panthers. Conflict among ourselves and against members of our own species was and is the privilege of the human race. But this sad privilege has sprung from a necessity of civilisation. In order to develop into what we have become we have been obliged to demand from nature more than she is in a position voluntarily to offer us ; and for many thousands of years there has been no way of obtaining it but that of satisfying our higher needs by a system of mutual plunder and oppression. And in this way want became a stimulus to conflict in the human struggle for existence. Note, therefore, that the fighting of man against man, with material care as the sharpest spur to the conflict, was not and is not the simple transfer-

ence to human society of a law everywhere prevalent in nature, but
an exceptional distortion of this great natural law under the influence of a certain phase of human development. We suffered want
not because nature compelled us to do so, but because we robbed
each other ; and we robbed each other because with civilisation there
arose a disproportion between our requirements and our natural
means of satisfying them. But now that civilisation has attained to control over the forces of nature, this disproportion is
removed ; in order to enjoy plenty and leisure we no longer need
to exploit each other. Thus, to put an end to the conflict of man
with man, and at the same time of material want, is not to depart
from the natural form of the struggle for existence, but in reality to
return to it. The struggle is not ended, but simply the unnatural
form of it. In its endeavour to raise itself above the level of the
merely animal nature, humanity was betrayed into a long-enduring
strife with nature herself; and this strife was the source of all the
unspeakable torture and suffering, crime and cruelty, the unbroken
catalogue of which makes up the history of mankind from the first
dawn of civilisation until now. But this dreadful strife is now
ended by a most glorious victory ; we have become what we have
endeavoured for thousands of years to become, a race able to win
from nature plenty and leisure for all its members; and by this
very re-acquired harmony between our needs and the means of
satisfying them have we brought ourselves again into unison with
nature. We remain subject to nature's unalterable law of the
struggle for existence ; but henceforth we shall engage in this
conflict in the same manner as all other creatures of nature—our
struggle will be an external, not an internal one, not against our
fellow-men nor prompted by the sting of material want.'

'But,' I asked, ' what will prompt men to struggle in the cause
of progress when want has lost its sting ? '

'Singular question! You show very plainly how difficult it is
to understand things which contradict the views we have drunk in
with our mother's milk, and which we have been accustomed to regard as the foundation-stones of order and civilisation, even when
those views most manifestly contradict the most conspicuous facts.
As if want had ever been the sole, or even the principal, spring of
human progress! The strife with nature, in which the disproportion between the needs of civilisation and the ability to satisfy those

needs led mankind through a long period of transition from barbarism to a state of culture worthy of human nature, had, it is true,
this result—viz. that the struggle for existence assumed not only its
natural forms, but also forms which were unnatural, and which did
violence to the real and essential character of most of nature's offspring; yet these latter forms never attained to absolute dominion.
In fact, as a rule nature has shown herself stronger than the human
institutions which were in conflict with her.   During the whole of
the history of civilisation we owe the best achievements of the
human intellect not to want, but to those other impulses which are
peculiar to our race, and which will remain so as long as that race
dominates the earth.   Thrice blind is he who will not see this!
The great thinkers, inventors, and discoverers of all ages and all
nations have not been spurred on by hunger; and in the majority
of cases it may be asserted that they thought and speculated, in-
vestigated and discovered, not *because* they were hungry, but *in
spite* of it.   Yet—so it may be objected—those men were the elect
of our race; the great mass of ordinary men can be spurred on
only by vulgar prosaic hunger to make the best use of what the
elect have discovered and invented.   But those who judge thus are
guilty of a most remarkable act of oversight.   Only those who are
strongly prejudiced can fail to see that it is just the well-to-do, the
non-hungry, who most zealously press forward.   Hunger is certainly
a stimulus to labour, but an unnerving and pernicious one; and
those who would point triumphantly to the wretches who can be
spurred on to activity only by the bitterest need, and sink into
apathy again as soon as the pangs of hunger are stilled, forget that
it is this very wretchedness which is the cause of this demoralisa-
tion.   The civilised man who has once acquired higher tastes will
the more zealously strive to gratify those tastes the less his mental
and physical energy has been weakened by degrading want, and the
less doubtful the result of his effort is.   For all unprejudiced persons
must recognise the most effective stimulus to activity not in hopeless
want, but in rational self-interest cheerfully striving after a sure
aim.   Now, *our* social order, far from blunting this self-interest, has
in reality for the first time given it full scope.   You may therefore
be perfectly certain of this: the superiority over other nations in
inventiveness and intellectual energy which you have already noted
among us is no accidental result of any transitory influences, but

the necessary consequence of our institutions. Every nation that adopts these institutions will have a similar experience. Just as little as we need the stimulus of the pangs of want to call forth those inventions and improvements which increase the amount and the variety of our material and intellectual enjoyments, so little will progress be checked in any other nation which, like us, finds itself in the happy position of enjoying the fruits of progress.'

I was deeply moved as my friend thus spoke like an inspired seer. 'When I look at the matter closely,' I said, 'it seems as if, according to the contrary conception, there can be progress only where it is to all intents and purposes useless. For the fundamental difference between you Freelanders and ourselves lies here—that you enjoy the fruits of progress, while we merely busy ourselves with the Danaidean vessel of over-production. No one doubts that Stuart Mill was right when he complained that all our discoveries and inventions had not been able to alleviate the sorrow and want of a single working-man; nevertheless, what terrible folly it would be to believe that that very want was necessary in order that further discoveries and inventions might be made!

'But,' I continued, 'to return to the point at which we started. you have not yet fully explained to me all the astonishing, heart-quickening cheerfulness which prevails everywhere in this land of the happy. Want and material care are here unknown : admitted. But there are outside of Freeland hundreds of thousands, nay millions, who are free from oppressive care : why do they not feel real cheerfulness? Compare, for instance, our respective fathers. Mine is unquestionably the richer of the two, and yet what deep furrows care has engraved upon his forehead, what traces of painful reflection there are about his mouth ; but what a gladsome light of eternal youth shines from every feature of your father! I might almost imagine that the air which one breathes in this country has a great deal to do with this ; for the folds and wrinkles in my father's features of which I have just spoken have in the fortnight of our stay here grown noticeably less, and I myself feel brighter and happier than ever I felt before.'

'You have forgotten the most important thing,' replied David—'the influence of public feeling upon the feelings of the individual. Man is a social being whose thoughts and feelings are derived only in part from his own head and his own heart, whilst a not less

important part of them—I might say the fundamental tone which
gives colour and character to the individual's intellectual and
emotional life—has its source in the social surroundings for the
time being. Everyone stands in a not merely external, but also an
internal, indissoluble relation of contact with those who are around
him ; he imagines that he thinks and feels and acts as his own
individuality prompts, but he thinks, feels, and acts for the most
part in obedience to an external influence from which he cannot
escape—the influence of the spirit of the age which embraces all
heads, all hearts, and all actions. Had the enlightened humane
freethinker of to-day been born three centuries ago, he would have
persecuted those who differed from him upon the most subtile, and,
as he now thinks, ridiculous points of belief, with the same savage
hatred as did all others who were then living. And had he seen
the light yet a few centuries earlier—say, among the pagan Saxons
of the days of Charlemagne—human sacrifices would have shocked
him as little as they did the other worshippers of the goddess
Hertha. And the man who, brought up as a pagan Saxon in the
forests of the Weser and the Elbe, would have held it honourable
and praiseworthy to make the altar-stone of Hertha smoke with the
blood of slaughtered captives, would in that same age have felt
invincible horror at such a deed, had he—with exactly the same
personal capabilities—by accident been born in imperial Byzantium
instead of among German barbarians. At Byzantium, on the other
hand, he would have indulged in lying and deceit without scruple,
whilst, if surrounded by the haughty German heroes, he—in
other respects the same man from head to foot—would have been
altogether incapable of such weak vices. Since this is so—since
the virtues and vices, the thoughts and the feelings, of those of our
contemporaries among whom we are born and brought up give the
fundamental tone to our own character, it is simply impossible that
the members of a community, maddened by a ceaseless fear of
hunger, should pass their lives in undisturbed serenity. Where an
immense majority of the people never know what the morrow may
bring forth—whether it may bring a continuance of miserable
existence or absolute starvation—under the dominion of a social
order which makes one's success in the struggle for existence depend
upon being able to snatch the bread out of the mouth of a competitor, who in his turn is coveting the bread we have, and is striving

with feverish anxiety to rob us of it—in a society where everyone is everyone's foe, it is the height of folly to talk of a real gladsome enjoyment of life. No individual wealth protects a man from the sorrow that is crushing the community. The man who is a hundred-fold a millionaire, and who cannot himself consume the hundredth part of the interest of his interest, even he cannot escape the sharp grip of the horrid hunger-spectre any more than the most wretched of the wretched who wanders, roofless and cold and hungry, through the streets of your great cities. The difference between the two lies not in the brain and in the heart, but simply in the stomach ; the second simply endures physical suffering over and above the psychical and intellectual suffering of the first. But the psychical and mental suffering is permanent, and therefore more productive of results. Look at him, your Crœsus plagued with a mad hunger-fever ; how breathlessly he rushes after still greater and greater gains ; how he sacrifices the happiness and honour, the enjoyment and peace, of himself and of those who belong to him to the god from whom he looks to obtain help in the universal need—the god Mammon. He does not possess his wealth, he is possessed by it. He heaps estate upon estate, imagining that upon the giddy summit of untold millions he shall obtain security from the sea of misery which rages horridly around him. Nay, so blinded is the fool that he does not perceive how it is merely this ocean of universal misery that fills him with horror ; but he rather cherishes the sad delusion that his dread will become less if but the abyss below be deeper and farther removed from his giddy seat above. And let it not be supposed that by this superstitious dread of hunger merely the foolishness of individuals is referred to. The whole age is possessed by it, and the best natures most completely so. For the more sensitive are the head and the heart, the more potent is the influence exerted by the common consciousness of universal want in contrast with transitory individual comfort. Only absolutely cold-hearted egoists or perfect idiots form here and there an exception ; they alone are able really to enjoy their wealth undisturbed by the hunger-spectre which is strangling millions of their brethren.

'This, Carlo, is what imprints upon the faces of all of you such Hippocratic marks of suffering. You can never give yourselves up to the unrestrained enjoyment of life so long as you breathe an atmosphere of misery, sorrow, and dread. And it is this community

Q

of feeling, which connects every man with his surroundings, that enables you here, only just arrived among a society to which this misery, this sorrow, this dread, are totally unknown, to enjoy that cheerful serenity of thought and emotion which is the innate characteristic of every healthy child of nature. And we, who have lived for a generation in the midst of this community from which both misery and the fear of misery are absent—we have almost completely got rid of that gloomy conception of human destiny of which we were the victims so long as the Old World was about us with its self-imposed martyrdom. I use the limiting expression "almost" with reference to those among us who had reached adult manhood before they came to Freeland. We younger ones, who were born and have grown up here without having ever seen misery, differ in this respect very considerably from our elders who in their youth saw the Medusa-head of servility face to face. It is five-and-twenty years since my father and mother, who were both among the first arrivals at the Kenia, escaped from the mephitic atmosphere of human misery, the degradation of man by man. But the recollection of the horrors among which they formerly lived, and which they shared without being able to prevent, will never quite fade out of their minds, and their hearts can never be fully possessed by that godlike calm and cheerful serenity which is the natural heritage of their children, whose hands have never been stained by the sweat and blood of enslaved fellow-men, and who have never had to appropriate for their own enjoyment the fruit of the labour of others—have never stood before the cruel alternative of being either the hammer or the anvil in the struggle for existence.'

You know me well enough to imagine what an overpowering impression these words would make upon me. But I recalled by accident at this very moment a conversation I had had with the elder Ney about savings and insurance in Freeland, and it occurred to me that these were both things that did not harmonise with the absence of care of which his son had just been speaking. So I asked David, 'Why do men save in a country in which everyone can reckon with certainty upon a constantly increasing return for his industry, and in which even those who are incapable of work are protected not merely against material want, but even against the lack of higher enjoyments? Does not this thrift prove that anxiety for the morrow is not after all quite unknown here?'

'Almost all men save in Freeland,' answered David; 'nay, I can with certainty say that saving is more general here than in any other country. The object of this saving is to provide for the future out of the superfluity of the present; and certainly it follows from this that a certain kind of care for the morrow is very well known among us also. The distinction between our saving and the anxious thrift of other peoples lies merely here, that our saving is intended not to guard us against want, but simply against the danger of a future diminution of the standard of our accustomed enjoyments; and that we pursue this aim in our saving with the same calm certainty as we do our aim in working. A contradiction between this and what was said just now is found only when you overlook the equivocal meaning of the *word* " care." We know no " care " so far as a *fear* concerning the morrow is implied by the word; but our whole public and private life is pervaded by *foresight*, in the sense of making precautionary arrangements to-day in order that the needs of to-morrow may be met. Fear and uneasiness about the future, the *atra cura* of the Latins, you will look for among us in vain. It is this care which poisons the pleasure of the present; whilst that other, which can only improperly be called care, but the real name of which is foresight, by means of the perfect sense of security which it creates concerning the morrow enhances the delight of present enjoyment by the foretaste to-day of future enjoyments already provided for. Herein lies the guarantee of the success of our institutions, that, while solidarity is secured between the interest of the individual and the interest of the community, the individual possesses, together with liberty of action, a part of the responsibility of his action. Only a part, because the action of the individual is not altogether without limitations. Everyone in Freeland is hedged in by the equal rights of all the others, even more and more effectually than elsewhere. Consequently, everyone's responsibility finds its limitations just where the responsibility of all can be substituted for his own. And the guarding against actual deprivation on the part of anyone is one of the obligations of the whole community, which thereby and at the same time protects itself. Just as among you, a noble family, acting in its own well-understood interest, would not allow any of its members to fall into sordid misery, so long as it could in any way prevent it, so we, who act upon the principle that all men are brothers of the *one*

noble race destined to exercise control over the rest of nature, do
not allow anyone who bears our family features to suffer want so
far as our means allow us to save him from it. An existence
altogether worthy of man, participation in all that the highest
culture makes *necessary*—this we guarantee to all who live in our
midst, even when they have left off working. But absolute necessaries do not include the whole of the good things attainable at any
given time ; whence it follows that the transition from labour to
the ever so well-earned leisure of age would be connected with the
deprivation of a number of highly prized customary enjoyments, if
the copious proceeds of former labour were not in part laid by for
use in this time of leisure. Take, for example, my father : if he
pleased to spend now the 1,440*l.* which he receives as one of the
Freeland executive, together with the 90*l.* which my mother's claim
for maintenance amounts to, he could not, after his retirement from
office, with the fifty-five per cent. of the maintenance-unit to which
he and my mother together would be entitled—that is, with 330*l.*—
carry on his household without retrenchments which, though they
might deprive him only of superfluities, would nevertheless be
keenly felt, because they would involve the giving up of what he
has accustomed himself to. It is true that a considerable number
of his present expenses consists of items which in part would cease
in the course of time, in part—*e.g.*, his contributions to benevolent
objects in other parts of the world—could not be expected from
persons who are receiving a maintenance from the commonwealth,
and in part would no longer accord with the tastes and capacities
of aged persons. But in spite of all this, my parents would have
to forego many things to which they are accustomed ; and to avoid
this is the purpose of their saving.

' In order that this end may be attained, we have an altogether
peculiar form of insurance. The insurance department of our
central bank supplies the stipulated insurance-money not in fixed
amounts, but in sums bearing a certain proportion to the common
maintenance-allowance, or—which amounts to the same thing—to
the average value of labour for the time being. As the aim of the
insured is to be completely saved from anxiety as to the future,
there must, in view of the continual increase in the profits of labour,
be maintained an exact correspondence between those profits and
the amount of insurance. For the requirements of the individual

are regulated by the standard of life around him, and when this is raised so are his requirements raised. The annuity secured by the insurance must therefore be variable, if its object is to be completely attained. Consequently, the premiums are regulated by the height of the profits of labour for the time being. Certainly the inevitable arbitrariness of the connection between the premium and the claim of the insured is thereby magnified; but we do not allow that to trouble us. Our experts have taken into consideration, with the most scrupulous attempt at accuracy, all the appertaining factors, and the premiums—the rates of which have, since the institution has been in existence, been slightly amended to bring them into harmony with the teaching of experience—were so fixed as to make it probable that they would suffice to cover all current demands. If, however, contrary to our expectation, we should find that we erred on one side or the other, we should not look upon this as a great misfortune. The satisfaction of having secured to ourselves means sufficient to meet our requirements at all times will not appear to us to have been too dearly bought even if it prove that we have paid a few shillings or pounds more than was necessary; and, on the other hand, if the premiums should prove to have been too small, the deficiency will be at once made up out of the resources of the commonwealth.

'Perhaps you will ask what right we have in this way to burden future generations to the profit of their ancestors? The same right that we have continually to project into the future the claims upon the maintenance-allowance. As you know, these are entirely discharged out of the current public revenue, no reserve being accumulated for this purpose, the principle acted upon being that the workers of the present have to support the invalids of the past. Our parents when incapable of working are maintained out of the proceeds of our labour; and when we in our turn become incapable of working, it will be the duty of our children to support us out of the proceeds of their labour. It is no favour which we show to our parents and expect from our children, but a right—a right based upon the fact that each successive generation enjoys not merely the fruits of its own labour, but also the fruits of the labour of its predecessors. Without the treasures of knowledge and inventiveness, of wealth and capital, which we accumulate and bequeath, our posterity would be very poorly provided for. And if the next generation should find itself called upon to make up any deficit in favour of those of their parents who—it is immaterial on what ground—held an extraordinary increase in their maintenance-allowance to be necessary, we should not find any injustice in that, because the payments of the insured at once found employment in such a way as to benefit not merely the present, but also the future. The insurance-premiums have already accumulated to milliards; they have been invested chiefly in railways, canals, factories—in short, in works in aid of labour, most of which will endure for many generations. You may therefore regard the additional sums which may *possibly* have to be paid by the workers of the future to the insured of to-day as an insignificant interest subsequently levied by the latter upon the former; or, what is simpler still, you can imagine that the fathers retain for their own use until the end of their lives a part of the wealth they themselves have earned, and then at their death bequeath their whole property to their descendants.'

Here David ended his instructions for the time; and I will imitate him.

_____

CHAPTER XVII

Eden Vale : Aug. 2, ——

For some time I have been deeply interested in the education of the young here, and the day before yesterday was devoted to the study of this subject. Accompanied by David, I first visited one of the many kindergartens which are pretty evenly distributed about the town in Eden Vale. In an enclosure consisting partly of sunny sward and partly of shady grove, some fifty boys and girls of from four to six years of age were actively occupied under the direction of two young women of about eighteen or twenty, and a young widow. The children sang, danced, indulged in all sorts of fun and frolic, looked at picture-books which were explained to them, listened sometimes to fairy-tales and sometimes to instructive narratives, and played games, some of which were pure pastime and others channels of instruction. Among the little people, who enjoyed themselves right royally, there was a constant coming and going. Now one mother brought her little one, and now another fetched hers away. In general the Freeland mothers prefer to have their children with them at home; only when they leave home or pay a visit, or have anything to attend to, do they take their little ones to the nearest kindergarten and fetch them away on their return. Sometimes the young people beg to be allowed to go to the kindergarten, and the mothers grant them their request. But that is an exception; as a rule the children sport about at home under the eyes of their parents, and the earliest education is the special duty of the mother. A Freeland wife seldom needs to be taught how this duty can be best fulfilled; if she does there is a kindergarten not far off, or, later, the pedagogium, where good advice can always be obtained. I was told that every Freeland child of six years can read, has some skill in mental arithmetic, and possesses a considerable amount of general information, without having seen anything but a picture-book.

After the kindergarten came the elementary school. These schools also are pretty evenly distributed about Eden Vale, and, like the kindergartens, are surrounded by large gardens. They have four classes, and girls and boys are taught together. The teaching is entirely in the hands of women, married or unmarried; only gymnastics and swimming are taught by men to the boys. These two subjects occupy both boys and girls an hour every day. At least thrice a week excursions of several hours' duration are made into the neighbouring woods and hills, accompanied by a teacher for each class, and during these excursions all kinds of object-teaching are pursued. I watched the pupils at their books and in the gymnasium, in the swimming-school and on the hills, and had abundant opportunity of convincing myself that the children possessed at least as much systematised knowledge as European children of the same age; whilst upon vaulting-horse and bars, climbing-pole and rope, they were as agile as squirrels; in the water they swam like fishes, and after a three hours' march over hill and dale they were as fresh and sprightly as roes.

We next went to the middle schools, in which boys and girls of from ten to sixteen years are taught apart, the former solely by men, the latter partly by women. Here still greater attention is paid to bodily exercises of all kinds, and in order to obtain the requisite space these schools are located on the outskirts of the town, in the neighbourhood of the woods. I was astonished at the endurance, strength, and grace of the boys and girls in gymnastics, running, jumping, dancing, and riding. The boys I also saw wrestling, fencing, and shooting. A few passes with the rapier and the sabre with several of the youngsters showed me, to my surprise, that they were not merely my equals, but in many points were superior to me, though you know that I am one of the best fencers in Italy, the country so renowned for this art. I was not less astonished at the splendid muscular development of the half-grown wrestlers and gymnasts, than at the ease with which the same youths overtook a horse at full gallop and threw themselves upon its back. But I was completely dumfounded with the skill with which the lads used their rifles. The target—scarcely so large as an ordinary dinner-plate—was seldom missed at a distance of 550 yards, and not a few of the young marksmen sent ball after ball into the bull's-eye. Altogether the upper classes of these middle schools gave me the impression that they were companies of picked young athletes ; at the same time these athletes showed themselves well acquainted with all those branches of learning which are taught in the best European secondary schools.

I learnt that, up to this age, the instruction given to all the children of Freeland is the same, except that among the girls less time is given to bodily exercises and more to musical training. At sixteen years of age begins the differentiation of the training of the sexes, and also the preparation of the boys for their several vocations. The girls either remain at home, and there complete their education in those arts and branches of knowledge, the rudimental preparation for which they have already received ; or they are sent as pupil-daughters, with the same view, to the house of some highly cultured and intellectually gifted woman. Others enter the pedagogic training institutions, where they are trained as teachers, or they hear a course of lectures on nursing, or devote themselves to æsthetics, art, &c.

The boys, on the other hand, are distributed among the various higher educational institutions. Most of them attend the industrial and commercial technical institutions, where they spend a year or two in a scientific and practical preparation for the various branches of commerce and industry. Every Freeland worker passes through one of these institutions, whether he intends to be agriculturist, spinner, metal-worker, or what not. There is a double object aimed at in this : first, to make every worker, without distinction, familiar with the whole circle of knowledge and practice connected with his occupation; and next to place him in the position of being able to employ himself profitably, if he chooses to do so, in several branches of production. The mere spinner, who has nothing to do but to watch the movements of his spindles, in Freeland understands the construction and the practical working of everything connected with his industry, and knows what are the sources whence it derives its materials and where its best markets are; from which it follows that when the functionaries of his association are to be elected, the worker is guided in voting by his technical knowledge, and it is almost impossible that the choice should fall upon any but the best qualified persons. But, further, this simple spinner in Freeland is no mere automaton, whose knowledge and skill begin and end with the petty details of his own business : he is familiar with at least one or several other branches of industry; and from this again it follows that the man can take advantage of any favourable circumstance that may occur in such other branch or branches of industry, and can exchange the plough for the loom, the turning-lathe for the hammer, or even any of these for the writing-desk or the counting-house; and by this means there can be brought about that marvellous equilibrium in the most diverse sources of income which is the foundation of the social order of the country.

Young persons who have given evidence of possessing superior intellectual ability attend the universities, in which Freeland's professors, the higher government officials, physicians, technicians, &c., are educated; or the richly endowed academies of art, which send forth the architects, sculptors, painters, and musicians of the country. Even in all these educational institutions great importance is attached to physical as well as to intellectual development. The industrial and commercial technical colleges have each their gymnasium, wrestling-hall, and riding-school, their shooting and fencing ground, just as the universities and academies have; and as in these places the youths are not so directly under the control of their teachers as are the boys in the intermediate schools, the institution of public local and national exercises prevents the students from relaxing in their zeal for bodily exercises. All young men between sixteen and twenty-two years of age are organised in companies of a thousand each, according to their place of abode; and, under officers chosen by themselves, they meet once a month for exercise, and in this way still further develop their physical powers and skill. Once a year, in each of the forty-eight districts into which Freeland is divided for administrative purposes, a great competition for prizes takes place, before a committee of judges selected from the winners of previous years. On these occasions there are first single contests between fencers, marksmen, riders, wrestlers, and runners, the competitors being champions chosen by each thousand from their own number; and next, contests between the thousands themselves as such. A few weeks later there is a national festival in a valley of the Aberdare range specially set apart for this purpose; at that festival the winners in the district contests compete for the national championship. I am assured that no Greek youth in the best age of Hellas more eagerly contended for the olive-branch at the Isthmian Games than do the Freeland youths for the prize of honour at these Aberdare games, although here also the prize consists of nothing but a simple crown of leaves—a prize which, certainly, is enhanced by the fanfares of triumph which resound from the Indian Ocean to the Mountains of the Moon and from Lake Tanganika to Lake Baringo, and by the enthusiastic jubilation of such districts and towns as may be fortunate enough to have sent successful competitors. Hundreds of thousands stream out of all parts of the country to these contests; and the places to which the victors belong, particularly the district of the conquering thousand, welcome back their youths with a series of the most brilliant festivals.

When I heard this, I could not refrain from remarking that such enthusiasm on the occasion of a mere pastime seemed to me to be extravagant; and I particularly expressed my astonishment that Freeland, the home of social equity, could exhibit such enthusiasm for performances which might appear important in warlike Hellas, but which here, where everything breathed inviolable peace, could have no value but as simple bodily exercises.

'Quite right,' answered David, 'only it is this very superiority in bodily exercises which secures to us Freelanders the inviolable peace which we enjoy. We have no military institutions; and if it were not for our superiority in all that appertains to bodily strength and skill we should be an easy prey to any military Power that coveted our wealth.'

'But you surely do not imagine,' I cried, not without a sarcastic

smile, 'that your boy-fencers and marksmen and the victors at your
Isthmian Games make you a match for any great military Power
that might really attack you? In my opinion, your safety lies in
the mutual jealousy of the European Powers, each of which is prevented by the others from seizing such a prize; and yet more in
your isolation, the sea and mountains saving you from such dangerous visits. But, to secure yourselves against contingencies, I
think it would be well for you to make some military provision, such
as a competent militia, and particularly a powerful fleet, the expense
of which would be nothing in comparison with your wealth.'

'We think differently,' said David. 'Not our war-games, but
our superior physical ability which is exhibited in those games
perfectly secures us against any attack from the most powerful foe
who, against our harmoniously developed men and youths perfected
in the use of every kind of arm, could bring into the field nothing
but a half-starved proletariat scarcely able to handle their weapons
when required to do so. We hold that in war the number of shots
is of less moment than the number of hits, and that the multitude
of fighters counts for less than their efficiency. If you had seen,
as I did, at the last year's national festival how the victorious
thousand won their prize, you would perhaps admit that troops
composed of such men, or of men who approached them in skill,
need fear no European army.'

On my asking what were the wonderful feats performed on the
occasion referred to, David gave me a detailed account of the proceedings, the substance of which I will briefly repeat. In the
contests between the thousands, the firing *en masse* is directed
against a gigantic movable target, which represents in life-size a
somewhat loosely ordered front-line of a thousand men; by a special
apparatus, the front line, when at a distance of about 1,300 yards, is
set quickly in motion towards the firing-party, and the mechanism
of the target is so arranged that every bullet which hits one of the
thousand figures at once throws that figure down, so that the row of
the imaginary foes gets thinner at every hit. The rule is that that
thousand is the victor which knocks down the whole of the figures
in the approaching target in the shortest time and with the least
expenditure of bullets. Of course these two conditions compensate
each other according to certain rules—that is, a small *plus* in time is
corrected by a corresponding *minus* in the ammunition consumed,

and *vice versâ*. At all events, it is incumbent to shoot quickly and accurately; and in particular the competing thousands must be so thoroughly well drilled and so completely under command that on no account are two or more marksmen to aim at the same figure in the target. This last condition is no trifling one; for if it is difficult in a line of a thousand men to allot to every marksman his particular aim, and that instantaneously, without reflection and without recall, the difficulty must be very much greater when the number of the objects aimed at is continually becoming less, whilst the number of tho marksmen remains the same. In addition to all this, in order to have any chance at all of winning the olive-branch, the firing must begin the moment the target is set in motion—that is, when the figures are at a distance of 1,300 yards. At the last contest, the victorious thousand emptied the target within 145 seconds from the moment of starting. The target during this time had only got within 924 yards of the marksmen, who had fired 1,875 shots. Of course, it is not to be inferred that the same results would necessarily be obtained from firing at living and not inactive foes. But if it be taken into consideration—so David thought—that the intensity of the excitement of the Freeland youth in front of a European army could scarcely be so great as on the competition-field, when they are striving to wrest the much-coveted prize from well-matched opponents—for the least successful of the competing forty-eight thousands emptied the target in 190 seconds, when it had got within a distance of 930 yards and had fired 2,760 shots; and when, further, it is remembered that, in the presence of an actual foe, the most difficult of the conditions of the contest—viz. that of the lowest number of shots—ceases to exist; then it must certainly be admitted that such firing would, probably in a few minutes, completely annihilate an equally numerous body of men within range, and that it would sweep away twice or thrice as many as tho shooters before the foe would be in a position to do the shooters any very material injury. There is no European army, however numerous it may be, which would be able to stand against such firing. It is not to be expected that men, who are driven forward by nothing but mere discipline, would even for a few minutes face such a murderous fusillade.

On my part I had no argument of weight to meet this. I did not deny that the soldiers in our gigantic European armies, who do nothing with their shooting-sticks but allay their helpless fears by shooting innumerable holes in the air, only one out of two hundred of their bullets reaching its billet, could do little with such antagonists. ' But how would you defend yourselves against the artillery of European armies ? ' I asked.

' By our own artillery,' answered David. ' Since these institutions of ours have the double purpose of stimulating zeal for physical development and of making us secure against attack without maintaining an army, we give considerable prominence in our exercises to practising with cannons of the most various calibres. And even this practice is begun at school. Those boys who, having reached the fourth class in the intermediate schools, have shown proficiency in other things, are promoted to artillery practice—and this, it may be observed, has proved to be a special stimulus to effort. The reason you have not seen the cannons is that the exercise-ground lies some distance outside of the town—a necessary arrangement, as some of the guns used are monsters of 200 tons, whose thunder would ill accord with the idyllic peace of our Eden Vale. The young men are so familiar with this kind of toy, and many of them have, after profound ballistic studies, brought their skill to such perfection, that in my opinion they would show themselves as superior to their European antagonists in artillery as they would in rifle-practice. The same holds good of our horsemen. In brief, we have no army ; but our men and youths handle all the weapons which an army needs infinitely better than the soldiers of any army whatever. And as, moreover, for the purposes of our great prize-contests there exists an organisation by means of which, out of the 2,500,000 men and youths whom Freeland now possesses capable of bearing arms, the best two or three hundred thousand are always available, we think it would be a very easy thing to ward off the greatest invading army—a danger, indeed, which we do not seriously anticipate, as we doubt if there is a European people that would attack us. Rifles and cannons collected for use against us would very soon—without our doing anything—be directed against those who wished us ill.'

To this I assented. We then discussed several other topics connected with the education of the young ; and I took occasion to ask how it was that the before-mentioned voluntary insurance against old age and death in Freeland was effected on behalf of only the insurer himself and his wife, and not of his children. According to all I had seen and heard, indifference towards the fate of the children could not be the reason. I therefore asked David to tell me why, whilst we in Europe saved chiefly for the children, here in Freeland nothing was laid by for them.

'The reason,' explained David, 'lies here; the children are already sufficiently provided for—as sufficiently as are those who are unable to work, and the widows. And this is necessarily involved in the principle of economic justice ; for if the children were thrown upon the voluntary thrift of their parents—as they are with you— they would be made dependent upon conduct upon which they in truth could exercise no influence. If I accustom myself to require- ments which my maintenance-allowance could not enable me to satisfy, it lies in my own power permanently to secure what I need by means of an insurance-premium. If I neglect to do this, it is my own fault, and I have no right to complain when I afterwards have to endure unpleasant privations. The case is the same with my wife, for she exercises the same influence over the management of the household as I do. My children, on the other hand, would suffer innocently if they were thrown upon our personal forethought for what they would need in the future. They must, therefore, be protected from any privation whatever, independently of anything that I may do. And that is the case. What we bequeath to our children, and bequeath it in all cases, is the immense treasure of the powers and wealth of the commonwealth delivered into their care and disposition. Just think. The public capital of Freeland already amounts to as much as 6,000*l.* for every working inhabitant ; and last year this property yielded to everyone who was moderately industrious a net income of 600*l.*, and the ratio of income is, more- over, constantly growing year by year.'

'But,' I interposed, 'suppose a child is or becomes incapable of work ? '

'If he is so from childhood, then the forty per cent. of the main- tenance-unit, to which in such a case he has a right, is abundantly sufficient to meet all his requirements, for he neither can nor should have an independent household. If he *becomes* incapable of work, after he has set up a household and perhaps has children of his own, it would be his own, not his parents' fault, if he had neglected to provide for this emergency—assuming, of course, that he con- sidered it necessary to make such provision.'

'Very well; I perfectly understand that. But how is it with

those who are orphaned in infancy ? Is no provision made for such ? It cannot possibly accord with the sentiments of Freeland parents who live in luxury to hand over their children to public orphanages?'

'As to orphanages, it is the same as with hospitals,' answered David. 'If by orphanages you mean those barracks of civilised Europe or America, in which the waifs of poverty are without love, and after a mechanical pattern educated into the poor of the future, there are certainly none such among us. But if you mean the institutions in which the Freeland orphans are brought up, I can assure you that the most sensitive parents can commit their children to them with the most perfect confidence. Of course, nothing can take the place of parental love ; but otherwise the children are cared for and brought up exactly as if they were in their parents' house. The sexes dwell apart by tens in houses which differ in nothing from other Freeland private houses ; and they are under the care of peda-gogically trained guardians, whose duty it is not to teach them, but to watch over them and attend to all their domestic wants. Food, clothing, play,—in short, the whole routine of life is in every respect similar to that of the rest of Freeland. They are taught in the public schools ; and after they have passed through the intermediate schools, the young people themselves decide whether they will go to a technical school or to a university. Until their majority they remain in the adoptive home selected for them by the authorities, and then, if they are not yet able to maintain themselves, they enjoy the general right of maintenance-allowance. What more could the most affectionate care of parents do for them ? Not even the most intangible reproach can attach to training in such a public orphanage, for the children are not the children of poverty, but simply orphans.'

'But I imagine that orphans from better houses are adopted by relatives or acquaintances, particularly if the parents make full provision for their support,' I answered.

'In case there are such houses to which the children can go, the parents need make no provision for their maintenance, but merely a testamentary declaration, and the children will then be transferred to such houses without becoming any pecuniary burden to their adoptive parents. For in such a case the commonwealth pays to the household in question an equivalent to what would have been the cost of maintenance at the orphanage ; and as, besides the

ordinary expenses of living in every Freeland house, the fee for
personal superintendence must be paid out of this equivalent, the
allowance will not be much more than the child will cost its foster-
parents. Thus no parental provision is needed to save the orphans
from being dependent upon the liberality or goodwill of strangers.
But I should tell you that this interposition of friendly or even
related families on behalf of orphans is exceptional. Unless circumstances are very much in favour of such an arrangement, Freeland parents prefer to leave their children to the care of the public
orphanages. And this is very intelligible to all who have had opportunities of observing the touching tenderness of the guardian angels
who rule in these houses, and of the intimate relations which quickly
develop between the children and their attendants. Our Board of
Maintenance, supported by our Board of Education, lays great
weight upon this part of its duty. Only the most approved masters
and mistresses—and the latter must also be experienced nurses—
are appointed as guardians of the orphans ; and to have been successfully occupied in this work for a number of years is a high
distinction zealously striven after, particularly by the flower of our
young women.'

   'I can quite understand that,' I said. ' May I, in this connection, ask how you deal with the right of inheritance in general, and
of inheritance of real property in particular ? For here, in property
in houses there seems to me to be a rock upon which your general
principles as to property in land might be wrecked. It is one of
the fundamental principles of your organisation that no one can have
a right of property in land ; but houses—if I have been rightly informed—are private property. How do you reconcile these things?'

   'Everyone,' answered David, 'can dispose freely of his own
property, at death as in life. The right of bequest is free and
unqualified ; but it must be noted that between husband and wife
there is an absolute community of goods, whence it follows that only
the survivor can definitively dispose of the common property. The
right of property in the house, however, cannot be divided ; and it
is not allowable to build more than one dwelling-house upon a
house-and-garden plot. Finally, the dwelling-house must be used
by the owner, and cannot be let to another. If the house-plot be
used for any other purpose than as the site of the owner's home,
the breach of the law involves no punishment, and no force will be

brought to bear upon the owner, but the owner at once loses his exclusive right as usufructuary of the plot. The plot becomes at once, *ipso facto*, ground to which no one has a special right, and to which everyone has an equal claim. For, according to our views, there is no right of property in land, and therefore not in the building-site of the house ; and the right to appropriate such ground to one's own house is simply a right of usufruct for a special purpose. Just as, for example, the traveller by rail has a claim to the seat which he occupies, but only for the purpose of sitting there, and not for the purpose of unpacking his goods or of letting it to another, so I have the right to reserve for myself, merely for occupation, the spot of ground upon which I wish to fix my home ; and no one has any more right to settle upon my building-site than he has to occupy my cushion in the railway, even if it should be possible to crowd two persons into the one seat. But neither am I at liberty to make room for a friend upon my seat ; for my fellow-travellers are not likely to approve of the inconvenience thereby occasioned, and they may protest that the legs and elbows of the sharer of my seat crowd them too much, and that the air-space calculated for one pair of lungs is by my arbitrary action shared by two pair. Just so my house-neighbours are not likely to approve of having my walls and roof too near to theirs, and will resent the arbitrary act by which I fill the air-space of the town with more persons than the commonwealth allows.

'Now, in the exercise of my right of usufruct of a definite plot of ground, I have inseparably connected with this plot something over which I have not merely the right of usufruct, but also the right of property—namely, a house. Consequently my right of usufruct passes over to the person to whom—whether gratuitously or not—I transfer my right of property in the house. Therefore I can sell, or bequeath, or give away my house without being prevented from doing so by the fact that I have no right of property in the building-site.

' But if, through any circumstances independent of my labour or of the building cost, the site on which my house stands acquires a value above that of other building-sites, this increased value belongs not to me, but to those who have given rise to it, and that is, without exception, the community. Let us suppose that building-ground in Eden Vale has acquired such an exceptional value, while there

R

are still sites available throughout Freeland for milliards of persons: this local increase of value can be attributed merely to the fact that the excellent streets, public grounds, splendid monuments, theatres, libraries—in short, the public institutions of Eden Vale—have made living in this town more desirable than in any other place in the country. But these public institutions are not my work—they are the work of the community; and I have no right to put into my pocket the increased ground-value derived from the common enjoyment of these institutions. All that I myself have expended upon the house and garden belongs to me, and on a change of ownership must be either made good to me or put to my credit; but the ground-price—and, indeed, the whole of it—belongs to the commonwealth; for building-sites which offer no advantages over any others are, in view of the still existing surplus of unoccupied ground, valueless. The commonwealth, therefore, has, strictly speaking, a right at any time to claim this value or an equivalent; and if the question were an important one, it would be advisable actually to exercise this right—that is, from time to time, or at least on a change of ownership, to assess the value of the sites of houses and gardens, and to appropriate the surplus of the sale-price to the public treasury.

'In reality, in view of our other arrangements, this question of the value of building-sites in Freeland is of no importance whatever. It must not be forgotten that our private houses are not lodging-houses, but merely family dwellings. As I have already said, every contract to let renders absolutely void the occupier's right of exclusive usufruct of the house-site. He who lets his house has, by the very act of doing so, made his plot masterless. A secret letting is prevented by our general constitution, and particularly by the central bank, which we will visit next. Thus the increased value which may be acquired by a building-plot cannot become a question of importance, and we are able to refrain altogether from interfering with free trade in houses. We buy, sell, bequeath, and give away our dwelling-houses, and no one troubles himself about it. I may remark, in passing, that up to the present there has been no noticeable increase in the prices of sites. A man pays for his house what the house itself is held to be worth, the trifling differences being due to the greater or less taste exhibited in the structure, the greater or less beauty of the garden, &c., &c. But that the Eden Vale plots, for example, as such, have a special value cannot be asserted, as there are still many thousands freely available to anyone, but which are not taken. The conveniences of life are pretty evenly distributed throughout Freeland, and no town can boast of attractions which are not balanced by attractions of other kinds in other towns. Eden Vale, for instance, possesses the most splendid buildings, and is distinguished by incomparable natural beauty; hence it is less adapted to industries, and has no agricultural colony in its neighbourhood. Dana City, on the other hand, which is specially suitable for industry, and is in the midst of agricultural land, is unattractive to many on account of its ceaseless and noisy business activity. And, in general, we Freelanders are not fond of large towns; we love to have woods and meadows as near us as possible, and those who are able to live in the country do it in preference to living in towns. Of course, there is not likely to be any lack of rural building-sites; hence there can never be any ground-price proper among us. If, however, building-ground should acquire a price, we are in any case protected by our way and manner of building and living from such prices as would give rise to any material derangement of our property relations. Whether a family residence has a higher or a lower value is, therefore, after all, only a question of subordinate interest, and it is not worth the trouble, in order to equalise the differences in value which arise, to bring into play an apparatus which, under the circumstances, might lead to chicanery.'

I agreed with him. Wishing, however, to understand this important matter in all its relations, I supposed a case in which the opportunity of gaining an extraordinarily high profit was connected with a certain definite locality, and asked what would happen then. 'Let us imagine that in a small valley surrounded by uninhabitable rocks or marshes, a mine of incalculable value is discovered, the exploitation of which would give twice or thrice as much profit as the average profit in Freeland at that time. Naturally everyone will labour at this mine until the influx of workers produces an equilibrium in the profits. If there were sufficient space round the mine for dwelling-houses, nothing would stand in the way of this equalisation of profits; but as, in the supposed case, the space is limited, only the first comers will be able to work at the mine; all later comers—unless they camp out—will be as effectually excluded

R 2

from competing as if an insuperable barrier had been raised round the mine. The fortunate usufructuaries of the few building-sites will, therefore, be in the pleasant situation of permanently pocketing twice or thrice the average proceeds of labour—let us say, for example, 1,600*l.* a year, whilst 600*l.* is the average. Consequently their early occupation of the ground will be worth 1,000*l.* a year to them, exactly the same as to a London house-owner the lucky circumstance that his ancestors set up their huts on that particular spot on the banks of the Thames is worth his 1,000*l.* or more a year. That this is the rule and is the principal source of wealth, not only in London, but everywhere outside of Freeland, whilst in this country it would require an extraordinary concurrence of circumstances to produce similar phenomena, makes no difference in the fact itself that it can occur everywhere, and that, if you know of no means to prevent it, the ground-rent you have fortunately got rid of might revive among you. Nay, in this—I will admit extreme—case the Freeland institutions would prove themselves a hindrance to the national exploitation of such a highly profitable opportunity for labour, the most intense utilisation of which would evidently be to the general interest. If such a case occurred in Europe or America, the fortunate owners would surround the mines with large lodging-barracks, from which certainly they would without any trouble derive enormous profits, but which at the same time would make it possible to extract the rich treasures from the earth. Your Freeland house-right, on the contrary, would in such a case prevent the exploitation of the treasure of the earth, merely in order that an exceptional increase of the wealth of individuals should be avoided. And yet it is characteristic of your institutions as a whole to render labour more productive than is possible under an exploiting system of industry. A correct principle, however, must be correct under all circumstances.'

'That is also my view,' answered David; 'but in such cases even your Western law affords a means of help—namely, expropriation. Let it be assumed that we could by no means whatever make the neighbourhood of the mine accommodate a greater number of dwelling-houses; then, in the public interest, we would redeem the houses already existing at the mine, and in their place we would erect large lodging-houses after the pattern of our hotels. If that would not suffice to accommodate as many workers as were required in order to bring the profit of labour at the mine into equilibrium with the average profit of the country, we would proceed to the last resource and expropriate the mine for the benefit of the commonwealth. By no means would even such a very improbable contingency present any serious difficulties to the carrying out of our principles. For you will certainly admit that the undertaking of a really monopolist production by the commonwealth is not contrary to our principles. If you would deny it, you must go farther, and assert that in working the railways, the telegraphs, the post, nay, even in assuming the ultimate control of the community, there is to be found a violation of the principle of individual freedom.'

'You are only too right,' I answered, 'and I cannot defend myself from the charge of harbouring a doubt which would have been seen to be superfluous if I had only been unreservedly willing to admit that the people of Freeland, whatever might happen, would probably make the wisest and not the stupidest provision against such a contingency as I imagined. The ground of that inconceivable stubbornness with which we adherents of the old are apt to resist every new idea is, that we imagine difficulties, which exist only in our fancy, and most unnecessarily suppose that there is no other way of surmounting those imaginary difficulties than the stupidest imaginable. We then triumphantly believe we have reduced the new ideas *ad absurdum*; whilst we should have done better to have been ashamed of our own absurdities.'

With this fierce self-accusation I will close my letter to-day; but not without telling you in confidence that in making it I was thinking less of myself than of—others.

CHAPTER XVIII

Eden Vale: Aug. 6, ——

YESTERDAY, accompanied by the two English agents, we inspected the Freeland Central Bank. The comprehensive and—as a necessary consequence—exceedingly simple clearing system excited the highest admiration of the two experienced gentlemen. The remarkably small amount of cash required to adjust the accounts of the whole of the gigantic business transactions drew from Lord E—— the inquiry why Freeland retained gold as a measure of value. He thought that, as the Freelanders already made the value of a unit of labour-time the standard of calculation in their most important affairs, the simplest plan would be to universalise this method—that is, to declare the labour-hour to be the measure of value, the money-unit. This would, he thought, far better harmonise with the general social order of Freeland, in which labour is the source and basis of all value.

The director of the bank (Mr. Clark) replied : ' That is a view which has been repeatedly expressed by strangers ; but it is based simply upon confounding the *measure of value* with the *source of income*. For labour alone is not the source of value, though most Socialists adopt this error of the so-called classical economists as the ground of their demands. If all value were derived from labour and from labour alone, then even among you in the old exploiting world everything would be in favour of the workers, for even there the workers have control over their working power. The misery among you is due to the fact that the workers have no control over the other things which are requisite for the creation of value, namely, the product of previous work—*i.e.* capital, and the forces and materials derived from nature. We in Freeland have guaranteed to labour the whole of what it assists to produce. But we do not base this right upon the erroneous proposition that labour is the sole source of the value of what it produces, but upon the proposition that the worker has the same claim to the use of those other factors requisite for the creation of value as he has to his working-power. But this is only by the way. Even if labour were the only source of and the only ingredient in value, it would still be in any case the worst conceivable *measure* of value ; for it is of all things that possess value the one the value of which is most liable to variations. Its value rises with every advance in human dexterity and industry ; that is, a labour-day or a labour hour is continuously being transformed into an increasing quantity of all imaginable other kinds of value. That the value of the product of labour differs as the labour-power is well or badly furnished with tools, well or badly applied, cannot be questioned, and never has been seriously questioned. Now, among us in Freeland *all* labour-power is as well equipped and applied as possible, because the perfect and unlimited freedom of labour to apply itself at any time to whatever will then create the highest value brings about, if not an absolute, yet a relative equilibrium of values; but, in order that this may be brought about, there must exist an unchangeable and reliable standard by which the value of the things produced by labour can be measured. That the labour expended by us upon shoe goods and upon textile fabrics, upon cereals and turnery goods, possesses the same value is shown by the fact that these various kinds of wares produced in the same period of time possess the same value; but this fact can be shown, not by a comparison between the respective amounts of labour-time, but only by a comparison with something that has a constant value in itself. If we concluded that the things which required an equal time to produce were of equal value because they were produced in an equal time, we might soon find ourselves producing shoes which no one wanted, while we were suffering from a lack of textile fabrics; and we might see with unconcern the superfluity of turnery wares, the production of which was increasing, while perhaps all available hands were required in order to correct a disastrous lack of cereals. To make the labour-day the measure of value—if it were not, for other reasons, impossible—involves Communism, which, instead of leaving the adjustment of the relations between supply and demand to free commerce, fixes those relations by authority; doing this, of course, without asking anyone what he wishes to enjoy, or what he wishes to do, but authoritatively prescribing what everyone shall consume, and what he shall produce.

'But we in Freeland strive after what is the direct opposite of Communism—namely, absolute individual freedom. Consequently we, more imperatively than any other people, need a measure of value as accurate and reliable as possible—that is, one the exchange-power of which, with reference to all other things, is exposed to as little variation as possible. This best possible, most constant, standard the civilised world has hitherto found rightly in gold. There is no difference in value between two equal quantities of gold, whilst one labour-day may be very materially more valuable than another; and there is no means of ascertaining with certainty the difference in value of the two labour-days except by comparing them both with one and the same thing which possesses a really constant value. Yet this equality in value of equal quantities of gold is the least of the advantages possessed by gold over other measures of value. Two equal quantities of wheat are of nearly equal value. But the value of gold is exposed to less *variation* than is the value of any other thing. Two equal quantities of wheat are of equal value at the same time ; but to-morrow they may both be worth twice as much as to-day, or they may sink to half their present value ; while gold can change its value but very little in a short time. If its exchange-relation to any commodity whatever alters suddenly and considerably, it can be at once and with certainty assumed that it is the value not of the gold, but of the other commodity, which has suddenly and considerably altered. And this is a necessary conclusion from that most unquestionable law of value according to which the price of everything is determined by supply and demand, if we connect with this law the equally unquestionable fact that the supply and demand of no other thing are exposed to so small a relative variation as are those of gold. This fact is not due to any mysterious quality in this metal, but to its peculiar durability, in consequence of which in the course of thousands of years there has been accumulated, and placed at the service of those who can demand it, a quantity of gold sufficient to make the greatest temporary variations in its production of no practical moment. Whilst a good or a bad wheat harvest makes an enormous difference in the supply of wheat for the time being, because the old stock of wheat is of very subordinate importance relatively to the results of the new harvest, the amount of gold in the world remains relatively unaltered by the variations, however great they may be, of even several years of gold-production, because the existing stock of gold is enormously greater than the greatest possible gold-production of any single year. If all the gold-mines in the world suddenly ceased to yield any gold, no material influence would be produced upon the quantity of available gold ; whilst a single general failure in the cereal crop would at once and inevitably produce the most terrible corn-famine. This, then, is the reason why gold is the best possible, though by no means an absolutely perfect, measure of value. But labour-time would be the worst conceivable measure of value, for neither are two equal periods of labour necessarily of equal value, nor does labour-time in general possess an unalterable value, but its exchange-power in relation to all other things increases with every step forward in the methods of labour.'

We were all convinced, but Lord E—— could not refrain from

remarking that the Freelanders did nevertheless estimate the value of many things in labour-equivalents. He at once received from my father the pertinent answer that, according to all they had yet heard, this happened only in cases in which an increase of payment had to run parallel with a rise in the value of labour. Salaries and maintenance-allowances *ought* to rise in proportion as the proceeds of labour and therewith the general consumption rose; and it was only when this relation had to be kept in view that the value of things could be estimated in labour-equivalents.

Mr. Clark now drew our attention to the comprehensive, transparent, and detailed publicity which marked all the pecuniary affairs of Freeland, in consequence of the entry in the bank books of all commercial and industrial relations. No one can deceive either himself or others as to his circumstances; and one of the most important social consequences of this is that no one has any desire to shine by extravagant spending. Extravagance is only too often prompted by a desire to make oneself appear in the eyes of the world richer than one really is; such an attempt in this country would only provoke a smile. And if anyone wished to spend in luxuries more than he earned, the bank would naturally refuse him credit for such a purpose; and without this credit the spendthrift would have to appeal to the liberality of his fellow-citizens before he could indulge in his extravagance. The amounts of all incomes and of all outgoings lie open to the day; all the world knows what everybody has and whence he gets it. And as everyone is free to engage in any branch of industry whatever, the difference of income can excite no one's envy.

But Lord E—— here asked whether the degree of authoritative arbitrariness inevitable in fixing salaries of different kinds—*e.g.* of officials – did not present some contradiction to the otherwise operative principle of unconditional freedom of choice of calling, and to the equilibrium in the proceeds of different kinds of labour which resulted from this freedom. 'When the profits of the woollen industry are higher than those of agriculture, fresh labour will be transferred to the former until an equilibrium has been established between the two profits; if a permanent excess of profit shows itself in one of these branches of production, it is evident under your institutions that this can be due solely to the fact that the labour in this more profitable industry is less agreeable, more exhausting, or

demands a higher or rarer knowledge or skill. No one has the
slightest ground to complain of injury; and so far the harmony
produced by freedom is worthy of all admiration. But when it
comes to appointments and salaries, this absolute freedom must
cease. You, as the head of a department of the government,
receive 1,400*l.*, your neighbour the hand-worker earns merely 600*l.*;
how do you know that the latter does not feel that he is wronged
thereby?'

'My lord,' said Mr. Clark, smiling, 'if you mean, how do I know
whether my neighbour does not feel himself wronged *by nature*
because he is not able, like me, to earn 1,400*l.* a year, I must answer
that I can speak only from conjecture, and that I really possess no
certain knowledge as to his feelings. But if you think that my
neighbour, or anyone else in Freeland, could find in my higher
salary an advantage conferred on me by an arbitrary exercise of
authoritative power, or by the favour of the electors, or for any
inadequate reason, I can certainly show that you are mistaken. For
my salary is, in the last resort, as much the result of free competition as is the labour-profit of my neighbour. Whether I am the
right man for my post is a question which is decided by the corporations by whom my election is made, and whose choice is controlled
or superseded by no automatically working contrivance; with what
salary my office must be endowed, in order that qualified men, or
let us say men who are held to be qualified, may be obtained, this
is regulated by exactly the same automatic laws as is the labour-
profit of a weaver or an agriculturist. And this holds good of the
salary of the youngest official up to that of the heads of the departments of the Freeland government. The fixing of the salaries in
every case depends upon the free judgment of the presidents or of the
electoral colleges; but these presidents or electoral colleges must
fix the salaries at such sums as will at any time attract a sufficient
number of qualified candidates. Of course, a pound more or less a
year would make no difficulty—it is a recognised principle that the
salaries should be high enough to attract rather a superfluity than a
lack of candidates; but when the number of candidates is greater
than a certain ratio, the salaries are reduced, whilst a threatened
lack of candidates is met by an increase of salaries. I will add, that
it is to be taken as a matter of course that in Freeland the unsuccessful candidates are not breadless aspirants. Success or failure

is never therefore a question of a livelihood, but of the gratification
of inclination and sometimes of vanity. A man gives up his office
when more profitable or more agreeable occupation attracts him
elsewhere. The public officials are not paid the same salaries in all
the branches of the public service. Specially trying work, or work
demanding special knowledge, obtains here higher profits, just as in
the various industries. And whilst the labour-earnings of ordinary
manual labour are the measure of the salaries of the lower officials,
so do the salaries of the various association-managers exercise a
regulative influence upon the salaries of the higher public officials.
You, also, have often experienced that the attractions of positions
connected with public activity have in no small degree brought down
the salaries of government officials, professors, &c., below the level
of the incomes of those who hold the chief posts in associations. As
a rule, it is found that with a rise in the general level of intelligence
there is a *relative*—by no means an absolute—sinking of the higher
salaries. While the directors of several large associations receive
as much as 5,000 hour-equivalents a year, the highest officials in the
Freeland central government at the present time receive only 3,600
more, and that because our persistent assertion of the relative
depreciation of the higher salaries is met by the parliaments with
an equally persistent resistance, and the parliaments yield to our
importunities only very slowly and very reluctantly. To be just, it
should be added that the same game is repeated in the associations.
The directors would often be satisfied with much lower salaries, for
they often really do not know what to do with their incomes, which,
in comparison with prices in Freeland, are in some cases exorbitant,
and increase with every increase in the value of labour. Particularly
during the last decade, since the value of the hour-equivalent has
increased so much, proposals from above to reduce salaries have
become a standing rule. I repeat, this reduction must be understood
to be merely relative—that is, to refer merely to the number of hour-
equivalents. The value of a labour-hour has quadrupled within the last
twenty years; those of us, therefore—we public officials, for example
—who receive twenty-eight per cent. fewer hour-equivalents than we
did originally, still have incomes which, when reckoned in money,
have been nearly tripled. As a rule, however, the associations will
not hear of even such a reduction. Though their directors openly
avow their willingness to accept lower salaries, the associations are

afraid of offending some one or other of the competing societies
which pay higher salaries ; and as a few hundred pounds are not
worth considering in view of the enormous sums which a great
association annually turns over, the reduction of the salaries goes
on but slowly. Nevertheless there is a gradual lessening of the
difference between the maximum and the minimum earnings, plainly
proving that even in this matter of salaries the law of supply and
demand is in full operation.'

Lord E—— thanked him for this explanation. But now Sir
B—— proposed a far weightier question. 'What struck me most,'
said he, 'when I was examining the enormous operations of your
central bank, and what I am not yet able to understand, is how it
is possible, without arbitrary exercise of authority and communistic
consequences, to accumulate the immense capital which you require,
and yet neither pay nor reckon any interest. That interest is the
necessary and just reward of the capitalist's self-denial I do not
indeed believe ; but I hold it to be the tribute which has to be paid
to the saver for sparing the community, by his voluntary thrift, the
necessity of making thrift compulsory. What I now wish to know
is, what were your reasons for forbidding the payment of interest?
Or are you in Freeland of opinion that it is unjust to give to the
saver a share of the fruits of his saving ? '

'We are not of that opinion,' answered the director. ' But first
I must assure you that you have started from an erroneous assumption. We *forbid* the payment of interest as little as we " forbid "
the undertaker's profit or the landlord's ground-rent. These three
items of income do not exist here, simply because no one is under
the necessity of paying them. If our workers needed an " undertaker " to organise and discipline them for highly productive
activity, no power could prevent them from giving up to him what
belonged to him—namely, the profit of the undertaking—and remaining satisfied themselves with a bare subsistence. Nothing in our
constitution, and no one among us, would interfere with such an
undertaker in the peaceable enjoyment of his share of the produce.
If the land needed——'

'Pardon my interruption,' said Sir B——. ' " If our workers
needed an undertaker to organise and discipline them, no power
could prevent them from giving up to him the whole of the produce "—these were your words. In the name of heaven, do not

your workers need such a man ? Do they need none over them to organise, discipline, guide, and overlook the process of production ? And when I hear you so coolly and distinctly assert that such a man has a right to the produce, and that neither for God's sake nor in the name of justice need he leave to the worker more than a bare subsistence, I am compelled to ask myself whether you, an authority in Freeland, are pleased to jest, or whether what we have hitherto seen and heard here rests upon a mere delusion ? '

' Forgive me for not having expressed myself more plainly,' answered the director to Sir B—— and to the rest of us who, like him, had shown our consternation at the apparent contradiction between the last words of our informant and the spirit of Freeland institutions. ' I said, " If our workers needed an *undertaker* " : I beg you to lay emphasis upon the word " undertaker." A man or several men to arrange, organise, guide the work, they certainly need; but such a man is not an undertaker. The difference between our workers and others consists in the fact that the former allow themselves to be organised and disciplined by persons who are dependent upon them, instead of being their masters. The conductors of our associations are not the masters, but the officials—as well as shareholders—of the working fellowship, and have therefore as little right to the whole produce as their colleagues abroad. The latter are appointed and paid by the " owner " of what is produced ; and in this country this owner is the whole body of workers as such. An undertaker in the sense of the old industrial system, on the other hand, is a something whose function consists in nothing but in being master of the process of production ; he is by no means the actual organiser and manager, but simply the owner, who, as such, need not trouble himself about the process of production further than to condescend to pocket the profits. That the undertaker at the same time bears the risks attendant upon production has to be taken into account when we consider the individual undertaker, but not when we consider the institution as such, for we cannot speak of the risk of the body of undertakers as a whole. I called the undertaker, not a man, but a something, because in truth it need not be a man with flesh and blood. It may just as well be a scheme, a mere idea ; if it does but appropriate the profits of production it admirably fulfils its duty as undertaker, for as such it is nothing more than the shibboleth of mastership. Let us not be misled by the fact that frequently—we will say, as a rule—the undertaker is at the same time the actual manager of the work of production ; when he is, he unites two economic functions in one person, that of the—mental or physical—labour and that of the undertakership. Other functions can just as well be associated together in him : the undertaker can be also capitalist or landlord ; nevertheless, the undertaker, as economic subject, has no other function than that of being master of other men's labour and of appropriating to himself the fruits of the process of production after subtracting the portions due to the other factors in production.

'And this master, whose function consists simply of an abstract mastership, is an inexorable necessity so long as the workers are servants who can be disciplined, not by their enlightened self-interest, but only by force. To throw the blame of this exclusively or only mainly upon "capital" was a fatal error, which for a long time prevented the clear perception of the real cause—the servile habits and opinions that had grown stronger and stronger during thousands of years of bondage. Capital is indispensable to a highly developed production, and the working masses of the outside world are mostly without capital ; but they are without it only because they are powerless servants, and even when in exceptional cases they possess capital they do not know how to do anything with it without the aid of masters. Yet it is frequently the capital of the servants themselves by means of which—through the intervention of the savings-banks—the undertaker carries on the work of production ; it none the less follows that he pockets the proceeds and leaves to the servants nothing but a bare subsistence over and above the interest. Or the servants club their savings together for the purpose of engaging in productive work on their own account ; but as they are not able to conceive of discipline without servitude, cannot even understand how it is possible to work without a master who must be obeyed, because he can hire and discharge, pay and punish— in brief, because he is master ; and as they would be unable to dispose of the produce, or to agree over the division of it, though this might be expected from them as possessors of the living labour-power,—they therefore set themselves in the character of a corporate capitalist as master over themselves in the character of workmen. In these productive associations, which the workers carry on with

money they have saved by much self-denial or have involved themselves in worry and anxiety by borrowing, they remain as workers
under a painful obligation to obey, and the slaves of wages; though
certainly in their character of small capitalists they transform themselves into masters who have a right to command and to whom the proceeds of production belong— that is, into undertakers. The example
of these productive associations shows, more plainly than anything
else can, that it was nothing but the incapacity of the working
masses to produce without masters that made the undertaker a
necessity. We in Freeland have for the first time solved the problem of uniting ourselves for purposes of common production, of disciplining and organising ourselves, though the proceeds of production belonged to us in our character of workers and not of capitalists.
And as the experiment succeeded, and when undertaken by intelligent men possessing some means must succeed, we have no further
need of the undertaker.

'But undertakership is not forbidden in Freeland. No one would
hinder you from opening a factory here and attempting to hire
workers to carry it on for wages. But in the first place you would
have to offer the workers at least as much as the average earnings
of labour in Freeland; and in the second place it is questionable
if you would find any who would place themselves under your
orders. That, as a matter of fact, no such case has occurred for
the past eighteen years—that even our greatest technical reformers,
in possession of the most valuable inventions, have without
exception preferred to act not as undertakers, but as organisers
of free associations—this is due simply to the superiority of free
over servile labour. It has been found that the same inventors are
able to accomplish a great deal more with free workers who are
stimulated by self-interest, than with wage-earners who, in spite of
constant oversight, can only be induced to give a mechanical attention to their tasks. Moreover, the system of authoritative mastership was as repugnant to the feelings of the masters as to those of
the men under them, and both parties found themselves uncomfortable in their unfamiliar *rôles*—as uncomfortable as formerly in the
rôles of absolutely co-equal associates in production. So considerable
was this mutual feeling of discomfort, and so evident was the
inferiority of the servile form of organisation, that all such attempts
were quickly given up, though no external obstacle of any kind had

been placed in their way. Certainly it must not be overlooked that every undertaker who needs land for his business is in constant danger of having claims made by others upon the joint use of the land occupied by him, for, of course, we do not grant him a privilege in this respect; neither he nor anyone else in Freeland can exclude others from a co-enjoyment of the ground. Nevertheless, as we have plenty of space, it would have been long before the undertaker would have had to strike his sail on this account. That the few who in the early years of our history made such attempts quickly transformed themselves into directors of associations, was due to the fact that, in spite of any advantages which they might possess, they could not successfully compete with free labour. Three of these undertakers failed utterly; they could fulfil their obligations neither to their creditors nor to their workmen, and must have had to submit to the disgrace of bankruptcy if their workmen, distinctly perceiving the one defect from which the undertakings suffered, had not taken the matter in hand. Since the inventions and improvements for the introduction of which these three undertakers had founded their businesses, were valuable and genuine, and the masters had during their short time of mastership shown themselves to be energetic and—apart from their fancy for mastership— sensible men, the workers stepped into the breach, constituted themselves in each case an association, took upon themselves all the liabilities, and then, under the superintendence of the very men who had been on the brink of ruin, carried on the businesses so successfully that these three associations are now among the largest in Freeland. Four other several individuals—also notable industrial inventors—avoided a threatened catastrophe only by a timely change from the position of undertakers to that of superintendents of associations; and they stand at present at the head of works whose workers are numbered by thousands, and have since realised continuously increasing profits, high enough to satisfy all their reasonable expectations. Thus, as I have said, undertakership is not forbidden in Freeland; but it cannot successfully compete with free association.'

Sir B—— and the others declared themselves perfectly satisfied with this explanation, and begged the bank director to proceed with his account which they had interrupted. 'You were saying,' intimated my father, 'that in Freeland interest was no more forbidden than undertaker's gains and ground-rent. As to undertaker's gains we now understand you ; but before you proceed to the main point of your exposition—to interest—I would like to ask for fuller details upon the question of ground-rent. How are we to understand that this is not forbidden in Freeland ? '

' How you are to understand that,' was the answer, ' will best be made plain to you if I take up my train of thought where I left off. If, in order to labour productively, we required the undertaker, no power in heaven or earth could save us from giving up to him what was due to him as master of the process of production, while we contented ourselves with a bare subsistence—that is what I said. I would add that we should also be compelled to pay the tribute due to the landlord for the use of the ground, if we could not till the ground without having a landlord. For property in land was always based upon the supposition that unowned land could not be cultivated. Men did not understand how to plough and sow and reap without having the right to prevent others from ploughing and sowing and reaping upon the same land. Whether it was an individual, a community, a district, or a nation, that in this way acquired an exclusive right of ownership of the land, was immaterial : it was necessarily an *exclusive* right, otherwise no one would put any labour into the land. Hence it happened, in course of time, that the individual owner of land acquired very considerable advantages in production over the many-headed owner ; and the result was that common property in land gradually passed into individual ownership. But this distinction is not an essential one, and has very little to do with our institutions. With us, the land—so far as it is used as a means of production and not as sites for dwelling-houses—is absolutely masterless, free as air; it belongs neither to one nor to many : everyone who wishes to cultivate the soil is at liberty to do so where he pleases, and to appropriate his part of the produce. There is, therefore, no ground-rent, which is nothing else than the owner's interest for the use of the land ; but a prohibition of it will be sought for in vain. In the fact that I have no right to prohibit anything to others lies no prohibition. It cannot even be said that I am prohibited from prohibiting anything, for I may do it without hindrance from anyone ; but everybody will laugh at me, as much as if I had forbidden people to breathe and had asserted that the atmospheric air was my own property. Where there is no power to enforce such pretensions, it is not necessary to prohibit

s

them; if they are not artificially called forth and upheld, they simply remain non-existent. In Freeland no one possesses this power because here no one need sequestrate the land in order that it may be tilled. But the magic which enables us to cultivate owner-less land without giving rise to disputes is the same that enables us to produce without undertakers—free association.

'Just as little do we forbid interest. No one in Freeland will prevent you from asking as high a rate of interest as you please; only you will find no one willing to pay it you, because everyone can get as much capital as he needs without interest. But you will ask whether, in this placing of the savings of the community at the disposal of those who need capital, there does not lie an injustice? Whether it is not Communism? And I will admit that here the question is not so simple as in the cases of the undertaker's gains and of ground-rent. Interest is charged for a real and tangible service essentially different from the service rendered by the under-taker and the landowner. Whilst, namely, the economic service of the two latter consists in nothing but the exercise of a relation of mastership, which becomes superfluous as soon as the working masses have transformed themselves from servants working under compulsion into freely associated men, the capitalist offers the worker an instrument which gives productiveness to his labour under all circumstances. And whilst it is evident that, with the establishment of industrial freedom, both undertaker and landowner become, not merely superfluous, but altogether objectless—*ipso facto* cease to exist—with respect to the capitalist, the possessor of savings, it can even be asserted that society is dependent upon him in an infinitely higher degree when free than when enslaved, because it can and must employ much more capital in the former case than in the latter. Moreover, it is not true that service rendered by capital—the giving wings to production—is compensated for by the mere return of the capital. After a full repayment, there remains to the worker, in proportion as he has used the capital wisely—which is his affair and not the lender's—a profit which in certain circumstances may be very considerable, the increase of the proceeds of labour obtained by the aid of the capital. Why should it be considered unreasonable or unjust to hand over a part of this gain to the capitalist—to him, that is, to whose thrift the existence of the capital is due? The saver, so said the earlier Socialists, has no right to demand any return for the service which he has rendered the worker; it costs him nothing, since he receives back his property undiminished when and how he pleases (the premium for risk, which may have been charged as security against the possible bad faith or bankruptcy of the debtor, has nothing to do with the interest proper). Granted; but what right has the borrower, who at any rate derives advantage from the service rendered, to retain all the advantage himself? And what certainty has he of being able to obtain this service, even though it costs the saver nothing to render it, if he (the borrower) does not undertake to render any service in return? It is quite evident that the interest is paid in order to induce the saver to render such a friendly service. How could we, without communistic coercion, transfer capital from the hands of the saver into those of the capital-needing producer? For the community to save and to provide producers with capital from this source is a very simple way out of the difficulty, but the right to do this must be shown. No profound thinker will be satisfied with the communistic assertion that the capital drawn from the producers in one way is returned to them in another, for by this means there does not appear to be established any equilibrium between the burden and the gain of the individual producers. The tax for the accumulation of capital must be equally distributed among all the producers; the demand for capital, on the other hand, is a very unequal one. But how could we take the tax paid by persons who perhaps require but little capital, to endow the production of others who may happen to require much capital? What advantage do we offer to the former for their compulsory thrift?

'And yet the answer lies close at hand. *It is true that in the exploiting system of society the creditor does not derive the slightest advantage from the increase in production which the debtor effects by means of the creditor's savings; on the other hand, in the system of society based upon social freedom and justice both creditor and debtor are equally advantaged.* Where, as with us, every increase in production must be equably distributed among all, the problem as to how the saver profits from the employment of his capital solves itself. The machinist or the weaver, whose tax, for example, is applied to the purchase or improvement of agricultural machines, derives, with us, exactly the same advantage from this as does the agriculturist; for, thanks to our institutions, the increase of profit effected in any locality is immediately distributed over all localities and all kinds of production.

'If anyone would ask what right a community based upon the free self-control of the individual, and strongly antagonistic to Communism, has to coerce its members to exercise thrift, the answer is that such coercion is in reality not employed. The tax out of which the capitalisation is effected is paid by everyone only in proportion to the work he does. No one is coerced to labour, but in proportion as a man does labour he makes use of capital. What is required of him is merely an amount proportional to what he makes use of. Thus both justice and the right of self-control are satisfied in every point.

'You see, it is exactly the same with interest as with the undertaker's gains and with ground-rent: the guaranteed right of association saves the worker from the necessity of handing over a part of the proceeds of his production to a third person under any plea whatever. Interest disappears of itself, just like profit and rent, for the sole but sufficient reason that the freely associated worker is his own capitalist, as well as his own undertaker and landlord. Or, if one will put it so, *interest, profit, and rent remain, but they are not separated from wages, with which they combine to form a single and indivisible return for labour.*'

And with this, good-night for the present.

_____

CHAPTER XIX

Eden Vale: Aug. 11, ——

WHAT we learnt from the director of the Freeland Central Bank occupied the thoughts of my father and myself for a long time. As this high functionary, who was a frequent visitor at the house of the Neys, dined with our hosts the next day, the table-talk ran mainly upon the Freeland institutions. My father began by asking whether the circumstance that the rest of the world, from which Freeland did not—and, in fact, in this matter could not—isolate itself, paid interest for loans, did not induce Freeland savers to seek foreign investments for their money; or whether at least some artificial means had not to be adopted to prevent this.

'There is nothing, absolutely nothing,' answered Mr. Clark.

' to prevent Freeland savers from investing their capital abroad ; in fact, at present—I have quite recently been referring to the statistics upon this point regularly published by our central bank—some two and a-half milliards (2,500,000,000*l.*) are invested partly in the large foreign banks, partly in European and American bonds. For example, a good half of your Italian national debt is in the hands of Freelanders. But what are such figures in comparison with the gigantic amounts of our savings and capital ? We cannot prevent, and have no reason whatever to prevent, many Freelanders from being induced by foreign interest to accumulate more capital than is needed here at home on the one hand, and more than they consider necessary to insure themselves against old age on the other. For what is required for these two purposes cannot go abroad.'

' And is not this last-mentioned fact a disadvantage to the Freeland saver ? ' I asked.

' A Freelander who thought so,' said Mr. Ney, ' must have a very imperfect knowledge of what is to his own advantage. The interest paid by foreign debtors can in no respect compare with the advantages offered by employment of the money in Freeland, those advantages being, as you know, equably distributed among all the members of our commonwealth. At the end of last year we had altogether thirty-four milliards sterling invested. The calculated profit of these investments amounted to seven milliards ; therefore, more than twenty per cent. Moreover, thanks to these same investments, every Freelander enjoys gratuitously the electric light, warming, the use of railways and steamships, &c., advantages the total value of which would very nearly equal the remunerative production effected by our investments. Anyone can now calculate how much more profitable Freeland investments of capital are than foreign ones. Moreover, the two and a-half milliards, of which friend Clark spoke, is a large sum in European and American financial operations, and it has actually contributed towards very considerably lowering from time to time the rate of interest in all the foreign money-markets ; but when this amount is compared with Freeland finances, the investment of it abroad is seen to be simply an insignificant and harmless whim. This large sum brings in, at the present rate of interest— you will understand that Freeland savers invest merely in the very best European or American bonds—about thirty-four millions sterling ; that is, not quite the two-hundredth part of the national revenue of Freeland. And there can be no doubt that this whim will—for us—lose much of even its present importance as Freeland continues to grow ; for the competition of our capital has already reduced the rate of discount of the Bank of England to one and a-quarter per cent., and raised the price of the One and a-Half per cent. Consols to 118 ; hence there can be no doubt that a large flow of Freeland savings to Europe and America must, in a near future, reduce the rate of interest to a merely nominal figure. That this whim of investing capital abroad will altogether vanish as soon as foreign countries adopt our institutions is self-evident.'

I now addressed to Mr. Clark the question in what way the Freeland commonwealth guarded against the danger of *crises*, which, in my opinion, must here be much more disastrous than in any other country.

'Crises of any kind,' was the answer, ' would certainly dissolve the whole complex of the Freeland institutions ; but here they are impossible, for lack of the source from which they elsewhere spring. The cause of all crises, whether called production-crises or capital-crises, lies simply in over-production—that is, in the disproportion between production and consumption ; and this disproportion does not exist among us. In fact, the starting-point of the Freeland social reform is the correct perception of the essential character of over-production arrived at twenty-six years ago by the International Free Society. Until then—and in the rest of the world it is still the case—the science of political economy found in this phenomenon an embarrassing enigma, with which it did not know how better to deal than to deny its existence. There was no real over-production—that is, no general non-consumption of products —so taught the orthodox political economists ; for, they contended, men labour only when induced to do so to supply a need, and it is therefore impossible in the nature of things that more goods should be produced than can be consumed. And, on our supposition, to which I will refer presently, this is perfectly correct. Everyone will use what he produces to meet a certain need ; he will either use his product himself or will exchange it for what another has produced. It matters not what that other product is, it is at any rate something that has been produced ; the question never need be what kind of product, but only whether some product is asked for. Let us assume that an improvement has taken place in the production of wheat: it is possible that the demand for wheat will not increase in proportion to the possibility of increasing its production, for it is not necessary that the producers of wheat should use their increased earnings in a larger consumption of wheat. But then the demand for something else would correspondingly increase—for example, for clothing, or for tools ; and if this were only known in time, and production were turned in that direction, there would never be a disturbance in the exchange-relations of the several kinds of goods. Thus the orthodox doctrine explains crises as due not to a surplus of products in general, not to a mere disproportion between production and consumption, but to a transient disturbance of the right relation between the several kinds of production ; and it adds that it is simply paradoxical to talk of a deficient demand in view of the misery prevailing all over the world.

'In this, in other respects perfectly unassailable reasoning, only *one* thing is forgotten—the fundamental constitution of the exploiting system of society. Certainly it is a cruel paradox to speak of a general lack of demand in view of boundless misery; but where an immense majority of men have no claim upon the fruits of their labour, this paradox becomes a horrible reality. What avails it to the suffering worker that he knows how to make right, good, and needful use of what he produces, if that which he produces does not belong to him ? Let us confine ourselves to the example of the increased production of wheat by improved methods of cultivation. If the right of disposal of the increased quantity of grain belonged to the agricultural producers, they would certainly eat more or finer bread, and thus themselves consume a part of the increased production ; with another part they would raise the demand for clothing, and with another the demand for implements, which would necessarily be required in order that more grain and clothing might be produced. In such a case it would really be merely a question of restoring the right relation between the production of wheat, of clothing, of implements, which had been disturbed by the increased production of one of these—wheat; and increased production, a condition of greater prosperity for all, would, after some transient disturbances, be the inevitable consequence. But since the increased proceeds of wheat-cultivation do not belong

to the workers, since those workers receive in any case only a bare
subsistence, the progress which has been made in their branch of
production does not enable them to consume either more grain or
more clothing, and therefore there can exist no increased demand
for implements for the production of wheat and textile fabrics.'

'But,' I objected, 'though this increased product is withheld
from the workers, it is not ownerless—it belongs to the undertakers ;
and these too are men who wish to use their gains to satisfy some
want or other. The undertakers will now increase their consumption ; and after all one might suppose it would be impossible that a
general disproportion should exist between supply and demand.
Certainly it would now be commodities of another kind, the production of which would be stimulated in order to restore an equilibrium
between the several branches of labour. If the increase belonged
to the workers, then would more grain, more ordinary clothing, and
more implements be required ; but since it belongs to a few undertakers there will be an increased demand only for luxuries—dainties,
laces, equipages—and for the implements requisite to produce these
luxuries.'

'Exactly !' said David, who here joined in the conversation.
'Only the undertakers are by no means inclined to apply, in any
considerable degree, the surplus derived from increased production
to an additional consumption of luxuries ; but they capitalise most
of it—that is, invest it in implements of production. Nay, in some
circumstances— as we heard yesterday—the " undertaker " is no man
at all possessing human wants, but a mere dummy that consumes
nothing and capitalises everything.'

'So much the better,' I said, 'wealth will increase all the more
rapidly ; for rapidly growing capital means rapidly increasing production, and that is in itself identical with rapidly increasing
wealth.'

'Splendid !' cried David. 'So, because the working masses
cannot increase their consumption, and the undertakers will not
correspondingly increase theirs, and consequently there can be no
increased consumption of any commodity whatever, therefore the
surplus power of production is utilised in multiplying the means of
production. That is, in other words, no one needs more grain—so
let us construct more ploughs ; no one needs more textile material
—so let us set up more spinning-mills and looms! Are you not

yet able to measure the height of absurdity to which your doctrine leads ? '

I think, Louis, you, like myself, will admit that there is simply no reply to reasoning so plain and convincing. An economic system which bars the products of human industry and invention from the only use to which they should finally be applied—namely, that of satisfying some human requirement—and which is then astonished that they cannot be consumed, narrowly escapes idiocy. But that such is the character of the system which prevails in Europe and America must in the end become clear to everyone.

' But, in heaven's name, what becomes of the productive power among us which thus remains unemployed ? ' I asked. 'We are, on the whole, as advanced in art, science, and technical skill as you are in Freeland ; I must therefore suppose that we could become as rich, or nearly so, as you, if we could only find a use for all our production. But we do not actually possess a tenth of your wealth, and yet there is twice as much hard work done among us as there is here. For though among you everyone works, and among us there are several millions of persons of leisure who live simply upon the toil of others, yet this is counterbalanced by the circumstance that our working masses are kept at their toil ten hours or more daily, whilst here an average working day is only five hours. Certainly among us there are millions of unemployed workers ; but that also is more than compensated for by the labour of women and children, which is unknown among you. Where then, I repeat, lies the immense difference between the utilisation of our powers of production and of yours ? '

' In the equipment of labour,' was the answer. ' We Freelanders do not work so hard as you do, but we make full use of all the aids of science and technics, whilst you are able to do this only exceptionally, and in no case so completely as we do. All the inventions and discoveries of the greatest minds are as well known to you as to us ; but as a rule they are taken advantage of only by us. Since your aristocratic institutions prevent you from enjoying the things the production of which is facilitated by those inventions, you are not able to take advantage of the inventions except in such small measure as your institutions permit.'

Even my father was profoundly moved by this crushing exposition of a system which he had always been accustomed to honour as the highest emanation of eternal wisdom. 'Incredible! shocking!' he murmured in a tone audible only to myself.

But Mr. Clark proceeded: 'Among us, on the contrary, the theorem of the so-called classical economics, that a general excess of production is impossible, has become a truth, for in Freeland consumption and production exactly tally. Here there can be over-production only temporarily and in *isolated* kinds of goods— that is, the equilibrium between different kinds of production may be temporarily disturbed. But we have no need to be afraid of even this trifling danger. The intimate connection of all productive interests springing from the nature of our institutions is an antecedent guarantee of equilibrium between all branches of production. A careful examination will show that the whole of Freeland is one great productive society, whose individual members are independent of one another, and yet are connected in one respect—namely, in respect of the proceeds of their labour. Just because everyone can labour where and how he pleases, but everyone's labour is alike in aiming at the highest possible utility, so—apart from any incidental errors—it is impossible but that an equal amount of labour should result in an equal amount of utility. All our institutions tend towards this one point. At first, as long as our commonwealth was in its initial stages, it sometimes happened that considerable inequalities had to be subsequently balanced; the producers did not always know until the year's accounts were closed what one and the other had earned. But that was a period of childhood long since outlived. At present, every Freelander knows, to within such trifling variations as may be due to little unforeseen accidents, exactly what he and others have earned, and also what they have every prospect of earning in the near future. He does not wait for inequalities to arise and then set about rectifying them; but he takes care that inequalities shall not arise. Since our statistics always show with unerring accuracy what at the time is being produced in every branch of industry, and since the demand as well as its influence upon prices can be exactly estimated from a careful observation of past years, therefore the revenue not only of every branch of industry, but of every separate establishment, can be beforehand so reliably calculated that nothing short of natural catastrophes can cause errors worth notice. If such occur, then comes in the assistance of the reciprocal insurance. In fact, in this country, not only are there no crises, but not even any considerable variations in the different productions. Our Statistical Department publishes an unbroken series of exact comparative statistics, from which can at any time be seen where either fresh demand or excess of labour is likely to arise; our supply of labour is controlled by these returns, and that is sufficient—with rare exceptions—to preserve a perfect equilibrium in production. It frequently occurs that here or there a newly started establishment comes to grief, particularly in the mining industry. Such a failure must not, however, be regarded as a bankruptcy—how can undertakers become bankrupt when they have neither ground-rent, nor interest, nor wages to pay, and who in any case still possess their highly priced labour-power?—but at the worst as a case of disappointed expectations. And should the very rare circumstance occur, that the community or an association loses the loaned capital through the premature death of the borrower, of what importance is that in the face of the gigantic sums safely employed in our business? And if a guaranty (*del credere*) were insisted upon to cover such a loss, it would amount to scarcely a thousandth part of one per cent., and would not be worth the ink used in writing it.'

'And do not foreign crises sometimes disturb the calm course of your Freeland production? Are not your markets flooded, through foreign over-production, with goods for which there is no corresponding demand?' I asked.

'It certainly cannot be denied that we are considerably inconvenienced by the frequent and sudden changes of price in the markets of the world caused by the anarchic character of the exploiting system of production. We are thereby often compelled to diminish our production in certain directions, and divert the labour thus set free to other branches of industry, though there is no actual change in the cost of production or in the relative demand. These foreign, sudden, and incalculable influences sometimes make a diversion of labour from one production to another necessary in order to preserve an equilibrium in the profits, though the regular and automatic migration of labour from one industry to another is sufficient to correct the disturbance in the relations between supply and demand due to natural causes. But these spasmodic foreign occurrences cannot produce a serious convulsion in our industrial relations. Just as it is impossible to throw out of equilibrium a liquid which yields to every pressure or blow, so our industry is able to preserve its equilibrium by means of its absolutely free mobility. It may be thrown into fruitless agitation, but its natural gravity at once restores the harmony of its relations. But, as I have said, such a disturbance is produced only by a partial over-production abroad. That this brings about a superabundance of all commodities, we care but little. Since foreign countries do not send us their goods for nothing, but demand other goods in return, what those other goods shall be is their business, not ours. We have no interest-bearing bonds or saleable property in land ; hence our export goods must be the produce of our labour. The fact that in Freeland every product must find a purchaser is therefore by no means affected by external trade.'

' That is very clear,' I admitted.

' But,' interposed my father, ' why do you not protect yourselves against disturbance due to foreign fluctuations in production, by a total exclusion of foreign imports ? '

' Because that would be to cut off one's hand in order to prevent it from being injured,' was Mr. Clark's drastic answer. ' We import only those goods which we cannot produce so cheaply our-selves. But since, as I have already taken the liberty of saying, the imported goods are not presented to us, but must be paid for by goods produced by us, it is of importance that we should be able to produce the goods with which we make the payment more cheaply —that is, with less expenditure of labour-power than we could the imported goods. For instance, we manufacture scarcely any cotton goods, but get nearly all such goods from England and America. We could, certainly, manufacture cotton goods ourselves, but it is plain that we should have to expend upon their manufacture more labour-power than upon the production of the corn, gold, machinery, and tools with which we pay for the cotton goods that we require. If it were not so, we should manufacture cotton goods also, for there is no conceivable reason for not doing so but the one just mentioned. If, therefore, our legislature prohibited the importa-tion of cotton goods, we should have to divert labour from other branches of industry for the sake of producing *less* than we do now. We should have either to put up with fewer goods, or to work more, to meet the same demand. Hence, in this country, to enact a protective duty would be held to be pure madness.'

'Then you hold,' said my father, 'that our European and American economists and statesmen who still in part adhere to the system of protection, are simply Bedlamites ; and you believe that the only rational commercial policy is that of absolute free trade ? '

'Allow me to say,' answered Mr. Clark, 'that Europe and America are not Freeland. I certainly cannot regard protection even abroad as rational, for the assumptions from which it starts are under all circumstances false. But neither do I think the foreign free trader is essentially wiser than the protectionist, for he also starts from assumptions which are baseless in an exploiting country. The prohibitionists think they are encouraging production : they are doing the opposite, they are hindering and hampering production ; and the free traders, in so far as they insist upon this fact, are perfectly correct. Both parties, however, fail to see that in an exploiting society, which is never able to utilise more than a small part of its power to produce, the influence of legislative interference with trade upon the good or the bad utilisation of productive power is a matter of very little importance. Of what advantage is it to the free traders that a nation under the domination of their commercial system *is able* to make the most prolific use of their industrial capacities, so long as the continuance of industrial servitude prevents this nation from enjoying more than enough to satisfy the barest necessities of life ? More than is consumed cannot, under any circumstances, be produced ; and consumption among you abroad is so infinitely small, that it is verily ridiculous to dispute over the question whether this or that commodity can be produced better at home or abroad.

' What alone interests us in this controversy among the foreign commercial politicians is that neither party has the slightest suspicion that what the free traders rightly reproach the protectionists with, and what the latter wrongly defend, is the very thing that gains so many adherents to protection—namely, the hindering and hampering of production. The protectionists have a right to boast that they compel their people to apply two day's labour or a double amount of capital to the production at home of a thing which, by means of external trade, might have been exchanged for things that are the product of merely half as much expenditure of home labour. We, who work in order to enjoy, would have a good right to treat as insane any persons among us

who proposed such a course as an "encouragement of home labour";
but among you, where labour and enjoyment are completely dis-
severed, where millions cry for work as a favour—among you, the
hampering of labour is felt to be a benefit because it makes more
toil necessary in order to procure an equal amount of enjoyment.
Among you it is also a somewhat dangerous narcotic, for protection
has a Janus head : it not merely increases the toil, it at the same
time still more diminishes the consumption by raising the price of
the articles in demand, the rise in price never being followed
immediately by a rise in wages ; so that, in the end, in spite of the
increased difficulty in production, no more labour and capital are
employed than before. But the intimate relation between these
things is as a book sealed with seven seals to both protectionists
and free traders. Had it been otherwise, they must long since
have seen that the cure for industrial evils must be looked for not
in the domain of commercial politics, but in that of social politics.'

'Now I begin to understand,' I cried out, 'the widespread
growth of economic reaction against which we Western Liberals are
waging a ridiculous Quixotic war with all our apparently irrefutable
arguments. We present to the people as an argument against
protection exactly that after which they are— unconsciously, it is
true—eagerly longing. Protective tariffs, trade guilds, and whatever else the ingenious devices of the last decades may be called,
I now understand and recognise as desperate attempts made by
men whose very existence is threatened by the ever-growing
disproportion between the power to produce and consumption—
attempts to restore to some extent the true proportion by curbing
and checking the power to produce. Whilst the protectionist is
eager to put fetters upon the international division of labour, to
keep at a distance the foreigner who might otherwise save him
some of his toil, the advocate of trade-guilds fights for hand-labour
against machine-labour and commerce. And when I look into the
matter, I find all these people are in a certain sense wiser than we
Liberals of the old school, who know no better cure for the malady
of the time than that of shutting our eyes as firmly as possible. It
is true, our intentions have been of the best ; but since we have at
length discovered how to attain what we wished for, we should at
once throw off the fatal self-deception that political freedom would
suffice to make men truly free and happy. Political freedom is

an indispensable, but not the sole, condition of progress ; whoever refuses to recognise this condemns mankind afresh to the night of reaction. For if, as our Liberal economics has taught, it were really contrary to the laws of nature to guarantee to all men a full participation in the benefits of progress, then not only would progress be the most superfluous thing imaginable, but we should have to agree with those who assert that the eternally disinherited masses can find happiness only in ignorant indifference. Now I realise that the material and mental reaction is the logically inevitable outcome of economic orthodoxy. If wealth and leisure are impossible for all, then it is strictly logical to promote material and mental reaction ; whilst it is absurd to believe that men will perpetually promote a growth of culture without ever taking advantage of it. I now see with appalling distinctness that if our toiling masses had not been saved by their social hopes from sharing our economic pessimism, we Liberals would long since have found ourselves in the midst of a reaction of a fearful kind : it is not through *us* that modern civilisation has been spared the destruction which overwhelmed its predecessors.'

After dinner, Mr. Ney invited us to accompany him to the National Palace, where the Parliament for Public Works was about to hold an evening session in order to vote upon a great canal project. He thought the subject would interest us. We accepted the invitation with thanks.

The Parliament for Public Works consists of 120 members, most of whom, as David—who was one of the party—told me, are directors of large associations, particularly of associations connected with building ; but among the members are also professors of technical universities, and other specialists. The body contains no laymen who are ignorant of public works ; and the parliament may be said to contain the flower and quintessence of the technical science and skill of all Freeland.

The project before the house was one which had been advocated for above a year by the directors of the Water and Mountain-Cultivation Associations of Eden Vale, North Baringo, Ripon, and Strahl City, in connection with two professors of the technical university of Ripon. The project was nothing less than the construction of a canal navigable by ships of 2,000 tons burden, from Lake Tanganika, across the Mutanzige and Albert Nyanza, whence the Nile could be followed to the Mediterranean Sea ; and from the mouth of the Congo, along the course of that river, across the Aruwhimi to the Albert lake ; thence following several smaller streams to the Baringo lake, along the upper course of the Dana, and thence to the Indian Ocean. The project thus included two water-ways, one of which would connect the great lakes of Central Africa with the Mediterranean Sea, and the other, crossing the whole of the continent, would connect the Atlantic with the Indian Ocean. Since a part of the immense works involved in this project would have to be carried through foreign territories—those of the Congo State and of Egypt—negotiations had been opened with those States, and all the necessary powers had been obtained. The readiness of the foreign governments to accede to the wishes of the Eden Vale executive is explained by the fact that Freeland did not propose to exact any toll for the use of its canals, thus making its neighbours a free gift of these colossal works. In connection with this project, there was also another for the acquisition of the Suez Canal, which was to be doubled in breadth and depth and likewise thrown open gratuitously to the world. The English government, which owned the greater part of the Suez Canal shares, had met the Freelanders most liberally, transferring to them its shares at a very low price, so that the Freelanders had further to deal with only holders of a small number of shares, who certainly knew how to take advantage of the situation. The British government stipulated for the inalienable neutrality of the canal, and urged the Freelanders to prosecute the work with vigour.

The following were the preliminary expenses :

	£
South-North Canal (total length 3,900 miles) . . .	385,000,000
East-West Canal (total length 3,400 miles) . . .	412,000,000
Suez Canal (purchase and enlargement) . . .	280,000,000
Total	£1,077,000,000

It was estimated that the whole would be completed in six years, and that therefore a round sum of 180,000,000*l.* would be required yearly during the progress of the work. The Freeland government believed that they were justified by their past experience in expecting that the national income would in the course of the coming six years increase from seven milliards—the income of the past year—to at least ten and a-half milliards, giving a yearly average of eight and a-half milliards for the six years. The cost of construction of the projected works would therefore absorb only two and one-eighth per cent. of the estimated national income, and would be covered without raising the tax upon this income above its normal proportion. The estimated cost was accompanied by detailed plans, and also by an estimate of the profits, according to which it was calculated that in the first year of use the canals would save the country 32,000,000*l*. in cost of transport ; and therefore, taking into account the presumptive growth of traffic, the canals would, in about thirty years, pay for themselves in the mere saving of transport expenses. Moreover, these future waterways were to serve in places as draining and irrigating canals ; and it was calculated that the advantage thus conferred upon the country would be worth on an average 45,000,000*l*. a year. Thus the whole project would pay for itself in fourteen years at the longest, without taking into account the advantages conferred upon foreign nations.

As the whole of the proposals and plans had been in the hands of the members for several weeks, and had been carefully studied by them, the discussion began at once. No one offered any opposition to the principle of the project. The debate was confined chiefly to two questions : first, whether it was not possible to hasten the construction ; and secondly, whether an alternative plan, the details of which were before the house, was not preferable. With reference to the first question, it was shown that, by adopting a new system of dredging devised by certain experienced specialists, quite six months could be saved ; and it was therefore resolved to adopt that system. As to the second question, after hearing the arguments of Mr. Ney, it was unanimously decided to adhere to the plan of the central executive. After a debate of less than three hours, the government found itself empowered to spend 1,077,000,000*l*., something more than the cost of all the canals in the rest of the civilised world. This amount was to be spent in five and a-half years, in constructing works which would make it possible for ocean steamers to cross the African continent from east to west, to pass from the Mediterranean as far as the tenth degree of south latitude, and to remove every obstacle and every toll from the passage of the Suez Canal.

I was absolutely dumfounded by all this. ' If I had not already resolved to strike the word " impossible " out of my vocabulary, I

T

should do it now,' I remarked to Mr. Ney on our way home. I must add that in the Freeland parliaments all the proceedings take place in the presence of the public, so that I had an opportunity of making a hasty examination of the details of the project which had just been adopted. You know that I understand such things a little, and I was therefore able to gather from the plans that the two central ship canals crossed several watersheds. One of these watersheds I accidentally knew something of, as we had passed a part of it on our journey hither, and a part of it we had seen in some of our excursions. It rises, as I reckon, at least 1,650 feet above the level of the canal. I asked Mr. Ney whether it was really proposed to carry a waterway for ships of 2,000 tons burden some 1,650 feet up and down—was it not impossible either to construct or to work such a canal?

'Certainly!' he replied, with a smile. 'But if you look at the plan more carefully, you will see that we do not *go over* such watersheds by means of locks, but *under* them by means of tunnels.'

I looked at him incredulously, and my father's face expressed no little astonishment.

'What do you find remarkable in that, my worthy guests? Why should it be impracticable to do on canals what has so long and extensively been done on railways, which could be much more easily carried *over* hills and valleys?' asked Mr. Ney. 'I admit that our canal tunnels are very costly; but as, in working, they spare us what is the most expensive of all things, human labour-time, they are the most practical for our circumstances. Besides, in several cases we had no alternative except to dispense with the canals or to construct tunnels. The watershed you speak of is not the most considerable one : our greatest boring—connecting the river system of the Victoria Nyanza with the Indian Ocean—is carried, in one stretch of ten and a-half miles, 4,000 feet below the watershed ; and altogether, in our new project, we have not less than eighty-two miles of tunnelling. Such tunnels are, however, not quite novelties. There are in France, as you know, several short water-tunnels ; we possess, in our old canal system, several very respectable ones, though certainly they cannot compare either in length or in size with the new ones, by means of which large ocean vessels—with lowered masts, of course—will be able to steam through the bowels of whole ranges of mountains. The cost is enormous; but you must remember that every hour saved to a Freeland sailor is already worth eight shillings, and increases in value year by year.'

'But,' said my father, ' what, after all, is inconceivable to me is the haste, I might almost say the *nonchalance*, with which milliards were voted to you, as if it was merely a question of the veriest trifle. I would not for a moment question the integrity of the members of your Parliament for Public Buildings; but I cannot refrain from saying that the whole assembly gave me the impression of expecting the greatest personal advantage from getting the work done as speedily and on as large a scale as possible.'

'And that impression was a correct one,' replied Mr. Ney. ' But I must add that every inhabitant of Freeland will necessarily derive the same personal profit from the realisation of this canal project. Just because it is so, just because among us there truly exists that solidarity of interests which among other peoples exists only in name, are we able to expend such immense sums upon works which can be shown to promise a utility above their cost. If, among you, a canal is constructed which increases the profitableness of large tracts of land, your recognised economics teaches you that it adds to the prosperity of all. But this is correct only for the owners of the ground affected by the canal, whilst the great mass of the population is not benefited in the least by such a canal, and perhaps the owners of other competing tracts of land are actually injured. The lowering of the price of corn—so your statesmen assert—benefits the non-possessing classes; they forget the little fact that the rate of wages cannot be permanently maintained if the price of corn sinks. Against this there is certainly to be placed as a consolation the fact that the non-possessing masses will not be permanently injured by the increased taxes necessitated by such public works; for he who earns only enough to furnish a bare subsistence cannot long be made to pay much in taxes. Therefore, in your countries, the controversy over such investments is a conflict of interests between different landowners and undertakers, some of whom gain, whilst others gain nothing, or actually lose. Among us, on the contrary, everyone is alike interested in the gains of profitable investments in proportion to the amount of work he does; and everyone is also called upon to contribute to the defraying of the cost in proportion to the amount of work he does : hence, a conflict

of interests, or even a mere disproportion in reaping the advantage,
is among us absolutely excluded. The new canals will convert
17,000,000 acres of bog into fertile agricultural land. Who will be
benefited, when this virgin soil traversed by such magnificent water-
ways annually produces so many more pounds sterling per acre
than is produced by other land? Plainly everyone in Freeland,
and everyone alike, whether he be agriculturist, artisan, professor,
or official. Who gains by the lowering of freights? Merely the
associations and workers who actually make use of the new water-
ways for transport? By no means; for, thanks to the unlimited
mobility of our labour, they necessarily share with everyone in
Freeland whatever advantage they reap. Therefore, with perfect
confidence, we commit the decision of such questions to those who
are most immediately interested in them. They know best what
will be of advantage to them, and as their advantage is everybody's
advantage, so everybody's—that is, the commonwealth's—treasury
stands as open and free to them as their own. If they wish to put
their hands into it, the deeper the better. We have not to inquire
whom the investment will benefit, but merely if it is profitable—
that is, if it saves labour.'

  ' Marvellous, but true!' my father was compelled to admit.
' But since in this country there exists the completest solidarity of
interests, I cannot understand why you require the repayment of
the capital which the commonwealth supplies to the different
associations.'

  ' Because not to do so would be Communism with all its inevitable consequences,' was the answer. ' The ultimate benefit of such
gratuitously given capital would certainly be reaped by all alike ;
but, in that case, who could guarantee that the investment of the
capital should be advantageous and not injurious? For an investment of capital is advantageous only when by its help more labour
is saved than the creation of the capital has cost. A machine that
absorbs more labour than it takes the place of is injurious. But we
are now secured against such wasteful expenditure, at least against
any known waste of capital. The commonwealth, as well as individuals, may be mistaken in its calculations ; both may consider
an investment profitable which is afterwards proved to be unprofitable—that is, which does not pay for the labour which it
costs. Nevertheless, the *intention* in all investments can only be to

save the expenditure of energy, for both the commonwealth and individuals must bear the cost of their own investments. If, however, the commonwealth had to be responsible for the investments of individuals—that is, of the associations—then the several associations would have no motive to avoid employing such mechanical aids as would save less labour than they cost. The necessary consequence of this liberality on the part of the commonwealth would therefore be that the commonwealth would assume a right of supervision and control over those who required capital ; and this would be incompatible with freedom and progress. All sense of personal responsibility would be lost, the commonwealth would be compelled to busy itself with matters which did not belong to it, and loss would be inevitable in spite of all arbitrary restraints from above.'

'That, again,' said my father, 'is as plain and simple as possible. But I must ask for an explanation of one other point. In virtue of the solidarity of interests which prevails among you, everyone participates in all improvements, wherever they may occur; this takes place in such a manner that everyone has the right to exchange a less profitable branch of production, or a less profitable locality, for a more profitable one. Then what interest has the *individual* producer—that is, the *individual* association— to introduce improvements, since it must seem to be much simpler, less troublesome, and less risky, to allow others to take the initiative and to attach oneself to them when success is certain ? But I perceive that your associations are by no means lacking in push and enterprise : how is this ? What prompts your producers to run risks—small though they may be—when the profit to be gained thereby must so quickly be shared by everybody ? '

'In the first place,' replied Mr. Ney, 'you overlook the fact that the amount of the expected profit is not the only inducement by which working-men, and particularly our Freeland workers, are influenced. The ambition of seeing the establishment to which one belongs in the van and not in the rear of all others, is not to be undervalued as a motive actuating intelligent men possessing a strong *esprit de corps*. But, apart from that, you must reflect that the members of the associations have also a very considerable *material* interest in the prosperity of their own particular undertaking. Freeland workers without exception have very comfortable,

nay, luxurious homes, naturally for the most part in the neighbourhood of their respective work-places; they run a risk of having to
leave these homes if their undertaking is not kept up to a level with
others. In the second place, the elder workmen—that is, those that
have been engaged a longer time in an undertaking—enjoy a constantly increasing premium ; their work-time has a higher value by
several units per cent. than that of the later comers. Hence, notwithstanding the solidarity of interest, the members of each association have to take care that their establishment is not excelled ;
and since the risk attending new improvements is very small indeed,
the spirit of invention and enterprise is more keenly active among
us than anywhere else in the world. The associations zealously
compete with each other for pre-eminence, only it is a friendly rivalry
and not a competitive struggle for bread.'

By this time it had grown late. My father and I would gladly
have listened longer to the very interesting explanations of our kind
host, but we could not abuse the courtesy of our friends, and so we
parted ; and I will take occasion also to bid you, Louis, farewell for
to-day.

CHAPTER XX

Eden Vale : Aug. 16, ——

In your last letter you give expression to your astonishment that
our host, with only a salary of 1,440*l.* as a member of the government of Freeland, is able to keep up such an establishment as I have
described, to occupy an elegant villa with twelve dwelling-rooms,
to furnish his table, to indulge in horses and carriages—in a word,
to live as luxuriously as only the richest are able to do among us at
home. In fact, David was right when he promised us that we
should not have to forego any real comfort, any genuine enjoyment
to which we had been accustomed in our aristocratic palace at
home. Our host does not possess capital the interest of which he
can use ; nor is Mrs. Ney a ' blue-stocking '—as you surmise—who
writes highly paid romances for Freeland journals ; nor does the
elder Ney draw upon his son's income as artist. It is true that
Mrs. Ney once possessed a large fortune which she inherited from
her father, one of the leading speculators of America ; but she lost
this to the last farthing in the great American crisis of 18—,

soon after her marriage. The domestic habits of the Neys were
not, however, affected in the least by this loss; for since her
migration to Freeland she had never made any private use of her
fortune, but had always applied its income to public purposes.
This does not prevent Mr. Ney from spending—over and above the
outlay you mention—very considerable sums upon art and science
and in benevolence : the last of course only abroad, for here no one
is in need of charity.   As it is not considered indiscreet in Freeland
to talk of such matters, I am in a position to tell you that last year
the Neys spent 92*l.* for objects of art, 75*l.* for books, journals, and
music, 120*l.* in travelling, and 108*l.*—the amount that remained to
their credit after defraying all the other expenses—in foreign charities
and public institutions.   Thanks to the marvellous organisation of
industry and trade, everything here is fabulously cheap—in fact,
many things which consume a great deal of money in Europe and
America do not add in the least to the expenses of a Freeland
household, as they are furnished gratuitously by the commonwealth,
and paid for out of the tax which has been subtracted in advance
from the net income of each individual.   For example, in the cost
of travelling, not a farthing has to be reckoned for railway or
steamship, since—as you have already learnt from my former letters
—the Freeland commonwealth provides free means of personal
transport.   The same holds, as I think I have already told you,
of the telegraphs, the telephones, the post, electric lighting, mechanical motive-power, &c.   On the other hand, the Freeland
government charges the cost of the transport of goods by land and
water to the owners of the goods.   I will take this opportunity of
remarking that almost every Freeland family spends on an average
two months in the year in travelling, mostly in the many wonderfully beautiful districts of their own land, and more rarely in foreign
countries.   Every Freelander takes a holiday of at least six, and
sometimes as much as ten weeks, and seeks recreation, pleasure,
and instruction, as a tourist.   The highlands of the Kilimanjaro,
the Kenia, and the Elgon, of the Aberdare range and the Mountains
of the Moon, as well as the shores of all the great lakes, swarm at
all seasons—except the two rainy seasons—with driving, riding,
walking, rowing, and sailing men, women, and children, in full
enjoyment of all the delights of travel.

An intelligent and hearty love of nature and natural beauty is a general characteristic of the Freelanders. They are proprietors in common of the whole of their country, and their loving care for this precious possession is everywhere conspicuous. It is significant that nowhere in Freeland are the streams and rivers poisoned by refuse-water; nowhere are picturesque mountain-declivities disfigured by quarries opened in badly selected localities. No such offences against the beauty of the landscape are anywhere to be met with. For why should these self-governing workers rob themselves of the real pleasure afforded by healthy and beautiful natural scenes, for the sake of a small saving which must be shared by everybody? Naturally, this intelligent regard for rural attractions benefits tourists also. Everywhere both the roads and the railways are bordered by avenues of fine palms, whose slender branchless trunks do not obscure the view, whilst their heavy crowns afford refreshing shade. In consequence of this simple and effective arrangement, one suffers far less from heat and dust here under the equator than in temperate Europe, where in the summer months a several hours' journey by rail or road is frequently a torture. At all the beautiful and romantic spots, the Hotel and Recreation Associations have employed their immense resources in providing enormous boarding-houses, as well as many small villas, in which the tourists may find every comfort, either in the company of hundreds or thousands of others, or in rural isolation, for hours, days, weeks, or months.

If you are astonished at the luxury in the house of the Noys, what will you say when I tell you that in this country every simple worker lives essentially as our hosts do? The villas merely have fewer rooms, the furniture is plainer; instead of keeping saddle-horses of their own, the simple workers hire those belonging to the Transport Association; less money is spent upon objects of art, books, and for benevolent purposes: these are the only differences. Take, for instance, our neighbour Moro. Though an ordinary overseer in the Eden Vale Paint-making Association, he and his charming wife are among the intimate friends of our host, and we have already several times dined in his neat and comfortable seven-roomed house. Even 'pupil-daughters' are not lacking in his house, for his wife enjoys—and justly, as I can testify—the reputation of possessing a special amount of mental and moral culture; and, as you know, pupil-daughters choose not the great house, but the superior housewife. And if it should strike you as remarkable that such a Phœnix of a woman should be the wife of a simple factory-hand, you must remember that the workers of Freeland are different from those of Europe. Here everybody enjoys sound secondary education; and that a young man becomes an artisan and not a teacher, or a physician, or engineer, or such like, is due to the fact that he does not possess, or thinks he does not possess, any *exceptional* intellectual capacity. For in this country the intellectual professions can be successfully carried on only by those who possess exceptional natural qualifications, since the competition of *all* who are really qualified makes it impossible for the imperfectly qualified to succeed. Among ourselves, where only an infinitely small proportion of the population has the opportunity of studying, the lack of means among the immense majority secures a privilege even to the blockheads among the fortunate possessors of means. The rich cannot all be persons of talent any more than all the poor can. Since we, however, notwithstanding this, supply our demand for intellectual workers—apart, of course, from those exceptional cases which occur everywhere—solely from the small number of sons of rich families, we are fortunate if we find one capable student among ten incapables; of which ten—since the one capable student cannot supply all our demand—at most only two or three of the greatest blockheads suffer shipwreck. Here, on the contrary, where everyone has the opportunity of studying, there are, of course, very many more capable students; consequently the Freelanders do not need to go nearly so low down as we do in the scale of capacity to cover their demand for intellectual workers. It does not necessarily follow that their cleverest men are cleverer than ours; but our incapables—among the graduates—are much, much more incapable than the least capable of theirs can possibly be. What would be of medium quality among us is here far below consideration at all. Friend Moro, for instance, would probably, in Europe or America, not have been one of the 'lights of science,' nor 'an ornament to the bar'; but he would at least have been a very acceptable average teacher, advocate, or official. Here, however, after leaving the intermediate school, it was necessary for him to take a conscientious valuation of his mental capacity; and he arrived at the conclusion that it would be better to become a first-rate factory-overseer than a mediocre teacher or official. And he could carry out this—perhaps too severe—resolve without socially degrading himself, for in Freeland manual labour does not degrade as it does in Europe and America, where the assertion that it does not degrade is one of the many conventional lies with which we seek to impose upon ourselves. Despite all our democratic talk, work is among us in general a disgrace, for the labourer is a dependent, an exploited servant—he has a master over him who can order him, and can use him for his own purpose as he can a beast of burden. No ethical theory in the world will make master and servant equally honourable. But here it is different. To discover how great the difference is, one need merely attend a social reunion in Freeland. It is natural, of course, that persons belonging to the same circle of interests should most readily associate together; but this must not be supposed to imply the existence of anything even remotely like a breaking up of society into different professional strata. The common level of culture is so high, interest in the most exalted problems of humanity so general, even among the manual labourers, that *savants*, artists, heads of the government, find innumerable points of contact, both intellectual and æsthetic, even with factory-hands and agricultural labourers.

This is all the more the case since a definite line of demarcation between head-workers and hand-workers cannot here be drawn. The manual labourer of to-day may to-morrow, by the choice of his fellow-labourers, become a director of labour, therefore a head-worker; and, on the other hand, there are among the manual labourers untold thousands who were originally elected to different callings, and who have gone through the studies required for such callings, but have exchanged the pen for the tool, either because they found themselves not perfectly qualified intellectually, or because their tastes have changed. Thus, for instance, another visiting friend of the Neys successfully practised as a physician for several years; but he now devotes himself to gardening, because this quiet calling withdraws him less than his work as physician from his favourite study, astronomy. His knowledge and capacity as astronomer were not sufficient to provide him with a livelihood, and as he was frequently called in the night from some interesting observation reluctantly to attend upon sick children, he determined to earn his livelihood by gardening, so that he might devote his nights to an undisturbed observation of the stars. Another man with whom I have here become acquainted exchanged the career of a bank official for that of a machine-smith, simply because he did not like a sedentary occupation; several times he might have been elected by the members of his association on the board of directors, but he always declined on the plea of an invincible objection to office work. But there is a still larger number of persons who combine some kind of manual labour with intellectual work. So general in Freeland is the disinclination to confine oneself *exclusively* to head-work, that in all the higher callings, and even in the public offices, arrangements have to be made which will allow those engaged in such offices to spend some time in manual occupations. The bookkeepers and correspondents of the associations, as well as of the central bank, the teachers, officials, and other holders of appointments of all kinds, have the right to demand, besides the regular two months' holiday, leave of absence for a longer or a shorter time, which time is to be spent in some other occupation. Naturally no wages are paid for the time consumed by these special periods of absence; but this does not prevent the greater part of all these officials from seeking a temporary change of occupation for several months once in every two or three years, as factory-hands, miners, agriculturists, gardeners, &c. An acquaintance of mine, a head of a department of the central executive, spends two months in every second year at one or other of the mines in the Aberdare or the Baringo district. He tells me he has already gone practically through the work of the coal, the iron, the tin, the copper, and the sulphur mines; and he is now pleasantly anticipating a course of labour in the salt-works of Elmeteita.

In view of this general and thorough inter-blending of the most ordinary physical with the highest mental activity, it is impossible to speak of any distinction of class or social status. The agriculturists here are as highly respected, as cultured gentlemen, as the learned, the artists, or the higher officials; and there is nothing to prevent those who harmonise with them in character and sentiment from treating them as friends and equals in society.

But the women—elsewhere the staunchest upholders of aristocratic exclusiveness—in this country are the most zealous advocates of a complete amalgamation of all the different sections of the population. The Freeland woman, almost without exception, has attained to a very high degree of ethical and intellectual culture. Relieved of all material anxiety and toil, her sole vocation is to ennoble herself, to quicken her understanding for all that is good and lofty. As she is delivered from the degrading necessity of finding in her husband one upon whom she is dependent for her livelihood, as she does not derive her social position from the occupation of her husband, but from her own personal worth, she is consequently free from that haughty exclusiveness which is to be found wherever real excellences are wanting. The women of the so-called better classes among us at home treat their less fortunate sisters with such repellent arrogance simply because they cannot get rid of the instinctive feeling that these poorer sisters would have very well occupied their own places, and *vice versâ*, had their husbands been changed. And even when it is not so, when the European 'lady' actually does possess a higher ethical and intellectual character, she is obliged to confess that her position in the opinion of the world depends less upon her own qualities than upon the rank and position of her husband—that is, upon another, who could just as well have placed any other woman upon the borrowed throne. Schopenhauer is not altogether wrong: women are mostly engaged in one and the same pursuit—man-hunting—and it is the envy of competition that lies at the bottom of their pride. Only he forgets to add, or rather he does not know, that this pursuit, which is common to all women, and which he lashes so unmercifully, is, with all its hateful evil consequences, the inevitable result of their lack of legal rights, and is in no way indissolubly bound up with their nature.

The women here, who are free and endowed with equal legal rights with the men in the highest sense of the words, exhibit none of this pride in the external relations of life. Even when the calling or the wealth of the husband might give rise to a certain social distinction, they would never recognise it, but allow themselves to be guided in their social intercourse simply by personal characteristics. It is the most talented, the most amiable woman whose friendship they most eagerly seek, whatever may be the position of the woman's husband. Hence you can understand that Mrs. Moro could select her husband without having to make the slightest sacrifice in her relation to Freeland 'society.'

Whilst we are upon this subject, let me say a few words as to the character of society here. Social life here is very bright and animated. Families that are intimate with each other meet together without ceremony almost every evening; and there is conversation, music, and, among the young people, not a little dancing. There is nothing particular in all this; but the very peculiar, and to the stranger at first altogether inexplicable, attraction of Freeland society is due to the prevailing tone of the most perfect freedom in combination with the loftiest nobility and the most exquisite delicacy. When I had enjoyed it a few times, I began to long for the pleasure of these reunions, without at first being able to account for the charm which they exercised upon me. At last I arrived at the conviction that what made social intercourse here so richly enjoyable must be mainly the genuine human affection which characterises life in Freeland.

Social reunions in Europe are essentially nothing more than masquerades in which those present indulge in reciprocal lying—meetings of foes, who attempt to hide under courtly grimaces the ill-will they bear each other, but who nevertheless utterly fail to deceive each other. And under an exploiting system of society this cannot be prevented, for antagonism of interests is there the rule, and true solidarity of interests a very rare and purely accidental exception. To cherish a genuine affection for our fellow-men is with us a virtue, the exercise of which demands more than an ordinary amount of self-denial; and everyone knows that nine-tenths of the wearers of those politely grinning masks would fall upon each other in bitter hatred if the inherited and acquired restraints of conventional good manners were for a moment to be laid aside. At such reunions one feels very much as those miscellaneous beasts may be supposed to feel who are confined together in a common cage for the delectation of the spectacle-loving public. The only difference is that our two-legged tigers, panthers, lynxes, wolves, bears, and hyenas are better trained than their four-legged types; the latter glide about fiercely snarling at each other, with difficulty restraining their murderous passions as they cast side-glances at the lash of their tamer, whilst the ill-will lurking in the hearts of the former is to be detected only by the closest observer through some malicious glance of the eye, or some other scarcely perceptible movement. In fact, so complete is the training of the two-legged carnivora that they themselves are sometimes deceived by it; there are moments when the hyenas seriously believe that their polite grinning at the tiger is honestly meant, and when the tiger fancies that his subdued growls conceal a genial affection and friendship towards his fellow-beasts. But these are only fleeting moments of fond self-deception; and in general one cannot get rid of the sensation of being among natural enemies, who, but for the external restraints, would fly at our throats. The Freelanders, on the contrary, feel that they are among true and honourable friends when they find themselves in the company of other men. They have nothing to hide from one another, they have no wish either to take advantage of or to injure one another. It is true that there is emulation between them; but this cannot destroy the sentiment of friendly comradeship, since the success of the victor profits the conquered as well. Genial candour, an almost childlike ingenuousness, are therefore in all circumstances natural to them; and it is this, together with their joyous view of life and their intellectual many-sidedness, which lends such a marvellous charm to Freeland society.

But let me go on with the story of my experiences here. Yesterday we saw for the first time in Freeland a drunken man! We—my father and I—had, after dinner, been with David for a short walk on the shore of the lake, where most of the Eden Vale hotels are situated. As we were returning home we met a drunken man, who staggered up to us and stutteringly asked the way to his inn. He was evidently a new-comer. David asked us to go the remaining few steps homewards without him, and he took the man by the arm and led him towards his inn. I joined David in this kindly act, whilst my father went home. When we had also got home we found my father engaged in a very lively conversation with Mrs. Ney over this little adventure. 'Only think,' cried he to me, 'Mrs. Ney says we should think ourselves fortunate in having seen what is one of the rarest of sights in this country! She has lived in Freeland twenty-five years, and has seen only three cases of drunkenness; and she is convinced that at this moment there is not another man in Eden Vale who has ever drunk to intoxication! You Freelanders'—he turned now to David—'are certainly no teetotallers; your beer and palm-wine are excellent; your wines leave nothing to be desired; and you do not seem to me to be people who merely keep these good things ready to offer to an occasional guest. Does it really never happen that some of you drink a little more than enough to quench your thirst?'

'It is as my mother says. We like to drink a good drop, and that not seldom; and I will not deny that on festive occasions the inspiration begotten of wine here and there makes itself pretty evident; nevertheless, a Freelander incapably drunk is one of the rarest phenomena. If you are so much surprised at this, ask yourself whether well-bred and cultured men are accustomed to get drunk in Europe and America. I know that happens even among you only very rarely, although public opinion there is less strict upon this point than it is here. But in Freeland there are no persons who are compelled to seek forgetfulness of their misery in intoxication, and the examples of such persons cannot therefore serve to accustom the public to the sight of this most degrading of all vices. Many, I know, think that the disgusting picture afforded by drunken persons is the best means of exciting a feeling of repugnance towards this vice—a view which is probably derived from Plutarch's statement that the Lacedemonians used to make their helots drunk in order to serve as deterring examples to the Spartan youth. This account may be true or false, but an argument in favour of the theory that example deters by its disgusting character can be based upon it only by the most thoughtless; for it is a well-attested fact that the Spartans—the rudest of all the Greeks—were more addicted to drunkenness than any other Hellenic tribe. The "deterring" example of the helots had therefore very little effect. It is because in this country drunkenness is so extremely rare that it excites such special disgust; and as, moreover, the principal source of this vice—misery—is removed, the vice itself may be regarded as absolutely extinct among us. This result has been not a little assisted by the circumstance that merrymakings and festivities in Freeland are always largely participated in by women. Since we honour woman as the embodiment and representative of human enjoyment, as the loftiest custodian of all that ennobles and adorns our earthly existence, we are unable to conceive of genuine mirth without the participation of women. You have seen enough of our Freeland women to understand that indecorous excesses of any kind in their presence are wellnigh inconceivable.'

'We are not so much surprised that you Freelanders are proof against this vice,' replied my father. 'But your respected mother tells us that even among the immigrants drunkards are as rare as white ravens. Now, I am not aware that teetotal apostles keep watch on your frontiers. The immigrants, at any rate many of them, belong to those races and classes which at home are by no means averse to drinking, and indeed to drunkenness in its most disgusting forms; what induces these people, when they get here, to become so persistently abstemious?'

'First, the removal of those things which in Europe and America lead to drunkenness. Sometimes, during my student-travels in Europe—when I studied not merely art, but also the manners and customs of your country—I have gone into the dens of the poor and have there found conditions under which it would have appeared positively miraculous if those who lived there had not sought in the dram-bottle forgetfulness of their torture, their shame, and their degradation. I saw persons to the number of twenty or thirty—all ages and sexes thrown indiscriminately together—sleeping in *one* room, which was only large enough for those who were in it to crowd close together upon the filthy straw that covered the floor—men who from day to day had no other home than the factory or the ale-house. And these were not the breadless people, but persons in regular employ; and not exceptional cases, but types of the labourers of large districts. That such men should seek in beastly intoxication an escape from thoughts of their degradation, of the shame of their wives and daughters—that they should lose all consciousness of their human dignity, never astonished me, and still less provoked me to indignation. I felt astonishment and indignation only at the folly which allowed such wretchedness to continue, as if it were in reality a product of an unchangeable law of nature. And it seems to me quite as natural that such men, when they get here—where they regain their dignity and their rights, where on every hand gladness and beauty smile upon them—should along with their misery cast away the vices of misery. These immigrants all gladly and eagerly adapt themselves to their new surroundings. Most of them cannot expect to become in all respects our equals : the more wretched, the more degraded, they were before, so much the more boundless is their delight, their gratitude, at being here treated by everyone as equals; on no account would they forfeit the respect of their new associates, and, as these latter universally avoid drunkenness, so the former avoid it also.'

'You have explained to us why there are no drunkards in this country,' I said. 'But it appears to me much more remarkable that your principle of granting a right of maintenance to all who are incapable of working, whatever may be the occasion of that incapacity, has not overwhelmed you with invalids and old people without number. Or have we yet to learn of some provisions made to defend you from such guests? And how, without exercising a painfully inquisitorial control, can you prevent the lazy from enjoying the careless leisure which the right of maintenance guarantees to real invalids? I can perfectly well understand that your intelligent Freelanders, with their multitudinous wants, will not be content with forty per cent., when a little easy labour would earn them a hundred per cent. But among the fresh immigrants there must certainly be many who at first can scarcely know what to do with the full earnings of their labour, and who at any rate—so I should suppose—would prefer to draw their maintenance-allowance and live in idleness rather than engage in what, from their standpoint, must appear to be quite superfluous labour. Perhaps, with respect to the right to a maintenance-allowance, you make a distinction between natives and immigrants; if so, what gives a claim to maintenance?'

'No distinction is made with respect to the right to a maintenance-allowance, a sufficient qualification for which is a certificate of illness signed by one of our public physicians, or proof of having attained to the age of sixty years. The greatest liberality is exercised on principle in granting the medical certificate; indeed, everyone has the right, if one physician has refused to grant a certificate, to go to any other physician, as we prefer to support ten lazy impostors rather than reject one real invalid. Nevertheless we have among us as few foreign idlers as native ones. In this matter also, the influence of our institutions is found to be powerful enough to nip all such tendencies in the bud. Note, above all, that the strongest ambition of the immigrant is to become like us, to become incorporated with us; in order to this, if he is healthy and strong, he must participate in our affairs. They understand human nature very imperfectly who think that proletarians in whom there lingers a trace of human dignity would, when they have an opportunity of taking part in important enterprises as fully enfranchised self-controlling men, forego that opportunity and prefer to allow themselves to be

U

supported by the commonwealth. The new-comers are *anxious* to
participate in all that is to be earned and done in this country ; in
ninety-nine cases out of a hundred no other stimulus to work is
needed than this. And the few to whom this stimulus is not sufficient, soon find themselves, when the novelty of their surroundings
has worn off, compelled by *ennui* and isolation to turn to some productive activity. We have here no public-house life in the European
sense, no consorting of habitual idlers: here a man *must* work if he
would feel at ease, and therefore everyone works who is capable of
doing so. The most stubborn indolence cannot resist for more than
a few weeks at the longest the magical influence of the thought that
in order to dare to salute the first in the land as an equal no other
title of honour or influence is necessary than any honest work.
Consequently, even among the immigrants strong healthy idlers are
extremely rare exceptions, which we allow to exist as cases of
mental disease. But even these must not suffer want among us.
Without possessing any recognised right to it, they receive what
they need, and even more than is absolutely necessary according to
European ideas.

'As to the question whether the right of maintenance does not
attract into this country all the bodily and mental incapables, the
cripples and the old people, of the rest of the world, I can only
answer that Freeland irresistibly attracts everyone who hears of the
character of its institutions ; and that therefore the proportion
between the immigrants who are capable of working and those who
are not is dependent simply upon whether such information reaches
the one class more quickly and more easily than it does the other.
We reject no one, and admit the cripple to our country as freely as
the able-bodied worker ; but it lies in the nature of things that the
ablest, the most vigorous, offer themselves in larger numbers than
those who are weak in body or in mind.

'From the founding of our commonwealth we have insisted
upon the ability to read and write sufficiently to be able to participate in all our rights. Freedom and equality of rights assume
the possession of a certain degree of knowledge, from which we
cannot exempt anyone. It is true we might resort to the expedient
of exercising guardianship over the untaught ; but to do this would
be to open up to the authorities a sphere of influence which we hold
to be incompatible with real freedom, and we therefore treat

illiterate immigrants as strangers, or, if you will, as guests whom
it is everyone's duty to assist as much as possible, and who, so far
as they show themselves capable of doing anything, suffer no
material disadvantage in comparison with the natives, but are
not allowed to exercise any political right.'

' But how,' asked my father—' how do you arrive at a knowledge
of the mental condition of your ignorant fellow-countrymen ? Have
you a special board for this purpose ; and do no unpleasantnesses
spring from such an inquisition ? '

' We make no inquiry, and no board troubles itself about the
knowledge of the people. At first, in order not to be overwhelmed
by foreign ignorance, we took the precaution of excluding illiterates
from gratuitous admission into Freeland, but for the last nineteen
years we have ceased to exclude any. Everyone, without any
exception, has since been free to settle gratuitously in any part
whatever of Freeland. No one asks him what he knows ; he is free
to make full use of all our institutions, to exercise all our rights ;
only he must do so in the same way as we, and that is impossible
to the illiterate. Whithersoever he goes—to the central bank, to
any of the associations, to the polling-places—he must read and
write, and as a matter of course write with understanding—must
be familiar with printed and written words; in short, he must
possess a certain degree of culture, from the possession of which we
cannot exempt him even if we would.'

' Then,' said my father, ' your boasted equality of rights exists
only for educated persons ? '

' Of course,' explained Mrs. Ney. ' Or do you really believe that
perfectly uneducated persons possess the power of disciplining
themselves ? Certainly, real freedom and equality of rights presuppose some degree of culture. The freedom and equality of
rights of poverty and barbarism can, it is true, exist among ignorant
barbarians, but wealth and leisure are the products of higher art
and culture, and can be possessed only by truly civilised men. He
who would make men free and rich must first give them knowledge
—this lies in the nature of things ; and it is not our fault, but yours,
that so many of your compatriots must be educated into freedom.'

' There you are right,' sighed my father. ' And what has been
your experience of these illiterate immigrants ? '

' The experience that this exclusion from perfect equality of

u 2

rights, being connected with no material disadvantage, operates as
an absolutely irresistible stimulus to acquire as quickly as possible
what was left unacquired in the old home. For the use of such
immigrants we have established special schools for adults; neighbours and friends interest themselves in them, and the people
learn with touching eagerness. They by no means content themselves with acquiring merely that amount of knowledge which is
requisite to the exercise of all the Freeland rights, but they honestly
endeavour to gain all the knowledge possible; and the cases are
very few in which the study of a few years has not converted such
immigrants into thoroughly cultured men.'

'And as to the immigrants who reach us in a really invalided
condition,' interposed David, 'we fulfil towards them the duty of
maintenance as if they had grown old and weak in Freeland workshops. We have not detected any considerable increase of our
annual expenditure in consequence. It is a characteristic fact,
moreover, that those who reach us as invalids make for the most
part only a partial use of their right to claim a maintenance-allowance. These pitiable sufferers as a rule take some time to accustom
themselves to the Freeland standard of higher enjoyments, and at
first they have no use for the wealth which streams in upon them.'

'I must ask you to remove yet one other difficulty, and one that
seems to me to be the greatest of all. What of the criminals,
against whose immigration you are not protected? To me it seems
most strange that, with the millions of your Freeland population,
you can dispense with both police and penal code; and I am
utterly at a loss to understand how you dispose of those vagabonds
and criminals who are sure to be drawn hither, like wasps by honey,
by your enticing lenity, which will not punish but merely reform
the bad? It is true you have told us that the justices of the peace
appointed to decide civil disputes have authority in the first instance
in criminal cases also, and that an appeal is allowed from these to
a higher judicial court; but you added that these judges had all
of them as good as nothing to do, and that only very rare cases
occurred in which the reformatory treatment adopted in this country
had to be resorted to. Have your institutions such a strong
ameliorating power over hardened criminals?'

'Certainly,' answered Mrs. Ney. 'And if you carefully consider
what is the essential and ultimate source of all crime, you will find

this is quite intelligible. Do not forget that justice and law in the exploiting form of society make demands on the individual which are directly opposed to human nature. The hungry shivering man is expected to pass by the abundance of others without appropriating that which he needs to satisfy the imperative demands of nature —nay, he must not indulge in envy and ill-will towards those who have in plenty what he so cruelly lacks! He is to love his fellow-man, though just where the conflict of interests is the most bitter, because it is waged around the very essentials of existence—just there, where his fellow-man is his rival, his tyrant, his slave, in every case his enemy, from whose injury he derives gain and from whose gain injury accrues to him! That for thousands of years all this has been inevitable cannot be denied; but it would be foolish to overlook the fact that the same cruel sequence which made the exploitation of man by man—that is, injustice—the necessary antecedent to the progress of civilisation, also called into existence crime —that is, the rebellion of the individual against the order which is both horrible in itself and yet indispensable to the welfare of the community. The exploiting system of society requires the individual to do what harms him, because the welfare of the community demands it, and demands it not as a specially commendable and pre-eminently meritorious act, which can be expected of only a few noble natures in whom public spirit has suppressed every trace of egoism, but as something which everyone is to do as a matter of course, the doing of which is not called a virtue, though the not doing of it is called a crime. The hero who sacrifices his life to his fatherland, to mankind, subordinates his own to a higher interest, and never will the human race be able to dispense with such sacrifices, but will always demand of its noblest that love of wife shall conquer love of self; nay, it may be stated as a logical consequence of progressive civilisation that this demand shall grow more and more imperative and meet with an ever readier response. But the name of this response is 'heroism,' its lack involves no crime; it cannot be enforced, but it is a voluntary tribute of love paid by noble natures. But in the economic domain a similar, nay, more difficult, heroism is required especially from the lowest and the most wretched, and must be required of such as long as society is based upon a foundation of exploitage, and 'criminal' must be the name of all those who show themselves to be less great than a Leonidas, or a Curtius, or a Winkelried on the battle-field, or than those generally nameless heroes of human love who have fearlessly sacrificed themselves in the conflict with the inimical powers of nature at the bidding of the holy voice within them—the voice of human love.

'But we in Freeland ask from no one such heroism as our right. In economic matters we require of the individual nothing that is antagonistic to his own interests; it follows as a matter of course that he never rebels against our laws. That which under the old order could be asserted only by self-complacent thoughtlessness, is a truth among us—namely, that economic morality is nothing but rational egoism. You will therefore find it intelligible that *reasonable* men cannot break our laws.

'But you ask, further, how does it happen that those unfortunates who in other countries are driven into crime, not by want, but by their evil disposition—and it cannot be denied that there are such —do not give us any trouble? Here also the question suggests its own answer. This hatred towards society and its members is not natural, is not innate in even the worst of men, but is the product of the injustice in the midst of which these habitual criminals live. The love of wife and of one's fellows is ineradicably implanted in every social animal—and man is such an animal; but its expression can be suppressed by artificially excited hatred and envy. It is true that long-continued exercise of evil instincts will gradually make them so powerfully predominant as to make it appear that the social nature of man has been transformed into that of the beast of prey, no longer linked to society by any residuum of love or attachment. But it only *seems* so. The most hardened criminal cannot long resist the influence of genuine human affection; hatred and defiance hold out only so long as the unfortunate sees himself deprived of the possibility of obtaining recognition in the community of the happy, as one possessed of equal rights with the others. If this hope is held out to him all defiance ceases.

'I question if there has ever been a large percentage of men of criminal antecedents among the immigrants into Freeland. As my son has already said, the proportion in which different categories of men have come hither depends not upon the greater or less degree of misery, but upon the intelligence of the men. Since the criminal classes in the five parts of the world know relatively less of Freeland than do the honest and intelligent workers,

I am convinced that relatively fewer of them have come hither. At any rate, we have seen very few signs of their presence here. We have a few dozen incorrigibly vicious persons in the country, but these are without exception incurable idiots. How these reached us I do not know ; but of course, as soon as their mental unsoundness was ascertained, they were placed in asylums.'

This point being cleared up, my father asked for a final explanation. He said he could perfectly understand that the Freeland institutions, being nothing else but a logical carrying out of the principle of economic justice, were thoroughly capable of meeting every fair and reasonable demand. He nevertheless expressed his astonishment at the perfect satisfaction which the people universally exhibited with themselves and their condition. Did not *unreasonable* party agitations create difficulties in Freeland ? Particularly he wished to know if Communism and Nihilism, which were ever raising their heads threateningly in Europe, gave no trouble here. 'In the eyes of a genuine Communist,' he cried, ' you are here nothing but arrant aristocrats ! There is not a trace of absolute equality among you ! What value can your boasted equality of *rights* have in the eyes of people who act upon the principle that every mouthful more of bread enjoyed by one than is enjoyed by another is theft ; and who therefore, to prevent one man from possessing more than another, abolish all property whatever ? And yet there are no police, no soldiers, to keep these Bedlamites in order ! Give us the recipe according to which the nihilistic and communistic fanaticism can be rendered so harmless.'

'Nothing easier,' answered Mrs. Ney. 'Supply everyone to satiety, and no one will covet what others have. Absolute equality is an hallucination of the hunger-fever, nothing more. Men are *not* equal, either in their faculties or in their requirements. Your appetite is stronger than mine ; perhaps you are fond of gay clothing, I would not give a farthing for it; perhaps I am dainty, while you prefer a plain diet; and so on without end. What sense would there be in attempting to assimilate our several needs ? I do not care to inquire whether it is possible, whether the violence necessary to the attempt would not destroy both freedom and progress; the idea itself is so foolish that it would be absolutely inconceivable how sane men could entertain it, had it not been a fact that one of us is able to satisfy neither his strong nor his weak appetite, his preference neither for fine nor for quiet clothing, neither for dainties nor for plain food, but must endure brutal torturing misery. When to that is added the mistake that my superfluity is the cause of your deficiency, it becomes intelligible why you and those who sympathise with you in your sufferings should call for division of property—absolutely equal division. In a word, Communism has no other source than the perception of the boundless misery of a large majority of men, together with the erroneous opinion that this misery can be alleviated only by the aid of the existing wealth of individuals. This view is inconceivably foolish, for it is necessary only to open one's eyes to see what a pitiful use is made of the power which man already possesses to create wealth. But this foolish notion was not hatched by the Communists; your orthodox economists gave currency to the doctrine that increased productiveness of labour cannot increase the already existing value—it was they, and not the Communists, who blinded mankind to the true connexion between economic phenomena. Communists are in reality merely credulous adherents of the so-called "fundamental truths" of orthodox economy; and the only distinction between them and the ruling party among you is that the Communists are hungry while the ruling classes are full-fed. When it is perceived that nothing but perfect equality of rights is needed *in order to create more than enough for all*, Communism disappears of itself like an evil tormenting dream. You may require—even if you do not carry it out—that all men shall be put upon the same bread rations, so long as you believe that the commonwealth upon which we are all compelled to depend will furnish nothing more than mere bread, for we all wish to eat our fill. To require that the same sorts and quantity of roast meats, pastry, and confections shall be forced upon everyone, when it is found that there is enough of these good things for all, would be simply puerile. Hence there is and can be no Communist among us.

'For the same reason Nihilism is impossible among us, for that also is nothing more than an hallucination due to the despair of hunger, and can flourish only on the soil of the orthodox view of the world. Whilst Communism is the practical application which hunger makes of the thesis that human labour does not suffice to create a superfluity for all, Nihilism is the inference drawn by despair from the doctrine that culture and civilisation are incompatible with equality of rights. It is orthodoxy which has given currency to this doctrine; certainly, as the spokesman of the well-to-do, it holds no other inference to be conceivable than that the eternally disinherited masses must submit to their fate in the interests of civilisation. But the party of the hungry turn in foaming rage against this civilisation, the very defenders of which assert that it can never help the enormous majority of men, and therefore can do nothing more for them than make them increasingly conscious of their misery. We have demonstrated that civilisation is not merely compatible with, but is necessarily implied in, the economic equality of rights. Hence Nihilism also must be unknown among us.'

'Then you think,' I said, 'that equality of actual income has nothing to do with equality *of rights*? For my part, I must admit that that useless heaping up of superfluous riches, which we have occasion to observe in our European society, has grown to be a very objectionable thing, even though I am convinced that the misery is not, in the slightest degree, caused by this accumulation of wealth in the hands of a few, and would not be materially alleviated by a general distribution of it. A social system that does not prevent this excessive accumulation in a few hands must remain imperfect, whatever provision it may make in other directions for the welfare of all.'

'And I cannot altogether get rid of the same feeling,' said my father. 'But my opinion is that in this revolt against inequality in itself we need see nothing more than the moral repulsion which every impartial thoughtful man feels against what have hitherto been the *causes* of the inequality. Among us at home, we see that large fortunes are very seldom acquired by means of pre-eminent individual talent, but are, as a rule, due to the exploitation of other men; and, when acquired, they are sure to be employed in further exploitation. This it is that arouses our indignation. If a fortune, however great, were acquired merely by pre-eminent talent, and employed to no other end than the heightening of the owner's personal enjoyment—as is the case in Freeland—the repugnance we now feel would soon pass away. What does our amiable hostess think upon this point?'

'The repugnance to excessively large fortunes,' replied Mrs. Ney, 'is not, in my opinion, based upon any injustice in their origin or use, but has a deeper cause—namely, the fact that, apart from very rare exceptions, the difference of capacity in men is not so great as to justify such enormous differences of fortune. Most of the wealth of a highly civilised society consists of what was bequeathed by the past; and the portion actually produced by existing individuals is so relatively small that a certain degree of equality—not merely of rights, but also of enjoyment and use—possesses a basis in fact and is a requirement of justice. Every advance in civilisation is synonymous with a progressive diminution of the differences. Carry your thoughts back to primitive conditions, when the individual, in his struggle for existence, was almost entirely shut up to the use of his congenital appliances, and you will find the differences were very great: only the strong, the agile, the cunning could hold their own; the less gifted were compelled to give way. As the growth of civilisation added to men's appliances, so that even the less gifted was able to procure what was necessary to his subsistence, the difference in the achievements of different individuals at first remained very great. The skilful hunter gets a far richer booty than the less skilful one; the strong and nimble agriculturist achieves with the spade a manifold greater result than the weak and the slow. The invention of the plough very materially reduces this difference, and—so far as the difference depends upon physical capacity—the invention of the power-machine reduces it almost to *nil*. Machinery more and more takes the place of the energy of human muscles; and, at the same time, the results of the talent and experience of previous generations accumulate and, in a growing ratio, exceed the invention of the actual living generation. It is true that in intellectual matters the individual differences do not diminish so completely as in matters dependent upon the corporal powers; but even the intellectual differences do not justify the colossal inequality suggested to the mind by the words "a large fortune." The man who drives a steam-plough may be either a giant or a dwarf, but he gets through the same amount of work. Quick-wittedness and discretion in conducting the process of production will considerably increase the result; but in the present day an achievement which shall exceed the average a hundredfold or a thousandfold in value is possible only to genius, and it is only to genius that our sense of justice would accord it.

'I believe that in this respect also our Freeland institutions have hit the mark. Among us inequality exists only so far as the difference of capacity justifies it; and we have seen that, in proportion as wealth increases, the distribution of it becomes automatically more and more equal. As in this country everything is controlled by a competition which is free in fact, and not in name merely, it follows as a necessary result that every kind of capacity is better paid the rarer it is. When we first founded our commonwealth knowledge and experience in business were rare—that is, the demand was greater than the supply; they were therefore able to command a higher price than ordinary labour. This is no longer the case; thanks to the general improvement in culture and the intensive participation of all in all kinds of business, head-work, as such, has lost its claim to exceptional wages. Only when superior intellectual gifts are connected with knowledge and experience in business can the man who performs head-work expect to obtain higher pay than the manual labourer. Yet even here there is to be seen a *relative* diminution of the higher pay. In the early years of Freeland a specially talented leader of production could demand six times as much as the average earnings of a labourer; at present three times as much as the average is a rare maximum, which in the domain of material production is exceeded only in isolated cases of pre-eminent inventors. On the other hand, the earnings of gifted authors and artists in this country have no definite limits; as their works are above competition, so the rewards they obtain bear no proportion to those obtainable in ordinary business.

'But in this way, I think, the most delicate sense of equality can be satisfied. Economic equality of rights never produces absolute and universal equality; but it is really accompanied by a general levelling of the enjoyments of all, and leaves unaffected only such incongruities as the most fastidious sense of justice will recognise as having their basis in the nature of things.'

Here ended this conversation, which will ever be a memorable one to me, because it confirmed my decision to become a Freelander.

CHAPTER XXI

Eden Vale: Aug. 20, ——

IN your last you say you think it very strange that in my letters I make no further mention of the young ladies who for the past six weeks have been under the same roof with me. When a young Italian—so argues your inexorable logic—has nothing to say about pretty girls with whom he associates, and among whom there is one whose first glance—according to his own confession—threw him into confusion, he has either been rejected by the lady in question or contemplates giving her an opportunity of rejecting him. Your logic is right, Louis : I am in love—indeed I was from the first sight I had of Bertha, David's splendid sister; and I have even had a narrow escape of being rejected. Not that my beloved has not returned my affection ; as soon as I could summon courage to propose to her, Bertha confessed, with that undisguised candour which is charming in her—more correctly, in all the women of Freeland—that on the very first evening of our acquaintance she felt she should either marry me or marry no one. And yet, on my first wooing her, I had to listen to a 'No' of the most determined character. The fact was that Bertha could not make up her mind to become an Italian duchess ; and my father, who—hear it and be astounded!—pleaded for me, had as a matter of course insisted that she should go to Italy with me, reside on our ducal estates there, weave the ducal diadems into her locks—they are of a ravishing blonde—and make it her life's duty to continue the noble race of the Falieri. My desire to settle in Freeland as a Freelander was regarded by my father as a foolish and extravagant whim. You know his views—a strange medley of honest Liberalism and aristocratic pride : rather, these were his views, but here in Freeland the democratic side of his character has considerably broadened and strengthened. Indeed, he became quite enthusiastic in his admiration of the Freeland institutions. If there were but another branch of the Falieri to which could be committed the transmission of the ducal traditions, *per Bacco !* my father would have at once assented to my wish, and, as he loves me tenderly, he would not hesitate long before he followed my example. But his enthusiasm,

noble and sincere as it is, would not permit me to lay the axe at
the root of the genealogical tree of a house whose ancestors had
fought among the first Crusaders, and had later, as petty Italian
princes, filled the world with deeds (of infamy). Against my loving
Bertha he made no objection—really and truly, my dear friend,
not the least. On the contrary, he was not a little proud of me
when, in answer to his question whether I was sure of the maiden's
love in return, I replied with a confident ' Yes.' ' Lucky dog you
are,' cried he, ' to win that splendid creature so quickly ! Who can
match us Falieris ! ' Bertha had captivated my father as she had
me; and as he entertained the greatest respect for the Freeland
women in general, he had no objection whatever to a *bourgeoise*
daughter-in-law. But only on condition that I gave up the ' insane '
idea of remaining here. ' The girl has more sense in her little
finger than you have in your whole body,' said he ; ' she would little
relish seeing her lover cast a shattered ducal crown at her feet. It
is very fine to be a Freeland woman—but, believe me, it is much
finer to be a duchess. Besides, these two very agreeable qualities
can easily be united. Spend the winter and spring in our palaces
at Rome and Venice ; summer and autumn you could enjoy freedom
on your lake and among your mountains—in my company, if you
had no objection. Let it stand so : I will get Bertha for you, but
not another word about a permanent settlement here.'

This did not please me. I assure you I had not formed the intention of becoming a Freelander for the sake of my beloved ; but
I could not think of her either in a ducal diadem or in the state
rooms of our castles. Nevertheless, I was fain to submit for a while
to the will of my father ; and I did not really know whether Bertha
and her relatives would show themselves so insensible to the attractions of a title and of princely wealth as would be necessary in
order that I might have them as confederates against my father.
In short, my father pleaded my case with Mr. Ney, and in the
presence of Bertha and myself asked her parents for the hand of
their daughter for his son, the Prince Carlo Falieri, adding that
immediately after the wedding he would hand over to me his estates
in the Romagna, Tuscany, and Venice, as well as the palaces at
Rome, Florence, Milan, Verona, and Venice ; and would retain for
himself merely our Sicilian possessions—as a reserve property, he
jestingly said. The elder Neys received these grandiose proposals

with a chill reserve that gave me little hope. After a silence of
some minutes, and after having thrown at me a searching and re-
proachful glance, Mr. Ney said, 'We Freelanders are not the
despots, but simply the counsellors, of our daughters; but in
this case our child does not need counsel : if Bertha is willing
to go with you to Italy as the Princess Falieri, we will not prevent her.'

With a proud and indignant mien Bertha turned—not to me,
but—to my father : 'Never, never !' she cried with quivering lips.
'I love your son more than my life; I should die if your son discarded me in obedience to you; but leave Freeland—leave it as
princess!—never, never ! Better die a thousand times !'

'But, unhappy child,' replied my father, quite horrified at the
unexpected effect of his proposal, 'you utter the word " princess "
as if it were to you the quintessence of all that is dreadful. Yes,
you should be princess, one of the richest, proudest of the princesses
of Europe—that is, you should have no wish which thousands should
not vie with each other in fulfilling; you should have opportunities
of making thousands happy; you should be envied by millions——'
'And cursed and hated,' interposed Bertha with quivering lips.
'What! You have lived among us six weeks, and you have not
learned what a free daughter of Freeland must feel at the mere
suggestion of leaving these happy fields, this home of justice and
human affection, in order, afar off in your miserable country, not to
wipe away, but to extort the tears of the downtrodden—not to
alleviate the horrors of your slavery, but to become one of the slave-
holders ! I love Carlo so much above all measure that I should be
ready by his side to exchange the land of happiness for that of
misery if any imperative duty called him thither ; but only on condition that his hands and mine remained free from foreign property,
that we ourselves earned by honest labour what we needed for our
daily life. But to become *princess*; to have thousands of serfs
using up their flesh and blood in order that I might revel in superfluity; to have thousands of curses of men tortured to death
clinging to the food I eat and the raiment I wear !' As she uttered
these words she shuddered and hid her face in her hands; then,
mastering herself with an effort, she continued : 'But reflect—if
you had a daughter, and some one asked you to let her go to be
queen among the cannibal Njam-Njam, and the father of her bride-

groom promised that a great number of fat slaves should be slaughtered for her—what would she say, the poor child who had drunk in with her mother's milk an invincible disgust at the eating of human flesh ? Now, see : we in Freeland feel disgust at human flesh, even though the sacrifice be slowly slaughtered inch by inch, limb by limb, without the shedding of blood ; to us the gradual destruction of a fellow-man is not less abhorrent than the literal devouring of a man is to you ; and it is as impossible for us to exist upon the exploitation of our enslaved fellows as it is for you to share in the feasts of cannibals. I cannot become a princess—I *cannot* ! Do not separate me from Carlo—if you do we shall both die, and—I have not learnt it to-day for the first time—you love not only him, but me also.'

This appeal, enforced by the most touching glances and a tender grasping of his hands, was more than my father could resist. ' You have verily made me disgusted with myself. So you think we are cannibals, and the only difference between us and your amiable Njam-Njam is that we do not slay our sacrifices with one vigorous blow and then devour them forthwith, but we delight in doing it bit by bit, inch by inch ? You are not far wrong ; at any rate, I will not force upon you the privileges of a position as to which you entertain such views. And my son appears in this point to share your tastes rather than those which have hitherto been mine. Take each other, and be happy in your own fashion. For myself, I will consider how I may to some extent free myself from the odour of cannibalism in my new daughter's eyes.'

Bertha flew first to me, then to my father, then in succession to her parents and brothers and sisters, and then again fell upon my father's neck. Her embrace of her father-in-law was so affectionate that I was almost inclined to be jealous. My father became at once so eager for our wedding that he asked the Neys forthwith to make all the necessary arrangements for this event. He expected to be obliged to return to Europe, provisionally, in about a month, and he should be pleased if we could be married before he went. Mrs. Ney, however, asked what further prelimi- naries were necessary ? We had mutually confessed our love, the blessing of the parents on both sides was not lacking ; we might, if agreeable to ourselves, start off somewhere that very day, by one of the evening trains, on our wedding-tour—perhaps to the Victoria

Nyanza, on whose shores she knew of a small delightfully situated country house.

I myself was somewhat surprised at these words, though they were evidently anticipated by my bride. But my father was utterly at a loss to know what to make of them. Of course his delicacy of feeling would not have allowed him to declare plainly that he thought it scandalous in the highest degree for a couple of lovers to start off on a journey together only a few hours after their betrothal, and that he could not conceive how a respectable lady could suggest what would bring such disgrace upon her house. There was a painful pause, until Mr. Ney explained to us that in Freeland the reciprocal declaration by two lovers that they wished to become husband and wife was all that was required to the conclusion of a marriage-contract. The young people had nothing further to do than to make such an express declaration, and they would be married.

'That is, indeed, extremely simple and charming,' said my father, shaking his head. 'But if the State or the commonwealth here has nothing to do with the marriage-contract, how does it know that such a contract has been entered into, and how can it give its protection to it?'

'Of course the marriage-contract is communicated to the Statistical Department as quickly as possible, but this enrolment has nothing to do with the validity of the contract; and as to the protection of the marriage-bond, we know of no other here than that which is to be found in the reciprocal affection of the married pair,' said Mrs. Ney.

My father thereupon began to ventilate the question whether it was not advisable on many grounds to attach to the marriage-contract some more permanent guarantee; but this suggestion was met, particularly on the part of Bertha, with such an evident and —to him—quite inexplicable resentment that he dropped the subject. Later, when we men were by ourselves, he inquired what the ladies found so offensive in the idea of giving to marriage some kind of protection against the changing fancies of the wedded pair? It was easy to see that the conversation had left upon him the impression that the women of Freeland held views upon this subject which were altogether too 'free.' But Mr. Ney gradually succeeded in convincing him—I had understood the matter from the beginning – that the reverse was the case; that the horror at the thought of being *compelled* to belong to a man who was not loved was not merely quite compatible with inviolable conjugal fidelity, but was a logical outcome of the highest and purest conception of marriage. At first he held out. He would not deny the ethical justness of the Freeland principle that marriage without love was objectionable ; only he questioned whether this principle could be strictly applied to practical life without opening the door to licentiousness. The fact that in Freeland divorces were quite unknown did not at once suffice to convince him. Mrs. Ney, who surprised us in the midst of this discussion, gave the finishing touch.

' If you take a comprehensive view of the whole complex of our economic and social institutions,' said she to my father, ' you will see why in Freeland man and wife must regard each other with different eyes than is the case in Europe or America. All your scruples will vanish, for the logical connection of economic justice with conjugal fidelity and honour lies as plain and open as does its connection with honour in questions of *meum* and *tuum*. That well-to-do intelligent men do not steal and rob, that in a highly cultivated society which guarantees to everyone the undiminished product of his own labour no one touches the fruits of another man's industry—this is not more self-evident than it is that the same principle of economic justice must smother in the germ all longing for the wife or the husband of another. For man is by nature a monogamous and monandrous being ; polygamy and poly-andry are inconsistent with the fundamental characteristics of his nature ; they are diseases of civilisation which would vanish spontaneously with a return to the healthy conditions of existence. Sexual honour and fidelity, like honesty in matters of property, are rare "virtues" only where they impose upon the individual the exercise of a self-denial which is not reconcilable with the instinct of self-preservation ; where, as among us, a harmony of interests is established even in this domain, where everyone gets the whole of what is his own, and no one is expected to forego in the common interest of the community what belongs to himself—here even this virtue is transformed into a rational self-interest which every accountable person exhibits spontaneously and without any compulsion from without, as something that he owes to himself. We are all

x

faithful because faithfulness does not impose upon any one of us the renunciation of his individuality.'

. 'I admire this sentiment,' answered my father, 'and do not wish to dispute the fact upon which it is based. It may be that in Freeland conjugal fidelity is without exception the rule, and that unfaithfulness is regarded as a kind of mental aberration; but if it is so, then the men and women of Freeland are themselves exceptions, and to deduce a formal law of nature from their behaviour seems to me to be premature. Because in this country—it matters not from what causes—sexual morality has become exceptionally high, because to your delicate ethical sense polygamy and polyandry in any form are repugnant, it does not follow that the inconstancy which has marked men and women in all stages of civilisation is to be at once regarded as "contrary to human nature." It were well, madam, if you were right, for that would mean that the last source of vice and crime was stopped; but, alas! the experience of all ages shows that unfaithfulness and love root themselves by turns deeply in human nature. I can understand that you, as a woman, should be influenced more by moral than by sober scientific views; but I am afraid that results which are based less upon nature than upon —certainly very admirable—moral experiments, will prove to be not too permanent.'

A delicate flush passed over the face of my mother as she heard this. I noticed that she did not feel quite comfortable in having to reply to this in the presence of men; but as my father was not to be convinced in any other way, she answered, at first with hesitancy, but she was afterwards carried away by her interest in the subject. She said:

'I am a woman of Freeland, and my sentiments are those of Freeland. I would not ascribe to nature what is merely the outcome of my own moral views. When I said that man is a monogamous being, and that polygamy and polyandry were repugnant to the conditions of his existence, were contrary to his real nature, I referred—far from speaking from an ethical standpoint—simply to the animal nature of man. We belong, to speak plainly, to a species of animals which nature intends to be monogamous and monandrous. A species, whose progeny takes nearly twenty years to arrive at maturity, cannot thrive without the united care of father and mother. It is the long-continued helplessness of our children that makes the permanent union of a single pair natural to man. The moral sentiments—which, certainly, in a healthy condition of human society also gravitate in the same direction— are nothing more than the outcome of these natural conditions of existence. If a man reached maturity in a single year our moral sentiments would permit, would perhaps imperatively demand, a change of partner after every child; for, without exception, we hold that alone to be beautiful and good which is requisite to the thriving of the species. Now the *genus homo* categorically demands, in order that it may thrive, that father and mother should foster the young for twenty years; in the meantime fresh offspring arrive; the natural command to rear children—you see I make use of the crassest expressions of natural history—therefore keeps the male and the female together until there ceases to be any reason for a separation. It would be simply contrary to nature if the natural sentiments and instincts of man were *not* in harmony with this command of nature. Conjugal attachment and fidelity *must* be and are natural instincts of man; all phenomena that appear to indicate the opposite are simply consequences of transitory ex- crescences of civilisation. It was social inequality which gave rise to sexual vices as to all the other vices. The same relation of mastership which gives the employer control over the labour of other men also gives him power over other women than his wife; and the same servitude which deprived the slave of his right to the produce of his own labour robs the woman of her right to herself. Love becomes an article of merchandise, *sold* in order to appease hunger and to cover nakedness, *bought* in order to gratify inconstant desires. You think I hold that to be unnatural because it is immoral? On the contrary, I hold it to be immoral because it is contrary to nature. That, your highness, is what I would impress upon you. A better acquaintance with this land of freedom will show you that fidelity and honour between husband and wife are here no rare exceptions, but the universal rule; but you must know at once that we do not therefore exercise any super- human virtue, but simply act in conformity with the real nature of man.'

I could plainly see, by the warm admiration expressed in the way in which he gallantly lifted Mrs. Ney's hand to his lips, that my father was already convinced; but, in order to mask his retreat,

he threw out the question whether there were not, in this country,
any other disturber of conjugal peace ?

'You mean harshness, love of domination, wrangling ? Even
these cannot occur in a really free society based upon perfect
equality of rights. It is the lack of freedom and of legal equality
which elsewhere sows discord between the sexes and makes them
like enemies by nature. The enslaved woman, robbed of her share
of the goods of the earth, is impelled, by inexorable necessity, to
trade upon the sexual desires and the weaknesses of man ; she
finds herself in a constant state of war with him, for she has no
alternative but to suffer wrong or to do wrong. What the other
sex has wrongly obtained from her sex the individual woman must
win back for herself from the individual man by stratagem and
cunning, and the individual man is forced into a continuous attitude
of defence by this injustice of his sex, and by the consequently
necessary attempts at re-vindication by the woman. In this respect,
also, Schopenhauer is not altogether wrong : there is no other
sympathy between man and woman than that of the epidermis ;
but he forgets here also to add that this is not the natural relation
of the sexes, but one resulting from the unnatural subjection of the
woman—that not man and woman as such, but slave and master,
are reciprocally opposed as strangers and foes. Remove the injustice which this disturbance of a relation so consonant with
nature has called forth, and it will at once be seen that the sympathy
between husband and wife is the strongest, the most varied, and
the most comprehensive of all. The woman possesses those very
excellences of heart and intellect which most charm the man, and
the excellences of the man are just those which the woman most
highly prizes. Nature, which has physically adapted the sexes to
each other, has also psychically formed them as complementary
halves. Nature, to accomplish whose purposes it is necessary
that man and wife should remain faithful for life, could not have
acted so inconsistently as to endow them with psychical attributes
which would prevent or render difficult such lifelong fidelity. The
instinct that preserves the race and is the occasion of so much
passionate physical enjoyment, this instinct must also inspire
the sexes with the strongest conceivable mutual sympathy with
each other's mental and ethical character. In Freeland every
disturbing discord is removed from the natural relation between

the sexes; what wonder that that relation shows itself in its perfect harmony and beauty! Every Freeland man is an enthusiastic worshipper of the women; every Freeland woman is a not less enthusiastic worshipper of the men. In the eyes of our men there is nothing purer, better, more worthy of reverence than the woman; and in the eyes of us, the women of Freeland, there is nothing greater, nobler, more magnanimous than the man. A man who ill-uses or depreciates his wife, who does not make it his pride to screen her from every evil, would be excluded from the society of all other men; and a wife who attempted to rule over her husband, who did not make it her highest aim to beautify his life, would be avoided by all other women.'

My father made no further objection. He was content that I should take my Bertha according to Freeland customs and without any formal ceremony. Only *one* condition he insisted upon: there should be a fortnight's interval between betrothal and wedding. I consented reluctantly to this delay; had I followed my own desires, we should have flown off together to the Victoria Nyanza that same day, and my betrothed also—for prudery is unknown here—did not hide the fact that she shared in my impatience. But during the last few hours my father had made such superhuman concessions that we owed him this—truly no small—sacrifice. On the 3rd of September, therefore, Bertha will become my wife; but from to-day you must look upon me as a citizen of Freeland.

Ungama: Aug. 24.

' 'Twixt cup and lip . . .'

When I finished my letter four days ago, and kept it back a little while in order to put in an enclosure from Bertha, who declared herself under an obligation to send to my friend a few words of apology for having stolen me, I had not the slightest presentiment that momentous events would come between me and the fulfilment of my ardent desires. The war in which we are engaged produces remarkably little excitement in my new fatherland; and if I were not in Ungama, I should not suspect that we were at war with an enemy who has repeatedly given serious trouble to several of the strongest military States of Europe. But I have not been a Freelander long enough not to be keenly sensible of the bitter disgrace and the heavy loss which my native land has lately suffered; and on all grounds—in my character of Freelander and also of quondam Italian—I held it to be my duty to take part personally in the war. Until this war is ended, there can of course be no thought of a wedding. In the meantime, the chance of war has brought me away from Eden Vale to the coast of the Indian Ocean. But I will tell my story in order.

Know then, first of all, that—for this is no longer a diplomatic secret—the efforts of my father and of his English and French colleagues to get permission for 300,000 or 350,000 Anglo-Franco-Italian troops to pass through Freeland, utterly failed. The Eden Vale government said that Freeland was at peace with Abyssinia, and had no right to mix itself up with the quarrels of the Western Powers. But the aspect of affairs would be entirely changed if those Powers resolved to adopt the Freeland constitution in their African territories; in which case those territories would be regarded as a part of the Freeland district, and as such would naturally be protected by Freeland. But then the military convention asked for would be superfluous, for Freeland would treat every attack upon its allies as a *casus belli*, and would with its own forces compel Abyssinia to keep the peace. The negotiations lasted for weeks without any result. Evidently the cabinets of London, Paris, and Rome did not attach any importance to the promise made by Freeland, though the ambassadors, and particularly my father, honestly did what they could to give the Western cabinets confidence in the military strength of Freeland. The Powers were not indisposed to recognise the Freeland law in their colonies on the Red and Indian Seas as a condition of alliance; but persisted, nevertheless, in asking for a military convention, to which Freeland would not consent. So the matter stood until a few days ago.

On the morning after my betrothal, as we were sitting at breakfast, a despatch in cypher came to my father from Ungama, the large port belonging to Freeland on the Indian Ocean. My father, when he had deciphered the despatch, sprang up pale and excited, and asked Mr. Ney forthwith to summon a session of the executive of the Freeland central government, as he had a communication of urgent importance to make. Remarking the sympathetic alarm of our friends, my father said, ' The matter cannot remain a secret—you shall learn the bad news from my lips. The despatch is from Commodore Cialdini, captain of one of our ironclads stationed at Massowah. It runs : " Ungama : Aug. 21, 8 A.M. Have just reached here with ironclad ' Erebus ' and two despatch-boats—one ours and one French—escaped from Massowah much damaged. The night before last, John of Abyssinia, contrary to existing treaty of peace, treacherously fell upon Massowah and took it with scarcely a blow struck. Our vessels lying in harbour, as well as the English and French, seventeen in number, were also surprised and taken, none escaping except ourselves and the two despatch-boats. The smaller coast fortresses which we passed are also all in the hands of the Abyssinians. As we are cut off from Aden by a number of the enemy's steamships that are following us, and the ' Erebus ' is not in a condition to fight, we have run into Ungama for refuge and to repair our damage. If the Abyssinians find us here, I shall blow up our ships." '

This was bad tidings, not only for the allies, but also for Freeland, for it meant war with Abyssinia, which the Freelanders had hoped to avoid. Though it had been resolved from the first to secure for the European Powers, as presumptive allies, peace with Abyssinia, yet, in reliance upon the great respect which Freeland enjoyed among the neighbouring peoples, the Freelanders had indulged in the hope of so imposing upon the defiant semi-barbarians by a determined attitude as to keep them quiet without a resort to arms. The treacherous attack, at the very time when the plenipotentiaries of the attacked Powers were in Eden Vale, destroyed this hope.

In the National Palace we found the Freeland ministers already assembled, and we were soon followed by the English and French plenipotentiaries. By his agitated demeanour, the French ambassador showed that he had already heard the unhappy tidings. It was some hours later when the English ambassador received direct tidings that their ironclad corvette ' Nelson ' had reached Ungama half-wrecked, having had a desperate encounter on her way with two of the vessels that had fallen into the hands of the Abyssinians, and one of which she bored and sank. In the meantime, more accurate and detailed accounts had reached the Freeland Foreign Office from different places on the coast, revealing the full extent of the misfortune. The Abyssinian attack had been made with vastly superior forces, assisted by treachery, and had been completely successful. As the treaty of peace with Abyssinia had several weeks to run, the garrisons of the—for the most part unhealthy—places on the coast were neither very strong nor very vigilant. The Abyssinians had simultaneously—at about two o'clock in the morning—attacked and taken Massowah, Arkiko, and Obok, the chief fortresses of the Italians, the English, and the French, as well as all the eight coast forts belonging to the same Powers. The garrisons, surprised asleep, were in part cut down, in part taken prisoners, and the vessels lying in the harbours were —with the exception of those already mentioned—captured at the same time. That as early as the next morning the Abyssinians were able to put to sea in some of these captured vessels is to be explained by the Negus's zealous enlistment of sailors already mentioned, which also proves that the attack had been long premeditated and was carefully planned. The treachery was so excellently well managed, that it was only a few minutes after the vessels were taken that the four which had escaped had to encounter a most destructive attack from the guns of the other ships. The vessels that fell into the hands of the Abyssinians in the three ports were : seven English, five French, and four Italian ironclads, including several of the first class ; and eleven English, eight French, and four Italian gunboats and despatch-boats. About 24,000 men were either killed or taken prisoners in the fortresses and vessels.

The plenipotentiaries of the three Powers had, upon receipt of this Job's tidings, telegraphed to their governments for instructions. They told the Freeland executive that in all probability the conclusion of the military convention would now be most strongly insisted upon. Now that the fortresses had fallen, it would be absolutely impossible to collect upon the inhospitable shores of the Red Sea an army sufficiently large to meet the Negus. In fact, this was almost categorically the collective demand of the three Powers which reached Eden Vale the same day. As categorical, however, was the rejection of the proposal, accompanied by the declaration that the Eden Vale government intended to carry on alone the war with Abyssinia which now seemed inevitable. Moreover, the allies were told that their armies could not be brought to the seat of war soon enough. Even if the Suez Canal had been practicable for the transport of troops, their proposed 350,000 could not be brought together under two months at the least ; and it was certain that, long ere that, the Negus John would have attempted to get possession of all the strategical positions of Freeland. And again, wherever the ships which the Abyssinians had taken could be utilised to block the Suez Canal, the allied forces, if they were called out, would at any rate arrive too late to prevent it. The overland route through Egypt could be so easily blocked by the Abyssinians that to select it as the base of operations would be simply absurd. The only route that remained was that round the Cape of Good Hope ; and how long it would take to transport 350,000 auxiliary troops that way to Freeland, the cabinets of Paris, Rome, and London could calculate for themselves. But the Powers need feel no uneasiness ; they should receive satisfaction sooner and more completely than they seemed to expect it. Before the English, French, and Italians could have got ready so great an expedition, we should have reckoned with the Negus. In the meantime, the allies might get their new garrisons ready to sail for the coast towns of the Red and Indian Seas ; they could despatch them by the usual route through the Suez Canal, for before their transport-ships reached the canal—which could not be until the end of the next month—Freeland would either have recaptured or destroyed the stolen fleet of Abyssinia.

The last statement in particular was received by the allied Powers and their ambassadors with intense astonishment ; and I must confess that I could not myself see how we, without a single ship of war, were to annihilate a fleet of sixteen first-class and twenty-three small vessels of war. It was not without some amount of bitter sarcasm that the ambassadors replied that, instead of making such grandiose proposals, it would be more practical to take measures that the wretchedly battered vessels now lying in the harbour at Ungama might be repaired and sent to sea again as quickly at possible. Even the possibility of saving them from the immensely superior force of the enemy rested upon the very uncertain hope that the foe would not at once look for them in the utterly defenceless port of Ungama.

'For the moment '—thus did one of the executive console the distressed diplomats—' that is, for the next few hours, you are certainly right. If before dark this evening a superior Abyssinian force appears before Ungama and begins at once by attacking your ships, those ships are in all human probability lost. But that holds good only for to-day. If the Abyssinian fleet shows itself, we have prepared for it a reception which will certainly not entice it to come again.'

' What have you done ? ' asked the ambassadors in astonishment. ' What can you do to protect the wretched remnant of our proud allied fleet ? ' While he said this, the eyes of the men whose patriotism had been so deeply wounded were anxiously fixed upon the members of the executive, and, in spite of my naturalisation in Freeland, I participated only too strongly in their feelings. You will understand that we were not concerned merely for the preservation of the few vessels ; but to have at last found a point of resistance to the daring barbarians, to know that our men were relieved from the necessity of renewing their shameful flight—this it was which had a sweet sound of promise in the ear. The executive hastened to give us a full explanation.

As I have already told you, the Education Department of the Freeland government possesses a large number of cannon of different calibre in all parts of the country for the exercise of the young men. The largest of these can pierce the strongest of the armour-plates now in use like a piece of card. As soon as the first news of the attack had been received, eighty-four of these giant guns had been put in motion towards Ungama from the adjoining districts. As all these monsters run upon rails that are in connection with the network of Freeland railways, they were all on their way towards the coast before noon, accompanied by the young men who were familiar with the handling of them ; and they would reach their destination in the course of the evening or during the night. As in Ungama, for purposes of ordinary harbour-service, several lines of rails ran along the coast in connection with the network of railways, the guns as they arrived could at once be placed in their several positions, which had been in the meantime—in course of the same day—provided with provisional earthworks. Later on, these earthworks were to receive armour-coating ; but at present, as the central executive calculated, eighty-four guns of the largest size, manned by the most experienced gunners, would suffice even without any special protection to keep any armour-clads manned by wandering adventurers at a respectful distance.

I could not endure to stay longer in Eden Vale. After bidding my father a hasty farewell, and taking a somewhat less hurried fare-well of Bertha, I started for Ungama. Two days later it was seen that the precautions which had been taken were neither superfluous nor insufficient. On the 23rd of August five Abyssinian ironclads and four gunboats appeared off Ungama ; and, as the harbour was thought to be quite defenceless, they attempted forthwith to steam in for the purpose of destroying the disabled vessels of the allies which lay there. A shot from the largest of our armour-crushers, at a distance of a little over six miles, carried away one of the funnels of the nearest ironclad frigates. This made them more cautious ; but they held on their way. Now our young gunners allowed the once-warned foe to steam in to within four miles and a-half of the shore, without giving a sign of their pre-sence ; then they opened fire simultaneously with thirty-seven can-nons. This, however, did not last long. The first volley sank a gunboat, and damaged the whole fleet so much that the enemy was thrown into visible disorder. Some of the vessels appeared to be about to return our fire, while others seemed disposed to turn about and steam away. Two minutes later our second volley swept over the waves ; it could be plainly seen that this time not one of the thirty-seven shots had missed its mark. All the enemy's ships showed severe damage, and the whole fleet had lost all desire to continue the unequal conflict. They reversed their engines and steamed off into the open sea with all possible speed. A third and a fourth salvo were sent after them, and a second gunboat and the largest of the ironclad frigates sank. Three other volleys did still further damage to the fleeing enemy, but failed to sink any more of the ships ; but we learnt from the Italian despatch-boat, which followed the Abyssinian ships at a distance, that an hour after the battle a third gunboat sank, and that one of the ironclad frigates had to be taken in tow in order to get her out of the reach of our strand batteries. These batteries had lost only two men.

With the account of this Freeland deed of arms—in which I was simply an astonished spectator—I close this letter. When, where, and whether I shall write you another is known only to the God of war.

CHAPTER XXII

Massowah ; Sept. 25, ——

IF I recollect rightly, it is just a month and a day since I sent you my last letter. During this brief time I have gone through experiences which must have afforded you in old Europe many a surprise, and which—if I am not mistaken in the views of my new countrymen—will, in their immediate consequences, be of decisive importance to the whole of the habitable globe. It is the freedom of the world, I believe, that has been won on the battle-fields of the Red Sea and the Galla country ; a victory has been gained, not merely over the unhappy John of Abyssinia, but also over many another tyranny which has held nations in bondage in your so-called civilised world. But why should I spend time in surmises about questions which the immediate future must bring to a decision ? My present letter shall serve the purpose of assuring you of my safety and health, as well as of describing the Freeland-Abyssinian campaign, in which I took part from the beginning to the end.

On the 25th of August, two days after the outbreak of the war, the Eden Vale central executive received the Negus's ultimatum, in which he declared that he bore no ill-will against Freeland, but he had taken up arms only in order to protect himself and Freeland against a European invasion, which, as he had learnt, would be forced upon Freeland. As we had not shown courage enough to keep the foe away from our frontiers, the duty of self-preservation compelled him to demand from us the surrender of several important strategical points. If we acceded to this request, he would otherwise respect our liberties and rights, and would even overlook the damage done to his vessels at Ungama. But, if we refused, he would make a hostile invasion into our territory ; and as, by the overthrow of the coast fortresses, he had guarded against our receiving any speedy assistance from Europe, the result could not be doubtful. He was already in motion with an army of occupation numbering 300,000 men, and expected within a week to have crossed our northern frontier. It was for us to decide whether we would receive him as a friend or as a foe. The answer to the Negus ran thus : He was mistaken in his supposition that Freeland thought of receiving foreign troops. Freeland was as little disposed to admit into its territory either English, French, or Italian, as to admit him for military purposes. We could, nevertheless, live at peace with him only on condition that he determined to maintain peace with the above-mentioned European Powers, and to make full compensation for the injury he had done to them. We did not wish to conceal from him that Freeland intended to enter into a friendly alliance with these European States, and would then hold itself bound to regard the enemies of its friends as its own enemies. He was warned against mistaking the conspicuously pacific character of Freeland for cowardice or weakness. A week would be given him to relinquish his threatening attitude and to furnish guarantees of peace and compensation. If within a week overtures of peace were not made, Freeland would attack him wherever he was found.

Of course, no one doubted the issue of this interchange of messages; and the preparations for the war were carried on with all speed.

Scarcely had the telegraph and the journals carried the first news of the Abyssinian attack through Freeland, before announcements and questions reached the central executive from all quarters, proving that the population of the whole country not merely had come to the conclusion that a war was imminent, but that, without any instruction from above, there had set themselves automatically in motion all those factors of resistance which could have been supplied by a military organisation perpetually on a war-footing. Freeland mobilised itself; and the event proved that this self-determined activity of millions of intelligent minds accustomed to act in common afforded very much better results than would have been obtained under an official system of mobilisation, however wisely planned and prepared for. From all the corps of thousands of the whole country there came in the course of the first few days inquiries whether the central executive thought the co-operation of the inquirers desirable. The corps of thousands of the first class, belonging to the twelve northern and north-eastern districts, comprising the Baringo country and Lykipia, announced at once that on the next day they should be fully assembled—with the exception of any who might be travelling—since they assumed that the prosecution of the war with Abyssinia would be specially their business. It was the general opinion in Freeland that from 40,000 to 50,000 men would be sufficient to defeat the Abyssinians; and as the northern districts possessed eighty-five of the corps of thousands that had gained laurels in the district exercises, no one doubted that the work of the war would fall upon these alone. Many a young man in the other parts of the country felt in his breast the stirrings of a noble ambition ; but there was nowhere manifested a desire to withdraw more labour from the country than was necessary, or to interfere with the rational plan of mobilisation by pushing corps into the foreground from a distance. While the other corps thus voluntarily held back, those of the northern districts threw themselves, as a matter of course, into the campaign. But those thousands which during recent years had been victors at the great Aberdare games expressed the wish—so many of them as did not belong to the mobilised districts—to participate in the mobilisation ; and all who had been victors in the individual contests at the last year's district and national games begged, as a favour, to be incorporated among the mobilised thousands. Both requests were granted ; and the additional material thus supplied amounted to four corps of thousands and 960 individuals. Altogether about 90,000 men prepared themselves—about twice as many as the general opinion held to be requisite. But the men themselves, of their own initiative, decided, on the next day, that merely the unmarried men of the last four years, between the ages of twenty-two and twenty-six, should take the field. The force was thereby reduced to 48,000, including 9,500 cavalry and 180 guns, to which last were afterwards added eighty pieces from the Upper Naivasha district.

Each thousand had its own officers. Some of them were married, but it was resolved that, notwithstanding this, they should be retained. The election of superior officers took place on the 23rd of August, after the four extra corps had arrived at the place in North Lykipia appointed for this purpose. The chief command was not given to one of the officers present, but to a young engineer named Arago, living at Ripon as head of the Victoria Nyanza Building Association. Arago of course accepted the position, but asked to have one of the head officials of the traffic department of the central executive as head of the general staff. Hastening from Ungama direct to North Lykipia, I applied to that official with the request that he would place me on the general staff—a request to which, as I was able to prove my possession of the requisite knowledge, and in consideration of my recent renunciation of my Italian birthright, he was doubly willing to accede. David arrived at the same time as myself, bringing me the tenderest greetings and the cordial consent of my bride to the step I was taking, declaring at the same time that he should not jog from my side while the campaign lasted.

All the thousands were abundantly furnished with weapons and ammunition ; and there was no lack of well-trained saddle-horses.

The commissariat was entrusted to the Food-providing Associations of Eden Vale and Dana City. The technical service— pioneering, bridge-construction, field-telegraphy, &c.—was undertaken by two associations from Central and Eastern Baringo ; and the transport service was taken in hand by the department of the central executive in charge of such matters. Within the Freeland frontiers, the perfection of the network of communication made the transport and maintenance of so small an army a matter of no difficulty whatever. But as the Freelanders did not intend to wait for the Abyssinians, but meant to carry the war into the Galla country and to Habesh, 5,000 elephants, 8,000 camels, 20,000 horses, and 15,000 buffalo oxen were taken with the army as beasts of burden. Tents, field-kitchens, conserves, &c., had to be got ready ; in short, provision had to be made that the army should want nothing even in the most inhospitable regions outside of Freeland.

All these preparations were completed by the 29th of August. Two days previously Arago had sent 4,000 horsemen with twenty-eight guns over the Konso pass into the neighbouring Wakwafi country, with instructions to spread themselves out in the form of a fan, to discover the whereabouts of the Abyssinians, whose approach we expected in that quarter. To be prepared for all contingencies, he sent smaller expeditionary corps of 1,200 and 900 men, with eight and four guns respectively, to watch the Endika and Silali mountain-ranges, which lay to the north-east and the north-west of his line of operations. Further, at the Konso pass he left a reserve of 6,000 men and twenty guns ; and on the 30th of August he crossed the Galla frontier with 36,000 men and 200 guns. In order to make long marches and yet to spare the men, each man's kit was reduced as much as possible. It consisted, besides the weapons— repeating-rifle, repeating-pistol, and short sword, to be used also as bayonet—of eighty cartridges, a field-flask, and a small knapsack capable of holding only *one* meal. All the other luggage was carried by led horses, which followed close behind the marching columns, and of which there were twenty-five to every hundred men. This very mobile train, accessible to the men at all times, carried water-proof tents, complete suits and shoes for change of clothing, mackintoshes, conserves and drink for several days, and a reserve of 200 cartridges per man. In this way our young men were furnished with every necessary without being themselves over-burdened, and they were consequently able to do twenty-five miles a day without injury.

The central executive had sent with the army a fully authorised commissioner, whose duty it was to carry out any wish of the leaders of the army, so far as the doing so was the business of the execu-tive; to conduct negotiations for peace should the Negus be disposed to come to terms; and, finally, to provide for the security and com-fort of the foreign military plenipotentiaries and newspaper corre-spondents who should join the campaign. Some of the latter accompanied us on horseback, while others were accommodated upon elephants; most of them followed the headquarters, and were thus kept *au courant* of all that took place.

On the third day's march—the 2nd of September—our mounted advance-guard announced that they had come upon the enemy. As Arago, before he engaged in a decisive battle, wished to test practi-cally whether he and we were not making a fatal mistake in imagining ourselves superior to the enemy, he gave the vanguard orders to make a forced reconnaisance— that is, having done what he could to induce the foe to make a full disclosure of his strength, to withdraw as soon as he was sure of the course the enemy was taking.

At dawn on the 3rd of September we came into collision (I was one of the advanced body at my own request) with the Abyssinian vanguard at Ardeb in the valley of the Jubba. The enemy, not much more in number than ourselves, was completely routed at the first onset, all their guns—thirty-six pieces—taken. as well as 1,800 prisoners, whilst we lost only five men. The whole affair lasted scarcely forty minutes. While our lines were forming, the Abys-sinian artillery opened upon us a perfectly ineffectual fire at three miles and three-quarters. Our artillery kept silent until the enemy was within a mile and a-half, when a few volleys from us silenced the latter, dismounted two of their guns, and compelled the rest to withdraw. Our artillery next directed its attention to the madly charging cavalry of the enemy, which it scattered by a few well-aimed shells, so that our squadron had nothing left to do but to follow the disordered fugitives and to ride down the enemy's infantry, thrown into hopeless confusion by their own fleeing cavalry. The affair closed with the pursuit of the panic-stricken foe and the bringing in of the prisoners. The enemy's loss in killed and wounded, though much greater than ours, was comparatively small.

Thus ended the prologue of the sanguinary drama. Our horse had scarcely got together again, and the prisoners, with the captured guns, sent to the headquarters, when dense and still denser masses of the enemy showed themselves in the distance. This was the whole of the Abyssinian left wing, numbering 65,000, with 120 guns. Twenty of our guns were stationed on a small height that commanded the marching route of the enemy, and opened fire about seven in the morning. The masses of the enemy's infantry were at once seen to turn aside, while ninety of the Abyssinian guns were placed opposite our artillery. The battle of cannons which now began lasted an hour without doing much harm to our artillery, for at so great a distance—three miles—the aim of the Abyssinian gunners was very bad, whilst our shells silenced by degrees thirty-four of the enemy's pieces. Twice the Abyssinians attempted to get nearer to our position, but were on both occasions driven back in a few minutes, so deadly was our fire at a shorter distance. As this did not answer, the enemy tried to storm our position. His masses of infantry and cavalry had deployed along the whole of our thin front, and shortly after eight o'clock the whole of the vastly superior force was in movement against us.

What next took place I should not have thought possible, notwithstanding what I had seen of the skill in the manipulation of their weapons possessed by the Freeland youth. Even the easily gained victory over the enemy's vanguard had not raised my expectations high enough. I confess that I regarded it as unjustifiable indiscretion, and as a proof of his total misunderstanding of the task which had been committed to him by the commander-in-chief, that Colonel Ruppert, the leader of our little band, should accept battle, and that not in the form of a covered retreat, but as a regular engagement which, if lost, must inevitably issue in the annihilation

Y

of his 4,000 men. For he had deployed his cavalry—who had all dismounted, and fired with their splendid carbines—in a thin line of over three miles, extending a little beyond the lines of the enemy, and with very weak reserves behind him. Thus he awaited the Abyssinians, as if they had been advancing as *tirailleurs* and not in compact columns. And I knew these storming columns well; at Ardeb and before Obok they had overthrown equal numbers of England's Indian veterans, France's Breton grenadiers, and Italy's *bersaglieri*; their weapons were equal to those of Freeland, their military discipline I was obliged to consider as superior to that of my present companions in arms. How could our thin line withstand the onset of fifteen times as many veteran warriors? I was firmly convinced that in another quarter of an hour they must be broken in pieces like a cord stretched in front of a locomotive; and then any child might see that after a few minutes' carnage all would be over. In spirit I took leave of distant loved ones—of my father—and I remembered you too, Louis, in that hour which I thought I had good reason to consider my last.

And, what was most astonishing to me, the Freelanders themselves all seemed to share my feelings. There was in their demeanour none of that wild lust for battle which one would have expected to see in those who – quite unnecessarily—engaged in the proportion of one against fifteen. A profound, sad earnestness, nay, repugnance and horror, could be read in the generally so clear and bright eyes of these Freeland youths and men. It was as if they, like myself, were all looking in the face of death. The officers also, even the colonel in command, evidently participated in these gloomy forebodings: then why, in heaven's name, did they offer battle? If they anticipated overthrow, why did they not withdraw in time? But what injustice had I done to these men! how completely had I mistaken the cause and the object of their anxiety! Incredible as it may sound, my comrades in arms were anxious not for their own safety. but on account of their enemies; they shuddered at the thought of the slaughter that awaited not themselves, but their foes. The idea that they, free men, could be vanquished by wretched slaves was as remote from their minds as the idea that the hare can be dangerous to him is from the mind of the sportsman. But they saw themselves compelled to shoot down in cold blood thousands of unfortunate fellow-creatures; and this excited in them, who held man to be the most sacred and the highest of all things, an unspeakable repugnance. Had this been told me *before* the battle, I should not have understood it, and should have held it to be braggadocio ; now, after what I have shudderingly passed through, I find it intelligible. For I must confess that a column advancing against the Freeland lines, and torn ·to pieces by their fire, is a sight which freezes the blood of even men accustomed to murder *en masse*, as I am. I have several times seen the destroying angel of the battlefield at work, and could therefore consider myself steeled against its horrors : but here . . . .

I will not describe my feelings, but what occurred. When the Abyssinians were a little less than a mile from us, Ruppert's adjutants galloped along our front for the last time and bade our men to fire : ' But not a shot after they begin to waver ! ' Then among us there was a stillness as of death, whilst from the other side the noise of the drums and the wild music grew louder and louder, n-terrupted from time to time by the piercing war-cries of the Abyssinians. When the enemy was within half a mile our men discharged a single volley : the front line of the enemy collapsed as if smitten by a blast of pestilence ; their ranks wavered and had to be formed anew. No second shot was as yet fired by the Free- landers ; but when the Abyssinians again pressed forward with wild cries, and now at a more rapid pace, there thundered a second volley ; and as the death-seeking brown warriors this time stormed forward over their shattered front rank, a third volley met them. This was enough for the enemy for the present ; they turned in wild confusion, and did not stop in their flight until they thought themselves out of our range. Our fire had ceased as soon as the enemy turned, and it was high time it did. Not that our position would have been at all endangered by a further advance of the enemy : the Abyssinians had advanced little more than a hundred yards, and were still, therefore, between six and seven hundred yards away, and it was most improbable that one of them could have reached our front. But it was this very distance, and the consequent absence of the special excitement of close combat, that made the horror of the slaughter too great for human nerves to have borne it much longer. Within a few minutes nearly a thousand Abyssinians had been killed or wounded ; and many of the Freeland officers afterwards declared to me that they were seized with faintness at the sight of the

breaking ranks and of the foes in the agonies of death. I can perfectly understand this, for even I felt ill.

The Freeland medical men and ambulance corps were already
at work carrying the wounded foes from the field, when the
Abyssinian artillery recommenced the battle, and their infantry at
the same time opened a tremendous fire. But as the infantry now
kept themselves prudently at the respectable distance of a mile and
a quarter, their fire was at first quite harmless and therefore was
not answered by our men. But when a ball or two had strayed into
our ranks, Colonel Ruppert gave orders that every tenth man
should step far enough out of the ranks to be visible to the enemy
and discharge a volley. This hint was understood; the enemy's
infantry-fire ceased at once, as the Abyssinians learnt from the
effects of this small volley that the Freeland riflemen could make
themselves so unpleasant, even at such a great distance, that it
would not be advisable to provoke them to answer an ineffective fire.
The stubborn fellows, who evidently could not bear the thought of
being driven from the field by such a handful of men, formed themselves afresh into storming columns, this time with a narrower
front and greater depth. But these columns met with no better
fate than their predecessors, the only difference being that they had
to meet a more rapid fire. After a few minutes they were compelled
to retire with a loss of eight hundred men, and could not be made
to move forward again. In order to get possession of the Abyssinian
wounded, who were much better cared for under Freeland treatment
than under that of their own people, Ruppert sent out an advance-
party before whom the enemy hastily retreated, so that we remained
masters of the field. Our losses amounted to eight dead and forty-
seven wounded; the Abyssinians had 860 killed, 1,480 wounded,
and left thirty-nine guns behind. Our first care was to place the
wounded—friend and foe alike—in the ambulance-waggons, of which
there was a large number, all furnished with every possible convenience, and to send them towards Freeland. Then the captured
guns and other weapons were hidden and the dead buried.

Just as the last duty was performed, and we had begun our
retreat to headquarters, strong columns of Abyssinians appeared in
the west, whilst at the same time the left wing of the enemy, which
had retreated towards the north, again came into sight. Ruppert
did not, however, allow himself to be diverted from his purpose.

Masses of the enemy's cavalry made a vigorous attempt to follow us, but were quickly repulsed by our artillery, and we accomplished our retreat to headquarters without further molestation.

We now knew from experience that the assumed superiority of Freeland troops over opponents of any kind was a fact. The Abyssinians had fought as bravely against us as they had formerly fought against European troops. Their equipment, discipline, and training, upon which despotism had brought all its resources to bear for many years, left, according to European ideas, nothing to be desired; and these dark-skinned soldiers had repeatedly shown themselves to be a match for equal numbers of European troops. But we had repulsed a number fifteen times as many as ourselves, without allowing the issue to be for a moment uncertain. That the fight lasted as long as it did, and did not much sooner end in the complete overthrow of the Abyssinians, was due to the fact that the leader of the advance-guard adhered to his orders, to compel the enemy to disclose his whole force. Had our commander at once thrown himself with full force upon the enemy, given him no time to deploy his troops, and energetically made use of his advantage, the 65,000 men of the enemy's left wing would have been scattered long before the centre could have come into action. Not that Colonel Ruppert was wrong in waiting and confining himself rather to defensive action. Even he had to learn, by the issue of the conflict, that the presumed superiority of the Freelanders was an absolute fact; and the more doubtful the ultimate victory of our cause appeared, the more decisively was it the duty of a conscientious leader to avoid spilling the blood of our Freeland youth merely to perform a deed of ostentatious heroism. He, like the rest of us, naturally concluded that this first lesson would abundantly suffice to show the Negus the folly of continuing the struggle.

We had not, however, taken into account the obtuseness of a barbaric despot. When the commissioner of the executive, who accompanied the expedition, sent next day a flag of truce into the Abyssinian headquarters, announcing to John that Freeland was still prepared to treat with him for the restoration of the captured fortresses and ships, and for the arrangement of peace guarantees, the Negus received the ambassadors haughtily, and asked them if they were come offering terms of submission. Because our advanced guard had retired, he treated the affair of the day before as an

Abyssinian victory. He said the officers of the five repulsed brigades were cowards ; we should see how *he* himself would fight. In short, the blinded man would not hear of yielding. He evidently hoped for a complete change of fortune from a not badly planned strategic flanking manœuvre which he had been meanwhile carrying out, and which had only one defect—it did not sufficiently take into account the character of his opponents. In short, more fighting had to be done.

On the 5th of September the two armies stood face to face. The Negus, with 265,000 men and 680 guns, had entrenched himself in a very favourable position, and seemed indisposed to take the offensive. Our commander also felt little inclined to storm the enemy's camp, a course which would have involved an unnecessary sacrifice. To lie here, on the Jubba river, in an inhospitable district in which his army must soon run short of provisions, could not possibly be the intention of the enemy. He merely wished to keep us here a little while until he could by stratagem outflank us. Arago, having guarded against that, determined to wait ; but in the meantime, in order to tire the enemy of waiting, he caused our cavalry to intercept the enemy's provisioning line. Our men lacked for nothing : the commissariat was managed admirably. Among the Abyssinians, on the contrary, Duke Humphrey was the host. Nevertheless the enemy kept quiet for three days in his evidently untenable position, and the field-telegraph first informed us of the motive of his doing so.

The Negus had sent out 45,000 men, who, making a wide circuit eastwards beyond our outposts, were to cross the Endika range of hills, and to effect an entrance into Freeland behind us, and in that way compel us to retreat. Even if his plot had succeeded it would have helped him but little, for the men left behind in the northern districts of Freeland would have very quickly overcome these 45,000 men. But a few days of Abyssinian activity might have been inconvenient for the prosperous fields and cities of North Baringo and Lykipia ; and it was therefore well that the passes of the Endika range were guarded by 1,200 Freeland soldiers and eight guns. The Abyssinians came upon these on the 7th of September, and through the whole day vainly attempted to force a passage. Next morning they found themselves shut in on their rear by our reserves, who had been left at the Konso pass, and who had hastened to the scene of action by forced marches. After a brief and desperate resistance the Abyssinians were compelled to lay down their arms.

This news reached us about noon on the 8th of September. This Job's message must have reached the Negus about the same time, for towards two o'clock we saw the enemy leaving the camp and preparing to give battle. Arago rightly judged that, in order to avoid useless bloodshed, the Abyssinians must this time be prevented from storming our lines in masses, and must be completely routed as quickly as possible and deprived of any power of offering further resistance. He therefore sent our artillery to the front, repelled an attack from the enemy's centre by a couple of sharp volleys from our mounted rifles, and at the same time moved 14,000 men on the left flank of the enemy. Thence he opened fire about half-past three, and, simultaneously making a vigorous attack on the front, he so completely broke up the Abyssinian order of battle that the columns which a little while before had been so well ordered were in a very short time crushed into a chaotic mass, which our lines of rifles swept before them as the beaters drive the game before the sportsmen. After the panic had once seized the enemy there was but little firing. It was fortunate that the Negus had posted on his left wing the troops that had learnt our mode of fighting at Ardeb. These poor fellows remembered, after they had received a murderous volley from our column advancing on their flank, that the Freelanders stop firing as soon as the enemy gives way. Hence they could not be made to stand again; and the cry of terror, ' Don't shoot, or you are dead men!' with which they threw themselves upon their own centre—which in the meantime had been attacked—was not calculated to stimulate the latter to resistance. By five o'clock all was over; the centre and the left wing of the Abyssinians were fleeing in wild confusion, the right wing, 54,000 men strong, was thrown, with the loss of all the artillery, into the entrenchment they had just left, and there laid down their weapons as soon as our guns began to play against the improvised earthworks. The other prisoners taken on the field and during the pursuit, which lasted until nightfall, amounted to 72,000; so that including the 41,000 unwounded men who had fallen into our hands in the Endika passes, we now had 167,000 prisoners. The second battle cost the enemy 760 killed and 2,870 wounded; our own losses in this last encounter were 22 killed and 105 wounded.

Assuming that the Negus succeeded in collecting the scattered remnants of his army, he would still have nearly 130,000 men at his disposal, and it was possible that he might still persist in the campaign. To prevent this, the pursuit was carried on with all possible energy. All the cavalry and a part of the artillery kept at the heels of the enemy; the rest of the army, after the wounded and prisoners were provided for and the dead were buried, followed rapidly the next morning. The retreating Abyssinians made no further serious resistance, but allowed themselves to be easily taken prisoners. In this way, during a five days' chase through the Galla country, 65,000 more men fell into our hands. John had lost nearly all his artillery in the engagement on the Jubba; during the pursuit he lost twenty-six more guns, and then had only seventeen left. With these, and about 60,000 utterly demoralised and for the most part disarmed men, the Negus succeeded on the 13th of September in reaching the southern frontier of his country, which he had recently left with such high hopes. Among the hill-districts of Shoa he attempted to stop our pursuit. In spite of the formidable natural advantages afforded him by his strong position, it would not have been difficult to drive him out by a vigorous attack in the front. But here again Arago shrank from causing unnecessary bloodshed, and by means of a skilful flank manœuvre he induced the Negus, on the next day, voluntarily to leave his position. Thence the pursuit continued without intermission through the provinces of Shoa, Anchara, and Tigre, to the coast. If the Negus had hoped to attract fresh troops on the way, or to inflame the national fanaticism of his subjects against us, he was disappointed. The utterly demoralised panic-stricken fragments of his army which he carried with him were a *Mene, Tekel*, which caused his own people to vanish wherever he came as if the ground had swallowed them up, to reappear after he had gone and to receive us (his pursuers) with palm-branches and barley, the Abyssinian emblems of peace. This led the hunted man, when he had reached the frontier of Tigre, to leave the rest of his army to their fate, and to throw himself, with a small guard of horsemen, into his newly acquired coast possessions. Arrived there, with masterly rapidity he concentrated all his available troops in the coast fortresses, which he hoped, with the help of the fleet, to be able to defend long enough to give time for a possible diversion in his favour among the hill-tribes at our rear. This was the state of things when, on the 18th of September, our advance-guard appeared before the walls of Massowah. The Negus did not then know how short a time his fancied security would last.

The fleet which the Negus had taken from the European Powers at this time still contained thirteen men-of-war and nineteen gun-boats and despatch-boats; at the attack on Ungama, three ironclad frigates and four smaller vessels had been either totally lost or so seriously damaged that the Abyssinians, who had no means of repairing them, could make no further use of them. A few days after the first unsuccessful attempt the Abyssinians reappeared in greater force before Ungama, whose well-known extensive wharves now for the first time seemed attractive to them; but at the first greeting from our giant guns they wisely vanished, and did not allow themselves to be sighted again.

On the other hand, they now watched all the more carefully the two entrances into the Red Sea—from Bab-el-Mandeb in the south, and from Suez in the north. They did not immediately expect any stronger naval power to come from the Indian Ocean, as, besides the two ironclads and the two despatch-boats which lay damaged at Ungama, there were no English, French, or Italian warships of importance for thousands of miles in those seas; and it would take months to get together a new fleet and send it round by the Cape of Good Hope. Moreover, the Abyssinian agents in Europe reported that the allies were preparing an expedition for the canal route, and not for the Cape route. The fact that the French were collecting materials at Toulon was not decisive evidence, as that Mediterranean port was as convenient for the one route as for the other. That the Italians concentrated their ships at Venice instead of at Genoa, which would be much more convenient for an Atlantic expedition, spoke somewhat more plainly; but that the English had chosen Malta as their rendezvous made the destination of the fleet clear to everybody. But the Abyssinians could not understand how the allies expected to pass the Suez Canal, which the Abyssinian guns were able so completely to command that any vessel entering the canal could be sunk ten times before it could fire a broadside. Besides, the Abyssinians cruising at the mouth of the canal had made it impassable by a sunken vessel laden with stones. To remove this obstacle under the fire of 184 heavy guns—the number possessed by the Abyssinian fleet—was an undertaking at which John grimly smiled when he thought of it. And as he now needed his ironclads at least as much at Massowah as at Suez and Bab-el-Mandeb, he had the larger part of them brought to him in order to keep the Freeland besieging army in check, while merely four ironclad frigates, two gunboats, and one despatch-boat remained at Suez, and one ironclad frigate, three gunboats, and two despatch-boats at Bab-el-Mandeb.

The ships ordered to Massowah reached that port on the 18th and 19th of September ; but our newly constructed Freeland fleet had already started from Ungama on the 16th.

Immediately after receiving news of the capture of the coast fortresses and the ships of the allies, the central executive had determined upon the construction of this fleet, and the work was not delayed an hour. There was no time to construct an armoured fleet; but they did not think they needed one. What the executive decided upon was the construction of fast wooden vessels with guns of such a range that their shots would destroy the ironclads without allowing the shots of the latter to reach our vessels. The government relied not merely upon the greater speed of the vessels and the longer range of the guns, but chiefly upon the superiority of our gunners. It was calculated that if our vessels could come within a certain distance of the enemy, our guns would destroy the strongest ship of the enemy before our vessels could be hit. The Freeland shipbuilding and other industries were fully capable, if the work were undertaken with adequate energy and under skilful organisation, of constructing and equipping a sufficient number of wooden vessels of from 2,000 to 3,500 tons in the course of a few weeks. As early as the 23rd of August the keels of thirty-six such vessels were laid at Ungama ; there was sufficient timber in stock, and the machine-works of Ungama also had in stock enough ship-engines of between 2,000 and 3,000 horse-power to furnish the new vessels, the larger of which were to be supplied with four such engines. The best and largest guns were collected from all the Freeland exercise-grounds ; twenty-four new ones, which threw all former ones into the shade, were made in the steel-works at Dana City. The work was carried out with such energy that within twenty-two days the final touch had been given to the last of the thirty-six floating batteries. These constructions were not perfect in elegance ; but in mechanical completeness they were faultless. They were flat-decked, so as to present as little surface as possible to the enemy's balls, and were divided into water-tight compartments to prevent their being sunk by shells striking them under the water-line. Each vessel had at least two engines working in complete independence of each other, so that it could not easily be deprived of its power of locomotion. Only the powder-magazines were armour-plated, but the plates used were of the strongest kind. The guns, which moved freely on the deck, weighed from 100 to 250 tons, and were distributed, to some vessels one, to others two, and to others three; altogether thirty-six vessels possessed seventy-eight guns. The maximum speed ranged for the different vessels from twenty-three to twenty-seven knots per hour.

As we had promised the Western Powers that we would open the Suez Canal to the European transport-ships, we had to proceed at once to carry this task into execution. On the evening of the 19th of September our vessels sighted the Abyssinian squadron cruising in the Straits of Bab-el-Mandeb. These, mistaking us for passenger-steamers, at once gave chase, and were not a little astonished to find that the harmless-looking crafts did not alter their course. It was not until the enemy had got within a little more than nine miles and had had a taste of a few of our heaviest shot, that they recognised their error and beat a hasty retreat. The greater part of our fleet kept on its way into the Red Sea ; only six of our largest and fastest vessels pursued the fleeing Abyssinians, sunk two of their ships by a well-directed fire, which, on account of the distance, the enemy could not effectively return, and drove the others ashore. Our sloops picked as many of the men as they could reach out of the water, and the vessels then proceeded on their way to Suez. The affair with the Bab-el-Mandeb squadron lasted only about two hours and a-half.

The greater part of our fleet steamed unperceived past Massowah in the night of the 19th–20th ; the other six were, however, in the early dawn, seen and pursued by a hostile cruiser. As it was not our intention to make a halt at Massowah or prematurely to warn the Abyssinian ships lying there by giving a lesson to a cruiser as we passed, our vessels did not answer the enemy's shots—though several of the latter struck us—but endeavoured to get out of reach as quickly as possible. They succeeded in doing this without suffering any serious damage. As we learnt afterwards, our vessels were mistaken at Massowah also for mail-ships which were heedlessly running into the hands of the cruisers guarding the canal. All that the Negus did was to set his vessels industriously cruising off Massowah for several nights in order to prevent the six supposed mail-steamers from escaping if they should turn back from Suez.

On the afternoon of the 22nd our fleet appeared off Suez, attacked the enemy's ships forthwith, and, after a short engagement, sank three of them. The others, including three ironclad frigates, ran ashore, and the crews were taken by the Egyptian troops. Our admiral provisionally handed over to the Egyptians the Abyssinian sailors and marines who had been rescued from drowning, and told off three of our vessels to assist the Egyptian and English canal officials in raising the sunken stone-ship. These officials told us that the allied fleet had reached Damietta the day before. If the last obstacle to the navigation of the canal could be removed so soon, the first ships of the allies could enter the Red Sea on the 24th, and the expedition might be expected at Massowah by the end of the month. In order to open Massoyah by that time, our fleet at once returned southwards, and on the 24th of September appeared off the Negus's last place of refuge.

The Freeland army had, in the meantime, remained inactive outside of Massowah, knowing that the co-operation of our vessels would enable us to take the place without difficulty. When those vessels appeared in the offing, several small Abyssinian war-ships steered towards them. A few shots from ours put the enemy's vessels to flight, and the Negus at last understood the situation. However, he still hoped to demolish our wooden ships, until the terrible execution effected by the first charges from our enormous guns taught him and his admirals better. Continually withdrawing out of range of the heavy ironclads as they steamed towards our vessels, the destructive long-ranged guns of the latter poured forth their shot and sank two of the frigates, before even one of the enemy's balls had struck a Freeland vessel. The enemy then turned and fled, but our vessels, keeping at the same advantageous distance, pressed hard after them, and, before the hostile fleet had reached the harbour, sank a third ironclad. Even in the harbour the enemy found as little security as in the open sea ; the dreadful armour-crushing guns sent in shot after shot ; a fourth ship sank, and then a fifth. At the same time our gigantic guns battered at the harbour bastions with tremendous effect, and we expected every moment to see the white flag as a token of surrender. Instead of that, the Negus, finding that he could not hold the fortress, and expecting no mercy from us, suddenly made a desperate sortie, in the hope of fighting his way through our lines to the hills. He succeeded in passing only our first line of outposts ; before he had reached the first Freeland line several volleys had brought his party to a standstill and had given him his death. The Abyssinians threw their arms away, and the war was ended.

To-morrow David and I return in the fastest of the Freeland vessels to Ungama, where Bertha awaits us. The fortnight my father bargained for has passed more than twice—I shall meet, not my betrothed, but my wife, on the Freeland seashore.

. . . .

Here end the Freeland letters of our new countryman, Carlo Falieri, to his friend the architect Luigi Cavalotti. The two friends have exchanged residences ; Cavalotti has migrated to Freeland, Falieri on the contrary, after spending a few delightful weeks on a paradisiacal island on Lake Victoria Nyanza, has been withdrawn from us for a time. He obeyed a call from his native land to assist in the carrying out of those reforms which had to be undertaken there, as elsewhere throughout the world, in consequence of the events described in his letters, and of other events which followed those. His wife accompanies him on his mission, in the furtherance of which our central government has placed the resources of Freeland at his disposal. But this carries us into the subject of the following book.

BOOK IV

CHAPTER XXIII

THE moral effect of our Abyssinian campaign was immense among all the civilised and half-civilised peoples who heard of it. We ourselves had expected the most salutary results from it, as we foresaw that the brilliant proof of our power which we had given to the world would make our adversaries more cautious and induce them to be more compliant to our just wishes. But the effect far exceeded our most sanguine expectations. The former opponents of economic justice were not merely silenced, but actually converted—a fact which seemed to astonish us Freelanders ourselves rather than our friends abroad. We could not clearly understand why people, who for decades had regarded our efforts as foolish or objectionable, should, simply because our young men had shown themselves to be excellent soldiers, suddenly conclude that it would be possible and beneficial to enable every worker to retain the full produce of his industry. The connection between the latter and the execution done by our rifles and cannons was not clear to us who lived under the dominion of reason and justice; but outside of Freeland, wherever physical force was still the ultimate ground of right, everybody—even those who in principle endorsed our ideas—held it to be a matter of course that the crushing blows under whose tremendous force the Negus of Abyssinia fell, were an unanswerable *argumentum ad hominem* for the superiority of our institutions as a whole. In particular, the sudden victorious appearance of our fleet operated abroad as a decisive proof that economic justice is no mere dream-Utopia, but a very real actuality; in short, our military successes proved to be the triumph of our social institutions. A strong feverish excitement took possession of all minds; and men everywhere now wished practically to adopt what until then had been seriously regarded by a comparatively small number as an ideal to be attained in the future, by many had been treated with disfavour, and by most had been altogether ignored.

And it was seen—which certainly did *not* surprise us—that the impatience and the revolutionary fever were the intenser the less the subjects of them had previously studied our principles. The most advanced liberal-minded nations, whose foremost statesmen had already been in sympathy with us, and had made well-meant, but disconnected, attempts to lead their working-classes into industrial freedom, applied themselves with comparative deliberateness to the task of effecting the great economic and social revolution with as little disturbance of the existing interests as possible. England, France, and Italy, which before the outbreak of the Abyssinian war were already prepared to introduce our institutions into their East African possessions, now resolved to co-operate with us in the conversion of their existing institutions into others analogous to ours—a course which they could take without involving themselves in any very revolutionary steps. Several other European Powers, as well as the whole of America and Australia, immediately followed their example. This gave rise to some stormy outbursts of popular feeling in the States in question; but beyond the breaking of a few windows no harm was done. There were more serious disturbances in the 'conservative' States of Europe and in some parts of Asia; there occurred violent uprisings and serious attacks upon unpopular ministers, who in vain asserted that they no longer had any objection to make to economic equity. Here and there the struggle led to bloodshed and confiscations. The working-classes mistrusted the wealthy classes, but were themselves not agreed upon the course that should be taken ; and the parties assumed a more and more threatening attitude towards each other. But the condition of affairs was worst where the governments had formerly acted in avowed opposition to the people, the wealthy had oppressed the masses, and the latter had been designedly kept in ignorance and poverty. In such countries there was no intelligent popular class possessing influence enough to control the outbursts of furious and unreasoning hatred ; cruelty and horrors of all kinds were perpetrated, the former oppressors slaughtered wholesale, and there would have been no means of staying the senseless and aimless bloodshed if, fortunately for these countries, our influence and authority had not ultimately quieted the raging masses and turned the agitation into proper channels. After one of the parties, which in those countries were fruitlessly tearing each other to pieces, had conceived the idea of calling in our intervention, the example was generally followed. Wherever anarchy prevailed in the east of Europe, in Asia, in several African States, requests were sent that we would furnish commissioners, to whom should be granted unlimited authority. We naturally complied most gladly with these requests; and the Freeland commissioners were everywhere the objects of that implicit confidence which was necessary for the restoration of quiet.

In the meantime those States also which were more advanced in opinion had asked for confidential agents from Freeland to assist, both with counsel and material aid, the governments in prosecuting the intended reforms. We say advisedly with counsel and *material aid*; for the people of Freeland, as soon as it was known that assistance had been asked for, granted to their delegates, whether acting as consultative members of a foreign government or as commissioners furnished with unlimited power, disposal over the material resources of Freeland for the benefit of the countries that had sent for them; the sums advanced being treated not as gifts, but as loans. The central government of Eden Vale formally reserved the right to give the final decision in the case of each loan; but as it was an understood principle that necessary help was to be afforded, and as only those who were on the spot could know what help was necessary, a discretionary right of disposal of the available capital really lay in the hands of the commissioners and confidential agents.

That we were able, in the course of a few months, to meet a demand from abroad for nearly two milliard pounds sterling is explained by the fact that our Freeland Insurance Department had at its disposal in an available form about one-fifth of its reserve of more than ten milliards sterling. The other four-fifths were invested—that is, it was lent to associations and to the commonwealth for various purposes; the one-fifth had been retained in the coffers of the bank as disposable stock for emergencies, and now could be used to meet the sudden demand for capital. This reserve, of course, was not kept in the form of gold or silver : had it been, it would not have been available when an accidental demand arose. It is not

gold or silver, but quite other things that are required in a time of
need : the precious metals can serve merely as suitable means of
procuring the things that are really required. In order that such
things may be acquired they must exist somewhere in a sufficient
quantity, and that they exist in sufficient quantity to meet a sudden
and exceptionally large demand cannot be taken for granted. He
who suddenly wants goods worth milliards of pounds will not be
able to buy them anywhere, because they are nowhere stored up to
that amount ; if he would be protected from the danger of not being
able to get such a demand met, he must lay up, not the money for
purchase, but the goods themselves which he expects to need.
Take, for example, the case of the Russians who had burnt and
destroyed the granaries of their landowners, the warehouses of their
merchants, the machines in their factories : what good would
have done them had the milliards of roubles which they needed to
make good—and to add to—what had been destroyed been sent to
them in the form of money for them to spend ? There were no
surplus supplies which they could have bought : had they taken
our money into the markets the only effect would have been to
raise all prices, and to have made all the neighbouring nations share
their distress. And in the same way all the other nations, which
we wished to assist in their endeavour to rise as quickly as possible
out of their misery into a state of wealth similar to our own, needed
not increased currency but increased food, raw material, and implements. And our reserve was laid up in the form of such things.
About half of it always consisted of grain, the other half of various
kinds of raw material, particularly materials for weaving, and
metals. When our commissioner in Russia asked at different times
for sums amounting altogether to 285,000,000*l.*, he did not receive
from us a farthing in money, but 3,040 cargoes of wheat, wool,
iron, copper, timber, &c. : the result was that the wasted country
did not suffer at all from want, but a few months later—certainly
less in consequence of the loans themselves than of the fact that
the loans were employed in the Freeland spirit—it enjoyed a prosperity which a short time before no one would have dreamt to be
possible. In the same way we made our resources useful to other
nations, and we resolved that should our existing means not suffice
to meet the demands, we would make up what was still needed
from the produce of the coming year.

z

We by no means intended to continue this *rôle* of economic and social providence to our brother peoples longer than was absolutely necessary. We did not shrink from either the burden or the responsibility; but we considered that in all respects it would be for the best if the process of social reconstruction, in which all mankind was now engaged, were to be carried out with the united powers of all, according to a well-considered common plan. We therefore determined at once to invite all the nations of the earth to a conference at Eden Vale, in which it might be decided what ought next to be done. It was not our intention that this congress should pass binding resolutions : it should remain, we thought, free to every nation to draw what conclusions it pleased from the discussions at the congress; but it seemed to us that in any case it would be of advantage to know what the majority thought of the movement now going on.

This suggestion met with no serious objection anywhere. Among the less advanced nations of Asia there was a strong feeling that, instead of spending the time in useless talk, it would be better simply to put into execution whatever we Freelanders advised. The constituent assemblies of several—and those not the least—nations said that they on their part would abide by what we said, whatever the congress might decide upon. But it was necessary only to point out that we could not advise them until we had heard them, and that a congress seemed to be the best means of making their wants known, to induce them to send delegates. We could not prevent many of the delegates from receiving instruction to vote with us Freelanders in all divisions whatever—an instruction which proved to be quite unnecessary, as the congress did not divide at all, except upon questions of form, upon other questions confining itself to discussion and leaving everyone to draw his own conclusions from the debates.

On the other hand, in the most advanced countries a small minority had organised an opposition, not, it is true, against the general principles of economic justice, but against many of the details involved in carrying out that principle. This opposition had nowhere been able to elect a delegate who should bear its mandate to the World's Congress; but it everywhere found strong advocates among the Freeland confidential agents and commissioners, who, while perfectly in harmony with the public opinion of Free-

land, endeavoured, as far as possible, to secure a representation of every considerable party tendency, in order that those who clung to the obsolete old economic order should have no right to complain that they could not make themselves heard. Sixty-eight nations were invited to take part in the congress; it was left to the nations themselves to decide how many delegates they should send, provided they did not send more than ten each. The sixty-eight countries elected 425 delegates, thus making with the twelve heads of departments of the Freeland government a total number of 437 members of the congress.

On the 3rd of March, in the twenty-sixth year after the founding of Freeland, the congress met in the large hall of the Eden Vale National Palace. On the right sat those who questioned the possibility of carrying out the proposed reform universally, in the centre the adherents of Freeland, on the left the Radicals to whom the most violent measures seemed best. The presidency was given to the head of the Freeland government, which position had been uninterruptedly occupied by Dr. Strahl since the founding of the commonwealth.

We give the following *résumé* of the six days' discussion from the official minutes:

FIRST DAY

The PRESIDENT, in the name of the Freeland people, welcomed the delegates of the nations who had responded to the Freeland invitation.

CHARLES MONTAIGNE (*Centre*), in the name of his colleagues, thanked the Freeland people for the magnanimous and extraordinary assistance which they had afforded to the other nations of the earth in their struggles after economic freedom. Not content with showing to the rest of the world the way to economic freedom and justice, Freeland had also made enormous material sacrifices. For his part, he did not know which was the more astonishing, the inexhaustibleness of the resources which Freeland had at its disposal or the disinterested magnanimity exhibited in the employment of those resources.

JAMES CLARK (*Freeland*): In the interest of sober truth, as well as with a view of furthering as much as possible the great work we all have at heart, I must explain that though the Freeland people

are always happy to make disinterested sacrifices for the good of
their brother peoples, and that in all they do in this way their object
is rather to develop and to promote the best interests of mankind
than to obtain any advantage for themselves, yet, as a matter of fact,
the milliards lent to foreign countries cost Freeland no material
sacrifice, but bring it considerable material profit. [Sensation.]
Under the *régime* of economic justice and freedom the solidarity of all economic interests is so universal and without exception, that in Freeland business becomes as profitable as it is
possible to conceive of its being while you, with our assistance, are
growing rich most rapidly. This would be true if we gave you the
milliards instead of lending them. You look at each other and at
me with an inquiring astonishment? You hold it to be impossible
to become rich by lending gratuitously or by absolutely giving away
a part of one's property? Yet nothing is simpler. The subject is a
very important one, and will come up for discussion again in the
course of our sittings; at present I will only briefly point out that
we have been prevented by the misery of the rest of the world from
making the right use of the advantages of international division of
labour. We have been obliged to manufacture for ourselves goods
which we might have obtained better from you; and we have therefore had to produce a smaller quantity of those things which we
could have produced most profitably. It is plain that we should be
far richer if we could give our attention chiefly to the production of
grain for ourselves and for you, and derive from you the supplies we
need to meet our demand for manufactured articles. For here the
soil yields for an equal amount of labour and capital ten times as
much as among you, while few manufactures here yield a larger
return for labour and capital than they do abroad. But, on account
of the system of exploitation which has prevailed and is not yet got
rid of among you—the cheap wages consequent upon which have
cramped your use of labour-saving machinery—we have been, and
still are, compelled to meet most of our demand for manufactured
articles by our own production, since you are scarcely able to produce for yourselves, to say nothing of producing for us, a great
number of goods which in the nature of things you ought to be able
to produce most profitably both for yourselves and for us, and in
exchange for which you would receive our foodstuffs and raw material.
We calculate that the removal of this hindrance to the complete

international division of labour must increase the productiveness of our labour so much that the resulting gain would be cheaply bought by a permanent sacrifice of many milliards. You need not wonder, then, at finding us always so eager in encouraging you to make the freest and fullest claims upon our resources. You will never dip so deeply into our pockets that we—in our own interest as well as in yours—will not wish to see you dip still deeper. Every farthing spent in hastening the development of your wealth is made good to us ten and twentyfold.

FRANCIS FAR (*Right*): If it is so much to the interest of Freeland to enrich us that Freeland is profited even by making us a gift of its capital, why has it not given us its capital sooner? Who would have hindered it from handing its milliards over to us? Why did it delay so long, and why does it now make its assistance conditional on our accepting its economic institutions?

JAMES CLARK: Because so long as you remained in servitude every farthing given to you for such a purpose would have been simply thrown away. Formerly we could do nothing more than support the victims of your social system and mitigate the misery and wretchedness you inflicted upon yourselves. As a matter of fact, there have long been large sums of Freeland capital—bearing interest, it is true—invested in Europe and America. What has been the result? This money has contributed to increase the amount of surplus capital among you: it could not increase the quantity of capital actually employed in production among you, for nothing could have done that but an increased consumption by the people outside of Freeland—and this was not compatible with what were then your economic principles. Therefore we have been able to help you only since you yourselves have held out the hand: our capital will benefit you only because you have at length decided to enjoy the fruits of it yourselves. [General assent.]

The PRESIDENT: In order to preserve a certain amount of order in our discussions, I propose that we at once agree upon a list of the questions to be considered. It may not always be possible to adhere strictly to the order in the list; but it is advisable that each speaker should endeavour as much as possible to confine himself to the subject under discussion. In order to expedite matters, the Freeland government has prepared a kind of agenda, which you can accept, or amend, or reject. The matters for discussion mentioned in this agenda, I may remark, were not introduced on our initiative, but were mentioned by the leaders of the different parties abroad as needing more detailed explanation : we, on our part, contented ourselves with arranging these questions. We propose, therefore, that the following be the order in which the subjects be discussed :

1. How can the fact be explained that never in the course of history, before the founding of Freeland, has there been a successful attempt to establish a commonwealth upon the principles of economic justice and freedom ?

2. Is not the success of the Freeland institutions to be attributed merely to the accidental, and therefore probably transient, co-operation of specially favourable circumstances ; or do those institutions rest upon conditions universally present and inherent in human nature ?

3. Are not want and misery necessary conditions of existence; and would not over-population inevitably ensue were misery for a time to disappear from the earth ?

4. Is it possible to introduce the institutions of economic justice everywhere without prejudice to inherited rights and vested interests ; and, if possible, what are the best means of doing this ?

5. Are economic justice and freedom the ultimate outcome of human evolution ; and what will probably be the condition of mankind under such a *régime* ?

Has anyone a remark to make upon our proposal ? No one has. Therefore I place point 1 upon the order of the day, and call upon delegate Erasmus Kraft to speak.

ERASMUS KRAFT (*Right*) : Wherever thinking men dwell upon this earth, we are preparing to exchange the state of servitude and misery in which from time immemorial our race has been sunk, for a happier order of things. The brilliant example which we have before our eyes here in Freeland seems to be a pledge that our attempt will—nay, must—succeed. But the more evident this certainty becomes, the more urgent, the more imperative, becomes the question why that which is now to be accomplished has not long since been done, why the genius of humanity slept so long before it roused itself to the task of completing this richly beneficent work. And the simpler—the more completely in harmony with human nature and with the most primitive requirements of sound reason—appears to be the complex of those institutions upon which the work of emancipation depends, so much the more enigmatical is it that earlier centuries and millenniums, when there was no lack of enlightened and noble minds, never seriously attempted to accomplish such a work. We see that it suffices to guarantee to everyone the full enjoyment of what he produces, in order to supply everyone with more than enough ; and yet through untold millenniums men have patiently endured boundless misery with all its consequences of sorrow and crime as if they were inevitable conditions of existence. Why was this ? Are we shrewder, wiser, juster than all our ancestors ; or, in spite of all the apparently infallible evidence in favour of the success of our work, are we not perhaps under a delusion ? It is true that the greatest and most important part of the history of mankind is veiled in the obscurity of primitive antiquity ; yet history is so old that it is scarcely to be assumed that the endeavour after the material well-being of all—an endeavour prompted by the most ardent desires of every creature—should now make its appearance for the first time. It must be that such an endeavour has been put forth, not *once* merely but repeatedly, even though no tradition has given us any trustworthy account of it. But where are its results ? Or did its results once exist though we know nothing of them ? Is the story of the Golden Age something more than a pious fable ; and are we upon the point of conjuring up another Golden Age ? And then arises the query, how long will this Golden Age last ; will it not again be followed by an age of bronze and an age of iron, perhaps in a more wretched, more humble form than that exhibited by the age from which we are preparing to part ? Is that fatalistic resignation, with which the ages known to us endured misery and servitude, a human instinct evolved during an earlier and bitter experience—an instinct which teaches mankind to endure patiently the inevitable rather than strive after a brief epoch of happiness and progress at the risk of a deeper fall ? In obedience to the hint from the chair, I will at present refrain from inquiring what might be the cause of such a relapse into redoubled misery, as this will be the theme of the third point in the list of subjects for discussion ; but I think that before we proceed to an exposition of all the conceivable consequences of the success of our endeavours it would be advisable first to find out *whether* those endeavours will really and in their full extent succeed ; and in order to find this out, it will again be advisable to ask why such endeavours have never succeeded before—nay, perhaps, why they have never before been made.

CHRISTIAN CASTOR (*Centre*): The previous speaker is in error when he asserts that history tells us of no serious attempt to realise the principle of economic justice. One of the grandest attempts of this kind is Christianity. Everyone who knows the Gospels must know that Christ and His apostles condemned the exploitation of man by man. The words of Scripture, ' Woe to him who waxes fat upon the sweat of his brother,' contain *in nuce* the whole codex of Freeland law and all that we are now striving to realise. That the official Christianity afterwards allowed its work of emancipation to drop is true ; but individual Fathers of the Church have again and again, in reliance upon the sacred text, endeavoured to realise the original purposes of Christ. And that during the Middle Ages, as well as in modern times, vigorous attempts to realise the Christian ideal—that is, the ideal of Christ, not that of the Church—have never been wanting is also well known. This is what I wished to point out. The elucidation of the question why all these attempts were wrecked I leave to other and better furnished minds.

VLADIMIR OSSIP (*Left*): Far be it from me to hold the noble Founder of Christianity responsible for what was afterwards made out of His teaching ; but our friend from the United States goes, in my opinion, too far when he represents Christ and His successors as *our* predecessors. We proclaim prosperity and freedom— Christ preached self-denial and humility ; we desire the wealth, He the poverty, of all ; we busy ourselves with the things of this world —He had the next world before His eyes ; we are—to speak briefly— revolutionaries, though pacific ones—He is the founder of a religion. Let us leave religion alone ; I do not think it will be of any use for us to call in question the *meum* and *tuum* as to Christianity.

LIONEL ACOSTA (*Centre*): I differ entirely in this case from the previous speaker, and agree with our colleague from North America. The teaching of Christ, though not explicit as to means and ends, is the purest and noblest proclamation of social freedom that has yet been heard, and it is this proclamation of social emancipation, and not any religious novelty, that forms the substance of the ' Good News.' It was a master-stroke of the policy of enslavement to represent Christ as a founder of a religion instead of a social reformer : the latter doctrine had quickly won the hearts of the oppressed masses because it promised them release from their sufferings, but the former doctrine was used to lull to sleep their awakening energy.

Christ did not concern Himself with religion—not a line in the Gospels shows the slightest trace of His having interfered with one of the ancient religious precepts of His country. The most orthodox Jew can unhesitatingly place the Gospels in the hands of his children, certain that they will find nothing therein to wound their religious sentiment. [A Voice : Then why was Christ crucified ?] I am asked why Christ was crucified if He had done nothing contrary to the Mosaic law. Do men commit murder from religious motives *merely* ? Christ was hurried to death because He was a *social*, not because He was a religious, innovator ; and it was not the pious but the powerful among the Jews who demanded His death. Scarcely a word is needed to set this matter right in the minds of all those who study without prejudice the momentous events of that saddest, but at the same time most glorious, of the days of Israel, upon which the noblest of her sons voluntarily sought and found a martyr's death. In the first place, it is a well-attested historical fact that in Judæa at that time death for religious heresy was as little known as in Europe during the last century. In the second place, the mode of execution—the cross, which was quite foreign to the Jews—shows that Christ was executed according to Roman, not Jewish, law. But the Romans, the most tolerant in religious matters of all peoples, would never have put a man to death for religious innovation ; they would not have allowed the execution to take place, much less have themselves pronounced sentence and carried out that sentence in their own method. The cross was among them the punishment for *riotous slaves* or their *instigators*. I do not say this for the purpose of shifting the responsibility for Christ's death from Judæa—it is the sad privilege of that people to have been the executioner of its noblest sons; and as only the Athenians killed Socrates, so none but the Jews killed Christ; the Romans were only the instruments of Jewish hatred—the hatred, that is, of those wealthy men among the Jews of the time who denounced the ' perverter of the people ' to the Governor because they trembled for their possessions. Indeed, it is quite credible that the Governor did not show himself willing to accede to the wishes of the eager denouncers, for he, the Roman, who had grown up in unshaken faith in the firmly established rights of property, did not understand the significance and bearing of the social teaching of Christ. The Gospels leave us little room to doubt—and it would be difficult to understand how it could be otherwise—that he held Christ to be a harmless enthusiast, who might have been let off with a little scourging. Generations had to pass away before the *Roman* world could learn what the teaching of Christ really was ; and then it fell upon His followers with a fury without a parallel— crucified them, threw them to the beasts; in short, did every- thing that Rome was accustomed to do to the foes of its system of law and property, but never to the followers of foreign religions. It was different with the *Jewish* aristocracy : these at once under- stood the meaning and the bearing of the Christian propaganda, for they had long since learnt the germ of these social demands in the Pentateuch and in the teaching of the earlier prophets. The year of Jubilee which required a fresh division of the land after every forty-nine years, the regulation that all slaves should be emanci- pated in the seventh year—what were these but the precursors of the universal equality demanded by Christ ? Whether all these ideas, which are to be found in the Sacred Scriptures of ancient Judæa, were ever realised in practice is more than doubtful. But they were currently known to every Jew ; and when Christ attempted to give them a practical form—when, in vigorous and rousing addresses, He denounced woe to the rich man who fattened upon his brother's sweat—then the powerful in Jerusalem at once recognised that their interests were threatened by a danger which was not clearly seen by non-Jewish property-owners until much later. There is not the slightest doubt that they made no secret of the true grounds of their anxiety to the Roman Governor, for Christ was executed, not as a sectary, but as an inciter to revolt.

But, of course, it could not be told to the people that the death of Christ was demanded because He wished to put into practice the principle of equality laid down in the sacred books and so often insisted on by the prophets. The people had to be satisfied with the fable of the religious heresy of the Nazarene, which fable, how- ever—except in the case of the unjudging crowd that collected together at the crucifixion—for a long time found no credence. Everywhere in Israel did the first Christian communities pass for good Jews ; they were called *Judaei* by all the Roman authors by whom they were mentioned. What they really were, in what respects alone they differed from the other communities of Jews, is sufficiently revealed in the Acts of the Apostles, notwithstanding the very natural caution of the writer, and the subsequent equally intelligible corruptions of the text. They were Socialists, to some extent Communists ; absolute economic equality, community of goods, was practised among them. Later, when the Christian Church sacrificed its social principle to peace with the State, and transformed itself from a cruelly persecuted martyr to equality into an instrument of authority and—perhaps because of this apostasy —of a doubly zealous persecuting authority, then first did she put forth as her own teaching the malicious calumny of her former maligners, and took upon herself the *rôle* of a new religion ; and since then she has, in fact, been the propounder of a new religion. And that she has succeeded, for more than 1,500 years, in connecting her new *rôle* with the name of Christ, is mainly the fault of the Jews, who, through the sanguinary persecutions which have been carried on against them in the name of the meek Sufferer of Golgotha, have allowed themselves to be betrayed into a blind and foolish hatred towards this their greatest and noblest son.

But it remains none the less true that Christ suffered death for the idea of social justice and for this alone—nay, that before His time this idea was not unknown to Judaism. And it is equally true that notwithstanding all subsequent obscuration and corruption of this world-redeeming idea, the propaganda of economic emancipation has never since been completely suppressed. It was in vain that the Church forbad the laity to read those books which were alleged to contain no teaching but that of the Church : again and again did the European peoples, languishing in the deepest degradation, derive from those forbidden Scriptures courage and inspiration to attempt their emancipation.

DARJA-SING (*Centre*) : I should like to add to what I have just heard that another people, six centuries before Christ, also conceived the ideas of freedom and justice—I mean the Indian people. The essence of Buddhism is the doctrine of the equality of all men and of the sinfulness of oppression and exploitation. Nay, I venture to assert that the already mentioned ideas of social freedom to be found in the Pentateuch, and held by the prophets, and consequently those also held by Christ, are to be referred back to Indian suggestion. At first sight this appears to be an anachronism, for Buddha lived six centuries before Christ, while the Jewish legends carry back the composition of the Pentateuch to the fourteenth century before Christ. But recent investigations have almost certainly established that these alleged books of Moses were composed in the sixth century B.C. at the earliest—at any rate, after the return of the Israelites from the so-called Babylonish captivity. Now, just at the time when the *élite* of the then existing Jews were carried to Babylon, Buddha sent his apostles through the whole of Asia; and it may safely be assumed that those who 'wept by the waters of Babylon' were specially susceptible to the teaching of such apostles.

When, therefore, certain eminent German thinkers assert that Christianity is a drop of foreign blood in the Arian peoples, they are certainly correct in so far as Christianity actually came to them as Semitism, as having sprung from Judaism; nevertheless the Arian world can lay claim to the fundamental conception of Christianity as its own, since it is most highly probable that the Semitic peoples received the first germ of it from the Arians. I say this not for the purpose of depreciating the service performed by the great Semitic martyr to freedom. I cannot, alas! deny that we Arians were not able to accomplish anything of our own strength with the divine idea that sprang from our bosom. While it is probable that the horrors of the Indian system of caste, that most shameful blossom that ever sprang from the blood-and-tear-bedewed soil of bondage, made India the scene of the first intellectual reaction against this scourge of mankind, it is certain, on the other hand, that that very system of caste so severely strained the energy of our Indian people as to make it impossible for them to give practical effect to the reaction. Buddhism was extinguished in India, and outside of India it was soon entirely robbed of its social characteristic. Those transcendental speculations to which even in the West it was *attempted* to limit Christianity have in Eastern Asia been in reality the only effects of Buddhism. Indeed, the idea of freedom took different forms in the minds of the founders—taking one form in the Indian Avatar which, notwithstanding all his sublimity, bore the mark of his nationality ; and taking another form in the Messiah of Judah who saw the light of the world in the midst of a people fired with a never-subdued yearning for freedom. Buddha could conceive of freedom only in the form of that hopeless self-renunciation which was falsely introduced into the Christian idea of freedom by those who did not wish to have their own enjoyments interfered with by the claims of others.

In fact, I am convinced that even our more vigorous kinsmen who had migrated to the West could not have given practical effect to the conception of freedom and equality if we—the Indian world —had transmitted to them that conception just as we had conceived it. For even those who migrated westward carried in their blood to Europe, and retained for a thousand years, the sentiment of caste. The idea that all men are equal, really equal here upon earth, would have remained as much beyond the grasp of the German noble and the German serf as it has remained beyond the grasp of the Indian Pariah or Sudra and the Brahman or Kshatriya. This conception had first to be condensed and permanently fixed by the genius of the strongly democratic little Semitic race on the banks of the Jordan, and then to be subjected to a severe—and, for a time, adverse—analytical criticism by the independent and logical spirit of research of Rome and Greece, before it could be transplanted and bear fruit in purely Arian races. It is very evident that the converted German kings adopted Christianity because they held it to be a convenient instrument of power. It was for the time being immaterial to them what the new doctrine had to say to the serfs ; for the serf who looked up to the ' offspring of the gods,' his master, with awful reverence, seemed to be for ever harmless, and the only persons against whom it was necessary for the masters to arm were their fellow lords, the great and the noble, who differed from the kings in nothing but in the amount of their power. The right to rule came, according to the Arian view, from God : very well, but the right of the least of the nobles sprang, like that of the king, from the gods. Now, the kings found in Christ the *one* supreme Lord who had conferred power upon them, and upon them alone. They alone now possessed a divine source of authority ; and therefore history shows us everywhere that it was the kings who introduced Christianity against the—often determined—opposition of the great, and never that the great were converted without, or against the will of, the kings. The masses of the people, the serfs, where were these ever asked? They have to do and believe what their masters think well; and without exception they do it, making no resistance whatever—allowing themselves to be driven to baptism in flocks like sheep, and believing, as they are commanded to do, that all power comes from *one* God, who bestows it upon *one* lord. For the Arian serf is a mere chattel without a will, and will not think for himself until he is educated to do so. This work of education has been a long time in progress; but, as the previous speaker rightly said, the idea of freedom has never slept.

ERICH HOLM (*Right*) : I do not think that any valid objection can be made to the statement that the general idea of economic justice is thousands of years old and has never been completely lost sight of. But it is a question whether this general idea of equality of rights and of freedom has much in common with that which *we* are now about to put into practice, or whether in many respects it does not differ from that ancient idea. And, further, it is a question whether that idea, which we have heard is already twenty-five centuries old, has ever been or can be realised.

With reference to the first question, I must admit that Christ, in contrast to Buddha, entertained not a transcendental and metaphysical, but a very material and literal idea of equality. It is true that He pronounced the poor in spirit blessed ; but the rich, who according to Him would find it harder to get into heaven than it is for a rope of camel's hair to go through a needle's eye, were not the rich in spirit, but the rich in earthly riches. It is also true that he said, 'My kingdom is not of this world' and ' Render unto Cæsar the things that are Cæsar's '; yet everyone who reads these passages in connection with their context must see that He is simply waiving all interference whatever with political affairs—that in wishing to gain the victory for social justice he is influenced not by political, but by transcendental aims for the sake of eternal blessedness. Whether Rome or Israel rules is immaterial to Him, if only justice be exercised ; yet only pious narrow-mindedness can deny that He wished to see justice exercised here below, and not merely in the next world. But is that which Christ understands by justice really identical with what we mean by it ? It is true that the ' Love thy neighbour as thyself,' which He preached in common with other Jewish teachers, would be a senseless phrase if it did not imply economic equality of rights. The man who exploits man loves man as he does his domestic animal, but not as himself: to require true 'Christian neighbourly love' in an exploiting society would be simply absurd, and what would come of it we have in times past sufficiently experienced. Indeed, the apostle removes all doubt from this point, for he expressly condemns the getting rich upon another's sweat.

So far, then, we are completely at one with Christ. But He just as emphatically condemns wealth and praises poverty, whilst we would make wealth the common possession of all, and therefore would place all our fellow-men in a condition in which—to speak with Christ—it would be harder to enter the kingdom of heaven than it is for a rope to go through a needle's eye. Here is a contradiction which it seems to me can scarcely be reconciled. We hold misery, Christ held wealth, to be the source of vice, of sin: our equality is that of wealth, His that of poverty. This is my first point.

In the second place, Christ did *not* succeed, modest as His aims were. Is not, then, an appeal to this noblest of all minds calculated to discourage rather than to encourage us in the pursuit of our aims?

EMILIO LERMA (*Freeland*): The previous speaker has brought the poverty which Christ praised and required into a false relation with the—alleged—miscarriage of His work of emancipation. Christ's work miscarried not in spite of, but *because* of, the fact that He attempted to base equality upon poverty. The equality of poverty cannot be established, for it would be synonymous with the stagnation of civilisation. However, it is not only possible, but necessary, to bring about the equality of wealth, as soon as the necessary conditions exist, because this is synonymous with the progress of civilisation. You will say that certainly this is so according to our view; but according to the view of Christ wealth is an evil. Very true. But when we examine the matter without prejudice, it is impossible not to see *that Christ rejected wealth only because it had its source in exploitation.* There is nothing in the life of Christ to suggest that He was such a gloomy ascetic as He must have been if He had held wealth, as such, to be sinful: numberless passages in the Gospels afford unequivocal evidence of the contrary. Christ's daily needs were very simple, but He was always ready to enjoy whatever His adherents offered him, and never saw any harm in getting as much

pleasure from living as was consistent with justice. This view of His
was not affected even by the hatred with which the rich of Jerusalem
persecuted Him, and the often-quoted condemnation of the rich has
in it something contrary to the spirit of the Gospels, if we tear
it away from its connection with the words, 'Woe unto him who
waxeth fat upon the sweat of his brother.' In condemning wealth,
Christ condemned merely its source; the kingdom of heaven was
closed to wealth because, and only because, wealth could not be
acquired except by exploiting the sweat of men. There can be no
doubt that Christ, like ourselves, would have become reconciled to
wealth if then, as in our days, wealth were possible without exploitation—nay, really possible only without it. We shall have further
occasion to discuss why this was impossible in Christ's day and
for many centuries afterwards ; at present it is enough to know that
it *was* impossible, that the only choice lay between poverty and
wealth with exploitation.

Christ rendered the immortal service of having recognised this
alternative more clearly than anyone before Him, and of having
attacked exploitation with soul-stirring fervour. It was inevitable
that He should be crucified for what He did, for in the antagonism
between justice and the claims of civilisation the first always suc-
cumbs. It was inevitable that He should die, because He unrolled
the banner of true human love, freedom, and equality—in short, of
all the noblest sentiments of the human heart—nearly two thousand
years too soon ; too soon, that is, for Him, not for us : for dull-witted
humanity needed those two thousand years in order fully to understand what its martyr meant. For humanity Christ died not a day
too soon. There is, then, no contradiction between the Christian
ideas and what we are striving for ; the difference between the two
lies simply herein : that the first announcement of the idea of
equality was made in an age when the material conditions necessary
for the practical realisation of this divine idea did not yet exist,
whilst our endeavours signify the 'Incarnation of the Word,' the
fruit of the seed then cast into the mind of mankind. It cannot,
therefore, be said that the Christian work of emancipation has
really ' miscarried ' : there merely lie two thousand years between
the beginning and the completion of the work undertaken by Christ.

On account of the lateness of the hour the President here closed
the sitting, the debate standing adjourned until the next day.

CHAPTER XXIV
SECOND DAY
(Adjourned Discussion upon the first point on the Agenda)

LEOPOLD STOCKAU (*Centre*) re-opened the debate : I think that the preliminary question, whether our present endeavours after economic justice really are without any historical precedent, was exhaustively discussed yesterday and was answered in the negative. At least, I am authorised by yesterday's speakers of the opposite party to declare that they are fully convinced that the teaching of Christ differs in no essential point from that which is practically carried out in Freeland, and which we wish to make the common property of the whole world. We now come to the main subject of the first question for discussion—namely, to the inquiry why the former attempts to base human industry upon justice and freedom have been unsuccessful.

The answer to this question has already been suggested by the last speaker of yesterday. Former attempts miscarried because they aimed at establishing the equality of poverty : ours will succeed because it implies the equality of wealth. The equality of poverty would have produced stagnation in civilisation. Art and science, the two vehicles of progress, assume abundance and leisure ; they cannot exist, much less can they develop, if there are no persons who possess more than is sufficient to satisfy their merely animal wants. In former epochs of human culture it was impossible to create abundance and leisure for all—it was impossible because the means of production would not suffice to create abundance for all even if all without exception laboured with all their physical power ; and therefore much less would they have sufficed if the workers had indulged in the leisure which is as necessary to the development of the higher intellectual powers as abundance is to the maturing of the higher intellectual needs. And since it was not possible to guarantee to all the means of living a life worthy of human beings, it remained a sad, but not less inexorable, necessity of civilisation that the majority of men should be stinted even in the little that fell to their share, and that the booty snatched from the masses should be used to endow a minority who might thus attain to abundance and leisure.

A A

Servitude was a necessity of civilisation, because that alone made possible the development of the tastes and capacities of civilisation in at least a few individuals, while without it barbarism would have been the lot of all.

It is, moreover, a mistake to suppose that servitude is as old as the human race : it is only as old as civilisation. There was a time when servitude was unknown, when there were neither masters nor servants, and no one could exploit the labour of his fellow-men ; that was not the Golden, but the Barbaric, Age of our race. While man had not yet learnt the art of *producing* what he needed, but was obliged to be satisfied with gathering or capturing the voluntary gifts of nature, and every competitor was therefore regarded as an enemy who strove to get the same goods which each individual looked upon as his own special prey, so long did the struggle for existence among men necessarily issue in reciprocal destruction instead of subjection and exploitation. It did not then profit the stronger or the more cunning to force the weaker into his service—the competitor had to be killed ; and as the struggle was accompanied by hatred and superstition, it soon began to be the practice to eat the slain. A war of extermination waged by all against all, followed generally by cannibalism, was therefore the primitive condition of our race.

This first social order yielded, not to moral or philosophical considerations, but to a change in the character of labour. The man who first thought of sowing corn and reaping it was the deliverer of mankind from the lowest, most sanguinary stage of barbarism, for he was the first producer—he first practised the art not only of collecting, but of producing, food. When this art so improved as to make it possible to withdraw from the worker a part of his produce without positively exposing him to starvation, it was gradually found to be more profitable to use the vanquished as beasts of labour than as beasts for slaughter. Since slavery thus for the first time made it possible for at least a favoured few to enjoy abundance and leisure, it became the first promoter of higher civilisation. But civilisation is power, and so it came about that slavery or servitude in one form or another spread over the world.

But it by no means follows that the domination of servitude must, or even can, be perpetual. Just as cannibalism—which was the result of that minimum productiveness of human labour by means of which the severest toil sufficed to satisfy only the lowest animal needs of life—had to succumb to servitude as soon as the increasing productiveness of labour made any degree of abundance possible, so servitude—which is nothing else but the social result of that medium measure of productiveness by which labour is able to furnish abundance and leisure to a few but not to all—*must* also succumb to another, a higher social order, as soon as this medium measure of productiveness is surpassed, for from that moment servitude has ceased to be a necessity of civilisation, and has become a hindrance to its progress.

And for generations this has actually been the case. Since man has succeeded in making the forces of nature serviceable in production —since he has acquired the power of substituting the unlimited elemental forces for his own muscular force—there has been nothing to prevent his creating abundance and leisure for all; nothing except that obsolete social institution, servitude, which withholds from the masses the enjoyment of abundance and leisure. We not merely can, but we shall be compelled to make social justice an actual fact, because the new form of labour demands this as imperatively as the old forms of labour demanded servitude. Servitude, once the vehicle of progress, has become a hindrance to civilisation, for it prevents the full use of the means of civilisation at our disposal. As it reduces to a minimum the things consumed by most of our brethren, and therefore does not call into play more than a very small part of our present means of production, it compels us to restrict our productive labour within limits far less than those to which we should attain if an effective demand existed for what would then be the inevitable abundance of all kinds of wealth.

I sum up thus: Economic equality of rights could not be realised in earlier epochs of civilisation, because human labour was not then sufficiently productive to supply wealth to all, and equality therefore meant poverty for all, which would have been synonymous with barbarism. Economic equality of rights not only can but *must* now become a fact, because—thanks to the power which has been acquired of using the forces of nature—abundance and leisure have become possible for all; but the full utilisation of the now acquired means of civilisation is dependent on the condition that everyone enjoys the product of his own industry.

SATZA-MUNI (*Right*): I think it has been incontrovertibly shown that economic equality of rights was formerly impossible, and that it *can* now be realised; but why it *must* now be realised does not seem to me to have been yet placed beyond a doubt. So long as the productiveness of labour was small, the exploitation of man by man was a necessity of civilisation—that is plain; this is no longer the case, since the increased productiveness of labour is now capable of creating wealth enough for all—this is also as clear as day. But this only proves that economic justice has become possible, and there is a great difference between the possible and the necessary existence of a state of things. It has been said—and the experience of the exploiting world seems to justify the assertion —that full use cannot be made of the control which science and invention have given to men over the natural forces, while only a small part of the fruits of the thus increased effectiveness of labour is consumed; and if this can be irrefutably shown to be inherent in the nature of the thing, there remains not the least doubt that servitude in any form has become a hindrance to civilisation. For an institution that prevents us from making use of the means of civilisation which we possess is in and of itself a hindrance to civilisation; and since it restrains us from developing wealth to the fullest extent possible, and wealth and civilisation are power, so there can consequently be no doubt as to why and in what manner such an institution must in the course of economic evolution become obsolete. The advanced and the strong everywhere and necessarily imposes its laws and institutions upon the unprogressive and the weak; economic justice would therefore—though with bloodless means—as certainly and as universally supplant servitude as formerly servitude—when it was the institution which conferred a higher degree of civilisation and power—supplanted cannibalism. I have already admitted that the modern exploiting society is in reality unable to produce that wealth which would correspond to the now existing capacity of production : hence it follows as a matter of fact that the exploiting society is very much less advanced than one based upon the principle of economic justice, and it also quite as incontrovertibly follows that the former cannot successfully compete with the latter.

But before we have a right to jump to the conclusion that the principles of economic justice must necessarily be everywhere victorious, it must be shown that it is the essential nature of the exploiting system, and not certain transitory accidents connected with it, which makes it incapable of calling forth all the capacity of highly productive labour. Why is the existing exploiting society not able to call forth all this capacity? Because the masses are prevented from increasing their consumption in a degree corresponding to the increased power of production—because what is produced belongs not to the workers but to a few employers. Right. But, it would be answered, these few would make use of the produce themselves. To this the rejoinder is that that is impossible, because the few owners of the produce of labour can use—that is, actually consume—only the smallest portion of such an enormous amount of produce ; the surplus, therefore, must be converted into productive capital, the employment of which, however, is dependent upon the consumption of those things that are produced by it. Very true. No factories can be built if no one wants the things that would be manufactured in them. But have the masters really only this *one* way of disposing of the surplus—can they really make no other use of it ? In the modern world they do as a matter of fact make no other use of it. As a rule, their desire is to increase or improve the agencies engaged in labour—that is, to capitalise their profits— without inquiring whether such an increase or improvement is needed ; and since no such increase is needed, so over-production —that is, the non-disposal of the produce—is the necessary consequence. But because this is the fact at present, *must* it necessarily be so? What if the employers of labour were to perceive the true relation of things, and to find a way of creating an equilibrium by proportionally reducing their capitalisation and increasing their consumption ? If that were to happen, then, it must be admitted, all products would be disposed of, however much the productiveness of labour might increase. The consumption by the masses would be stationary as before ; but luxury would absorb all the surplus with exception of such reserves as were required to supply the means of production, which means would themselves be extraordinarily increased on account of the enormously increased demand caused by luxury.

And who will undertake to say that such a turn of affairs is altogether impossible ? The luxury of the few, it is said, cannot possibly absorb the immense surplus of modern productiveness. But why not ? Because a rich man has only one stomach and one body ; and, moreover, everyone cannot possibly have a taste for

luxury. Granted; luxury, in its modern forms, cannot possibly
consume more than a certain portion of the surplus produce of
modern labour. But are we shut up to these modern kinds of
luxury? What if the wealthy once more have recourse to a mode
of spending repeatedly indulged in by antiquity in order to dispose
of the accumulating proceeds of slave-labour? In ancient Egypt a
single king kept 200,000 men busy for thirty years building his
sepulchre, the great pyramid of Ghizeh. This same Pharaoh probably built also splendid palaces and temples with a no less profligate
expenditure of human labour, and amassed treasures in which infinite
labour was crystallised. Contemporaneously with him, there were
other Egyptian magnates, priests, and warriors in no small number,
who sought and found in similar ways employment for the labour
of their slaves. If the luxury of the living did not consume enough,
then costly spices, drink-offerings and burnt-offerings were lavished
upon the dead, and thus the difficulty of disposing of the accumulated produce of labour was still further lightened. And this succeeded admirably. The Egyptian slave received a few onions and a
handful of parched corn for food, a loin-cloth for clothing; and yet,
notwithstanding a comparatively highly developed productiveness
of the labour of countless slaves exploited by a few masters, there
was no over-production. In ancient India the men in power
excavated whole ranges of hills into temples, covered with the most
exquisite sculptures, in which an infinite amount of labour was
consumed; in ancient Rome the lords of the world ate nightingales'
tongues, or instituted senseless spectacles, in order to find employment for the superfluous labour of countless slaves who, despite the
considerable productiveness of labour, were kept in a condition of the
deepest misery. And it answered. Why should not such a course
answer in modern times? Because, thanks to the control we
have acquired over nature, the productiveness of labour has become
infinitely greater. Labour may have become infinitely more productive; indeed, I think it probable that it is no longer possible for
the maddest prodigality of the few wealthy to give *full* employment
to the whole of the labour-energy at present existing without admitting the masses to share in the consumption; but it would be
possible for the wealthy to consume a very large portion of the
possible produce. Then why does the modern exploiting society
build no pyramids, no rock palaces; why do the lords of labour

institute no costly cultus of the dead; why do they not eat nightingales' tongues, and keep the exploited populace busy with circus
spectacles and mock sea-fights? They could indulge in these and
countless other things, if they only discovered that the surplus must
be consumed and not capitalised. But as long as they continue to
multiply the instruments of labour, and only the instruments of
labour, so long are they simply increasing over-production, and can
become richer only in proportion as the consumption accidentally
increases. As soon, however, as they adopt the above-mentioned
expedient, the connection between their wealth and the lot of the
masses is broken. Why does not this happen?

I hope it is not necessary for me expressly to assert that I
am far from wishing for such a turn in affairs; rather, I should
look upon it as the greatest misfortune that could befall mankind,
for it would mean that, despite the enormously increased productiveness of labour, exploitation was not necessarily a hindrance
to civilisation, and consequently would not necessarily be superseded
by economic justice. But Confucius says rightly, that what is to be
deplored is not always to be regarded as impossible or even as only
improbable.

JOHN BELL (*Centre*): The last speaker, who in other respects
shows himself to be a profound thinker, overlooks the fact that the
completest utilisation of the existing means of civilisation and the
corresponding evolution of wealth are not the only determining
criteria in the struggle for existence among nations. The strength
of a nation that employs its wealth in fostering the higher development of the millions of its subjects, will ultimately become very
different from that of a nation which consumes an equal amount
of wealth merely in increasing the enjoyment, nay, the senseless
luxury, of the ruling classes.

ARISTID-KOLOTRONI (*Centre*): The last speaker is correct in
what he says, although it may be objected that the wealthy are not
necessarily obliged to consume their wealth in senseless luxury:
they might just as well gratify their pride by boundless benevolence,
accompanied by enormous expenditure in all imaginable kinds of
scientific, artistic and other institutions of national utility. But I
think we are getting away from the main point, which is: is such a
turn of affairs possible? The fact that it has not occurred, despite
all the evils of over-production, that on the contrary a continually

growing desire to capitalise all surplus profits dominates the modern world, should save us from a fear of such a contingency.

KURT OLAFSOHN (*Freeland*): I must agree with Satza-Muni, the honourable member for Japan, so far as to admit that the bare fact that such a contingency has not yet been realised cannot set our minds completely at rest. The consideration advanced by the two following speakers as to whether an exploiting society in which the consumption by the wealthy increases indefinitely must, under all circumstances, succumb to the influence of the free order of society, appears arbitrary and inconclusive. I venture to think that the free society does not possess the aggressive character of the exploiting society, and that therefore the latter, even though it should prove to be decidedly the weaker of the two, may continue to exist for some time side by side with the other so far as it does not itself recognise the necessity of passing over to the other. And this recognition would be materially delayed by the fact that the ruling classes profit by the continuance of exploitation. The change could then be effected universally only by sanguinary conflicts, whilst we lay great stress upon the winning over of the wealthy to the side of the reformers. It is the enormous burden of over-production that opens the eyes of exploiters to the folly of their action ; should this spur be lacking, the beneficial revolution would be materially delayed. The member for Japan is also correct in saying that repeatedly in the course of history the surplus production which could not be consumed in a reasonable manner has led the exploiting lords of labour to indulge in senseless methods of consumption. It may therefore be asked whether what has repeatedly happened cannot repeat itself once more ; but a thorough investigation of the subject will show that the question must be answered with a decided *No*.

No, it *can* never happen again that full employment for highly productive labour will be found except under a system of economic justice ; for since it last occurred, a new factor has entered into the world which makes it for all times an impossibility. This factor is the mobilisation of capital and the consequent separation of the process of capital-formation from the process of capital-using. Anyone who in Ancient Egypt or Ancient Rome had surplus production to dispose of and wished to invest it profitably, therefore in the form of aids to labour, must either himself have had a need of aids to labour, or must have found someone else who had such a need and

was on that account prepared to take his surplus, at interest of
course. It was impossible for anyone to invest capital unless someone could make use of such capital ; and if this latter contingency
did not occur, it was a matter of course that the possessor of the
surplus production, unusable as capital, should seek some other
mode of consuming it. Many such modes offered themselves, dif-
fering according to the nature of the several kinds of exploiting
society. If the constitution of the commonwealth was a patriarchal
one, the labour which had become more productive would be utilised
in improving the condition of the serfs, in mitigating the severity of
their labour. In a commonwealth of a more military character the
increasing productiveness of labour would serve to enlarge the non-
labouring, weapon-bearing class. If—as was always the case when
civilisation advanced—the bond between lord and serf became laxer,
the lord merely increased his luxury. But, in any case, the surplus
which could not be utilised in the augmentation or improvement of
labour was consumed, and there could therefore be no over-production. As now, however, the possessor of surplus produce can—even
when no one has a need of his savings—obtain what he wants,
viz. interest, he has ceased to concern himself as to whether that
surplus is really required for purposes of production, but is anxious
to capitalise even that which others can make as little use of as he
can.

And this, in reality, is the result of the mobilisation of capital.
Since this discovery has been made, all capital is as it were thrown
into one lump, the profits of capital added to it, and the whole
divided among the capitalists. No one needs my savings, they are
absolutely superfluous, and can bear no fruit of any kind ; nevertheless I receive my interest, for the mobilisation of capital enables me
to share in the profits of profit-bearing, that is, of really working,
capital. I deposit my savings at interest in a bank, or I buy a share
or a bill and thereby raise the price of all other shares or bills
correspondingly, and thus make it appear as if the capital which
they represent had been increased, while in truth it has remained
unchanged. And the produce of this working capital has not increased through the apparent addition of my capital ; the interest
paid on the whole amount of capital including mine is not more
than that paid on the capital before mine was added to it. The
addition of my superfluous capital has lowered the *rate* of interest,

or, what comes to the same thing, has raised the price of a demand for the same rate of interest as before ; but even a diminished rate of interest is better than no interest at all. I continue, therefore, to save and capitalise, despite the fact that my savings cannot be used productively as capital ; nay, the above-mentioned diminution of the rate of interest impels me, under certain circumstances, to save yet more carefully, that is, to diminish my consumption in proportion as my savings become less remunerative. It is evident that my surplus produce cannot find any productive employment at all, yet there is no way out of this circle of over-production. Luxury cannot come in as a relief, because the absence of any profitable employment for the surplus renders that surplus valueless, and the ultimate result is the non-production of the surplus. Only exceptionally is there an actual production of unconsumable and, consequently, valueless things ; the almost unbroken rule is that the things which no one can use, and which therefore are valueless, will not be produced. Since the employer leaves to the worker only a bare subsistence, and can apply to capitalising purposes only so much as is required for the production of consumable commodities, every other application of the profits being excluded by capitalism, he cannot produce more than is enough to meet these two demands. If he attempts to produce more, the inevitable result is not increased wealth, but a crisis.

We have, therefore, no ground to fear that the ruling classes will again, as in pre-capitalistic epochs, be able to enjoy the fruits of the increasing productiveness of labour without allowing the working masses to participate in that enjoyment. Capitalism, though by no means—as some socialistic writers have represented—the cause of exploitation, is the obstacle which deprives modern society of every other escape from the fatal grasp of over-production but that of a transition to economic justice. It is the last stage in human economics previous to that of social justice. From capitalism there is no way forward but towards social justice ; for capitalism is at one and the same time one of the most effectual provocatives of productivity and the bond which indissolubly connects the increase of the effective production of wealth with consumption.

WILHELM OHLMS (*Right*): Then how is it that the Freeland institutions, which are to become those of the whole of civilised mankind, have broken with capitalism ?

HENRI FARR (*Freeland*): So far as by capitalism is to be understood the conversion of any actual surplus production into working capital, we in Freeland are far from having broken with it. On the contrary, we have developed it to the utmost, for much more fully than in the exploiting capitalistic society are our savings at all times at the disposal of any demand for capital that may arise. But our method of accumulating and mobilising capital is a very different and much more perfect one : the solidarity of interest of the saver with that of the employer of capital takes the place of interest. This form of capitalism can never lead to over-production, for under it—as in the pre-capitalistic epoch—it is the demand for capital that gives the first impulse to the creation of capital. But that this kind of capitalisation is impracticable in an exploiting society needs no proof. For such a society there is no other means of making the spontaneously accumulating capital serviceable to production than that of interest ; and as soon as the mobilisation of capital dissolves the immediate personal connection between saver and employer of capital, creditor and debtor, interest inevitably impels to over-production, from which there is no escape except in economic justice— or relapse into barbarism. [Loud and general applause.]

The PRESIDENT here asked if anyone else wished to speak upon point 1 of the Agenda ; and, as no one rose, he declared the discussion upon this subject closed.

The Congress next proceeded to discuss point 2 :—

Is not the success of the Freeland institutions to be attributed merely to the accidental and therefore probably transient co-operation of specially favourable circumstances ; or do those institutions rest upon conditions universally present and inherent in human nature ?

GEORGE DARE (*Right*) opened the debate : We have the splendid success of a first attempt to establish economic justice so tangibly before us in Freeland, that there is no need to ask whether such an attempt *can* succeed. It is another question whether it *must* succeed, and that everywhere, because it has succeeded in this one case. For the circumstances of Freeland are exceptional in more than one respect. Not to mention the pre-eminent abilities, the enthusiasm and the spirit of self-sacrifice which marked the men who founded this fortunate commonwealth, and some of whom still stand at its head, men such as it is certain will not everywhere be

found ready at hand, it must not be overlooked that this country is
more lavishly endowed by nature than most others, and that a
broad band of desert and wilderness protected it—at least at first—
from any disturbing foreign influence. If men of talent, enjoying
the unqualified confidence of their colleagues, are able on a soil
where every seed bears fruit a hundredfold to effect the miracle of
conjuring inexhaustible wealth for millions out of nothing, of exter-
minating misery and vice, of developing the arts and sciences to the
fullest extent,—all this is, in my opinion, no proof that ordinary men,
given perhaps to squabbling with each other, and to being mutually
distrustful, will achieve the like or even approximately similar
results on poorer land and in the midst of the turmoil of the world's
competitive struggle. My doubts upon this point will appear the
more reasonable when it is remembered that in America we have
witnessed hundreds upon hundreds of social experiments which
have all either proved to be in a greater or less degree miserable
fiascos, or at least have only assumed the proportion of isolated
successful industrial enterprises. It is true that some of our efforts
at revolutionising modern society have had remarkable pecuniary
results ; but that has been all : a new, practicable foundation of the
social organisation they have not furnished, not even in germ. I
wished to give expression to these doubts ; and before allowing ourselves to be intoxicated by the example of Freeland, I wished to invite
you to a sober consideration of the question whether that which is
successful in Freeland must necessarily succeed in the rest of the
world.

THOMAS JOHNSTON (*Freeland*) : The previous speaker makes a
mistake when he ascribes the success of the Freeland undertaking
to exceptionally favourable conditions. That our soil is more
fertile than that of most other parts of the world is, it is true, a
permanent advantage, which, however, accrues to us merely in the
item of cost of carriage ; for, after allowing for this, the advantage
of the fertility of our soil is equally shared by all of you everywhere,
wherever railways and steam-vessels can be made use of. Isolation
from the market of the world by broad deserts was at first an
advantage ; but it would now be a disadvantage if we had not made
ourselves masters of those deserts. And as to the abilities of the
Freeland government, I must—not out of modesty, but in the
name of truth—decline the compliments paid us. We are not

abler than others whom you might find by the dozen in any civilised country. Only in one point were we in advance of others, namely, in perceiving what was the true basis of human economics. But the advantage which this gave us was only a temporary one, for at present you have men in abundance in every part of the civilised world who have become as wise as we are even in this matter. The advantage we derived from being the first in this movement was that we have enjoyed for nearly a generation the happiness in which you are only now preparing to participate. Freeland's advantages are due simply to the date of its foundation, and have now lost their importance. Now that the establishment of a world-wide freedom is contemplated, there will no longer be any national advantages or disadvantages. What belongs to us belongs to you also, and what is wonderful is that we as well as you will become richer in proportion as each of us is obliged to allow all the others to share quickly, easily, and fully our own wealth. We have suffered from being compelled to enjoy our wealth alone, and we shall become richer as soon as you share that wealth ; and in the same way will you become richer as others share in your wealth. For herein lies the solidarity of interest that is associated with true freedom, that every existing advantage in production—such as wealth is—can be the more fully utilised the wider the circle of those who enjoy its fruits.

That those attempts, of which the last speaker spoke, all miscarried is due to the fact that they were all based upon wrong principles. The only thing they have in common with what we have carried out in Freeland, and what you now wish to imitate, is the endeavour to find a remedy for the misery of the exploiting world ; but the remedy which we seek is a different one from that which they sought, and in that—not in exceptional advantages which we may have had—lies the cause of our success and of their miscarriage.

For it was not by the aid of economic justice that they sought to attain their end ; they sought deliverance from the dungeon of exploitation, whether by a way which did not lead out of it, or by a way which, though it led out of that dungeon, yet led into another and more dreadful one. In none of those American or other social experiments, from the Quaker colonies to the Icaria of Cabet, was the full and undiminished produce of labour ever assured to the worker; on the contrary, the produce belonged either to small capitalists who, while themselves taking part in the undertaking as workers, shared the produce according to the amount of capital they had invested, or it belonged to the whole as a body, who as such had a despotic right of disposal over both the labour and the produce of the labour of every individual. These reformers were, without exception, associated small capitalists or communists. They were able, if they had specially good fortune, or if they were under specially able direction, to achieve transient success ; but a revolution of the current industrial system by them was not to be thought of.

(*End of Second Day's Debate*)

CHAPTER XXV
Third Day
(*Debate on Point 2 of the Agenda, continued*)

Johann Storm (*Right*): I think that the lack of any analogy between the frequent attempts to save society undertaken by small capitalists or communists and the institutions of Freeland has been made sufficiently clear. I think also that we are convinced that the exceptional external advantages, which may have at any rate favoured and assisted the success of Freeland, are not of a kind to suggest a fear that our proposed work will fail for the want of such advantages. But we do not yet know whether the success of social reform is exposed to danger from any conditions inherent in human nature, and therefore universally to be met with. We have, in our discussion upon the first point of the agenda, established the fact that, thanks to the control which has been acquired over the forces of nature, exploitation has become an obstacle to civilisation, and its removal a necessity of civilisation. But severe criticism cannot be satisfied with this. For is everything which is necessary to the progress of civilisation consequently also possible ? What if economic justice, though an extraordinary vehicle of civilisation, were for some reason unfortunately impracticable ? What if that marvellous prosperity, which astonishes us so much in Freeland, were only a transient phenomenon, and carried in itself the germ of decay, despite, nay, because of, its fabulous magnitude ? In a word, what if mankind could not permanently, and as a whole, participate in that progress the necessary condition of which is economic justice ?

The evidence to the contrary, already advanced, culminates in the proposition that the exploitation of man by man was necessary only so long as the produce of human labour did not suffice to provide abundance and leisure for all. But what if other influences made exploitation and servitude necessary, influences the operation of which could not be stayed by the increased productiveness of labour, perhaps could never be stayed? The most powerful hindrance to the permanent establishment of a condition of economic justice, with its consequences of happiness and wealth, is recognised by the anxious student of the future in the danger of over-population. But as this is a special point in the agenda, I, like my colleagues who have already spoken, will postpone what occurs to my mind upon the subject. There are, however, other and not less important difficulties. Can a society, which lacks the stimulus of self-interest, permanently exist and make progress, and succeed in making public spirit and rational enlightenment take the place thoroughly, and with equal effectiveness, of self-interest? Does not the same apply to private property? Self-interest and private property are not altogether set aside by the institutions of Freeland. I readily admit this, but they are materially restricted. Even under the rule of economic justice the individual is himself responsible for the greater or less degree of his prosperity—the connection between what he himself does and what he gets is not altogether dissolved ; but as the commonwealth unconditionally protects every man in all cases against want, therefore against the ultimate consequences of his own mistakes or omissions, the stimulating influence of self-responsibility is very materially diminished. Just so we see private property abolished, though not entirely, yet in its most important elements. The earth and all the natural forces inherent in it are declared ownerless ; the means of production are common property ; will that, can that, remain so everywhere, and for all time, without disastrous consequences ? Will public spirit permanently fill the office of that affectionate far-seeking care which the owner bestows upon the property for which he alone is responsible ? Will not the gladsome absence of care, which has certainly hitherto been brilliantly conspicuous in Freeland, eventually degenerate into frivolity and neglect of that for which no one in particular is responsible ?

The fact that this has not yet happened may perhaps be due —for it is not yet a generation since this commonwealth was founded—to the dominant enthusiasm that marked the beginning. New brooms, it is said, sweep clean. The Freelander sees the eyes of the whole world fixed upon him and his doings ; he feels that he is still the pioneer of new institutions ; he is proud of those institutions, every worker here to the last man holds himself responsible for the way and manner in which he fulfils the apostolate of universal freedom to which he is called. Will this continue permanently : in particular, will the whole human race feel and act thus ? I doubt it ; at least, I am not fully convinced that it must necessarily be so. And what if it is not so ? What if, we will not say all, but many nations show themselves to be unable to dispense with the stimulus of want-inspired self-interest, the lure of unconditioned private property, without sinking into mental stagnation and physical indolence ? These are questions to which we now require answers.

RICHARD HELD (*Centre*) : The previous speaker finds that self-interest and private property are such powerful spurs to activity that, without their full and unrestricted influence, permanent human progress is scarcely conceivable, and that it is extremely uncertain whether public spirit would be an effective substitute for them. I go much farther. I assert that without these two means of activity no commonwealth can be expected to thrive, unless human nature is radically changed, or labour ceases to require effort. Every attempt in the domain of economics to substitute public spirit or any other ethical motive for self-interest must immediately, and not merely in its ultimate issue, prove an ignominious fiasco. I think it quite unnecessary to give special proof of this; but for the very reason that self-interest and its correlative, private property, are the best incitements to labour, and can be effectively replaced by no surrogate—for this very reason, I contend, are the institutions of economic justice immensely superior in this respect to those of the exploiting system of industry. For they alone really give full play to self-interest and the right of private ownership : the exploiting system only falsely pretends to do this.

For servitude is, in truth, the negation of self-interest. Self-interest assumes that the worker serves his ' own ' interest by the trouble he takes ; does this apply to the *régime* of exploitation : does the servant work for his *own* profit ? With reference to the question of self-interest, anyone who would show that economic justice was less advantageous than servitude would have to assert that labour was the most productive and profitable when the worker produced, *not* for his own, but for some one else's profit. But it will perhaps be objected that the employer produces for his own profit. Right. But, apart from the fact that this, strictly speaking, has nothing to do with the stimulating effect of self-interest upon labour—for here it is not the profit of his own but of some one else's labour that comes in question—it is clear that a system which secures to only a minority the profit of work must be infinitely less influential than the one we are now considering, which secures the profit to every worker. In reality the exploiting world, with very few exceptions, knows only men who labour without getting the profit themselves, and men who do not labour themselves yet get profit from labour; in the exploiting world to labour for one's own profit is quite an accidental occurrence. With what right, then, does exploitation dare to plume itself upon making use of *self*-interest as a motive to labour? *Some one else's* interest is the right description of the motive to labour that comes into play under exploitation; and that this should prove itself to be more effective than the self-interest which economic justice has to introduce into the modern world as a novelty it would be somewhat difficult to demonstrate.

It is nearly the same with private property. What boundless presumption it is to claim for a system which robs ninety-nine per cent. of mankind of all and every certainty of possessing property, and leaves to them nothing that they can call their own but the air they breathe—what presumption it is to claim for such a system that it makes use of private property as a stimulus to human activity, and to urge this claim as against another system which converts all men without exception into owners of property, and in fact secures to them unconditionally, and without diminution, all that they are able in any way to produce! Or does, perhaps, the superiority of the 'private property' of the exploiting system lie in the fact that it extends to things which the owner has *not* himself produced? Unquestionably the adherents of the old system have no clear conception of what is *mine* and what is *thine*. What properly belongs to *me*? 'Everything you can take from anyone,' would be their only answer, if they were but to speak honestly. Because this appropriation of the property of others has, in the course of thousands of years,

B B

been formulated into certain established rules, consecrated by cruel necessity, the adherents of the old system have completely lost the natural conception of private property, the conception which is inherent in the nature of things. It passes their comprehension that, though force can possess and make use of whom it pleases, yet the free and untrammelled use of one's own powers is the inalienable property of everyone, and that consequently any political or social system which overrides this inalienable personal right of every man is based, not upon property, but upon robbery. This robbery may be necessary, nay, useful—we have seen that for thousands of years it actually was useful—but ' property ' it never will be, and whoever thinks it is has forgotten what property is.

After what has been said, it seems to me scarcely necessary to spend many words in dispelling the fear that frivolity or carelessness in the treatment of the means of production will result from a modified form of property. As to frivolity, it will suffice to ask whether hopeless misery has proved itself to be such a superior stimulus to economic prudence as to make it dangerous to supersede it by a personal responsibility which, though it lacks the spur of misery, is of a thoroughly comprehensive character. And as to the fear lest carelessness in the treatment of the means of production should prevail, this fear could have been justified only if in the former system the workers were owners of the means of production. Private property in these will, it is true, not be given to them by the new system, but instead of it the undiminished enjoyment of the produce of those means ; and he whose admiration of the beauties of the existing system does not go so far as to consider the master's rod a more effective stimulus to foresight than the profit of the workers may rest satisfied that even in this respect things will be better and not worse.

CHARLES PRUD (*Right*): I do not at all understand how the previous speaker can dispute the fact that in the former system self-interest is that which conditions the quantity of work. No one denies that the workers must give up a part of the profit of their labour ; but another part remains theirs, hence they labour for their own profit, though not exclusively so. At any rate they *must* labour if they do not wish to starve, and one would think that this stimulus is the most effectual one possible. So much as to the denial that self-interest is the moving spring of so-called exploited labour. As to the attack upon the conception of property advanced by those of us who defend, not exactly the existing evil condition of things, but a rational and consistent reform of it, I would with all modesty venture to remark that our sense of justice was satisfied because no one compelled the worker to share with the employer. He made a contract as a free man with the employer . . . [General laughter.] You may laugh, but it is so. In countries that are politically free nothing prevents the worker from labouring on his own account alone; it is, therefore, at any rate incorrect to call the portion which he surrenders to the employer robbery.

BÉLA SZÉKELY (*Centre*) : It seems to me to be merely a dispute about a word which the previous speaker has attempted to settle. He calls wages a part of the profit of production. It may be that here and there the workers really receive a part of the profit as wages, or as an addition to the wages. With us, and, if I am rightly informed, in the country of the speaker also, this was not generally customary. We rather paid the workers, who were quite unconcerned about the profits of their work, an amount sufficient to maintain them ; profits—and losses when there were any—fell exclusively to the lot of the production, the employers. He could have said with nearly as much justice that his oxen or his horses participated in the profits of production. When I say ' nearly,' I mean that this could as a rule be said *more* justly of oxen and horses, for, while those useful creatures are for the most part better fed when their labour has enriched their master, this happens very rarely.in the case of our two-legged rational beasts of labour.

Then the previous speaker made hunger absolutely identical with self-interest. The masses *must* labour or starve. Certainly. But the slave must labour or be whipped : thus this strange logic would make it appear that the slave is also stimulated to labour by self-interest. Or will the arguer fall back upon the assertion that self-interest refers merely to the acquisition of material goods ? That would be false ; self-interest does not after all either more or less prompt men to avoid the whip than to appease hunger. But I will not argue about such trifles : we will drop the rod and the whip as symbols of activity stimulated by self-interest. But how does it stand with those slave-holders who—probably in the interest of the ' freedom of labour '—do not whip their lazy slaves,' but allow them to starve ? Is it not evident that the previous speaker would, under their *régime*, set self-interest upon the throne as the inciter to work? That hunger is a very effectual means of *compulsion*, a more effectual one than the whip, no one will deny; hence it has everywhere superseded the latter, and very much to the advantage of the employer. But self-interest? The very word itself implies that the profit of the labour is the worker's own. So much as to hunger.

And now as to the security against the injustice of exploitation, for my own part I do not understand this at all. The workers were ' free,' nothing compelled them to produce for other men's advantage? Yes, certainly, nothing but the trifle—hunger. They could leave it alone, if they wished to starve! Just the ' freedom ' which the slave has. If he does not mind being whipped, there is nothing to compel him to work for his master. The bonds in which the ' free ' masses of the exploiting society languish are tighter and more painful than the chains of the slave. The word ' robbery ' does not please the previous speaker? It is, indeed, a hard and hateful word ; but the ' robber ' is not the individual exploiter, but the exploiting society, and this was formerly, in the bitter need of the struggle for existence, compelled to practise this robbery. Is the slaughter in battle any the less homicide because it is done at the command, not of the individual, but of the State, which is frequently acting under compulsion? It will be said that this kind of killing is not forbidden by the penal law, nay, that it is enjoined by our duty to our country, and that only forbidden kinds of killing can be called ' homicide.' *Juridically* that is quite correct ; and if it occurred to anyone to bring a charge of killing in battle before a court of justice he would certainly be laughed at. But he would make himself quite as ludicrous who, because killing in war is allowed, would deny that such killing was homicide if the point under consideration was, not whether the act was juridically penal, but how to define homicide as a mode of violently putting a man to death. So exploitation is no robbery in the eye of the penal law ; but if every appropriation to one's self of the property of another can be called robbery—and this is all that the present case is concerned with— then is robbery and nothing else the basis of every exploiting society, of the modern ' free ' society no less than of the ancient or mediæval slave-holding or serf-keeping societies. [Long-continued applause, in which Messrs. Johann Storm and Charles Prud both joined.]

JAMES BROWN (*Right*): Our colleague from Hungary has so pithily described the true characteristics of self-interest and property in the exploiting society, that nothing more is to be said upon that subject. But even if it is correct that these two motive springs of labour can be placed in their right position only by economic justice, it still remains to be asked whether the only way of doing this— namely, the organisation of free, self-controlling, unexploited labour —will prove to be everywhere and without exception practicable. Little would be gained by the solemn proclamation of the principle that every worker is his own master, and the complete concession to all workers of a right of disposal of the means of production, if those workers were to prove incapable of making an adequate use of such rights. The final and decisive question, therefore, is whether the workers of the future will always and everywhere exhibit that discipline, that moderation, that wisdom, which are indispensable to the organisation of truly profitable and progressive production? The exploiting industry has a routine which has taken many thousands of years for its development. The accumulated experience of untold generations teaches the employer under the old system how to proceed in order to control a crowd of servants compelled dumbly to obey. He, nevertheless, frequently fails, and only too often are his plans wrecked by the insubordination of those under him. The leaders of the workers' associations of the future have as good as no experience to guide them in the choice of modes of association ; they will have as masters those whom they should command, and yet we are told that success is certain, nay, success must be certain if the associated free society is not to be convulsed to its very foundations. For whilst the exploiting society confines the responsibility for the fate of the separate undertakings to those undertakings themselves, the so-often-mentioned solidarity of interests in the free society most indissolubly connects the weal and the woe of the community with that of every separate undertaking. I shall be glad to be taught better ; but until I am, I cannot help seeing in what has just been said grounds for fear which the experience of Freeland until now is by no means calculated to dissipate. The workers of Freeland have understood how to organise and discipline themselves: does it follow from this that the workers everywhere will be equally intelligent ?

MIGUEL SPADA (*Left*) : I will confine myself to a brief answer to the question with which the previous speaker closed. It certainly does not follow that the attempt to organise and discipline labour without capitalist employers must necessarily succeed among *all* nations simply because it has succeeded among the Freelanders, and will unquestionably succeed among numerous other peoples. It is possible, nay, probable, that some nations may show themselves incapable of making use of this highest kind of spontaneous activity; so much the worse for them. But I hope that no one will conclude from this that those peoples who are not thus incapable— even if they should find themselves in the minority—ought to refrain from such activity. The more capable will then become the instructors of the less capable. Should the latter, however, show themselves to be, not merely temporarily incapable, but permanently intractable, then will they disappear from the face of the earth, just as intractable cannibals must disappear when they come into contact with civilised nations. The delegate who proposed the question may rest assured that the nation to which he belongs will not be numbered among the incapable ones.

VLADIMUR TONOF (*Freeland*) : The honourable member from England (Brown) has formed an erroneous conception of the diffi· culties of the organisation and discipline now under consideration, as well as of the importance of any miscarriage of individual enterprises in a free community. As to the former matter, I wish to show that in the organisation of associated capital, which is well known to have been carried out for centuries, there is an instructive and by no means to be despised foreshadowing of associated labour, so far as relates to the modes of management and superintendence to be adopted in such cases. Of course there are profound distinctions which have to be taken into consideration ; but it has been proved, and it is in the nature of things, that the differences are all in favour of associated labour. In this latter, for instance, there will not be found the chief sins of associations of capitalists—namely, lack of technical knowledge and indifference to the objects of the undertaking on the part of the shareholders ; and therefore it is possible completely to dispense with those useless and crippling kinds of control-apparatus with which the statutes of the companies of capitalists are ballasted. As a rule, the single shareholder understands nothing of the business of his company, and quite as seldom dreams of interfering in the affairs of the company otherwise than by receiving his dividends. Notwithstanding, *he* is the master of the undertaking, and in the last resort it is his vote that decides the fate of it; what provisions are therefore necessary in order to protect this shareholder from the possible consequences of his own ignorance, credulity, and negligence! The associated workers, on the contrary, are fully acquainted with the nature of their undertaking, the success of which is their chief material interest, and is, without exception, recognised as such by them. This is a decisive advantage. Or does anyone see a special difficulty in the fact that the workers are placed under the direction of persons whose appointment depends upon the votes of the men who are to be directed? On the same ground might the authority of all elective political and other posts be questioned. The directors have no means of *compelling* obedience? A mistake; they lack only the right of arbitrarily dismissing the insubordinate. But this right is not possessed by many other bodies dependent upon the discipline and the reasonable co-operation of their members; nevertheless, or rather on this very account, such bodies preserve better discipline than those confederations in which obedience is maintained by the severest forcible measures. It is true that where there is no forcible compulsion discipline cannot so easily pass over into tyranny; but this is, in truth, no evil. Moreover, the directors of free associations of workers can put into force a means of compulsion, the power of which is more unqualified and absolute than that of the most unmitigated tyranny: the all-embracing reciprocal control of the associates, whose influence even the most obstinate cannot permanently withstand. It is certainly indispensable that the workers as a whole, or a large majority of them, should be reasonable men whose intelligence is sufficient to enable them to understand their own interests. But this is the first and foremost *conditio sine quâ non* of the establishment of economic justice. That economic justice—up to the present the highest outcome of the evolution of mankind—is suitable only to men who have raised themselves out of the lowest stage of brutality, is in no respect open to question. Hence it follows that nations and individuals who have not yet reached this stage of development must be educated up to it; and this educational work is not difficult if it be but undertaken with a will. We doubt that it could altogether fail anywhere, if undertaken seriously and in the right way.

And now let us look at the second side of the question which has been thrown out. Is it correct that, in consequence of the solidarity of interests which exists in the free community, the weal and woe of the whole are indissolubly bound up with the success of any individual undertaking? If it be meant by this that in such a community everyone is interested in the weal of everyone else, and consequently in the success of every undertaking, then it fully expresses what is the fact; but—and this was evidently the meaning of the speaker—if it is meant that the weal of such a community is dependent upon the success of every single undertaking of its members, then it is utterly groundless. If an undertaking does not thrive, its members leave it and turn to one that is more prosperous—that is all. On the other hand, this mobility of labour, bound up with the solidarity of interests, protects the free community from the worse consequences of actual miscarriage. If there should be an ill-advised choice of directors, the unqualified officials can do but relatively little mischief; they see themselves— that is, the undertaking under their control—promptly forsaken by the workers, and the losses are insignificant because confined within a small area. In fact, this mobility proves itself to be in the last resort the most effectual corrective of all kinds of mistakes, the agency by which all the defective forms of organisation and the less capable minds are thrust aside and automatically superseded by better. For the undertakings which, from any cause whatever, fail to thrive are always in a comparatively short time absorbed by better, without involving in ruin—as happens under the exploiting system of society—those who were engaged in the former undertakings. Hence it is not necessary that these free organisations should in all cases strike the highest note at the very beginning in order eventually to attain to perfect order and excellence; for in the friendly competition what is defective rapidly vanishes from sight, being merged in what is proved to be superior, which then alone holds the field.

JOHN KILMEAN (*Right*): Let us grant, then, that the associations of free labour are organised as well as, or better than, the capitalists' associations of the old exploiting world. Is there, nevertheless, no ground to fear that they will exhibit serious defects in comparison with undertakings conducted by individual employers? That self-interest, so far as concerns the workers themselves, can for the first time have full play in stimulating activity is true; but with respect to the management the reverse is the fact. At least one would think that the interest of the individual undertaker in the success of the business belonging to him alone must be a keener one than that of directors, who are nothing more than elected functionaries whose industrial existence is in no way indissolubly connected with the undertaking. The advantages which the private undertaking conducted by the individual proprietor has hitherto exhibited over the joint-stock company, it must, in the nature of things, also have over the free associations.

THEODOR YPSILANTI (*Freeland*) : Let us assume, for the present, that this is so. But are the advantages of the individual undertaker over the joint-stock company really so great ? It is not necessary to theorise for and against, since practice has long ago pronounced its verdict. And what is this ? Simply that the joint-stock undertaking has gradually surpassed, nay, in the most important and the most extensive branches of business totally superseded, the much-lauded private undertaking. It can be confidently asserted that in every kind of undertaking which is large enough to support the—certainly somewhat costly—apparatus of a joint-stock company, the joint-stock company is undisputed master of the field, so that there remains to the private undertaking, as its domain, nothing more than the dwarf concerns with which our free society does not meddle. It cannot be said that this is due to the larger money power of the combined capital, for even relatively small undertakings, whose total capital is many times less than that of a great many private millionaires, prefer, I may say choose exclusively, the joint-stock form. It is quite as great a mistake to ascribe this fact to the reluctance of private capitalists to run the risk involved in certain undertakings, and to their consequent preference for joint-stock undertakings ; for, in the first place, it is generally the least risky branches of business in which the joint-stock form most exclusively prevails ; and in the second place, we see only too often that individual capitalists place enormous sums in single companies, and even found undertakings in a joint-stock form with their own capital. But a decisive proof of the superiority of the joint-stock company is the universal fact that the great capitalists are everywhere entrusting the control of their property to joint-stock companies. If the account-books of the wealthy in every civilised exploiting country were to be examined, it would

unquestionably be found that at least nine-tenths of the capitalists
had employed the greatest part of their capital which was not
invested in land in the purchase of shares. This, however, simply
shows that the rich prefer not to manage their wealth themselves,
but to allow it to be managed by joint-stock companies.

The orthodox theory, spun out of the flimsiest fictions, is not
able to do anything with this fact ; it therefore ignores it, or seeks
to explain it by a number of fresh fictions, such as the fable of
divided risk, or some other similar subterfuge. The truth is that
the self-interest of the employer has very little to do with the real
direction of the businesses belonging to him—so far as concerns
great undertakings—for not the employer, but specially appointed
wage-earners, are, as a rule, the actual directors ; the alleged
advantage of the private undertaking, therefore, does not exist at
all. On the other hand, the undertaking of the private capitalist is
at a very heavy disadvantage in competition with that of the joint-
stock company, inasmuch as the latter almost always attracts by
far the greater amount of intelligence. The capitalist, even the
largest, is on the average no cleverer than other men—that is,
generally speaking, he is *not* particularly clever. It may, perhaps,
be objected that he would scarcely have attained to great wealth
had he not possessed superior abilities ; but apart from the fact
that it has yet to be established whether in the modern exploiting
society it is really special mental gifts, and not rather other things,
that lead to the accumulation of great wealth, most large fortunes
are no longer in the hands of the original acquirers, but in those of
their heirs. Consequently, in private undertakings, if not the
actual direction, yet certainly the highest authority, and particularly
the final decision as to the choice of the actual directors, lies in the
hands of men who, shall we say, half of them, possess less than
the average, nine-tenths of the rest about the average, and only
one-twentieth of them more than the average of human intelligence.
Naturally nineteen-twentieths of the undertakings thought out
and established by such men will be either indifferent or bad. It
will be further objected that it is in the main the same men to
whom a similar *rôle* falls in the creation and officering of joint-
stock companies. Very true. But here it is usual for the few able
men among the wealthy to take the *rôle* of leaders ; the stupid or
the moderately gifted are changed from autocratic despots into a

herd of common docile cattle, who, led by the instinct of self-interest, blindly follow the abler men. And even when it is otherwise, when the incapable rich man stubbornly insists upon thrusting forward his empty pate, he finds himself compelled to give reasons for what he does, to engage in the game of question and answer with his fellow shareholders, and ordinarily he is thus preserved from the gross follies which he would be sure to commit if the whole responsibility rested upon himself. In a word, capitalists acting together as joint-stock companies as a rule exhibit more ability than capitalists acting independently. But even if it were not so, the selections which they make—as shareholders—in appointing the chief managers of their business are infinitely better than those made by private capitalists, because a whole category of intelligences, and that of the highest and best kind, stands at the disposal of the joint-stock company, but not of the private undertaker. Many persons who offer themselves as directors, members of council of administration, presidents, of joint-stock companies, would never condescend to enter into the service of an individual. The general effect of all this is, that joint-stock companies in the greater number of cases possess far abler, more intelligent managers than private undertakings—a circumstance which no one will overlook who is but even moderately well acquainted with the facts of the case.

The alleged superiority of the private undertaking, supposed to be due to the personal care and oversight of the owner, is therefore nothing more than one of the many fables in which the exploiting world believes in spite of the most obvious lack of truth. But even the trifling advantages which the private undertaking really has over the joint-stock company cannot be claimed as against freely associated labour. Colleague Tonof has already pointed out that ignorance and indifference, those most dangerous characteristics of most shareholders, are not to be feared in those who take part in labour associations. Here it can never happen that an unscrupulous minority will obtain control of the management and exploit the undertaking for the benefit of some private interest; here it is natural that the whole body of members, who are interested in the successful conduct of the business, should incessantly and attentively watch the behaviour of the officials they have elected; and in view of the perfect transparency of all the business transactions in the free community, secret practices and crooked ways—those inevitable expedients of dishonour—are not to be thought of. In a word, the form of labour organisation corresponding to the higher stage of civilisation proves itself to be infinitely superior in every respect to the form of organisation prevalent in the past—a fact which, strictly speaking, is a matter of course.

It does not follow that this form of organisation is the most suitable for every kind of labour ; there are branches of production —I mention merely the artistic or the scientific—in which the individual must stand by himself ; but we do not apply the principle of association to these branches. For no one would forcibly impose this principle, and the individual freedom that is nowhere interfered with is able of itself to take care that what is done is everywhere done in the way that has been found to be most consistent with nature, and best.

MIGUEL DIEGO (*Right*) : We know now that the new system unites in itself all the natural requisites of success ; it has been shown before that its introduction was demanded by the progress of civilisation. How comes it that, in spite of all, the new system enters the world, not as the product of the co-operation of elementary automatically occurring historical events, but rather as a kind of art-product, as an artificially produced outcome of the efforts of certain individuals ? What if the International Free Society had not been formed, or if its appeal had been without response, its work crushed in the germ, or in some other way made to miscarry ? It will be admitted that these are conceivable contingencies. What would have become of economic justice if any one of these possibilities had occurred ? If social reform is in truth an inevitable necessity, it must ultimately be realised in spite of the opposition of the whole world ; it must show itself to be indissolubly bound up with forces which will give it the victory over prejudice, ill-will, and adverse accident. Thus alone would proof be given that the work in which we are engaged is something more than the ephemeral fruit of fallible human ingenuity—that rather those men who gave it the initial impulse and watched over its development were acting simply as the instruments of the universal force which, if *they* had not done the work, would have found other instruments and other ways to attain the inevitable end.

HENRI NEY (*Freeland*) : If the existence of economic justice as an established fact depended upon the action of the founders of

Freeland, little could have been said, not merely as to its necessary character, but also as to the certainty of its continuance. For what individual men attempt, other men can frustrate. It is true that, as far as outward appearances go, all historical events are human work; but the great necessary events of history are distinguished from merely accidental occurrences by the fact that in them all the actors are clearly seen to be simply the instruments of destiny, instruments which the genius of mankind calls into being when it is in need of them. We do not know who invented language, the first tool, writing; but whoever it was, we know that he was a mere instrument of progress, in the sense that, with the same certainty with which we express any other natural law, we can venture to assert that language, the tool, writing, would have been invented even if their respective accidental inventors had never seen the light. The same holds good of economic freedom : it would have been realised, even if none of us who actually realised it for the first time had existed. Only in such a case the form of its entrance into the world of historical fact would probably have been a different, perhaps a more pacific, a more joyous one still than that of which we are the witnesses; but perhaps it might have been a violent and horrible one.

In order to show this in a manner that excludes all doubt, it must first be demonstrated that the continuance of modern society as it has been evolved in the course of the last century is in the very nature of things an impossibility. For this purpose you must allow me to carry you back some distance.

In the original society of barbarism, when the productiveness of labour was so small that the weaker could not be exploited by the stronger, and one's own prosperity depended upon the suppression and annihilation of competitors, a thirst for blood, cruelty, cunning, were not merely necessary to the self-preservation of the individual, but they were obviously serviceable to the society to which the individual belonged. They were, therefore, not only universally prevalent, but were reckoned as virtues. The most successful and most merciless slayer of men was the most honourable member of his tribe, and was lauded in speech and song as an example worthy of imitation.

When the productiveness of labour increased, these 'virtues' lost much of their original importance ; but they were not converted into vices until slavery was invented, and it became possible to utilise the labour instead of the flesh of the conquered. Then bloodthirsty cruelty, which hitherto had been profitable, became injurious, since, for the sake of a transient enjoyment—that of eating human flesh—it deprived the victorious individual, as well as the society to which he belonged, of the permanent advantage of augmented prosperity and increased power. Consequently, the bestial thirst for blood gradually disappeared in the new form of the struggle for existence, and from a cherished virtue it passed into a characteristic which met with increasing disapproval—that is, it became a vice. It necessarily became a vice, for only those tribes which were the subjects of this process of moral transformation could enjoy all the advantages of the new forms of labour and of the new social institution, slavery, and could therefore increase in civilisation and power, and make use of their augmented power to extirpate or to bring into subjection the tribes that persisted in their old cannibal customs. In this way, in the course of thousands of years, there grew up among men a new ethics which, in its essential features, has been preserved until our days—the ethics of exploitation.

But to call this ethics 'philanthropy' is the strangest of mistakes. It is true that the savage bloodthirsty hatred between man and man had given place to milder sentiments; but it is a long way from those sentiments to genuine philanthropy, by which we understand the recognition of our fellow-man as our equal, and not merely that chilly benevolence which we entertain towards even dumb animals. Real philanthropy is as inconsistent with exploitation as with cannibalism. For though the new form of the struggle for existence abhors the death of the vanquished, it substitutes for it the oppression and subjugation of man by man as an imperative requirement of social prosperity. And it should be clearly understood that real and unselfish philanthropy is not merely not demanded by the kind of struggle for existence which is carried on by the exploiting society, but is known to be distinctly injurious, and is quite impracticable as a universally operative race-instinct. Individuals may love their fellow-men as themselves; but as long as exploitation is in force, such men must remain rare, and by no means generally esteemed, exceptions. Only hypocrisy or gross self-deception will question this. Certainly the so-called civilised nations of the West have for more than a thousand years written upon their banners the words ' Love thy neighbour as thyself,' and have not shrunk from asserting that they lived up to those words, or that at least they endeavoured to do so. But in truth they loved their fellow-man, in the best of cases, as a useful domestic animal, have without the slightest scruple profited by his painful toil, by his torture, and have not been prevented by any sentiment of horror from slaughtering him in cold blood when such a course was or seemed to be profitable to them. And such were not the sentiments and feelings of a few particularly hard-hearted individuals, but of the whole body of society ; they were not condemned but imperatively demanded by public opinion, lauded as virtues under all sorts of high-sounding names, and, so far as deeds and not empty phrases were in question, their antithesis, the genuine philanthropy, passed at best as pitiable folly, or more generally as a crime worthy of death. He who uttered the words quoted above, and to Whom prayers were offered in the churches, would have been repeatedly crucified, burnt, broken on the wheel, hanged by them all, in the most recent past perhaps imprisoned, had He again ventured, as He did nineteen centuries ago, to preach in the market-place, in burning living words that could not be misunderstood, that which men's purblind eyes and their minds clouded by a thousand years of ancient self-deception read, but did not understand, in the writings of His disciples.

But the decisive point is, that in the epoch of exploitation mankind could not have thought or felt, not to say acted, otherwise. They were compelled to practise exploitation so long as this was a necessity of civilisation ; they were therefore unable either to feel or exercise philanthropy, for that was as little in harmony with exploitation as repugnance to homicide was with cannibalism. Just as in the first barbaric epoch of mankind that which the exploiting period called ' humanity ' would have been detrimental to success in the struggle for existence, so, later, that which *we* call humanity, the genuine philanthropy, would have placed any nation that had practised it at a disadvantage. To eat or to be eaten—that was the alternative in the epoch of cannibalism ; to oppress or to be oppressed, in the epoch of exploitation.

A change in the form and productiveness of labour has recently been effected ; neither social institutions nor moral sensibilities can

FREELAND

escape the influence of that change. But—and here I come to the
last decisive point—there are certainly several alternatives conceivable. The first is that with which we have hitherto been exclusively occupied: the social institutions accommodate themselves to
the change in the form of labour, and the modification of the
struggle for existence thus brought about leads to a corresponding
revolution in moral sentiments; friendly competition and perfect
solidarity of interests supersede the reciprocal struggle for
advantage, and the highest philanthropy supersedes the exploitation
of man.

If we would once for all remove the last doubt as to the unqualified necessity of this phase of evolution, let us suppose that the
contrary has happened, that the adaptation of the social institutions
to the modified form of labour is not effected. At any rate the
mind can imagine such a possibility ; and I hold it to be superfluous,
at this point in the demonstration, to discuss the probability or the
improbability of such a supposition—we simply assume the case.
But it would be absurd likewise to assume that this persistence of
the old form of the social institutions could occur without being
necessarily accompanied by very material reactions both upon the
forms of labour and upon the moral instincts of mankind. Those
over-orthodox but not less thoughtless social politicians who accept
the above assumption, hold it to be possible for a cause of such
enormous and far-reaching importance as is an increased productiveness of labour, that makes it possible for all men to enjoy
abundance and leisure, to remain without the slightest influence
upon the course of human evolution. They overlook the fact that the
struggle for existence in human society must in any case be changed
under the influence of this factor, whether the social institutions
undergo a corresponding adaptation or not, and that consequently
the inquiry must in any case be made what reaction this changed
form of the struggle for existence can or must exercise upon the
totality of human institutions ?

And in what consists the change in the struggle for existence,
in such a case as that indicated above? *Simply in a partial reversion to the form of struggle of the first, the cannibal, epoch of
mankind !*

We have seen that exploitation transformed the earlier struggle,
that aimed at annihilating the competitor, into one directed

towards his subjugation. But now, when the productiveness of labour is so great that the consumption, kept down by exploitation, is no longer able to follow it, the suppression, the—if not the physical, yet the industrial—annihilation of the competitor is once more a necessary condition of everyone's prosperity, and the struggle for existence assumes at once the forms of subjugation and annihilation. In the domain of industry it now profits little to have arbitrary authority over any number of human subjects of exploitation; if the exploiter is not able to drive his co-exploiter from the market, he must succumb in the struggle for existence. And the exploited now have not merely to defend themselves from the harsh treatment of their masters : they must, if they would ward off hunger, fight with tooth and claw for the only too few places at the food-crib in the 'labour market.' Is it conceivable that such a terrible alteration in the fundamental conditions of the struggle for existence can remain without influence upon human ethics ? Cause and effect *must* correspond—the ethics of the cannibal epoch *must* triumphantly return. In consequence of the altered character of the conflict of annihilation, the former cruel and malicious instincts will undergo a modification, but the fundamental sentiment, the unqualified animosity against one's fellow-man, must return. During the thousands of years when the struggle was directed towards the making use of one's neighbour, and especially when the exploited had become accustomed to reverence in the exploiter a higher being, there was possible between master and servant at least that degree of attachment which exists between a man and his beast. Neither masters nor servants had any necessary occasion to hate each other. Mutual considera- tion, magnanimity, kindness, gratitude, could in such a condition become—certainly very sparingly—substitutes for philanthropy. But now, when exploitation and suppression are at one and the same time the watchwords of the struggle, the above-mentioned virtues must more and more assume the character of obstacles to a successful struggle for existence, and must consequently disappear in order to make room for mercilessness, cunning, cruelty, malice. And all these disgraceful characteristics must not merely become universally prevalent : they must also become universally esteemed, and be raised from the category of the most shameful kinds of baseness to that of 'virtues.' As little as it is possible to conceive

of a 'humane' cannibal or of an exploiter under the influence of
real philanthropy, so little is it possible to think of a magnanimous and—in the former sense—virtuous exploiter permanently
under the colossal burden of over-production; and as certainly as
the cannibal society was compelled to recognise the thirst for murder
as the most praiseworthy of all virtues, so certainly must the exploiting society, cursed by over-production, learn to reverence the
most cunning deceiver as its ideal of virtue. But it will be objected that, logically unassailable as this position may be, it is
contradicted by facts. Over-production, the disproportion between
the productivity of labour and the capacity for consumption as
conditioned by the existing social institutions, has practically existed for generations; and yet it would be a gross exaggeration to assert that the moral sensibilities of civilised humanity
had undergone such a terrible degeneration as is indicated above.
It is certainly true that, in consequence of the increasingly reckless
industrial competitive struggle, many kinds of valueless articles are
produced in larger and larger quantities—nay, that there is beginning to prevail a certain confusion in public opinion, which is
no longer able clearly to distinguish between honest services and
successful roguery; but it is equally true, on the other hand, that
never before was humanity in all its forms so highly esteemed and
so widely diffused as it is in the present. These undeniable facts,
however, do not show that over-production can ultimately lead
to any other than the above-indicated results—which would be
logical nonsense; they only show, on the one hand, that this
dreadful morbid phenomenon in the industrial domain of mankind has not yet been long enough in existence to have fully matured its fruit, and that, on the other hand, the moral instinct of
mankind felt a presentiment of the right way out of the economic dilemma long before that right way had become practicable.
It is only a few generations since the disproportion between productivity and consumption became unmistakably evident: and what
are a few generations in the life of mankind? The ethics of exploitation needed many centuries in order to subvert that of
cannibalism: why should the relapse into the ethics of cannibalism
proceed so much more rapidly? But the instinctive presentiment that
growing civilisation will be connected, not with social stagnation and
moral retrogression, but with both social and moral progress—this

yearning for liberty, equality, and fraternity ineradicably implanted
in the Western mind, despite all the follies and the horrors to which
it for a time gave rise—it was just this ' drop of foreign blood in the
European family of nations,' this Semitic-Christian leaven, which,
when the time of servitude was past, preserved that Western mind
from falling even temporarily into a servile and barbarous decay.
Things will *not* follow the last indicated course of evolution—exploitation will *not* persist alongside of increased productivity ; and
that is the reason why the indicated moral consequences will not
ensue. If, however, it be assumed that material progress and exploitation combined are the future lot of mankind, this cannot logically
be conceived otherwise than as accompanied by a complete moral relapse. Yet a third form of evolution may be assumed as conceivable :
in the antagonism between the productivity of labour and the current
social rights, the former—the new form of labour—might succumb ;
in the face of the impossibility of making full use of the acquired
industrial capacity, mankind might lose this capacity again. In
such a case, the concord between productivity and consumption,
labour and right, would have recovered the old basis, and as a
consequence the ethics of mankind might also remain in the same
track. Progress towards genuine philanthropy would necessarily
be suspended, for the struggle for existence would, as before, be based
upon the subjugation of one's fellow-men, but the necessity for the
struggle of annihilation would be avoided. The presentiment of the
possibility of such a development was not foreign to the Western
mind ; there have not been wanting, particularly during the last
generations, attempts, partly conscious and partly unconscious, to
lead men's minds in this direction. Alarmed and driven nearly to
distraction by the strangling embrace of over-production, whole
nations have at times attacked the fundamental sources of production,
sought to choke the springs of the fruitfulness of labour, and persecuted with violent hatred the progress of civilisation, whose fruits
were for the time so bitter. These attacks upon popular culture,
upon the different kinds of division of labour, upon machinery,
cannot be understood except in connection with the occasional
attempts to end the discord between production and distribution by
diminishing the former. It is impossible not to see that in this way
morality also would be preserved from a degeneracy the real cause
of which this sort of reformers certainly did not understand, but

which hovered before their mind's eye as an indistinct presentiment. And now, having noticed *seriatim* the three conceivable forms of evolution—namely, (1) the adaptation of social rights to the new and higher forms of labour and the corresponding evolution of a new and higher morality ; (2) the permanent antagonism between the form of labour and social rights, and the corresponding degeneracy of morality ; (3) the adaptation of the form of labour to the hitherto existing social rights by the sacrifice of the higher productivity, and the corresponding permanence of the hitherto existing morality—we now ask ourselves whether in the struggle between these three tendencies any but the first can come off as conqueror. They all three are conceivable ; but is it conceivable that material or moral decay can assert itself by the side of both moral and material progress, or will ultimately triumph over these ? It is possible, we will say even probable, that but for our successful undertaking begun twenty-five years ago, mankind would for the most part still longer have continued to traverse the path of moral degeneracy on the one hand, and of antagonism to progress on the other ; yet there would never therefore have been altogether wanting attempts in the direction of social deliverance, and the ultimate triumph of such attempts could be only a question of time. No ; mankind owes us nothing which it would not have obtained without us : if we claim to have rendered any service, it is merely that of having brought about more speedily, and perhaps with less bloodshed, that which must have come. [Vehement and long-continued applause and enthusiastic cheers from all sides. The leaders of the opposition one after another shook the hands of the speaker and assured him of their support.]

(End of Third Day's Debate)

CHAPTER XXVI

Fourth Day

THE PRESIDENT (Dr. Strahl) : We have reached the third point in the agenda : *Are not want and misery necessary conditions of existence; and would not over-population inevitably ensue were misery for a time to disappear from the earth ?* I call upon Mr. Robert Murchison.

ROBERT MURCHISON (*Right*) : I must first of all, in the name of myself and of those of my colleagues who entertained doubts of the practicability of the work of social reform, formally declare that we are now thoroughly convinced, not only of the practicability, but also of the inevitable accomplishment of that reform. Moreover, what has already been advanced has matured our hope that the other side will succeed in removing as completely the doubts that still cling to our minds. In the meantime I hold it to be my duty, in the interest of all, to seek explanations by strongly stating the grounds of such doubts as I am not yet able to free myself from. By far the most important of these doubts, one which has not yet been touched upon, is the subject now before us for discussion. It refers not to the practicability, but to the durability of the work of universal freedom and prosperity. Economic justice must and will become an accomplished fact : that we know. But have we a right to infer that it will permanently assert itself ? Economic justice will be followed by wealth for all living. Want and misery, with their retinue of destructive vices, will disappear from the surface of the earth. But together with these will disappear those restraints which have hitherto kept in check the numerical growth of the human race. The population will increase more and more, until at last—though that day may be far off—the earth will not be able to support its inhabitants. I will not trouble you with a detailed repetition and justification of the well-known principle of my renowned countryman, Malthus. Much has been urged against that principle, but hitherto nothing of a convincing character. That the increase in a geometric ratio of the number of living individuals has no other natural check than that of a deficiency of food is a natural law to which not merely man but every living being is inexorably subject. Just as herrings, if they could freely multiply, would ultimately fill the whole of the ocean, so would man, if the increase of his numbers were not checked by the lack of food, inevitably leave no space unoccupied upon the surface of the globe. This cruel truth is confirmed by the experience of all ages and of all nations ; everywhere we see that it is lack of food, want with its consequences, that keeps the number of the living within certain limits ; and it will remain so in all future times. Economic justice can very largely extend the area included in these sad limits, but can never altogether abolish the limits. Under its *régime* the food-supply can be increased tenfold, a hundredfold, but it cannot be increased indefinitely. And when the inevitable limit is reached, what then ? Wealth will then gradually give place to privation and ultimately to extreme want ; a want that is the more dreadful and hopeless because there will be no escape from its all-embracing curse—not even that partial escape which exploitation had formerly offered to a few. Will, then, mankind, after having passed from cannibalism to exploitation and from that to economic justice, revert to exploitation, perhaps even to cannibalism ? Who can say ? It seems evident that economic justice is not a phase of evolution which our race could enjoy for any great length of time. It is true that Malthus and others after him have proposed to substitute for the repressive law of misery certain preventives of over-population. But these preventives are all based upon artificial and systematic suppression of the increase of population. If they could be effectively employed at all, such an employment of them is conceivable only in a poor population groaning under the worst consequences of misery ; I cannot imagine that men enjoying abundance and leisure, and in possession of the most perfect freedom, will subject themselves to sexual privations. In my opinion, this kind of prevention could not under the most favourable circumstances, come into play in a free society until the pressure of over-population had become very great, and the former prosperity, and with that perhaps the sense of individual liberty also, had been materially diminished. This is not a pleasant prospect, quite apart from the moral repulsiveness of all such violent interference with the relations of the sexes—relations which would be specially delicate under the *régime* of economic justice. The perspective shows us in the background a picture which contrasts sadly with the luxuriant promise of the beginning. Do the men of Freeland think that they are able to defend their creation from these dangers ?

Franzisko Espero (*Left*) : Man differs from other living beings in having to prepare food for himself, and, in fact, in being able, with increasing civilisation, to prepare it the more easily the denser the population becomes. Carey, an eminent American economist, has pointed this out, and has thereby shown that the otherwise indisputably operative natural law, according to which a species has an inevitable tendency to outgrow its means of sustenance, does not apply to man. The fact that want and misery have, notwithstanding, hitherto always operated as checks upon the growth of the population is not the result of a natural law but of exploitation. The earth would have produced enough for all if everyone had but been able to make free use of his powers. But, as we have seen, exploitation is an institution of men, not of nature. Get rid of that, and you have driven away the spectre of hunger for ever.

STEFAN VALÓ (*Freeland*): I think it will be well at once to state what is the Freeland attitude towards the subject now under discussion. The honourable member from Brazil (Espero) is correct in connecting the actual misery of mankind—in the epoch of exploitation—with human institutions instead of with the operation of natural forces. The masses suffered want because they were kept in servitude, not because the earth was incapable of yielding more copious supplies. I will add that this actual misery never prevented the masses from multiplying up to the point at which the further increase of population was checked by other factors—nay, that as a rule misery acted as a stimulus to the increase of the population. Our friend from Brazil is in error, however, when, relying upon the empty rhetoric of Carey, he denies that the growth of the population, if it could go on indefinitely, would necessarily at last lead to a lack of food. The first of the speakers of to-day has rightly remarked that in such a case the time must come when there would no longer be space enough on the earth for the men who were born. But can we conceive the condition possible in which our race should cover the surface of the earth like a plague of locusts? Nay, a really unlimited and continuous increase in the number of human beings would not merely ultimately cover the whole surface of the earth, but would exhaust the material necessary for the crowded masses of human bodies. The growth of the population *must*, therefore, have some limit, and so far are Malthus and his followers correct. Whether this limit is to be found exactly in the supply of food is another question—a question which cannot be satisfactorily answered in the affirmative until it has been positively shown, or at any rate rendered plausible, that other factors do not come into play long before a lack of food is felt—factors whose operation is such that the limit of necessary food-supply is never, except in very rare cases, even approximately reached, to say nothing of its being crossed.

ARTHUR FRENCH (*Right*): What I have just heard fills me with astonishment. The member of the Freeland government admits

—what certainly cannot reasonably be denied—that unlimited growth of population is an impossibility; and yet he denies that a lack of food is the sought-for check of over-population. It may be at once admitted that Malthus was in error in supposing that this natural check had already been operative in human society. Men have suffered hunger because they were prevented from supplying themselves with food, not because the earth was incapable of copiously—or, at least, more copiously—nourishing them all. Exploitation has therefore proved to be a check upon over-population operating before the limit of necessary food has been reached; it has been a kind of hunger-cure which man has applied to himself before nature had condemned him to suffer hunger. I am less able to understand what the speaker means when he says the misery artificially produced by exploitation has sometimes proved to be, not a check, but rather a stimulus to the growth of population. But I should particularly like to hear more about those other factors which are alleged to have acted as effective checks, and which the speaker evidently anticipates will in future regulate the growth of the population. These factors are to produce the wonderful effect of preventing the population from ever getting even approximately near to the limit of the necessary food-supply. They cannot be artificial and arbitrarily applied means, otherwise a member of the Freeland government, of this commonwealth based upon absolute freedom, would not speak of them so confidently. But apart from all this, how can there be any doubt of the operation of such an elementary factor of restriction as the lack of food in human society, whilst it is to be seen so conspicuously throughout the whole of organic nature? Is man alone among living beings exempt from the operation of this law of nature; or do the Freelanders perhaps know of some means that would compel, say, the herrings so to control their number as not to approach the limit of their food-supplies, or, rather, induce them to preserve such a reasonable rate of increase as would be most conducive to the prosperous continuance of their species?

This cutting apostrophe produced a great sensation. The tension of expectancy was still further increased when several members of the Freeland government—including Stefan Való, who had already spoken—urgently begged the President to take part in the debate. The whole assembly seemed conscious that the discussion

—not merely the special one of the day, but the general discussion of the congress—had reached its decisive point. If the advocates of economic justice were able successfully to meet the objections now urged by their opponents, and to show that those objections were groundless, then the great argumentative battle was won. What would follow would not concern the question *whether,* but merely the question *how,* the new social order could be well and lastingly established. But if the Freeland evidence failed upon this point—if the structure of Opposition argumentation could not in this case be blown down like a house of cards—then all the previous successes of the advocates of economic justice would count for nothing. To remove the misery of the present merely to prepare the way for a more hopeless misery in the future, was not that which had aroused men's enthusiasm. If there remained only a shadow of such a danger, the death-knell of economic justice had been sounded.

Amid breathless silence, Dr. STRAHL rose to speak, after he had given up the chair to his colleague Ney, of the Freeland government.

Our friend of the Right (he began) ended his appeal to us with the question whether we in Freeland knew of any means which would compel the herrings to confine the increase in their numbers within such bounds as would best conduce to the prosperous continuance of their species. My answer is brief and to the point: Yes, we know of such a means. [Sensation.] You are astonished? You need not be, dear friends, for you know of it as well as we do ; and what leads you to think you do not know of it is merely that peculiar mental shortsightedness which prevents men from perceiving the application of well-known facts to any subject upon which the prejudices they have drunk in with their mother's milk prevent them making a right use of their senses and their judgment. So I assert that you all know of the means in question as well as we do. But I do not say, as you seem to assume, that either you or we were in a position to teach this prudence to the herrings—a task, in fact, which would be scarcely practicable. I assert, rather, that our common knowledge of the means in question is derived not from our gift of invention, but from our gift of observation—in other words, that the herrings have always acted in the way in which, according to the opinion of the propounder of the question, they need to be taught

how to act by our wisdom ; and that, therefore, in order to attain to
a knowledge of the mode of action in question, we need merely
first, open our eyes and see *what* goes on in nature, and secondly,
make some use of our understanding in order that we may find out
the *how* of this natural procedure.

Let us, then, first open our eyes--that is, let us remove the
bandages with which inherited economic prejudices have blinded us.
To make this the easier, my friends, I ask you to fix your mind upon
any living thing—the herring, for example—without thinking of any
possible reference which it may have to the question of population
in human society. Do not seek among the herrings for any explanation of human misery, but regard them simply as one of the many
kinds of boarders at the table of nature. It will then be impossible
for you not to perceive that, though this species of animal is represented by very many individuals, yet those individuals are not too
numerous to find places at nature's table. Nay, I assert that—
always supposing you keep merely the herring in mind, and are not
at the same time looking at human misery in the background—you
would think it absurd to suppose for a moment that the herrings,
if they were more numerous than they are, would not find food
enough in the ocean—that there were just as many of them as
could be fully fed at the table of nature. Or let us take another
species of animal, the relations between which and its food-supply
we are not obliged to arrive at by reflection, but, if necessary,
could easily discover by actual observation—namely, the elephant.
Malthus calculated how long it would take for a pair of elephants
to fill the world with their descendants, and concluded that it
would be lack of food which would ultimately check their indefinite increase. Does not the most superficial glance show you
that nowhere on the earth are there nearly so many elephants as
would find nourishment in abundance? Would you not think
anyone a dotard who would try to convince you of the contrary ?
Thus you all know—and I wish first of all to make sure of this
—that every kind of animal, whether rare or common, more or less
fruitful, regularly keeps within such limits as to its numerical increase as are far, infinitely far, removed from a deficiency in the
supply of food. I go further : you not merely know that this is so—
you know also that it must be so, and why it must be so. Careful
observation of natural events teaches you that a species which

regularly increased to the very limit of the food-supply, and was, therefore, regularly exposed to hunger and privations, must necessarily degenerate – nay, you cannot fail to see that to many kinds of animals such an increase to the limit of the food-supply would mean sudden destruction. For the animals sow not, neither do they reap ; they do not store up provisions for the satisfaction of future needs : and if at any time they were obliged to consume all the food that nature had produced for them, they would thereby, as a rule, destroy the source of their future food-supply, and would not merely suffer hunger, but would all starve. You know, therefore, that that inexhaustible abundance which, in contrast to the misery of human society, everywhere prevails in nature, and which, because of this contrast, the thinkers and poets of all ages have spoken and sung about, is not due to accident, but to necessity ; and it only remains now to discover that natural process, that causal connection, by virtue of which this state of things necessarily exists. Upon this point men were treated to nothing but vague phrases when Malthus lived. The veil which hid the history of the evolution of the organic world had not then been lifted ; men were therefore obliged to content themselves with explaining all that took place in the kingdoms of animals and plants as the work of Providence or of the so-called vital force—which naturally even then prevented no one from seeing and understanding the fact as well as the necessity of this formerly inexplicable natural phenomenon. But you, living in the century of Darwin, cannot for a moment entertain any doubt upon this last point. You know that it is through the struggle for existence that the living beings have developed into what they are—that properties which prove to be useful and essential to the well-being of a species are called forth, perfected, and fixed by this struggle ; and, on the other hand, properties which prove to be detrimental to the well-being of a species are suppressed and removed. Now, since the property of never increasing to the limit of the food-supply is not only advantageous but absolutely necessary to the well-being--nay, to the existence—of every species, it must have been called forth, perfected, and fixed as a permanent specific character by the struggle for existence. You knew all this, my friends, before I said it ; but this knowledge was so consciously present to your mind as to be of use in the process of thinking only when purely botanical or zoological questions were under consideration : as soon as in your organ of thought the strings of social or economic problems were struck, there fell a thick, opaque veil over this knowledge which was so clear before. The world no longer appeared to you as it is, but as it looks through the said veil of acquired prejudices and false notions; and your judgment no longer obeyed those universal laws which, under the name of ' logic,' in other cases compelled your respect, but indulged in singular capers which—if the said veil had not fallen over your senses—could not have failed to make you laugh. Indeed, so accustomed have you become to mistake the pictures which this veil shows to you for the actual world that you are not able to free yourselves from them even after you have roused yourselves to tear the veil in pieces. The false notions and erroneous conclusions of the Malthusian theory arose from the fact that its author was not able to discover the true source of the misery of mankind. He asked himself why did the Irish peasant and the Egyptian fellah suffer hunger ? He was prevented by the above-mentioned veil from seeing that they suffered hunger because the produce of their labour was taken away from them—because, in fact, they were not permitted to labour. But he perceived that the masses everywhere and always suffered hunger—in some places and at some times less severely than in other places and at other times : yet, in spite of all their painful toil and industry, they perpetually suffered hunger, and had done so from time immemorial. Hence he at last came to the conclusion that this universal hungering was a consequence of a natural law. He further concluded that the fellah and the Irish peasant and the peoples of all parts of the world and of all times had suffered and still suffer hunger because there are too many of them; and there are too many of them because it is only hunger that prevents them from becoming still more numerous. That the world, perplexed by the enigma of misery, should believe *this* becomes intelligible when one reflects that misery must have a cause, and erroneous explanations must obtain credence when right ones are wanting. But it is remarkable, my friends, that you, who have recognised in exploitation and servitude the causes of misery, should still believe in that strange natural law which Malthus invented for the purpose of constructing out of it the above-mentioned makeshift. This means that, though you have torn the veil in pieces, your mind and your senses are still enveloped in its tatters. You have released yourselves sufficiently to see why the fellah and the Irish peasant suffer hunger to-day, but you tremble in fear that our posterity will have to endure the horrors of over-population. You still see the herring threatened with starvation, and the elephant wandering with an empty stomach over the bare-eaten forest-lands of Hindostan and Africa; and you pass in thought from the herring and the elephant to our poor over-populated posterity.

Tremendous applause burst forth from all parts of the hall when Dr. Strahl had finished. As he passed from the speaker's tribune to the President's chair, he was cordially shaken by the hand, not only by his friends who crowded around him, but also by the leaders of the Opposition, who gladly and unreservedly acknowledged them-selves convinced. The excitement was so great that it was some time before the debate could be resumed. At last the President obtained a hearing for one of the previous speakers.

ROBERT MURCHISON (*Right*): I rise for the second time, on behalf of those who sit near me, first to declare that we are fully and definitively convinced. You will readily believe that we do not regret our defeat, but are honestly and heartily glad of it. Who would not be glad to discover that a dreadful figure which filled him with terror and alarm was nothing but a scarecrow? And even a sense of shame has been spared us by the magnanimity of the leader of the opposite party, who laid emphasis upon the fact that not merely we, but even his adherents outside of Freeland, still cherished in their hearts the same foolish anxiety, begotten of ac-quired and hereditary prejudices and false notions. The phantoms fled before his clear words, our laughter follows them as they flee, and we now breathe freely. But, if we might still rely upon the magnanimity of the happy dwellers in Freeland, the after-effects of the anxiety we have endured still linger in us. We are like children who have been happily talked out of our foolish dread of the 'black man,' but who nevertheless do not like to be left alone in the dark. We would beg you to let your light shine into a few dark corners out of which we cannot clearly see our way. Do not despise us if we still secretly believe a little in the black man. We will not forget that he is merely a bugbear; but it will pacify us to hear from your own mouths what the true and natural facts of the case are. In the first place, what are, in your opinion, the means em-ployed by nature, in the struggle for the existence of species, to keep

the growth of numbers from reaching the limit of the food-supply ?
Understand, we ask this time merely for an expression of opinion—
of course, you cannot, any more than anyone else, *know* certainly
how this has been done and is being done in individual cases ; and
if your answer should happen to be simply, ' We have formed no
definite opinion upon the subject,' we should not on that account
entertain any doubt whatever as to the self-evident truth that every
living being possesses the characteristic in question, and that the
origin of that characteristic must be sought somewhere in the
struggle for existence.   In order to be convinced that the stag has
acquired his fleetness, the lion his strength, the fox his cunning, in
the struggle for existence, it is not necessary for us to know exactly
how this has come about ; yet it is well to hear the opinions as to
such subjects of men who have evidently thought much about them.
Therefore we ask for your opinions on the question of the power of
adaptation in fecundity.

LOTHAR WALLACE (*Freeland*) : We think that the characteristic
in question, as it is common to all organisms, must have been acquired in a very early stage of evolution of the organic world ; from
which it follows that we are scarcely able to form definite conceptions of the details of the struggle for existence of those times—as,
for example, of the process of evolution to which the stag owes his
swiftness.   We can only say in general that between fecundity and
the death-rate an equilibrium must have been established through
the agency of the mode of living.   A species threatened with extinction would increase its fecundity or (by changing its habits)
diminish its death-rate ; whilst, on the other hand, a species
threatened with a too rapid increase would diminish its fecundity
or (again by changing its habits) increase its death-rate.   Naturally
the death-rate in question is not supposed to depend upon merely
sickness and old age, but to be due in part to external dangers.   The
great fecundity, for example, of the herring would, according to this
view, be both cause and effect of its habits of life, which exposed it
in its migrations to enormous destruction.   Whether the herring
and other migratory fishes adopted their present habits because of
their exceptional fecundity—the origin of which would then have
to be sought in some other natural cause—or whether those habits
were originally due to some other cause, and provoked their exceptional fecundity, we cannot tell.   But that a relation of action and

reaction exists and must necessarily exist here is evident, since a species whose death-rate is increased by an increase of danger must die out if this increase of death-rate is not accompanied by an increased fecundity; and, in the same way, increased fecundity, when not followed by an increased death-rate, must in a short time lead to deterioration. At any rate, it can be shown that, whether deterioration or extermination has been the agent, species have died out; and it can be inferred thence that some species do not possess this power of effecting an equilibrium between fecundity and death-rate. But this conclusion would be too hasty a one. All natural processes of adaptation take place very gradually; and if a violent change in external relations suddenly produces a very considerable increase in the death-rate, it may be that the species cannot adapt its fecundity to the new circumstances rapidly enough to save itself from destruction. To infer thence that the species in question did not possess this power of adaptation at all would be as great a mistake as it would be to argue that, for example, because the stag, or the lion, or the fox, notwithstanding their fleetness, strength, or cunning, are not protected from extermination in the face of overpowering dangers, therefore these beasts do not possess swiftness, strength, or cunning, or that these properties of theirs are not the outcome of an adaptation to dangers called forth in the struggle for existence.

Since there can be no doubt that the power of adaptation, of which we have just spoken, was absolutely necessary to the perpetuation of any species in the struggle for existence in the very beginning of organic life upon our planet, it must have been acquired in immemorial antiquity, and must consequently be a part of the ancient heritage of all existing organisms. There certainly was a time, in the very beginning of life, when this power of adaptation was not yet acquired; but nature has an infallible means of making not only useful but necessary characters the common property of posterity, and this means is the extirpation of species incapable of such a power of adaptation. The selection in the struggle for existence is effected by the preservation of those only who are capable of development and of transmitting their acquired characters to posterity until those characters become fixed, such individuals as revert to the former condition being exterminated as they appear.

The reciprocal adaptation of fecundity to death-rate has thus belonged unquestionably for a long time to the specific character of all existing species without exception. Its presence is manifested not merely in the great universal fact that all species, despite many varying dangers—leaving out of view sudden external catastrophes and attacks of special violence—are preserved from either extermination or deterioration, but also in isolated phenomena which afford a more intimate glimpse into the physiological processes upon which the adaptation in question depends. Human knowledge does not yet extend very far in this direction, but accident and investigation have already given us a few hints. Thus, for example, we know that, as a rule, high feeding diminishes the fecundity of animals; stallions, bulls, etc., must not become fat or their procreative power is lessened, and the same has been observed in a number of female animals. As to man, it has long been observed that the poor are more fruitful than the rich, and, as a rule, notwithstanding the much greater mortality of their children, bring up larger families. The word 'proletarian' is derived from this phenomenon as it was known to the Romans; in England, Switzerland, and in several other countries the upper classes—that is, the rich—living in ease and abundance, have relatively fewer children—nay, to a great extent decrease in numbers. The census statistics in civilised countries show a general inverse ratio between national wealth and the growth of the population—a fact which, however, will be misinterpreted unless one carefully avoids confounding the wealth of certain classes in a nation with the average level of prosperity, which alone has to be taken into account here. In Europe, Russia takes the lead in the rate of growth of population, and is without question in one sense the poorest country in Europe. France stands lowest, the country which for more than a century has exhibited the most equable distribution of prosperity. That the English population increases more rapidly, though the total wealth of England is at least equal to that of France, is explained by the unequal distribution of its wealth. Moreover, it is not merely wealth that influences the growth of population—the ways in which the wealth is employed appear to have something to do with it. In the United States of America, for example, we find—apart from immigration—a large increase with an average high degree of prosperity, offering thus an apparent exception to our rule. Yet if we bear in mind the national character of the Yankees, excitable and incapable of calm enjoyment, the exception is sufficiently explained, and it is brought into harmony with the above principle. But the study of this subject is still in its infancy, and we cannot expect to see it clearly in its whole complex; nevertheless the facts already known show that the connection between the habits and life of fecundity is universally operative.

JOHN VUKETICH (*Right*): Certain phenomena connected with variations in population appear, however, to contradict the principles that disastrous circumstances act as stimuli to fecundity. For example, the fact that the number of births suddenly increases after a war or an epidemic, in short when the population has been decimated by any calamity, is to be explained by the sudden increase in the relative food-supply on account of the diminution of the number of the people. In this case, the greater facility of supplying one's wants produces a result which our theory teaches us to expect from a greater difficulty in doing so.

JAN VELDEN (*Right*): I know that this is the customary explanation of the well-known phenomenon just mentioned, and I must admit that an hour ago I should have accepted this explanation as plausible. Now, however, I do not hesitate to pronounce it absurd. Or can we really allow it to be maintained that, after a war or an epidemic, it is easier to get a living, wealth is greater, than before these misfortunes? I think that generally the contrary is the fact; after wars and epidemics men are more miserable than before, and on that account, and not because it is easier to get a living, their fecundity increases.

The conception to which our friend has just appealed is exactly like that concerning the famishing herrings or elephants; it has been entertained only because economic prejudice was in want of it, and it prevails only so far as this prejudice still requires it. If we were not now discussing the population question, but were speaking merely of war and peace, disease and health, the previous speaker would certainly regard me with astonishment, would indeed think me beside myself, if I were to be guilty of the absurdity of contending that, for example, after the Thirty Years' War the decimated remains of the German nation enjoyed greater prosperity and found it easier to live, or that the survivors of the great plagues of antiquity and the Middle Ages were better off than was the case before the plagues. His sound judgment would at once reject this singular notion; and if I showed myself to be obstinate, he could speedily refute me out of the old chronicles which describe in such vivid

D D

colours the fearful misery of those times. But since it is the population question which is under consideration, and some of the shreds of that veil of which our honoured President spoke seem to flutter before his eyes, he heedlessly mistakes the absurdity in question for a self-evident truth which does not even ask for closer examination. The misery that follows war and disease now becomes—and is treated as if it must be so, as if it cannot be imagined otherwise—a condition in which it is easier to obtain a supply of food, since—thus will the veil of orthodoxy have it—misery is produced only by over-population. Since men suffer want because they are too numerous, it *must* be better for them when they have been decimated by war and disease. From this categorical ' must ' there is no appeal, either to the sound judgment of men, or to the best known facts ; and should rebellious reason nevertheless venture to appeal, something is found wherewith to silence her too loud voice, as for example the reminder that the survivors would find their wealth increased by what they inherited from the dead, that the supply of hands—the demand is simply conveniently forgotten in this connection—has been lessened, and so on.

EDMOND RENAULD (*Centre*) : I wish to draw attention to another method of violently bringing the fact that the growth of the population bears an inverse ratio to the national prosperity into harmony with the Malthusian theory of population, or at least of weakening the antagonism to this theory. For example, in order to explain the fact that the French people, ' in spite of their greater average well-being,' increase more slowly than many poorer nations, the calumny is spread abroad that the blame attaches to artificial prevention, the so-called ' two-children system.' Even in France many believe in this myth, because they—ensnared by Malthus's false population law—are not able to explain the fact differently. Yet this two-children system is a foolish fable, so far as the nation, and not merely a relatively small section of the nation, is concerned. It is true that in France there are more families with few children than there are in other countries ; but this is very easily explained by the fact that the French, on account of their greater average prosperity, are on the whole less fruitful than most other peoples. But that the Frenchman intentionally limits his children to two is an absurdity that can be believed only by the bitter adherents of a theory which, finding itself contradicted by facts, distorts and moulds the facts in order to make them harmonise with itself. It should not be overlooked that such a limitation would mean, where it was exercised, not a slow increase, but a tolerably rapid extinction. Nothing, absolutely nothing, exists to prove that French parents exercise an arbitrary systematic restraint ; the irregularity of chance is as conspicuous here as in any other country, with only the general exception that large families are rarer and small ones more frequent than elsewhere, a fact which, as has been said, is due to diminished fecundity and not to any ' system ' whatever.

At the same time, I do not deny that the wealthy classes, particularly where the bringing up of children is exceedingly costly, do to some extent indulge in objectionable preventive practices, which, however, are said to be not altogether unknown in other countries.

ALBERT MOLNÁR (*Centre*) : The just mentioned fable of the two-children system is also prevalent among certain races living in Hungary, particularly among the Germans of Transylvania and among the inhabitants of certain Magyar districts on the Theiss. The truth here also is, that—apart, of course, from a few exceptions —the cause of the small increase in population must be sought in a lower degree of fecundity, which fecundity—and I would particularly emphasise this—everywhere in Hungary bears an inverse proportion to the prosperity of the people. The slaves of the mountainous north, who live in the deepest poverty, and the Roumanians of Transylvania, who vegetate in a like miserable condition, are all very prolific. Notwithstanding centuries of continuous absorption by the neighbouring German and Magyar elements, these races still multiply faster than the Germans and the Magyars. The Germans, living in more comfortable circumstances, and the few Magyars of the northern palatinate, are far less prolific, yet they multiply with tolerable rapidity. The Germans and Magyars of the plains, in possession of considerable wealth, are almost stationary, as are the already mentioned Saxons of Transylvania.

ROBERT MURCHISON (*Right*) : In the second place, we would ask whether, contrary to the former assumption that man in his character of natural organism was subject to a universal law of nature imposing no check upon increase in numbers but that of deficiency of food—we would ask whether, on the contrary, the power acquired by man over other creatures does not constitute him an exception to that now correctly stated law of nature which provides that an equilibrium between fecundity and death-rate shall automatically establish itself before a lack of food is experienced. Our misgiving is strengthened by the fact that among other animals, as a rule, it is not so much the change that occurs in the fecundity of the species, as that which occurs in the relation of the species to external foes, that restores the equilibrium when the death-rate has been altered by any cause. Let us assume, for example, the herrings have lost a very dangerous foe—say that man, for some reason or other, has ceased to catch them—it is probable that their indefinite increase will not in the first instance be checked by a change in their fecundity, but an actual large increase in the number of the herrings will most likely lead to such an increase in the number and activity of their other natural foes that an equilibrium will again be brought about by that means.

Man, as lord of the creation, especially civilised man, has generally no other foe but himself to fear. Here, then, when the death-rate happens to be diminished by the disappearance of evils which he had brought upon himself, the equilibrium could be restored *only* by a diminution of fecundity; here it would be as if nature was prevented from employing that other expedient which, in the world of lower animals, she, as a rule, resorts to at once, the increase of the death-rate by new dangers. I admit that several facts mentioned by the last speaker belonging to the Freeland government show that nature would find this, her only remaining expedient—the spontaneous diminution of fecundity—quite sufficient. It cannot be denied that the number of births decreases with increasing prosperity; but is it certain that this will take place to a sufficient extent permanently and radically to avert any danger whatever of over-population? For, apart from very rare exceptions which are too insignificant to make a rule in such an important matter, the births have everywhere a little exceeded the deaths, though the latter have hitherto been everywhere unnaturally increased by misery, crime, and unwholesome habits of life; and if in future it remains the rule that the births preponderate, let us say to only a very small extent, then eventually, though not perhaps for many thousands of years, over-population must occur, for the lack of any external check.

In order permanently to prevent this, there must be established sooner or later an absolute equilibrium between births and deaths. Can we really depend upon nature spontaneously to guarantee us this? Is it absolutely certain that nature will, as it were, say to man : 'My child, you have by the exercise of your reason emancipated yourself from my control in many points. You have made ineffectual and inapplicable all but one of those means by which I protected your animal kindred from excessive increase, and the one means you have left untouched is just that which I have been accustomed to employ only in extreme cases. Do not look to me alone to furnish you with effectual protection against that evil, but make use of your reason for that purpose—*for that also is my gift.*'

The supposition that, in this matter, nature really indicates that man is to exercise some kind of self-help gains weight when one recalls the course of human evolution. Our Freeland friends have very appositely and strikingly shown us how the men of the two former epochs of civilisation treated each other, first as beasts for slaughter and then as beasts of burden. And what was it but want that drove them to both of these courses? Is not the conviction forced upon us that our ancestors were compelled at first to eat each other, and, when they refrained from that, to decimate each other, simply because they had become too strong to be saved from over-population by the interposition of nature ? In the first epoch of civilisation man protected himself against a scarcity of food by slaying and, driven by hunger, straightway devouring, his competitor at nature's table. What happened in the second epoch of civilisation was essentially the same : men were consumed slowly, by piecemeal, and a check put upon their increase by killing them and their offspring slowly through the pains and miseries of servitude. In short, since man has learnt to use his reason he has ceased to be a purely natural creature, his own will has become partly responsible for his fate ; and it seems to me that in the population question of the future he will not be left to the operation of nature alone, but must learn how to help himself.

LOTHAR MONTFORT (*Freeland*) : That man, by the exercise of his reason, has made himself king of nature, and has no special need to fear any foe but himself, is certainly true ; and it is just as true that he can and ought to use this reason of his in all the relations of the struggle for existence. Moreover, I do not doubt that

if it were really true, as the previous speaker apprehended, that man
has become too strong for nature to save him from over-population
in the same way in which she saved his lower fellow-creatures, then
man would be perfectly able to solve this problem by a right use of
his own reason. Should he actually be threatened by over-population after he had left off persecuting his fellow men, recourse could
and would be had to the voluntary restriction of the number of
children.

In the first place, it is not too much to expect that physiology
would be able to supply us with means which, while they were
effectual, would not be injurious to health or obnoxious to the
æsthetic sentiment, and would involve the exercise of no ascetic
continence ; though all the means hitherto offered from different
quarters, and here and there actually employed, fail to meet at least
one or more of these conditions. In the second place, it is certain
that public opinion would be in favour of prevention as soon as
prevention was really demanded in the public interest. That the
declamations of the apostles of prevention, powerful as they have
been, have not succeeded in winning over the sympathies of the
people is due to the fact that those apostles have been demanding
what was altogether superfluous. There has hitherto been, and
there is now, no over-population ; the working classes would not be
in the least benefited by refraining from the begetting of children ;
hence, prevention would in truth have been nothing but a kind of
offering up of children to the Moloch of exploitational prejudice.
The popular instinct has not allowed itself to be deceived, and moral
views are determined by the moral instincts, not by theories. On
the other hand, if there were a real threat of over-population, in
whatever form, the restriction of the number of births would then
be a matter of general interest, and the public views upon prevention
would necessarily change. Should such a change occur, it would
be quite within the power of society to regulate the growth of population according to the needs of the time. It may safely be assumed
that no interference on the part of the authorities will be called for ;
the exercise of compulsion by the authorities is absolutely foreign to
the free society, and cannot be taken into consideration at all. The
modern opinion concerning the population question, the opinion
that is gradually acquiring the force of a moral principle—viz. that
it is reprehensible to beget a large number of children—must prove

itself to be sufficiently powerful for the purpose, it being taken for granted, of course, that means of prevention were available which were absolutely trustworthy, and did not sin against the æsthetic sentiment. But if this did not suffice, the incentive to restriction would be furnished by the increased cost of bringing up children, or by some other circumstance.

But it is really superfluous to go into these considerations, for in this matter nature has no need whatever of the conscious assistance of man. Man is, in this respect, no exception ; what he expects from nature has been given in the same degree to other creatures, and all that is essential has already been furnished to him.

As to the first point, I need merely remark that, though man is the king of animals, he is in no way different from all the others as to the point under consideration. There are animals which, when the danger from one foe diminishes, may be exposed to increased danger from other foes, and in the case of such, therefore, as the previous speaker quite correctly said, the restoration of the disturbed equilibrium does not necessarily presuppose a diminution of fecundity. But there are other animals which, in this matter, are exactly in the same position as man. They have no foes at all whom they need fear, and a change of death-rate among them can therefore be compensated for only by a corresponding change in the power of propagation. The great beasts of prey of the desert and the sea, as well as many other animals, belong to this category. What foe prevents lions and tigers, sperm-whales, and sharks from multiplying until they reach the limit of their food supply ? Does man prevent them? If anyone is really in doubt as to this, I would ask who prevented them in those unnumbered thousands of years in which man was not able to vie with them, or did not yet exist ? But they have never—as species—suffered from lack of food ; consequently nature must have furnished to them exactly what *we* expect from her.

In fact, as I have said, she has already furnished us with it. For it is not correct that, in the earlier epochs of civilisation, man assisted nature in maintaining the requisite equilibrium between the death-rate and the fecundity of his species. It is true that men assisted in increasing their own death-rate by slaying each other, and by torturing each other to death ; but they did not in this way

restore an equilibrium that had been disturbed by too great
fecundity or too low a mortality ; on the contrary, they disturbed
an equilibrium already established by nature, and compelled nature
to make good by increased fecundity the losses occasioned by the
brutal interference of man. The previous speaker is in error when
he ascribes the rise of anthropophagy in the first competitive
struggles in human society to hunger, to the limitation of the food
supply, by which the savages were driven to kill, and eventually to
eat, their fellow savages. Whether the opponent was killed or not
made no material difference in the relations between these two-
legged beasts of prey and their food supply. Nature herself took
care that they never increased to the actual limit of their food
supply ; if they had been ten times more numerous they would have
found the food in their woods to be neither more nor less abundant.
They opposed and murdered each other out of ill-will and hatred,
impelled not by actual want but by the claim which each one made
to everything (without knowing how to be mutually helpful in
acquiring what all longed for, as is the case under the *régime* of
economic justice). Whether there were many or few of them is a
matter of indifference. Put two tribes of ten men each upon a given
piece of land, and they will persecute each other as fiercely as if
each tribe consisted of thousands. It is true that the popular
imagination generally associates cannibalism with a lack of food or
of flesh ; but this mistake is possible only because the doctrine of
exploitation fills the minds of its adherents with the hallucination
of over-population. Certainly cannibals do not possess abundance
in the sense in which civilised men do, but this is because they are
savages who have not, or have scarcely, risen out of the first stage
of human development. To suppose that they were driven into
cannibalism by over-population and the lack of food, is to exhibit a
singular carelessness in reasoning. For it is never the hungry who
indulge in human flesh, but those who have plenty, the rich ;
human flesh is not an article of food to the cannibal, but a dainty
morsel, and this horrible taste is always a secondary phenomenon ;
the cannibal acquires a taste for a practice which originally sprang
from nothing but his hatred of his enemy.

Again, neither is the action of the exploiter induced by a diminution of the food supply, nor would such a diminution prevent future
over-population. Men resort to mutual oppression, not because food

is scarcer, but because it is more abundant, and more easily obtainable than before ; and the misery which is thereby occasioned to the oppressed does not diminish but increases their number. It is true that misery at the same time decimates those unfortunates whose fecundity it continually increases ; but experience shows that the latter process exceeds the former, otherwise the population could not increase the more rapidly the more proletarian the condition of the people became, and become the more stationary the higher the relative prosperity of the people rose.

That, apart from insignificant exceptions, an actually stationary condition has never been known is easily explained from the fact that actual prosperity, real social well-being, has never yet been attained. When once this becomes an accomplished fact the perfect equilibrium will not be long in establishing itself. The same applies to every part of nature in virtue of a great law that dominates all living creatures ; and there is nothing to justify the assumption that man alone among all his fellow-creatures is *not* under the domination of that law.

(*End of Fourth Day's Debate*)

CHAPTER XXVII

FIFTH DAY

THE fourth point in the Agenda was : *Is it possible to introduce the institutions of economic justice everywhere without prejudice to inherited rights and vested interests ; and, if possible, what are the proper means of doing this ?*

ERNST WOLMUT (*belonging to no party*) opened the debate : I do not think it necessary to lay stress upon the fact that the discussion of the subject now before us cannot and ought not materially to influence our convictions. Whether it be everywhere possible or not to protect vested interests will hinder no one from adopting the principle of economic justice, and that at once and with all possible energy. We are not likely to be prevented from according a full share of justice to the immense majority of our working fellow-men by a fear lest the exploiting classes should suffer, any more than the promoters of the railroads were stayed in their work by the knowledge that carriers or the innkeepers on the old highways would suffer. It is, however, both necessary and useful to state the case clearly, and as speedily as possible to show to those who are threatened with inevitable loss what will be the extent of the sacrifice they will have to make. For I take it to be a matter of course that such a sacrifice is inevitable. No one suffered anything through the establishment of the Freeland commonwealth; but this was because there were here no inherited rights or vested interests to be interfered with. There were no landlords, no capitalists, no employers to be reckoned with. It is different with us in the Old World. What is to be done with our wealthy classes, and how shall we settle all the questions concerning the land, the capital, and the labour over which the wealthy now have complete control? Will it not be humane, and therefore also prudent, to make some compensation to those who will be deprived of their possessions? Will not the new order work better if this small sacrifice is made, and embittered foes are thereby converted into grateful friends?

ALONSO CAMPEADOR (*Extreme Left*): I would earnestly warn you against such pusillanimous sentimentality, which would not win over the foes of the new order, but would only supply them with the means of attacking it, or shall we say allow them to retain those means. If we would exercise justice towards them, we should give to them, as to all other men, an opportunity of making a profitable use of their powers. They cannot or will not labour. They are accustomed to take their ease while others labour for them. Does this constitute a just claim to exceptional treatment? But it will be objected that they ask for only what belongs to them, nay, only a part of what belongs to them. Very well. But what right have they to this so-called property? Have they cultivated the ground to which they lay claim? Is the capital which they use the fruit of *their* labour? Does the human labour-force which carries on their undertakings belong to them? No; no one has a natural right to more than the produce of his own labour; and since in the new order of things this principle deprives no one of anything, but, on the contrary, leads to the greatest possible degree of productiveness, no one has any ground for complaint—that is to say, no one who is content with what is his own and does not covet what rightly belongs to some one else. To acknowledge the claims of those who covet what is not theirs would be like acknowledging the claims of the robber or thief to the property he has stolen.

It will be said that owners possess what they have *bonâ fide*; their claim is based upon laws hitherto universally respected. Right. Therefore we do not *punish* these *bonâ fide* possessors; we simply take from them what they can no longer possess *bonâ fide*. But the owners have paid the full value for what they must now give up: why should they lose their purchase-money, seeing that the purchase was authorised by the law then in force? Is the new law to have a retrospective force? These are among the questions we hear. But no one need be staggered by these questions unless he pleases. For the purchase-money rightly belonged to the possessor of it as little as the thing purchased; he who buys stolen goods with stolen money has *no* claim for compensation. If he acts in good faith he is not obnoxious to punishment--but entitled to compensation?

Yet—and this is the last triumph of the faint-hearted—the purchase-money, that is, the capital sunk in land or in any business, can be legally the property of the possessor even in our sense of the term. The possessor may have produced it by his own labour and saved it: is he not in that case entitled to compensation? Yes, certainly; in this case, to refuse compensation for such capital would be robbery; but is not the establishment of economic justice, which gives a right to the produce of any kind of future labour, a fully adequate compensation for that capital which has really been produced by the possessor's own labour? Consider how poorly a man's own labour was remunerated under the exploiting system of industry, what capital could be saved out of what was really one's own labour, and you will not then say that a real worker who possessed any such savings will not find a sufficient compensation in the ten-fold or hundred-fold increase of the produce of his labour. But perhaps a difficulty is found in the possibility that this small capitalist might no longer be capable of work? Granted; and provision is made for this in the new order of things. The honest worker receives his maintenance allowance when his strength has left him; even *he* will have no occasion to sigh for what he had saved in the exploiting times of the past. To these maintenance allowances I refer also those other exploiters whose habits have robbed them of both desire and ability to work. The free com-munity of the future will be magnanimous enough not to let them suffer want; even they have, as our fellow-men, this claim upon the new order; but any right beyond this I deny.

STANISLAUS LLOWSKI (*Freeland*): We in Freeland take a dif-ferent standpoint. The exploiting world could, without being false to itself, forcibly override acquired rights in order to carry out what might be the order of the day; it could—and has almost always done so—carry into force any new law based upon the sword, with-out troubling itself about the claims of the vanquished; it could do all this because force and oppression were its proper foundation. Its motto was, 'Mine is what I can take and keep'; therefore he who took what another no longer had the power to keep acted in perfect accordance with his right, whether he could base his claim upon the fortune of war or upon a parliamentary majority. If we recognised this ancient right, matters would be very simple : we have become the stronger and can take what we please. The hypocrisy of the modern so-called international law, which has a horror of brutal confiscations, need not stand in our way any more than it has ever stood in the way of anyone who had power. Conquerors no longer deprived the conquered of their land, they no longer plundered or made men their slaves; but in truth, it was only in appearance that these practices had ceased : it was only the form, not the essence of the thing, that had changed. The victor retained his right of legislating for the vanquished; and the earnings of the vanquished were more effectually than ever transferred to the pockets of the victors in the forms of all kinds of taxes, of restrictions, and rights of sovereignty. 'Property' was 'sacred,' not even that of the subjugated was touched; merely the fruits of property were taken by the strong. This we, too, could do. Take the property from its owners? How brutal; what a mockery of the sacred rights of property! But to raise the taxes until they swallowed up the whole of the property—who in the exploiting world would be able to say *that* was contrary to justice? Yet we declare it to be so, for we recognise no right to treat the minority of possessors differently from the minority of workers; and as in our eyes property is sacred, we must respect it when it belongs to the wealthy classes as much as when it belongs to ourselves.

But—objects the member on the Left—the victorious majority

make no claim of right of private property in the land and in the productive capital. Certainly; but they do not possess anything which they will have to renounce in the future, while the minority does; hence to dispossess the possessors in favour of those who did not possess, in order that equality of right might prevail in future, would not be to treat both alike.

But—and this is the weightiest argument in the eyes of our friend—the minority is said to have at present no valid title to their property; they owe it to exploitation, and we do not recognise this as a just title; exploitation is robbery, and he who has stolen, though he did it in good faith, possesses no claim to compensation. This reasoning is also false. Exploitation is robbery only in an economic, not in a juridical, sense; it was not merely *considered* to be permissible—it *was* so. The exploiter did not act illegally though in good faith; rather he acted legally when in his day he exploited; and acted legally not merely on the formal ground that the law, as it then existed, allowed him thus to act, but because he could not act otherwise. This appropriation of other men's earnings, which, in an economic sense, we are compelled, and rightly so, to call robbery, was—let us not forget that—the necessary condition of any really productive highly organised labour whatever, so long as the workers were not able to freely organise and discipline themselves. Economic robbery, the relation of master held by the few towards the many, constituted an effective economic service that had the strongest right to claim the profit of other men's labour, which was in fact rendered profitable by it. Subsequently to confiscate the thus acquired compensation for the services rendered, because such services had become superfluous or indeed detrimental, would in truth be robbery, not merely in an economic sense, but in a legal sense—an offence against the principles of economic justice.

Then are those who have been exploiters to retain undiminished the fruit of their ' economic robbery ' ? Yes; but two things must be noted. In all ages it has been held to be the right of the community to dispossess owners of certain kinds of property without committing any offence against the sacredness of property, provided full compensation was offered to the owners. In the abolition of slavery, of serfdom, of certain burdens on the land, and the like, no one has ever found anything that was reprehensible, provided the owner of the slaves or of the land was compensated to the full value of the property taken from him. In the second place, it is to be noted that the community is bound to guarantee to the owners their property, but not the profit which has hitherto been obtained from it.

If you apply these two principles to the acquired rights which the Free Society found existing, you will find that, while the land is taken from the landowners, the value of it must be paid; the Society has nothing to do with movable capital, and the same holds good of the profit which the employers have hitherto drawn from their relation to the workers. The Society can also claim the right of obtaining possession of the movable productive property, so far as it may appear to be to the public interest to do this. Such an interest does not here come in question, for, apart from the fact that movable means of production can be created in any quantity that is required, there is no reason to fear that the owners will hold back theirs when they find what is both the only and the absolutely best employment for it in dealing with the associated workers. But, in the future, capitalists will not receive interest for their property, or, if they do, it will be only temporarily. There is as little occasion as there is right to forbid the receiving of interest; but, as every borrower will be able to get capital without interest, the paying of interest will cease automatically. Just as little can or need the Free Society forbid the former employers to hire workers to labour for them for stipulated wages; such workers will no longer be found.

ALI BEN SAFI (*Right*): Where is the Free Commonwealth to obtain the means to purchase all the land, and at the same time to furnish the workers with business capital? It is possible that some rich countries may be able to accomplish this by straining all their resources; but how could we in Persia find the 125,000,000*l.*, at which the fixed property was estimated at the last assessment, to say nothing of the hitherto totally lacking business capital?

FRANÇOIS RENAUD (*Right*): On the contrary, I fear that the—from a legal standpoint certainly unassailable—justice to the former owners will occasion the greatest difficulties to just the richest countries. Their greater means involve the heavier claims upon those means; for in proportion as those countries are really richer will the value of the land be higher, and the workers, because more skilful in carrying on highly developed capitalistic methods of industry, will at once require larger amounts of business capital, which the community will have to furnish. So far, then, the greater strength and the heavier burden balance each other. But to this it must be added that in the more advanced countries the amount of mobile capital requiring compensation is far greater than that of poor countries. As interest is to cease, all these numberless invested milliards then bearing interest will be withdrawn : whence will the means be suddenly obtained promptly to meet all these calls ?

CLARK (*Freeland*) : The last two speakers entertain unnecessary fears. The sums required to get possession of the land, to pay back the circulating capital, and to furnish the workers with more abundant means for carrying on business, are certainly enormous —are at any rate larger than the material advance of any country whatever can even approximately supply quickly enough to place the country in a position to bear such burdens in their full extent. Certainly, if the transition to economic justice were followed imme- diately by its full results—if, for example, such transition lifted any country at once to that degree of wealth which we enjoy in Free- land—comparatively little difficulty would be experienced in re- sponding to the heavy demands that would be made ; but this condition would not be reached for years ; the tasks you must undertake would be more than you could perform, if you had at once to discharge the whole of your responsibilities. But you have no reason whatever to fear this. Simply because interest will cease will neither landowner nor capitalist have any motive for insisting upon immediate payment, but will be quite content to accept pay- ment in such instalments as shall suit the convenience of the community or the private debtors—should there be any such—and which could be easily accommodated to the interests of those who were entitled to receive the payment. When it is considered that the latter would be compelled either to let their capital lie idle or to consume it, it will appear evident that, if only the slightest advan- tage were offered them, they would prefer to receive their property in instalments, so far as they did not actually want to use it them- selves.

You have quite as little reason to fear the demand which will be made for supplying the workers with the means of carrying on business. If your exploited masses already possessed the ability

to make use of all those highly developed capitalistic implements of
industry which we employ in Freeland, then certainly the Old World
would have to renounce any attempt even approximately to meet at
once the enormous demand for capital which would be made upon it.
In such a case the milliard and a-half of souls who would pass over
to the new order of things would require two billions of pounds ; but
the two milliards of men will not require these two billions, because
they would not know what to do with the enormous produce of the
labour called forth by such means of production.   To dispose of so
much produce it would be necessary for every family in the five
divisions of the globe to possess the art of consuming a minimum
of from 600l. to 700l. per year, as our Freeland families do ; and,
believe us, dear friends, your masses, just escaped from the servitude
of many thousands of years, at present entirely lack this art.   You
will not produce more than can be consumed.   You have not been
able to do so yet, and will certainly not be able to do it when the
consumption of the workers is able to supply the only reason for
production.   The extent and the intensity of production have been
and remain the determinating factors in the extent and kind of the
means of production.   You will at any time be able to create what
you are able to make use of; and if here and there the demand
grow somewhat more rapidly than can be conveniently met out of
the surplus acquired by the continually increasing productiveness
of labour, you must for a time be content to suffer inconvenience—
that is, you must temporarily forego the gratification of some of
your newly acquired wants in order the more rapidly to develop
your labour in the future.

For the rest, I can only repeat that the Freeland commonwealth will always be prepared, in its own interests, to place its
means at your disposal, so far as they will go.   We calculate that
your wealth—that is, looking at the subject from the standpoint of
our material interests, your ability to purchase those commodities
which we have special natural facilities for producing, and your
power of producing those commodities which we can take in
exchange for ours with the greatest advantage to you—will, in the
course of the next two or three years, at least double, and probably
treble and quadruple.   From this we promise ourselves a yearly
increase of about a milliard pounds sterling in our Freeland income.
We have determined to apply this increase for a time, not to the

extension of our consumption and of our own investments, but to place it at your disposal, as we have already done the unemployed surplus of our insurance reserve fund, and to continue to do this as long as it may seem necessary. [Tremendous applause.]

The PRESIDENT: I believe I am expressing the wish of the assembly when I ask William Stuart, the special representative of the American Congress, who arrived at Eden Vale this morning, to state to us the proposals laid before the congress of his country by the committee entrusted with the drawing up of the scheme for adopting the *régime* of economic equality of rights.

WILLIAM STUART: In the name of the representatives of the American people, I ask the kind attention of this distinguished assembly, and particularly of the representatives of Freeland who are present, to a series of legislative enactments which it is proposed to make for the purpose of carrying us—with the energy by which we are characterised, and, at the same time, without injury to existing interests—out of the economic conditions that have hitherto existed into those of economic equality of rights. Our government found themselves obliged to take this step because our nation is the first outside of Freeland—at least, so far as we are aware—which has passed the stage of discussion, and is about immediately to take action and carry out the work. The institutions of economic justice are no longer novelties; we can follow a well-proved precedent, the example of Freeland, and we intend to follow that example, with a few unessential modifications rendered necessary by the special characteristics of the American country and people. On the other hand, we lack experience; and as, notwithstanding our well-known 'go-ahead' habits, we would rather have advice before than after undertaking so important a task, I am sent to ask your opinion and report it to the American Congress before the recommendations of the committee have become law.

It is proposed to declare all the land in the United States to be ownerless, but to pay all the present owners the full assessed value. In order to meet the cases of those who may think they have not received a sufficient compensation, special commissions of duly qualified persons will be appointed for the hearing of all appeals, and the public opinion of the States is prepared to support these commissions in treating all claims with the utmost consideration. It is proposed to deal with buildings in the same way, with the

E E

proviso that dwelling-houses occupied by the owners may be excepted at the owners' wish. The purchase-money shall be paid forthwith or by instalments, according to the wish of the seller, with the proviso that for every year over which the payment of the instalment shall be extended a premium of one-fifth per cent. shall be given, to be paid to the seller in the form of an additional instalment after the whole of the original purchase-money has been paid. The payment is not to extend over more than fifty years. Suppose a property be valued at ten thousand dollars; then the owner, if he wishes to have the whole sum at once, receives his ten thousand, with which he can do what he pleases; but if he prefers, for example, to receive it in ten yearly instalments of 1,000 dollars, he has a right to ten premiums of 20 dollars each, which will be paid to him in a lump sum of 200 dollars as an eleventh instalment. If he wishes the payment to be in fifty instalments of 200 dollars, then his premiums will amount to fifty times twenty dollars—that is, to 1,000 dollars—which will be paid in five further instalments of 200 dollars. The national debt is to be paid off in the same way.

The existing debit and credit relations of private individuals remain intact, except that the debtor shall have the right of immediate repayment of the borrowed capital, whatever may have been the terms originally agreed upon. As the commonwealth will be prepared to furnish capital for any kind of production whatever, the private debtor will be in a position to exercise the right abovementioned ; but, according to the proposal of the committee, the commonwealth shall, for the present, demand of its debtors the same premium which it guarantees to its creditors. The object of this regulation is obvious : it is to prevent the private creditors—in case no advantage accrues to them—from withdrawing their capital from business and locking it up. If those who needed capital had their needs at first supplied without cost, simply upon undertaking gradually to repay the borrowed capital, they would not be disposed to make any compensatory arrangement with their former creditors, whilst, should the committee's proposal be adopted, they would be willing to pay to those creditors the same premiums as they would have to pay to the commonwealth.

The opinions of the committee were at first divided as to the amount of the premiums to be guaranteed and demanded. A

minority was in favour of fixing a maximum of one in a thousand
for each year of delayed payment: they thought that would be
sufficient to induce most of the capitalists to place in the hands of
the commonwealth or of private producers the property which
otherwise they must at once consume or allow to lie idle. Eventually,
however, the minority came over to the view of the majority, who
preferred to fix the maximum higher than was necessary, rather
than by untimely parsimony expose the commonwealth to the
danger of seeing the capital withdrawn which could be so profitably
used in the equipment of production. The voting was influenced
by the consideration that we, as the first, outside of Freeland,
among whom capital would receive no interest, must be prepared,
if only temporarily, to stand against the disturbing influences of
foreign capital. That such disturbing influences have not been felt
in Freeland, though here no premium of any kind has ever been in
force, whilst interest has been paid everywhere else in the world,
was an example not applicable to our case, as we have not to
decide—as you in Freeland have—what to do with capital which we
do *not* need, and which, after all conceivable demands on capital
have been met, still remains disposable; but, on the other hand, we
have to attract and to retain capital of which we have urgent need.
But that the proposed one-fifth per cent. will suffice for this purpose
we are able with certainty to infer from the double circumstance
that, in the first place, the anticipated adoption of this proposal,
which naturally became known at once to our world of capitalists,
has produced a decided tendency homewards of our capital invested
abroad. It is evident, therefore, that capitalists scarcely expect to
get elsewhere more for large amounts of capital than we intend to
offer. In the second place, the capitalistic transactions which have
recently been concluded or are in contemplation show that our
home capital is already changing hands at a rate of interest corresponding to our proposed premium. Anyone in the United States
who to-day seeks for a loan gets readily what he wants at one-fifth
per cent., particularly if he wishes to borrow for a long period.
Such seekers of capital among us at present are, of course, in
most cases companies already formed or in process of formation.

Thanks to the fact that the election for the Constituent Congress
has been the means of universally diffusing the intelligence that
it was intended to act upon the principle of respecting most

scrupulously all acquired rights, productive activity during the period of transition has suffered no disturbance, but has rather received a fresh impetus. The companies in process of formation compel the existing undertakers to make a considerable rise in wages in order to retain the labour requisite for the provisional carrying on of their concerns; and as this rise in wages has suddenly increased the demand for all kinds of production it has become still more the interest of the undertakers to guard against any interruption in their production. These two tendencies mutually strengthen each other to such a degree that at the present time the minimum wages exceed three dollars a day, and a feverish spirit of enterprise has taken possession of the whole business world. The machine industry, in particular, exhibits an activity that makes all former notions upon the subject appear ridiculous. The dread of over-production has become a myth, and since the undertakers can reckon upon finding very soon in the associations willing purchasers of well-organised concerns, they do not refrain from making the fullest possible use of the last moments left of their private activity. Even the landlords find their advantage in this, for the value of land has naturally risen very materially in consequence of the rapidly grown demand for all kinds of the produce of land. In short, everything justifies us in anticipating that the transition to the new order of things with us will take place not only easily and smoothly, but also in a way most gratifying to *all* classes of our people.

The PRESIDENT asked the assembly whether they would continue the debate on the fourth point on the Agenda, by at once discussing the message from the American Congress; or whether they would first receive the report which the Freeland commissioner in Russia had sent by a messenger who had just arrived in Eden Vale. As the congress decided to hear the report,

DEMETER NOVIKOF (messenger of the Freeland commissioner for Russia) said: When we, the commissioners appointed by the Freeland central government at the wish of the Russian people, arrived in Moscow, we found quiet—at least externally—so far restored that the parties which had been attacking each other with reckless fury had agreed to a provisional truce at the news of our arrival. Not merely the cannons and rifles, but even the guillotine and the gallows were at rest. Radoslajev, our plenipotentiary

commissioner, called the chiefs of the parties together, induced
them to lay down their weapons, to give up their prisoners, to
dissolve the seven different parliaments, each one of which had been
assuming the authority of exclusive representative of the Russian
people ; and then, after he had furnished himself for the interim
with a council of reliable men belonging to the different parties, he
made arrangements for the election of a constituent assembly with
all possible speed.

As production and trade were nearly at a standstill, the misery
was boundless. To be an employer was looked upon by several of
the extreme parties as a crime worthy of death ; hence no one
dared to give workers anything to do. In most parts of the
empire the ignorant masses, who had been held down in slavish
obedience, were altogether incapable of organising themselves ; and
as the most extreme of the Nihilists had begun to guillotine the
organisers of the free associations as 'masters in disguise,' it
seemed almost as if mutual slaughter could henceforth be the only
occupation that would be pursued in Russia.

The proclamation, in which Radoslajev called upon the people
to elect an assembly, and in which he insisted upon the security of
the person and of property as *conditio sine quâ non* of our continued
assistance, calmed the minds of the people, but it did not suffice to
produce a speedy growth of productive activity. When, therefore,
the constituent assembly met, Radoslajev proposed a mixed system
as transition stage into the *régime* of economic justice. In this
mixed system a kind of transitory Communism was to be combined
with the germs of the Free Society and with certain remnants of the
old industrial system.

In the first place, however, order had to be restored in the
existing legal relationships. During the reign of terror previous to
our arrival, all fixed possessions were declared to be the property of
the nation, without giving any compensation to the former owners.
All existing debts were simply cancelled ; and the first business now
was to make good as far as practicable the injury done by these
acts of violence. But at first the new national assembly showed
itself to be intractable upon these points. Hatred of the old order
was so universal and so strong that even those who had been dis-
possessed did not venture to endorse our views. The private
property of the epoch of exploitation was considered to be merely

robbery and theft, the claims for compensation were so obnoxious
to many that a deputation of former landowners and manufacturers,
headed by two who had borne the title of grand-duke, conjured
Radoslajev to desist from his purpose, lest the scarcely sleeping
nihilistic fanaticism should be awaked anew. The latter, nevertheless, persisted in his demands, after he had consulted us Freelanders who had been appointed to assist him. He announced to
the national assembly that we were far from wishing to force our
views upon the Russian nation, but that, on the other hand,
Russia could not require us to take part in a work based—in our eyes
—upon robbery; and this threat, backed by our withdrawal, finally
had its effect. The national assembly made another attempt to
evade the task of passing a measure which it disliked: it offered
Radoslajev the dictatorship during the period of transition. After
he had refused this offer, the assembly gave in and reluctantly
proceeded with the consideration of the compensation law. Radoslajev drafted a bill according to which the former owners were to be
paid the full value in instalments; and the old relations between the
debtors and creditors were to be restored, and the debts discharged
in full also in instalments. However, Radoslajev could not get
this bill passed unaltered. The national assembly unanimously
voted a clause to the effect that no one claim for compensation
should exceed 100,000 rubles; if debts were owing to the owner,
the amount was to be added, yet no claim for compensation for
debts owing to any one creditor was to exceed 100,000 rubles. For
property that had been devastated or destroyed a similar maximum
of compensation was voted.

In the meantime we had made all the necessary arrangements
for organising production upon the new principles. Private undertakers did not venture to come forward, though the field was left
open to them; on the other hand, free associations of workers, after
the pattern of those in Freeland, were soon organised, particularly
in the western governments of Russia. The great mass of the
working population, however, proved to be as yet incapable of
organising themselves, and the government was therefore compelled
to come to their assistance. Twenty responsible committees were
appointed for twenty different branches of production, and these
committees, with the help of such local intelligence as they found at
their disposal, took the work of production in hand. The liberty

of the people was so far respected that no one was compelled to engage in any particular kind of work; but those who took part in the work organised by the authorities had to conform to all the directions of the latter. At present there are 83,000 such undertakings at work, with twelve and a-half millions of workers. The division of the profits in these associations is made according to a system derived in part from the principles of free association and in part from those of Communism. One half of the net profits is equally divided among the whole twelve and a-half millions of workers; the other half is divided by each undertaking among its own workers. In this way, we hope on the one hand to secure every undertaking from the worst consequences of any accidental miscarriage in its production, and on the other to arouse the interest of the workers in the success of each individual undertaking. The managers of these productive corporations are paid according to the same mixed system.

The time of labour is fixed at thirty-six hours per week. Every worker is forced to undergo two hours' instruction daily, which instruction is at present given by 65,000 itinerant teachers, the number of whom is being continually increased. This obligation to learn ceases when certain examinations are passed. Down to the present time, 120,000 people's libraries have been established, to furnish which with the most needful books a number of large printing works have been set up in Russia, and the aid of the more important foreign printing establishments has also been called in ; the Freeland printing works alone have already supplied twenty-eight million volumes. And as the teaching of children is being carried on with all conceivable energy—780 teachers' seminaries either have been or are about to be established ; large numbers of teachers, &c., have been brought in from other Slav countries, particularly Bohemia—we hope to see the general level of popular culture so much raised in the course of a few years that the communistic element may be got rid of.

In the meantime, the control provisionally exercised over the masses who willingly submit to it will be utilised in the elevation and ennoblement of their habits and needs. Spirituous liquors, notably brandy, are given out in only limited quantities; on the other hand, care is taken that breweries are erected everywhere. The workers receive a part of their earnings in the form of good

clothing; the wretched mud huts and dens in which the workmen
live are being gradually superseded by neat family dwellings with
small gardens. At least once a month the authorities appoint a
public festival, when it is sought to raise the æsthetic taste of the
participators by means of simple but good music, dramatic
performances and popular addresses, and to cultivate their material
taste by viands fit for rational and civilised beings. Special care is
devoted to the education of the women. Nearly 80,000 itinerant
women-teachers are now moving about the country, teaching the
women—who are freed from all coarse kinds of labour—the
elements of science as well as a more civilised style of household
economy. These teachers also seek to increase the self-respect and
elevate the tastes of the women, to enlighten them as to their new
rights and duties, and particularly to remove the hitherto prevalent
domestic brutality. As these apostles of a higher womanhood—as
well as all the teachers—are supported by the full authority of the
government, and devote themselves to their tasks with self-denying
assiduity, very considerable results of their work are already visible.
The wives of the working classes, who have hitherto been dirty, ill-
treated, mulish beasts of burden, begin to show a sense of their
dignity as human beings and as women. They no longer submit
to be flogged by their husbands; they keep the latter, themselves,
and their children clean and tidy; and emulate one another in acquiring useful knowledge. Thanks to the maintenance allowance
for women, which was at once introduced, an incredible progress—
nay, a veritable revolution—has taken place in the morals of the
people. Whilst formerly, particularly among the urban proletariate, sexual licence and public prostitution were so generally
prevalent that—as our Russian friends assure us—anyone might
accost the first poorly clad girl he met in the streets without anticipating refusal, now sexual false steps are seldom heard of. Moreover, it is particularly interesting to observe the difference which
public opinion makes between such offenders in the past and those
of the present. Whilst the mantle of oblivion is thrown over the
former, public opinion has no indulgence for the latter. 'The
woman who sold herself in former times was an unfortunate; she
who does it now is an abandoned woman,' say the people. The
woman who in former times was a prostitute but is now blameless
carries her head high, and looks down with haughty contempt upon

the girl or the wife who, 'now that we women are no longer compelled to sell ourselves for bread,' commits the least offence.

(*End of Fifth Day's Debate*)

CHAPTER XXVIII

SIXTH DAY

THE business begins with the continuation of the debate upon point 4 of the Agenda.

IBRAHIM EL MELEK (*Right*): The very instructive reports from America and Russia, heard yesterday, afford strong proof that the transition to the system of economic justice is accomplished not merely the more easily, but also the more pleasantly for the wealthy classes, the more cultured and advanced the working classes are. In view of this, it will cause no wonder that we in Egypt do not expect to effect the change of system without painful convulsions. The nearness of Freeland, with the consequently speedy advent of its commissioners, who were received by the violently excited fellaheen with almost divine honours, has preserved us from scenes of cruel violence such as afflicted Russia for weeks. No murders and very little destruction of property have taken place; but the Egyptian national assembly, called into being by the Freeland Commissioners, shows itself far less inclined than its Russian contemporary to respect the compensation claims of the former owners. In this I see the ruling of fate, against which nothing can be done, and to which we must therefore submit with resignation. But I would exculpate from blame those who have had to suffer so severely. Though no one has expressly said it, yet I have an impression that the majority of the assembly are convinced that those who have composed the ruling classes are now everywhere suffering the lot which they have prepared for themselves. As to this, I would ask whether the landlords, capitalists, and employers of America, Australia, and Western Europe were less reckless in taking advantage of their position than those of Russia or Egypt? That they could not so easily do what they pleased with their working classes as the latter could is due to the greater energy of the American national character and to the greater power of resistance possessed by the masses, and not to the kindly disposition of the masters. Hence I cannot think it just that the Russian boyar or the Egyptian bey should lose his property, whilst the American speculator, the French capitalist, or the English lord should even derive profit from the revolution.

LIONEL SPENCER (*Centre*): The previous speaker may be correct in supposing that the wealthy classes of England, like those of America, will come out of the impending revolution without direct loss. There cannot be the slightest doubt that in England, as well as in France and in several other countries in which the government has had a democratic character, nothing will be taken from the wealthy classes for which they will not be fully compensated. But I am not able to see in this the play of blind fate. Observe that the sacrifices involved in the social revolution everywhere stand in an inverse ratio to what has hitherto been the rate of wages, which is the chief factor in determining the average level of popular culture. Where the masses have languished in brutish misery, no one can be surprised that, when they broke their chains, they should hurl themselves upon their oppressors with brutish fury. Again, the rate of wages is everywhere dependent upon the measure of political and social freedom which the wealthy classes grant to the masses. The Russian boyar or the Egyptian bey may be personally as kindly disposed as the American speculator or the English landlord; the essential difference lies in the fact that in America and England the fate of the masses was less dependent upon the personal behaviour of the wealthy classes than in Russia and Egypt. In the former countries, the wealthy classes—even if perhaps less kindly in their personal intercourse—were politically more discreet, more temperate than in the latter countries, and it is the fruit of this political discretion that they are now reaping. It may be that they knew themselves to be simply compelled to exercise this discretion : they exercised it, and what they did, and not their intentions, decided the result. Those that were the ruling classes in the backward countries are now atoning for the excessive exercise of their rights of mastership; they are now paying the difference between the wages they formerly gave and the—meagre enough—general average of wages under the exploiting system.

TEI FU (*Right*): The previous speaker overlooks the fact that the rate of wages depends, not upon the will of the employer, but upon supply and demand. That the receiver of a hunger-wage has been degraded to a beast is unfortunately too true, and the massacres with which the masses of my fatherland, driven to desperation, everywhere introduced the work of emancipation are, like the events in Russia, eloquent proofs of this fact. But how could any political discretion on the part of the ruling classes have prevented this? The labour market in China was over-crowded, the supply of hands was too great for any power on earth to raise the wages.

ALEXANDER MING-LI (*Freeland*): My brother, Tei Fu, thinks that wages depend upon supply and demand. This is not an axiom that was thought out in our common fatherland, but one borrowed from the political economy of the West, but which, in a certain sense, is none the less correct on that account. It holds good of every commodity, consequently of human labour so long as that has to be offered for sale. But the price depends also upon two other things—namely, on the cost of production and the utility of the commodity: in fact, it is these two last-named factors that in the long run regulate the price, whilst the fluctuations of supply and demand can produce merely fluctuations within the limits fixed by the cost of production and the utility. In the long run as much must be paid for everything as its production costs; and in the long run no more can be obtained for a thing than its use is worth. All this has long been known, only unfortunately it has never been fully applied to the question of wages. What does the production of labour cost? Plainly, just so much as the means of life cost which will keep up the worker's strength. And what is the utility of human labour? Just as plainly, the value of what is produced by that human labour. What does this mean when applied to the labour market? Nothing else, it seems to me, than that the rate of wages—apart from the fluctuations due to supply and demand— is in the long run determined by the habits of the worker on the one hand, and by the productiveness of his labour on the other. The first affects the demands of the workers, the second the terms granted by the employers.

But now, I beg my honoured fellow-countryman particularly to note what I am about to say. The habits of the masses are not unchangeable. Every human being naturally endeavours to live as comfortably as possible; and though it must be admitted that

custom and habit will frequently for a time act restrictively upon
this natural tendency to expansion in human wants, yet I can
assert with a good conscience that our unhappy brethren in the
Flowery Land did not go hungry and half-clad because of an invincible dislike to sufficient food and clothing, but that they would
have been very glad to accustom themselves to more comfortable
habits if only the paternal wisdom of all the Chinese governments
had not always prevented it by most severely punishing all the
attempts of the workers to agitate and to unite for the purpose of
giving effect to their demands. Workers who united for such purposes were treated as rebels; and the wealthy classes of China—
this is their folly and their fault—have always given their approval
to this criminal folly of the Chinese government.

I call this both folly and crime, because it not merely grossly
offended against justice and humanity, but was also extremely detrimental to the interests of those who thus acted, and of those who
approved of the action. As to the government, one would have
thought that the insane and suicidal character of its action would long
since have been recognised. A blind man could have seen that the
government damaged its financial as well as its military strength in
proportion as its measures against the lower classes were effective.
The consumption by the masses has been in China, as in all other
countries, the principal source of the national income, and the physical
health of the people the basis of the military strength of the country.
But whence could China derive duties and excise if the people were
not able to consume anything; and how could its soldiery, recruited
from the proletariate, exhibit courage and strength in the face of
the enemy? This oppression of the masses was equally injurious
to the interests of the wealthy classes. While the Chinese people
consumed little they were not able to engage in the more highly
productive forms of labour—that is, their labour had a wretchedly
small utility because of the wretchedly small cost at which it was
produced.

Thus the Chinese employer could pay but little for labour, because the worker was prevented from demanding much in such a way
as would influence not merely the individual employer, but the
labour market in general. The individual undertaker could have
yielded to the demands of his workers to only a limited degree, since
he as individual would have lost from his profits what he added to

wages. But if wages had risen throughout the whole of China, this would have increased the demand to such a degree that Chinese labour would have become more productive—that is, it would have been furnished with better means of production. The employers would have covered the rise in wages by the increased produce, not out of their profits ; in fact, their profits would have grown—their wealth, represented by the capitalistic means of labour in their possession, would have increased. Of course this does not exclude the possibility that some branches of production might have suffered under this general change, for the increase of consumption resulting from better wages does not affect equally all articles in demand. It may be that while the average consumption has increased tenfold, the demand for a single commodity remains almost stationary—in fact, diminishes ; but in this case it is certain that the demand for certain other commodities will increase more than ten-fold. The losses of individual employers are balanced by the proportionately larger profits of other employers ; and it may be taken as a general rule that the wealth of the wealthy classes increases in exact proportion to the increase of wages which they are obliged to pay. It cannot be otherwise, for this wealth of the wealthy classes consists mainly of nothing else than the means of production which are used in the preparation of the commodities required by the whole nation.

Perhaps my honoured fellow countryman thinks that in the matter of rise of wages we move in a circle, inasmuch as on the one hand the productiveness of labour—that is, the utility of the power expended in labour—certainly cannot increase so long as the nation's consumption—that is, the amount which the labour power itself costs —does not increase, while on the other hand the latter increase is impossible until the former has taken place. If so, I would tell him that this is just the fatal superstition which the wealthy classes and the rulers of so many countries have now so cruelly to suffer for. Since, in the exploiting world, only a part, and as a rule a very small part, of the produce of labour went to wages, the employers— with very rare exceptions—were well able to grant a rise in wages even before the increase of produce had actually been obtained, and had resulted in a *universal* rise in wages. I would tell him that, especially in China, on the average even three or four times the wages would not have absorbed the whole profits—that is, of course, the old profits uninfluenced by the increase of produce. The employers *could* pay more, but they *would not*. From the standpoint of the individual this was quite intelligible ; everyone seeks merely his own advantage, and this demands that one retains for one's self as large a part of any utility as possible, and hands over as little as possible to others. In this respect the American speculators, the French capitalists, and the English landlords, were not a grain better than our Chinese mandarins. But as a body the former acted differently from the latter. Notwithstanding the fact that the absurdity that wages *cannot* be raised was invented in the West and proclaimed from all the professorial chairs, the Western nations have for several generations been compelled by the more correct instinct of the people to act as if the contrary principles had been established. In theory they persisted in the teaching that wages could not be increased ; in practice, however, they yielded more and more to the demands of the working masses, with whose undeniable successes the theory had to be accommodated as well as possible. You, my Chinese brethren, on the contrary, have in your policy adhered strictly to the teaching of this theory : you have first driven your toiling masses to desperation by making them feel that the State is their enemy ; and you have then immediately taken advantage of every excess of which the despairing people have been guilty to impose ' order ' in your sense of the word. Your hand was always lifted against the weaker : do not wonder that when they had become the stronger they avenged themselves by making you feel some small part of the sufferings they had endured.

This does not prevent us in Freeland—as our actions show—from condemning the violence that has been offered to those who formerly were oppressors, and from trying to make amends for it as well as we can. Hence we hold that the people of Russia, Egypt, and China—in short, everybody—would do well to follow the example given by the United States of America. We think thus because this wise generosity is shown to be advantageous not merely for the wealthy classes, but also for the workers. Unfortunately it is not in our power at once to instil into the Russian muzhik, the Egyptian fellah, or the Chinese cooley such views as are natural to the workers of the advanced West. History is the final tribunal which will decree to everyone what he has deserved.

As no one else was down to speak on this point of the Agenda, the President closed the debate upon it, and opened that upon the fifth point :

Are economic justice and freedom the ultimate outcome of human evolution; and what will probably be the condition of mankind under such a régime ?

ENGELBERT WAGNER (*Right*) : We are contemplating the inauguration of a new era of human development; want and crime will disappear from among men, and reason and philanthropy take possession of the throne which prejudice and brute force have hitherto occupied. But the apparent perfection of this condition appears to me to involve an essential contradiction to the first principle of the doctrine of human blessedness—namely, that man in order to be content needs discontent. In order to find a zest in enjoyment, this child of the dust must first suffer hunger ; his possessions satiate him unless they are seasoned with longing and hope ; his striving is paralysed unless he is inspired by unattained ideals. But what new ideal can henceforth hover before the mind of man—what can excite any further longing in him when abundance and leisure have been acquired for all ? Is it not to be feared that, like Tannhäuser in the Venusberg, our descendants will pine for, and finally bring upon themselves, fresh bitternesses merely in order to escape the unchangeable monotony of the sweets of their existence ? We are not made to bear unbroken good fortune ; and an order of things that would procure such for us could therefore not last long. That the world if once emancipated from the fetters of servitude will again cast itself into them, that the old exploiting system shall ever return, is certainly not to be feared, according to what we have just heard ; even a relapse into the material misery of the past through overpopulation is out of the question. But the more irrefragably the evidence of the impossibility of the return of any former kind of human unhappiness presses upon us, so much the more urgently is an answer demanded to the question : What will there be in the character of man's future destiny, what new ideals will arise, to prevent him from being swamped by a surfeit of happiness ?

The PRESIDENT (Dr. Strahl) : I take upon myself to answer this question from the chair, because I hope that what I am about to say will close the discussion upon the point of the Agenda now before us, and consequently the congress itself. From the nature of the subject we cannot expect any practical result to follow from the debate upon this last question, which was added to the Agenda merely because our foreign friends wished to learn, by way of conclusion to the previous discussions, what were our ideas as to the future. No mortal soul can have any definite ideas as to the future, for we can know only the past and the present. I venture to make only one positive assertion—namely, that the order of things which we propose to inaugurate will be in harmony with the general laws of evolution, as every foregoing human order has been ; that it cannot be permanent and eternal; and that consequently it will by no means put an end to human striving and change and improvement. This holds good even with respect to the material conditions of mankind. In the future, as in the past, labour will be the price of enjoyment, and there is no reason to fear that in future the wish will lag behind the effort necessary to realise it. Thus mankind will not lack even the material stimulus to progress and to further striving. But man possesses intellectual as well as material needs, and the less imperative the latter become, so much the more widely and powerfully do the former make themselves felt. Intellectual hunger is a far more influential stimulus to effort than material hunger ; and at present at least we are forced to believe that the former will never be appeased.

The fear that our race will sink into stagnation when the aims which have hitherto almost exclusively dominated its circle of ideas have been attained, is like the fancy of the child that the youth will give himself up to idleness as soon as he escapes the dread of the rod. It would be useless to attempt to make the child understand those other, and to him unknown, motives for activity by which the youth is influenced; and so we, standing now on the threshold of the youthful age of mankind and still half enslaved by the ideas of the childhood of our race, cannot know what new ideas mankind will conceive after the present ones have been realised. We can only say that they will be different, and presumably loftier ones. The new conditions of existence in which man will find himself in consequence of the introduction of economic freedom, will bring to maturity new properties, notions, and ideas, which no sagacity, no gift of mental construction possessed by anyone now living, is able to prefigure with accuracy. If, nevertheless, I venture to indicate some of the features of the future, I ask you not to attach to them any greater importance than you would to the fancies of a savage who, standing on the threshold leading from cannibalism to exploitation, might thousands of years ago have undertaken to form a conception of those changes which the invention of agriculture and of slavery would produce in the circumstances of his far-off successors. In this respect I have only one advantage over our remote ancestor : I know his history, while that of his ancestors was unknown to him. I can, therefore, seek counsel of the past in order to understand the future, while for him there was merely a present. I will now make use of this advantage ; the course of human evolution in the past shall give us a few hints as to the significance of that phase of evolution into which we are now passing.

The original condition of mankind was freedom and peace in the animal sense—that is, freedom and peace among men, together with absolute dependence upon nature. The first great stage in evolution reached its climax when man turned against his fellow-men the weapon which had in the beginning been employed only in conflict with the world of beasts : dependence upon nature remained, but peace among men was broken.

The second stage in evolution is distinguished by the fact that man turns against nature, who had hitherto been his sovereign mistress, the intelligence which he had employed in mutually destructive warfare. He discovers the art of compelling nature to yield what she will not offer voluntarily—he produces. The chain by which the elements hold him bound is in this way loosened ; but the first use which man makes of this gleam of deliverance from the bonds of merely animal servitude is to place fetters upon himself. The relaxing of dependence upon external nature and the alleviation of the conflict among men themselves—these are the acquisition of the second period.

The third stage of development begins with the dominion over nature gradually acquired by controlling the natural forces, and ends with the deliverance of mankind from the bonds of servitude. Independence of external control, freedom and peace among men, are its distinguishing features.

Here I would point out that the theatre of each of these phases of human progress has been a different one. The original home of our race was evidently the hottest part of the earth ; under the tropics, in our struggles with the world of animals, we gained our

F F

first victories, and developed ourselves into warlike cannibals ; but against the forces of nature, which reign supreme in that hot zone, we in our childhood could do nothing. Production, and afterwards slavery, could be carried on only outside of the tropics. On the other hand, it is quite as certain that man could not remove himself very far from the tropics so long as the productivity of his labour was still comparatively small, and he could not compel nature to furnish him with much more than she offered voluntarily. It is no mere accident that all civilisation began and first flourished exclusively in that zone which is equally removed from the equator and from the polar circle. In that temperate zone were found united all the conditions which protected the still infantile art of production from the danger of being crushed on the one hand or stunted on the other by the overwhelming power or the parsimony of nature. But this mean temperature, so favourable to the second phase of evolution, proved itself altogether unsuitable to the last step towards perfect control over nature. As human labour met with a generous reward, there was nothing to stimulate man's inventiveness to compel nature to serve man by her own, instead of by human, forces. This could happen only when the civilisation, which had acquired strength in the temperate zone, was transplanted into colder and less friendly regions, where human labour alone could no longer win from reluctant nature wealth enough to satisfy the claims of the ruling classes. Then first did necessity teach men how to employ the elemental forces in increasing the productiveness of human labour ; the moderately cold zone is the birthplace of man's dominion over nature.

But when the third phase of evolution has found its close in economic justice, there will be, apparently, yet another change of scene. It might be said, if we cared to look for analogies, that this change of scene will be of a double character, corresponding to the double character of the change in institutions. The perfected control over nature will be seen in the fact that the whole earth, subjugated to man, has become man's own property ; on the other hand, peace and freedom—which in themselves represent nothing new to mankind, but are as it were merely the return of the primitive relation of man to man—will find their analogies in the return to the primitive home of our race, the tropical world. That vigorous nature, which had formerly to be left lest civilisation should be killed in the very germ, can no longer be a hindrance, can only be a help to civilisation now that man, awaked to freedom, has attained to a full control over those forces which can be made serviceable to him. It will probably need several centuries before the civilised nations, whose northern wanderings and experiences have made them strangers in their birthplace, have afresh thoroughly acclimatised themselves here. In the meantime, the charming highlands which nature has placed—one might almost believe in anticipation of our attempt—directly under the equator, offer to the wanderers the desired dwelling-places, and, at any rate, the agriculture of the now commencing epoch of civilisation will have its headquarters here. Slowly but surely will man, who henceforth may freely choose his dwelling-place wherever productiveness and the charms of nature attract him, press towards the south, where merely to breathe and to behold is a delight beyond anything of the kind which the north has to offer. The notion that the torrid zone engenders stagnation of mind and body is a foolish fancy. There have been and there are strong and weak, vigorous and vigourless peoples in the north as well as in the south; and that civilisation has celebrated its highest triumphs under ice and snow is not due to anything in chilly temperatures essentially and permanently conducive to progress, but simply to the temporary requirements of the transition from the second to the third epoch of civilisation. In the future the centres of civilisation will have to be sought in proximity to the equator; while those countries which, during the last centuries—a short span of time—have held up the banner of human progress will gradually lose their relative importance.

That man, having attained to control over the forces of nature and to undivided proprietorship of the whole planet, will ever actually take possession of and productively exploit the whole of the planet, is scarcely to be expected. In fact, past history almost tempts us to believe that the population of the earth has undergone scarcely any material change since civilisation began. Certainly, Europe to-day is several times more populous than it was thousands of years ago; and in America—putting out of sight the unquestionable extraordinary diminution in the population of Mexico and Peru—there has undeniably been a large increase in the number of inhabitants. Against all this we have to place the fact that large parts of Asia and Africa are at present almost uninhabited, though they formerly were the homes of untold millions. Thus, taking everything into consideration, the variations in population can never have exceeded a few hundred million souls. But assuming that the introduction of the new order of things, with its sudden and general diminution of the death-rate, will produce a revolution in this respect, that man's control over nature will be connected with a general increase in the number of the earth's masters, yet it may be considered as highly improbable that this increase will be particularly rapid, and that it will go on for any great length of time.

In one respect, certainly, there can and will be a sudden and considerable increase in the number of the living. In consequence of the greater longevity which will be the necessary result of rational habits of life, generations that have hitherto been consecutive will then be contemporaneous. In the exploiting world, on the average the father, worn out by misery, toil, and vice, died ere the son had reached maturity; in the future the parents will be buried by their great-grandchildren, and thus the number of the living will be speedily raised from a milliard and a-half to two milliards or to two and a-half, without any increase in human fecundity. But assuming that there be for a time an actual growth in population over and above that caused by this greater longevity, I hold it to be in the highest degree improbable that this growth can be a rapid one, and still less a continuous one. My opinion—based, it is true, upon analogy—is that a doubling of the population is the utmost we need reckon upon, so that the maximum population of the world may grow to five milliards. This number, very small in proportion to the size and productive capacity of our planet, will find abundant room and food in the most beautiful, most agreeable, and most fertile parts of the earth. Ninety-nine per cent. of the land superficies of the earth will be either not at all or very sparsely populated—so far as the population depends upon the production of the locality—and ninety per cent. will be cultivated either not at all or only to a very trifling extent.

That under the new order the earth will be transformed into a swarming ant-hill of thickly crowded inhabitants, that complete control over the elemental forces will lead to a destruction of all primitive natural fertility, there is therefore no reason whatever to fear. On the contrary, the more rationally distributed inhabitants will not crowd upon each other in the way in which they do at present in most civilised countries; and the greater fertility of the cultivated land of the future, in connection with the improved methods of cultivation, will make it possible to obtain from a smaller area a ten-fold greater supply for a double or a triple number of people than can be now obtained by the plough. The beauty and romance of nature are exposed to no danger whatever of being destroyed by the levelling instruments of future engineers; nay, it may be anticipated that a loving devotion to nature will be one of the chief pleasures of those future generations, who will treasure and guard in every natural wonder their inalienable and undivided property.

It is impossible to predict what course the development of material progress will take under the dominion of the new social principle. So much is evident, that the spirit of invention will apply itself far more than it has hitherto done to the task of finding out fresh methods of saving labour. This is a logical consequence of the fact that arrangements for the sparing of labour will now become profitable and applicable under all circumstances—which has hitherto been the case only exceptionally. But it is probable that the future will surpass the present also in its comparative estimate of intellectual as more valuable than material progress. Hitherto the reverse has been the case: material wealth and material power have been the exclusive aims of human endeavour; intellectual culture has been at best prized merely as the means of attaining what was regarded as the real and final end. There have always been individuals who looked upon intellectual perfection as an end in itself; but there have always been isolated exceptions who have never been able to impress their character upon the whole race. The immense majority of men have been too ignorant and rude even to form a conception of purely intellectual endeavour; and the few who have been able to do so have been so absorbed in the reckless struggle for wealth and power, that they have found neither time nor attention for anything else. In fact, it lay in the essence of the exploiting system that under its dominion intellectual interests should be thrust into the background. In the mutual struggle for supremacy only those could succeed in becoming the hammer instead of the anvil who knew how to obtain control of material wealth; hence it was only these latter who could imprint their character upon the society they dominated, whilst the 'impractical,' who chased after intellectual aims, were forced down into the great subjugated herd. And the teaching of the history of civilisation compels us to admit that in the earlier epochs the chase after wealth could legitimately claim precedence over purely intellectual endeavour. It is true that intellectual perfection is the highest and final end of man ; but as a certain amount of wealth is an indispensable condition of success in that highest sphere of effort, man must give to the acquisition of wealth his chief attention until that condition of higher progress is attained. That condition has now been attained, that amount of wealth has been acquired which makes the supply of the highest intellectual needs possible to all men ; and there can be no doubt whatever that man will now awake to a consciousness of his proper destiny. That which he has hitherto striven after only incidentally, and, as it were, accidentally, will now become the object of his chief endeavour.

That this intellectual progress must produce a radical revolution in the sentiments and ideas of the coming generations is a matter of course. This holds good also of religious ideas. These have always been the faithful and necessary reflection of the contemporary conditions of human existence. In primitive times, so long as man carried on the struggle for existence only passively, like the beasts, he, like them, was without any religious conceptions. When he had taken the first step towards active engagement in the struggle for existence, and his dependence upon nature was to some extent weakened, but peace had not yet been broken with his fellow-men, he began to believe in helpful higher Powers that should fill his nets and drive the prey into his hands. When the war of annihilation broke out between man and man, then these higher Powers acquired a cruel and sanguinary character corresponding to the horribly altered form of the struggle for existence ; the devil became the undisputed master of the world, which, regarded as thoroughly bad, was nevertheless worshipped as such. Next the struggle for supremacy superseded the struggle of annihilation ; the first traces of humanity, consideration for the vanquished, showed itself, and in harmony with this the good gods were associated with the gods of evil, Ormuzd with Ahriman ; and the more the horrors of cannibalism were forced into the background by the chivalrous virtues of the new lords of the world, the more pronounced became the authority of the good gods over the bad. But since it was the dominant classes who created the new faith, and since they needed

for their prosperity the obedience of the subjugated, they naturally
transplanted the principle of servitude into their heaven. The gods
became severe, jealous masters; they demanded blind obedience,
and punished with tyrannical cruelty every resistance to their
will. This did not prevent the rulers from holding this to be
the best of all worlds, despite its servitude and its vices; for to
them servitude was well-pleasing, and as to the vices, they would
be rid of the 'evil gods' if only the last remnant of resistance and
disobedience—the only sources of all evil—were rooted out.

This kind of despotism was first attacked when the slaves found
spokesmen. The most logical of these was Buddha, who, as he
necessarily must from the standpoint of the slaves, again declared
the world to be evil, and thence arrived at the only conclusion consistent with this assumption—namely, that its non-existence, Nirvana,
was to be preferred to its continued existence. Christ, on the other
hand, opposed to the optimism of domination the optimism of
redemption. Like Buddha, he saw evil in oppression, not in disobedience; whilst, in the imagination of other nations, the good
gods had fought for the conquerors and the bad ones for the subjugated, he now represented the Jewish Jehovah as the Father of the
poor and Satan as the idol of those who were in power. To him
also the world was bad, but—and this was the decisive difference
between him and Buddha—not radically so, but only because of the
temporary sway of the devil. It was necessary, not to destroy the
world, but to deliver it from the power of the devil, and therefore,
in contrast to Buddhistic Quietism, he rightly called his church a
'militant' one. Both founders, however, being ignorant of the
law of natural evolution, were at one in regarding the contemporary
condition of civilisation as a permanent one, and therefore they
agreed that oppression could be removed only by condemning
riches and declaring poverty to be the only sinless state of man.
The Indian king's son, familiar with all the wisdom of the Indians of
his day, saw that reversion to universal poverty meant deterioration,
therefore destruction, and, in his sympathy with the oppressed in
their sorrow, he did not shrink from even this. The carpenter's Son
from Galilee held the equality of poverty to be possible, and He was
therefore far removed from the despondent resignation of His Indian
predecessor—He proclaimed the optimism of poverty.

The later official Christianity has nothing at all in common with this teaching of Christ. The official Christianity is the outcome of the conviction, derived from experience, that the millennial kingdom of the poor preached by Christ and the Apostles is an impossibility, and of the consequent strange amalgamation of practical optimism with theoretical pessimism. Jehovah now again became the gaoler of the powerful, Satan the tempter who incites to disobedience to the commands of God ; at the same time, however, the order of the world—though instituted by God—was declared to be fundamentally bad and incapable of improvement, the work of redemption no longer being regarded as referring to this world, but merely to the next. The exploiting world for the last fifteen centuries has naturally adhered to the new doctrine, leaving asceticism to a few anchorites and eccentric persons, whose conduct has remained without influence upon the sphere of practical human thought. Not until the last century, when the old industrial system approached its end, and the incipient control of man over nature gradually made the institution of servitude a curse to the higher classes, did pessimism—this time, philosophic pessimism—lift up its head once more. The world became more and more unpleasant even to the ruling classes ; they were made to feel fettered and anxious by the misery around them, which they had previously been able easily to explain by a reference to the inscrutable counsels of God ; they were seized by a dislike to those enjoyments which could be obtained only by the torture of their brethren, and, as they held this system, despite its horrible character, to be unchangeable, they gave themselves up to pessimism—the pessimism of Buddha, which looked for redemption only in the annihilation of just those more nobly constituted minds who did not allow themselves to be forced by the hereditary authoritative belief to mistake a curse for a blessing.

But another change is now about to be effected. The gods can no longer rule by terror over a race that has robbed the clouds of their lightning and the underworld of its fire ; and, now that servitude has ceased to be the basis of the terrestrial order, it must also disappear from the celestial. The fear of God is as inconceivable as pessimism of any kind whatever as a characteristic of the coming generations, who, released from the suffering of the world, will pass their existence in the enjoyment of a lifelong happiness. For the great thinkers who, looking beyond their own times, give expression to truths the full meaning of which is understood only by subsequent generations, have never failed to see that this suffering, this 'original sin,' is based upon nothing else than the injustice of exploitation. The evils which mankind brought upon itself—want and vice—were what converted earth into hell; what nature imposed upon us—sickness and death—can no more embitter life to us than it can any other kind of living creatures. Sickness cannot, because it is only transitory and exceptional, especially since misery and vice no longer minister to it; and death cannot, because, in reality, it is not death, but merely the fear of it, which is an evil.

But it will be said that this fear of death, foolish as it may be in itself, is a real evil which is infinitely more painful to man, who reflects upon the future, than to the animal that lives merely in the present and knows of and fears death only when it is imminent. This was, in fact, the case, but it will not continue to be so when man, by his return to the innocence of nature, has won back his right to the painlessness of death. The fear of death is only one of the many specific instincts by which nature secures the perpetuation of species. If the beasts did not fear destruction, they would necessarily all perish, for their means of warding off the powerful dangers with which they are threatened are but weak. It is different with man, who has not merely become king of the living world, but has at last made himself master of the elements. In order to preserve the human species from perishing, nature needed to give to man the blind fear of death only so long as he had to defend himself against himself and his fellow-men. So long as he was the victim of the torture of subjection, man had also to think of death with emotions of invincible shuddering if he would not prefer destruction to suffering. Just because it was so painful, life had to be fenced round with the blind dread of death even in the case of that highest species, man, which did not need protection from external dangers. But now is this last and worst danger overcome; the dread of death has become superfluous even as a protection against suicide; it has no longer any use as a specific instinct of man, and it will disappear like every specific character which has become useless. This evil, also, will vanish with injustice from mankind; life spreads out full of serene joyousness before our successors, who, free from the crippling influence of pessimism, will spend their days in unending progress towards perfection.

But we, my friends, now hasten to open the doors to this future!

Here closed the sixth and last day of the Universal Congress of Eden Vale.

CONCLUSION

THE history of 'Freeland' is ended. I could go on with the thread of the narrative, and depict the work of human emancipation as it appears to my mental eye, but of what use would it be? Those who have not been convinced, by what I have already written, that we are standing on the threshold of a new and happier age, and that it depends solely upon our discernment and resolve whether we pass over it, would not be convinced by a dozen volumes.

For this book is not the idle creation of an uncontrolled imagination, but the outcome of earnest, sober reflection, and of profound scientific investigation. All that I have described as really happening *might* happen if men were found who, convinced as I am of the untenability of existing conditions, determined to act instead of merely complaining. Thoughtlessness and inaction are, in truth, at present the only props of the existing economic and social order. What was formerly necessary, and therefore inevitable, has become injurious and superfluous; there is no longer anything to compel us to endure the misery of an obsolete system; there is nothing but our own folly to prevent us from enjoying that happiness and abundance which the existing means of civilisation are capable of providing for us.

It will perhaps be objected, 'Thus have numberless reformers spoken and written, since the days of Sir Thomas More; and what has been proposed to mankind as a panacea for all suffering has always proved to be Utopian.' And I am willing to admit that the dread of being classed with the legion of authors of Utopian romances at first filled my mind with not a few qualms as to the form which I had chosen for my book. But, upon mature deliberation, I decided to offer, not a number of dry abstractions, but as vivid a picture as possible, which should clearly represent in concrete conceptions what abstract ideas would have shown in merely shadowy outlines. The reader who does not for himself discover the difference between this book and the works of imagination above referred to, is lost to me; to him I should remain the 'unpractical enthusiast' even if I were to elaborate ever so dry a systematic treatise, for it is enough for him to know that I believe in a change of the existing system to condemn me as an enthusiast. It matters not, to this kind of readers, in what form I state my proofs; for such readers, like fanatics in the domain of religion, are simply disqualified to estimate aright the evidence which is pointed against what exists.

The impartial reader, on the other hand, will not be prevented by the narrative form of this book from soberly endeavouring to discover whether my propositions are essentially true or false. If he should find that I have started from false premisses, that the system of freedom and justice which I have propounded is inconsistent in any way with the natural and universally recognised springs of human action—nay, if, after reading my book, he should not have attained to the firm conviction that the realisation of this new order—apart, of course, from unimportant details—is absolutely inevitable, then I must be content to be placed in the same category as More, Fourier, Cabet, and the rest who have mistaken their desires for sober reality.

I wish once more expressly to state that the intrinsic practicability of my book extends beyond the economic and ethical principles and motives underlying it, to the actual stage upon which its scenes are placed. The highlands in Equatorial Africa exactly correspond to the picture drawn in the book. In order that 'Freeland' may be realised as I have drawn it, nothing more is required, therefore, than a sufficient number of vigorous men. Shall I be privileged to live until these men are found?

PRINTED BY
SPOTTISWOODE AND CO., NEW-STREET SQUARE
LONDON

www.ingramcontent.com/pod-product-compliance
Lightning Source LLC
Chambersburg PA
CBHW031821270326
41932CB00008B/497